## STEPS TO AN ECOLOGY OF MIND

Here is the book which develops a new way of thinking about the nature of order and organization in living systems, a unified body of theory so encompassing that it illuminates all particular areas of study of biology and behavior. It is interdisciplinary, not in the usual and simple sense of exchanging information across lines of discipline, but in discovering patterns common to many disciplines.

*"In this invaluable book, systemic intellectual clarity and moral clarity convene and evoke a convincing ethic of what is sacred, what is right for life. I owe more understanding than I know to Gregory Bateson and Steps to an Ecology of Mind."*

—STEWART BRAND
EDITOR, WHOLE EARTH CATALOG

# STEPS TO AN ECOLOGY OF MIND

## Gregory Bateson

BALLANTINE BOOKS • NEW YORK

Library of Congress Catalog Card Number: 75-169581

ISBN 0-345-33291-1

This edition published by arrangement with Chandler Publishing Company

Printed in Canada

First Ballantine Books Edition: March 1972
Thirteenth Printing: October 1985

# TABLE OF CONTENTS

# Preface

I have been one of Gregory Bateson's students for three years and I was able to help him select the essays which are here brought together for the first time in one volume. I believe that this is a very important book, not only for those who are professionally concerned with the behavioral sciences, biology, and philosophy, but also and especially for those of my generation—the generation born since Hiroshima—who are searching for a better understanding of themselves and their world.

The central idea in this book is that we create the world that we perceive, not because there is no reality outside our heads (the Indochinese war *is* wrong, we *are* destroying our ecosystem and therefore ourselves, whether we believe it or not), but because we select and edit the reality we see to conform to our beliefs about what sort of world we live in. The man who believes that the resources of the world are infinite, for example, or that if something is good for you then the more of it the better, will not be able to see his errors, because he will not look for evidence of them.

For a man to change his basic, perception-determining beliefs—what Bateson calls his epistemological premises—he must first become aware that reality is not necessarily as he believes it to be. This is not an easy or comfortable thing to learn, and most men in history have probably been able to avoid thinking about it. And I am not convinced that the unexamined life is never worth leading. But sometimes the dissonance between reality and false beliefs reaches a point when it becomes impossible to avoid the awareness that the world no longer makes sense. Only then is it possible for the mind to consider radically different ideas and perceptions.

Specifically, it is clear that our cultural mind has come to such a point. But there is danger as well as possibility in our situation. There is no guarantee that the new ideas will be an improvement over the old. Nor can we hope that the change will be smooth.

Already there are psychic casualties of the culture change. The psychedelics are a powerful educational tool. They are the surest way to learn the arbitrariness of our ordinary perception. Many of us have had to use them to find out how little we knew. Too many of us have become lost in the labyrinth, have decided that if reality doesn't mean what we thought it did then there is no meaning in it at all. I know that place. I have been lost there myself. As far as I know, there are only two ways out.

One is religious conversion. (I tried Taoism. Others are choosing various versions of Hinduism, Buddhism, and even Christianity. And such times always produce a host of self-proclaimed messiahs. Also, a few of those who study radical ideologies do so for religious rather than political reasons.) This solution may satisfy some, although there is always the danger of satanism. But I think that those who choose ready-made systems of belief lose the chance to do some truly creative thinking, and perhaps nothing less will save us.

This second way out—thinking things through and taking as little as possible on faith—is the more difficult. Intellectual activity—from science to poetry—has a bad reputation in my generation. The blame falls on our so-called educational system, which seems designed to prevent its victims from learning to think, while telling them that thinking is what you do when you study a textbook. Also, to learn to think, you must have a teacher who can think. The low level of what passes for thinking among most of the American academic community can perhaps only be appreciated by contrast with a man like Gregory Bateson, but it's bad enough to cause many of our best minds to give up looking for better.

But the essence of all our problems is bad thinking, and the only medicine for that is better thinking. This book is a sample of the best thinking I've found. I commend it to you, my brothers and sisters of the new culture, in the hope that it will help us on our journey.

—*Mark Engel*
*Honolulu, Hawaii*
*April 16, 1971*

# Foreword

Some men seem able to go on working steadily with little success and no reassurance from outside. I am not one of these. I have needed to know that somebody else believed that my work had promise and direction, and I have often been surprised that others had faith in me when I had very little in myself. I have, at times, even tried to shrug off the responsibility which their continued faith imposed on me by thinking, "But they don't really know what I am doing. How can they know when I myself do not?"

My first anthropological field work among the Baining of New Britain was a failure, and I had a period of partial failure in research with dolphins. Neither of these failures has ever been held against me.

I therefore have to thank many people and institutions for backing me, at times when I did not consider myself a good bet.

First, I have to thank the Council of Fellows of St. John's College, Cambridge, who elected me to a Fellowship immediately after my failure among the Baining. My daughter Mary Catherine Bateson also contributed much, including a fictional image of herself in the metalogue.

Next, in chronological order, I owe a deep debt to Margaret Mead, who was my wife and very close co-worker in Bali and New Guinea, and who since then has continued as a friend and professional colleague.

In 1942, at a Macy Foundation conference, I met Warren McCulloch and Julian Bigelow who were then talking excitedly about "feedback." The writing of *Naven* had brought me to the very edge of what later became cybernetics, but I lacked the concept of negative feedback. When I returned from overseas after the war, I went to Frank Fremont-Smith of the Macy Foundation to ask for a conference on this then-mysterious matter. Frank said that he had just arranged such a conference with McCulloch as chairman. It thus happened that I was privileged to be a member of the famous Macy Conferences on Cybernetics. My debt to Warren McCulloch, Norbert Wiener, John von Neumann, Evelyn Hutchinson, and other members of these conferences is evident in everything that I have written since World War II.

In my first attempts to synthesize cybernetic ideas with anthropological data, I had the benefit of a Guggenheim Fellowship.

In the period of my entry into the psychiatric field, it was Jurgen Ruesch, with whom I worked in the Langley Porter Clinic, who initiated me into many of the curious features of the psychiatric world.

From 1949 to 1962, I had the title of "Ethnologist" in the Veterans Administration Hospital at Palo Alto, where I was given singular freedom to study whatever I thought interesting. I was protected from outside demands and given this freedom by the director of the hospital, Dr. John J. Prusmack.

In this period, Bernard Siegel suggested that the Stanford University Press republish my book, *Naven*, which had fallen flat on its face when first published in 1936; and I was lucky enough to get film footage of a sequence of play between otters in the Fleishhacker Zoo which seemed to me of such theoretical interest as to justify a small research program.

I owe my first research grant in the psychiatric field to the late Chester Barnard of the Rockefeller Foundation, who had kept a copy of *Naven* for some years by his bedside. This was a grant to study "the role of the Paradoxes of Abstraction in Communication."

Under this grant, Jay Haley, John Weakland, and Bill Fry joined me to form a small research team within the V.A. Hospital.

But again there was failure. Our grant was for only two years, Chester Barnard had retired, and in the opinion of the Foundation staff we did not have enough results to justify renewal. The grant ran out, but my team loyally stayed with me without pay. The work went on, and, a few days after the end of the grant, while I was writing a desperate letter to Norbert Wiener for his advice about where to get the next grant, the double bind hypothesis fell into place.

Finally Frank Fremont-Smith and the Macy Foundation saved us.

After that there were grants from the Foundations Fund for Psychiatry and from the National Institute of Mental Health.

Gradually it appeared that for the next advances in the study of logical typing in communication I should work with animal material, and I started to work with octopus. My wife, Lois, worked with me, and for over a year we kept about a dozen octopuses in our living room. This preliminary work was promising but needed to be repeated and extended under better conditions. For this no grants were available.

At this point, John Lilly came forward and invited me to be the director of his dolphin laboratory in the Virgin Islands. I worked there for about a year and became interested in the problems of cetacean communication, but I think I am not cut out to administer a laboratory dubiously funded in a place where the logistics are intolerably difficult.

It was while I was struggling with these problems that I received a Career Development Award under the National Institute of Mental Health. These awards were administered by Bert Boothe, and I owe much to his continued faith and interest.

In 1963, Taylor Pryor of the Oceanic Foundation in Hawaii invited me to work in his Oceanic Institute on cetacean and other problems of animal and human communication. It is here that I have written more than half of the present book, including the whole of Part V.

While in Hawaii, I have also been working recently with the Culture Learning Institute of the East-West Center in the University of Hawaii, and owe some theoretical insights regarding Learning III to discussions held in that Institute.

My debt to the Wenner-Gren Foundation is evident from the fact that the book contains no less than four position papers written for Wenner-Gren conferences. I wish also to thank personally Mrs. Lita Osmundsen, the Director of Research of that Foundation.

Many also have labored along the road to help me. Most of these cannot be mentioned here, but I must particularly thank Dr. Vern Carroll, who prepared the bibliography, and my secretary, Judith Van Slooten, who labored with accuracy through long hours in preparing this book for press and compiling the index.

Finally there is the debt that every man of science owes to the giants of the past. It is no mean comfort, at times when the next idea cannot be found and the whole enterprise seems futile, to remember that greater men have wrestled with the same problems. My personal inspiration has owed much to the men who over the last 200 years have kept alive the idea of unity between mind and body: *Lamarck*, the founder of evolutionary theory, miserable, old, and blind, and damned by Cuvier, who believed in Special Creation; *William Blake*, the poet and painter, who saw "through his eyes, not with them," and knew more about what it is to be human than any other man; *Samuel Butler*, the ablest contemporary critic of Darwinian evolution and the first analyst of a schizophrenogenic family; *R. G. Collingwood*, the first man to recognize—and to analyze in crystalline prose—the nature of context; and *William Bateson*, my father, who was certainly ready in 1894 to receive the cybernetic ideas.

## Selection and Arrangement of Items

The book contains almost everything that I have written, with the exception of items too long to be included, such as books and extensive analyses of data; and items too trivial or ephemeral, such as book reviews and controversial notes. A complete personal bibliography is appended.

Broadly, I have been concerned with four sorts of subject matter: anthropology, psychiatry, biological evolution and genetics, and the new epistemology which comes out of systems theory and ecology. Essays on these subjects make up Parts II, III, IV, and V of the book, and the order of these parts corresponds to the chronological order of four overlapping periods in my life in which these subjects have been central to my thinking. Within each part, the essays are in chronological order.

I recognize that readers are likely to attend most carefully to those parts of the book dealing with their particular subjects. I have therefore not edited out some repetition. The psychiatrist interested in alcoholism will encounter in "The Cybernetics of 'Self'" ideas which appear again in more philosophic dress in "Form, Substance, and Difference."

*Oceanic Institute, Hawaii*
*April 16, 1971*

# Introduction:

# The Science of Mind and Order*

The title of this book of collected essays and lectures is intended precisely to define the contents. The essays, spread over thirty-five years, combine to propose a new way of thinking about *ideas* and about those aggregates of ideas which I call "minds." This way of thinking I call the "ecology of mind," or the ecology of ideas. It is a science which does not yet exist as an organized body of theory or knowledge.

But the definition of an "idea" which the essays combine to propose is much wider and more formal than is conventional. The essays must speak for themselves, but here at the beginning let me state my belief that such matters as the bilateral symmetry of an animal, the patterned arrangement of leaves in a plant, the escalation of an armaments race, the processes of courtship, the nature of play, the grammar of a sentence, the mystery of biological evolution, and the contemporary crises in man's relationship to his environment, can only be understood in terms of such an ecology of ideas as I propose.

The questions which the book raises are ecological: How do ideas interact? Is there some sort of natural selection which determines the survival of some ideas and the extinction or death of others? What sort of economics limits the multiplicity of ideas in a given region of mind? What

*This essay, written in 1971, has not been published elsewhere.

are the necessary conditions for stability (or survival) of such a system or subsystem?

Some of these questions are touched upon in the essays, but the main thrust of the book is to clear the way so that such questions can be meaningfully asked.

It was only in late 1969 that I became fully conscious of what I had been doing. With the writing of the Korzybski Lecture, "Form, Substance, and Difference," I found that in my work with primitive peoples, schizophrenia, biological symmetry, and in my discontent with the conventional theories of evolution and learning, I had identified a widely scattered set of bench marks or points of reference from which a new scientific territory could be defined. These bench marks I have called "steps" in the title of the book.

In the nature of the case, an explorer can never know what he is exploring until it has been explored. He carries no Baedeker in his pocket, no guidebook which will tell him which churches he should visit or at which hotels he should stay. He has only the ambiguous folklore of others who have passed that way. No doubt deeper levels of the mind guide the scientist or the artist toward experiences and thoughts which are relevant to those problems which are somehow his, and this guidance seems to operate long before the scientist has any conscious knowledge of his goals. But how this happens we do not know.

I have often been impatient with colleagues who seemed unable to discern the difference between the trivial and the profound. But when students have asked me to define that difference, I have been struck dumb. I have said vaguely that any study which throws light upon the nature of "order" or "pattern" in the universe is surely nontrivial.

But this answer only begs the question.

I used to teach an informal course for psychiatric residents in the Veterans Administration Hospital at Palo Alto, trying to get them to think some of the thoughts that are in these essays. They would attend dutifully and even with intense interest to what I was saying, but every year the question would arise after three or four sessions of the class: "What is this course all about?"

I tried various answers to this question. Once I drew up a sort of catechism and offered it to the class as a sampling of the questions which I hoped they would be able to discuss after completing the course. The questions ranged from "What is a *sacrament*?" to "What is *entropy*?" and "What is *play*?"

As a didactic maneuver, my catechism was a failure: it silenced the class. But one question in it was useful:

> A certain mother habitually rewards her small son with ice cream after he eats his spinach. What additional information would you need to be able to predict whether the child will: a. Come to love or hate spinach; b. Love or hate ice cream, or c. Love or hate Mother?

We devoted one or two sessions of the class to exploring the many ramifications of this question, and it became clear to me that all the needed additional information concerned the context of the mother's and son's behavior. In fact, the phenomenon of *context* and the closely related phenomenon of *"meaning"* defined a division between the "hard" sciences and the sort of science which I was trying to build.

Gradually I discovered that what made it difficult to tell the class what the course was about was the fact that my way of thinking was different from theirs. A clue to this difference came from one of the students. It was the first session of the class and I had talked about the cultural differences between England and America—a matter which should always be touched on when an Englishman must teach Americans about cultural anthropology. At the end of the session, one resident came up. He glanced over his shoulder to be sure that the others were all leaving, and then said rather hesitantly, "I want to ask a question." "Yes." "It's—do you want us to *learn* what you are telling us?" I hesitated a moment, but he rushed on with, "Or is it all a sort of example, an illustration of something else?" "Yes, indeed!"

But an example of what?

And then there was, almost every year, a vague complaint which usually came to me as a rumor. It was alleged that "Bateson knows something which he does not tell you," or "There's something behind what Bateson says, but he never says what it is."

Evidently I was not answering the question, "An example of what?"

In desperation, I constructed a diagram to describe what I conceive to be the task of the scientist. By use of this diagram, it became clear that a difference between my habits of thought and those of my students sprang from the fact that they were trained to think and argue *inductively* from data to hypotheses but never to test hypotheses against knowledge derived by *deduction* from the fundamentals of science or philosophy.

The diagram had three columns. On the left, I listed various sorts of uninterpreted data, such as a film record of human or animal behavior, a description of an experiment, a description or photograph of a beetle's leg, or a recorded human utterance. I stressed the fact that "data" are not events or objects but always records or descriptions or memories of events or objects. Always there is a transformation or recoding of the raw event which intervenes between the scientist and his object. The weight of an object is measured against the weight of some other object or registered on a meter. The human voice is transformed into variable magnetizations of tape. Moreover, always and inevitably, there is a selection of data because the total universe, past and present, is not subject to observation from any given observer's position.

In a strict sense, therefore, no data are truly "raw," and every record has been somehow subjected to editing and transformation either by man or by his instruments.

But still the data are the most reliable source of information, and from them the scientist must start. They provide his first inspiration and to them he must later return.

In the middle column, I listed a number of imperfectly defined explanatory notions which are commonly used in the behavioral sciences— "ego," "anxiety," "instinct," "purpose," "mind," "self," "fixed action pattern," "intelligence," "stupidity," "maturity," and the like. For the sake of politeness, I call these "heuristic" concepts; but, in truth, most of them are so loosely derived and so mutually irrelevant that they mix together to make a sort of conceptual fog which does much to delay the progress of science.

In the right-hand column, I listed what I call "fundamentals." These are of two kinds: propositions and systems of propositions which are truistical, and propositions or "laws" which are generally true. Among the truistical propositions I included the "Eternal Verities" of mathematics where truth is tautologically limited to the domains within which man-made sets of axioms and definitions obtain: "*If* numbers are appropriately defined and *if* the operation of addition is appropriately defined; *then* $5 + 7 = 12$." Among propositions which I would describe as scientifically or generally and empirically true, I would list the conservation "laws" for mass and energy, the Second Law of Thermodynamics, and so on. But the line between tautological truths and empirical generalizations is not sharply definable, and, among my "fundamentals," there are many propositions whose truth no sensible man can doubt but which cannot easily be classified as either empirical or tautological. The "laws" of probability cannot be stated so as to be understood and not be believed, but it is not easy to decide whether they are empirical or tautological; and this is also true of Shannon's theorems in Information Theory.

With the aid of such a diagram, much can be said about the whole scientific endeavor and about the position and direction of any particular piece of inquiry within it. "Explanation" is the mapping of data onto fundamentals, but the ultimate goal of science is the increase of fundamental knowledge.

Many investigators, especially in the behavioral sciences, seem to believe that scientific advance is predominantly inductive and should be inductive. In terms of the diagram, they believe that progress is made by study of the "raw" data, leading to new heuristic concepts. The heuristic concepts are then to be regarded as "working hypotheses" and tested against more data. Gradually, it is hoped, the heuristic concepts will be corrected and improved until at last they are worthy of a place in the list of fundamentals. About fifty years of work in which thousands of clever men have had their share have, in fact, produced a rich crop of several hundred heuristic concepts, but, alas, scarcely a single principle worthy of a place in the list of fundamentals.

It is all too clear that the vast majority of the concepts of contemporary psychology, psychiatry, anthropology, sociology, and economics are totally detached from the network of scientific fundamentals.

Molière, long ago, depicted an oral doctoral examination in which the learned doctors ask the candidate to state the "cause and reason" why opium puts people to sleep. The candidate triumphantly answers in dog Latin, "Because there is in it a dormitive principle (*virtus dormitiva*)."

Characteristically, the scientist confronts a complex interactive system—in this case, an interaction between man and opium. He observes a change in the system—the man falls asleep. The scientist then explains the change by giving a name to a fictitious "cause," located in one or other component of the interacting system. Either the opium contains a reified dormitive principle, or the man contains a reified need for sleep, an adormitosis, which is "expressed" in his response to opium.

And, characteristically, all such hypotheses are "dormitive" in the sense that they put to sleep the "critical faculty" (another reified fictitious cause) within the scientist himself.

The state of mind or habit of thought which goes from data to dormitive hypothesis and back to data is self-reinforcing. There is, among all scientists, a high value set upon *prediction*, and, indeed, to be able to predict phenomena is a fine thing. But prediction is a rather poor test of an hypothesis, and this is especially true of "dormitive hypotheses." If we assert that opium contains a dormitive principle, we can then devote a lifetime of research to studying the characteristics of this principle. Is it heat-stable? In which fraction of a distillate is it located? What is its molecular formula? And so on. Many of these questions will be answerable in the laboratory and will lead on to derivative hypotheses no less "dormitive" than that from which we started.

In fact, the multiplication of dormitive hypotheses is a symptom of excessive preference for induction, and this preference must always lead to something like the present state of the behavioral sciences—a mass of quasi-theoretical speculation unconnected with any core of fundamental knowledge.

In contrast, I try to teach students—and this collection of essays is very much concerned with trying to communicate this thesis—that in scientific research you start from *two* beginnings, each of which has its own kind of authority: the observations cannot be denied, and the fundamentals must be fitted. You must achieve a sort of pincers maneuver.

If you are surveying a piece of land, or mapping the stars, you have two bodies of knowledge, neither of which can be ignored. There are your own empirical measurements on the one hand and there is Euclidean geometry on the other. If these two cannot be made to fit together, then either the data are wrong or you have argued wrongly from them *or* you have made a major discovery leading to a revision of the whole of geometry.

The would-be behavioral scientist who knows nothing of the basic structure of science and nothing of the 3000 years of careful philosophic and humanistic thought about man— who cannot define either entropy or a sacrament—had better hold his peace rather than add to the existing jungle of half-baked hypotheses.

But the gulf between the heuristic and the fundamental is not solely due to empiricism and the inductive habit, nor even to the seductions of quick application and the faulty educational system which makes professional scientists out of men who care little for the fundamental structure of science. It is due also to the circumstance that a very large part of the fundamental structure of nineteenth-century science was inappropriate or irrelevant to the problems and phenomena which confronted the biologist and behavioral scientist.

For at least 200 years, say from the time of Newton to the late nineteenth century, the dominant preoccupation of science was with those chains of cause and effect which could be referred to forces and impacts. The mathematics available to Newton was preponderantly quantitative, and this fact, combined with the central focus upon forces and impacts, led men to measure with remarkable accuracy quantities of distance, time, matter, and energy.

As the measurements of the surveyor must jibe with Euclidean geometry, so scientific thought had to jibe with the great conservative laws. The description of any event examined by a physicist or chemist was to be founded upon budgets of mass and energy, and this rule gave a particular kind of rigor to the whole of thought in the hard sciences.

The early pioneers of behavioral science not unnaturally began their survey of behavior by desiring a similar rigorous base to guide their speculations. Length and mass were concepts which they could hardly use in describing behavior (whatever that might be), but energy seemed more handy. It was tempting to relate "energy" to already existing metaphors such as "strength" of emotions or character or "vigor." Or to think of "energy" as somehow the opposite of "fatigue" or "apathy." Metabolism obeys an energy budget (within the strict meaning of "energy"), and energy expended in behavior must surely be included in this budget; therefore it seemed sensible to think of energy as a determinant of behavior.

It would have been more fruitful to think of _lack_ of energy as preventive of behavior, since in the end a starving man will cease to behave. But even this will not do: an amoeba, deprived of food, becomes for a time _more_ active. Its energy expenditure is an inverse function of energy input.

The nineteenth-century scientists (notably Freud) who tried to establish a bridge between behavioral data and the fundamentals of physical and chemical science were, surely, correct in insisting upon the need for such a bridge but, I believe, wrong in choosing "energy" as the foundation for that bridge.

If mass and length are inappropriate for the describing of behavior, then energy is unlikely to be more appropriate. After all, energy _is_ Mass $\times$ Velocity$^2$, and no behavioral scientist really insists that "psychic energy" is of these dimensions.

It is necessary, therefore, to look again among the fundamentals for an appropriate set of ideas against which we can test our heuristic hypotheses.

But some will argue that the time is not yet ripe; that surely the fundamentals of science were all arrived at by inductive reasoning from experience, so we should continue with induction until we get a fundamental answer.

I believe that it is simply not true that the fundamentals of science began in induction from experience, and I suggest that in the search for a bridgehead among the fundamentals we should go back to the very beginnings of scientific and philosophic thought; certainly to a period before science, philosophy, and religion had become separate activities separately pursued by professionals in separate disciplines.

Consider, for example, the central origin myth of the Judaeo-Christian peoples. What are the fundamental philosophic and scientific *problems* with which this myth is concerned?

> In the beginning God created the heaven and the earth. And the earth was without form, and void; and darkness was upon the face of the deep. And the Spirit of God moved upon the face of the waters.

> And God said, Let there be light: and there was light. And God saw the light, that it was good: and God divided the light from the darkness. And God called the light Day, and the darkness he called Night. And the evening and the morning were the first day.

> And God said, Let there be a firmament in the midst of the waters, and let it divide the waters from the waters. And God made the firmament, and divided the waters which were under the firmament from the waters which were above the firmament: and it was so. And God called the firmament Heaven. And the evening and the morning were the second day.

> And God said, Let the waters under the heaven be gathered together unto one place, and let the dry land appear: and it was so. And God called the dry land Earth; and the gathering together of the waters called he Seas: and God saw that it was good.

> *Authorized version*

Out of these first ten verses of thunderous prose, we can draw some of the premises or fundamentals of ancient Chaldean thought and it is strange, almost eerie, to note how many of the fundamentals and problems of modern science are foreshadowed in the ancient document.

(1) The problem of the origin and nature of *matter* is summarily dismissed.

(2) The passage deals at length with the problem of the origin of *order*.

(3) A separation is thus generated between the two sorts of problem. It is possible that this separation of problems was an error, but—error or not—the separation is maintained in the fundamentals of modern science. The conservative laws for matter and energy are still separate from the laws of order, negative entropy, and information.

(4) Order is seen as a matter of sorting and dividing. But the essential notion in all sorting is that some difference shall cause some other difference at a later time. If we are sorting black balls from white balls, or large balls from small balls, a difference among the balls is to be followed by a difference in their location—balls of one class to one sack and balls of another class to another. For such an operation, we need something like a sieve, a threshold, or, *par excellence,* a sense organ. It is understandable, therefore, that a perceiving Entity should have been invoked to perform this function of creating an otherwise improbable order.

(5) Closely linked with the sorting and dividing is the mystery of classification, to be followed later by the extraordinary human achievement of *naming*.

It is not at all clear that the various components of this myth are all products of inductive reasoning from experience. And the matter becomes still more puzzling when this origin myth is compared with others which embody different fundamental premises.

Among the Iatmul of New Guinea, the central origin myth, like the Genesis story, deals with the question of how dry land was separated from water. They say that in the beginning the crocodile Kavwokmali paddled with his front legs and with his hind legs; and his paddling kept the mud suspended in the water. The great culture hero, Kevembuangga, came with his spear and killed Kavwokmali. After that the mud settled and dry land was formed. Kevembuangga then stamped with his foot on the dry land, *i.e.,* he proudly demonstrated "that it was good."

Here there is a stronger case for deriving the myth from experience combined with inductive reasoning. After all, mud does remain in suspension if randomly stirred and does settle when the stirring ceases. Moreover, the Iatmul people live in the vast swamps of the Sepik River valley where the separation of land from water is imperfect. It is understandable that they might be interested in the differentiation of land from water.

In any case, the Iatmul have arrived at a theory of order which is almost a precise converse of that of the book of Genesis. In Iatmul thought, sorting will occur if randomization is prevented. In Genesis, an agent is invoked to do the sorting and dividing.

But both cultures alike assume a fundamental division between the problems of material creation and the problems of order and differentiation.

Returning now to the question of whether the fundamentals of science and/or philosophy were, at the primitive level, arrived at by inductive reasoning from empirical data, we find that the answer is not simple. It is difficult to see how the dichotomy between substance and form could be arrived at by inductive argument. No man, after all, has ever seen or experienced formless and unsorted matter; just as no man has ever seen or experienced a "random" event. If, therefore, the notion of a universe "without form and void" was arrived at by induction, it was by a monstrous—and perhaps erroneous—jump of extrapolation.

And even so, it is not clear that the starting point from which the primitive philosophers took off was observation. It is at least equally likely that dichotomy between form and substance was an unconscious *deduction* from the subject-predicate relation in the structure of primitive language. This, however, is a matter beyond the reach of useful speculation.

Be that as it may, the central—but usually not explicit—subject matter of the lectures which I used to give to psychiatric residents and of these essays is the bridge between behavioral data and the "fundamentals" of science and philosophy; and my critical comments above about the metaphoric use of "energy" in the behavioral sciences add up to a rather simple accusation of many of my colleagues, that they have tried to build the bridge to the *wrong half* of the ancient dichotomy between form and substance. The conservative laws for energy and matter concern substance rather than form. But mental process, ideas, communication, organization, differentiation, pattern, and so on, are matters of form rather than substance.

Within the body of fundamentals, that half which deals

with form has been dramatically enriched in the last thirty years by the discoveries of cybernetics and systems theory. This book is concerned with building a bridge between the facts of life and behavior and what we know today of the nature of pattern and order.

Illustrations for "A Re-examination of 'Bateson's Rule'" (p. 379).

Fig. 5 *Pterostichus mühlfeldii*, No. 742. Semidiagrammatic representation of the left middle tibia bearing the extra tarsi upon the antero-ventral border of the apex. *L*, the normal tarsus; *R*, the extra right; *L'* the extra left tarsus. (The property of Dr. Kraatz.) From Bateson, W., *Materials for the Study of Variation*, London: Macmillan, 1894, p 485.

Fig. 8 A mechanical device for showing the relations that extra legs in Secondary Symmetry bear to each other and to the normal leg from which they arise. The model *R* represents a normal right leg. *SL* and *SR* represent respectively the extra right and extra left legs of the supernumerary pair. *A* and *P*, the anterior and posterior spurs of the tibia. In each leg the *morphologically anterior* surface is shaded, the posterior being white. *R* is seen from the ventral aspect and *SL* and *SR* are in Position VP. From Bateson, W., *Materials for the Study of Variation*, London: Macmillan, 1894, p. 480.

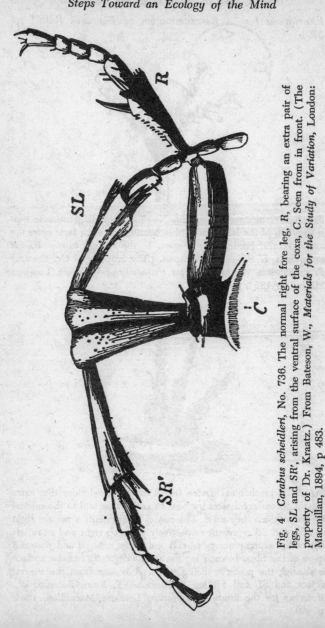

Fig. 4 *Carabus scheidleri*, No. 736. The normal right fore leg, R, bearing an extra pair of legs, SL and SR′, arising from the ventral surface of the coxa, C. Seen from in front. (The property of Dr. Kraatz.) From Bateson, W., *Materials for the Study of Variation*, London: Macmillan, 1894, p 483.

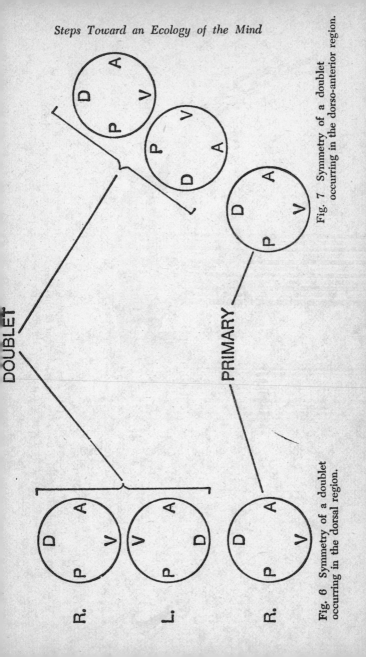

Fig. 7 Symmetry of a doublet occurring in the dorso-anterior region.

Fig. 6 Symmetry of a doublet occurring in the dorsal region.

# Part I: Metalogues

DEFINITION: A *metalogue* is a conversation about some problematic subject. This conversation should be such that not only do the participants discuss the problem but the structure of the conversation as a whole is also relevant to the same subject. Only some of the conversations here presented achieve this double format.

Notably, the history of evolutionary theory is inevitably a metalogue between man and nature, in which the creation and interaction of ideas must necessarily exemplify evolutionary process.

# Part I Mentalogues

# Metalogue: Why Do Things Get in a Muddle?*

Daughter:  Daddy, why do things get in a muddle?

Father:  What do you mean? Things? Muddle?

D:  Well, people spend a lot of time tidying things, but they never seem to spend time muddling them. Things just seem to get in a muddle by themselves. And then people have to tidy them up again.

F:  But do your things get in a muddle if you don't touch them?

D:  No—not if *nobody* touches them. But if you touch them—or if anybody touches them—they get in a muddle and it's a worse muddle if it isn't me.

F:  Yes—that's why I try to keep you from touching the things on my desk. Because my things get in a worse muddle if they are touched by somebody who isn't *me*.

D:  But do people *always* muddle other people's things? Why do they, Daddy?

F:  Now, wait a minute. It's not so simple. First of all, what do you mean by a muddle?

D:  I mean—so I can't find things, and so it *looks* all muddled up. The way it is when nothing is straight—

F:  Well, but are you sure you mean the same thing by muddle that anybody else would mean?

D:  But, Daddy, I'm sure I do—because I'm not a very

---

*Written in 1948; not previously published.

3

tidy person and if *I* say things are in a muddle, then I'm sure everybody else would agree with me.

F: All right—but do you think you mean the same thing by "tidy" that other people would? If your mummy makes your things tidy, do you know where to find them?

D: Hmm . . . *sometimes*—because, you see, I know where she puts things when she tidies up—

F: Yes, I try to keep her away from tidying my desk, too. I'm sure that she and I don't mean the same thing by "tidy."

D: Daddy, do you and I mean the same thing by "tidy?"

F: I doubt it, my dear—I doubt it.

D: But, Daddy, isn't that a funny thing—that everybody means the same when they say "muddled" but everybody means something different by "tidy." But "tidy" is the opposite of "muddled," isn't it?

F: Now we begin to get into more difficult questions. Let's start again from the beginning. You said "*Why do things always get in a muddle?*" Now we have made a step or two—and let's change the question to "Why do things get in a state which Cathy calls 'not tidy?'" Do you see why I want to make that change?

D: . . . Yes, I think so—because if I have a special meaning for "tidy" then some of other people's "tidies" will look like muddles to me—even if we do agree about most of what we call muddles—

F: That's right. Now—let's look at what *you* call tidy. When your paint box is put in a tidy place, where is it?

D: Here on the end of this shelf.

F: Okay—now if it were anywhere else?

D: No, that would not be tidy.

F: What about the other end of the shelf, here? Like this?

D: No, that's not where it belongs, and anyhow it would have to be *straight*, not all crooked the way you put it.

F: Oh—in the right place *and* straight.

D: Yes.

F: Well, that means that there are only very few places which are "tidy" for your paint box—

D: Only *one* place—

F: No—very *few* places, because if I move it a little bit, like this, it is still tidy.

D: All right—but very, very few places.

F: All right, very, very few places. Now what about the teddy bear and your doll, and the Wizard of Oz and your sweater, and your shoes? It's the same for all the things, isn't it, that each thing has only a very, very few places which are "tidy" for that thing?

D: Yes, Daddy—but the Wizard of Oz could be anywhere on that shelf. And Daddy—do you know what? I hate, hate it when my books get all mixed up with your books and Mummy's books.

F: Yes, I know. (Pause)

D: Daddy, you didn't finish. Why do my things get the way I say isn't tidy?

F: But I *have* finished—it's just because there are more ways which you call "untidy" than there are ways which you call "tidy."

D: But that isn't a reason why—

F: But, yes, it is. And it is the real and only and very important reason.

D: Oh, Daddy! Stop it.

F: No, I'm not fooling. That is the reason, *and all of science is hooked up with that reason*. Let's take another example. If I put some sand in the bottom of this cup and put some sugar on the top of it, and now stir it with a teaspoon, the sand and the sugar will get mixed up, won't they?

D: Yes, but, Daddy, is it fair to shift over to talking about "mixed up" when we started with "muddled up?"

F: Hmm . . . I wonder . . . but I think so—Yes—because let's say we can find somebody who thinks it is more tidy to have all the sand underneath all the sugar. And if you like *I*'ll say I want it that way—

D: Hmm . . .

F: All right—take another example. Sometimes in the movies you will see a lot of letters of the alphabet all scattered over the screen, all higgledy-piggledy and some even upside down. And then something shakes the table so that the letters start to move, and then as the shaking goes on, the letters all come together to spell the title of the film.

D: Yes, I've seen that—they spelled DONALD.

F: It doesn't matter what they spelled. The point is that you saw something being shaken and stirred up and instead of getting more mixed up than before, the letters came together into an order, all right way up, and spelled a word—they made up something which a lot of people would agree is *sense*.

D: Yes, Daddy, but you know . . .

F: No, I don't know; what I am trying to say is that in the real world things never happen that way. It's only in the movies.

D: But, Daddy . . .

F: I tell you it's only in the movies that you can shake things and they seem to take on more order and sense than they had before . . .

D: But, Daddy . . .

F: Wait till I've finished this time . . . And they make it look like that in the movies by doing the whole thing backwards. They put the letters all in order to spell DONALD and then they start the camera and then they start shaking the table.

D: Oh, Daddy—I knew that and I did so want to tell *you* that—and then when they run the film, they run it backwards so that it looks as though things had happened forwards. But really the shaking happened backwards. And they have to photograph it upside down . . . *Why* do they, Daddy?

F: Oh God.

D: Why do they have to fix the camera upside down, Daddy?

F: No, I won't answer that question now because we're in the middle of the question about muddles.

D: Oh—all right, but don't forget, Daddy, you've got to answer that question about the camera another day. Don't forget! You won't forget, will you, Daddy? Because I may not remember. Please, Daddy.

F: Okay—but another day. Now, where were we? Yes, about things never happening backwards. And I was trying to tell you why it is a reason for things to happen in a certain way if we can show that that way has more ways of happening than some other way.

D: Daddy—don't begin talking nonsense.

F: I'm not talking nonsense. Let's start again. There's only one way of spelling DONALD. Agreed?

D: Yes.

F: All right. And there are millions and millions and millions of ways of scattering six letters on the table. Agreed?

D: Yes. I suppose so. Can some of these be upside down?

F: Yes—just in the sort of higgledy-piggledy muddle they were in in the film. But there could be millions and millions and millions of muddles like that, couldn't there? And only one DONALD?

D: All right—yes. But, Daddy, the same letters might spell OLD DAN.

F: Never mind. The movie people don't want them to spell OLD DAN. They only want DONALD.

D: Why do they?

F: Damn the movie people.

D: But you mentioned them first, Daddy.

F: Yes—but that was to try to tell you why things happen that way in which there are most ways of their happening. And now it's your bedtime.

D: But, Daddy, you never did finish telling me why things happen that way—the way that has most ways.

F: All right. But don't start any more hares running—one is quite enough. Anyhow, I am tired of DONALD, let's take another example. Let's take tossing pennies.

D: Daddy? Are you still talking about the same question we started with? "Why do things get in a muddle?"

F: Yes.

D: Then, Daddy, is what you are trying to say true about pennies, and about DONALD, and about sugar and sand, and about my paint box, and about pennies?

F: Yes—that's right.

D: Oh—I was just wondering, that's all.

F: Now, let's see if I can get it said this time. Let's go back to the sand and the sugar, and let's suppose that somebody says that having the sand at the bottom is "tidy" or "orderly."

D: Daddy, does somebody have to *say* something like that before you can go on to talk about how things are going to get mixed up when you stir them?

F: Yes—that's just the point. They say what they hope will

happen and then I tell them it won't happen because there are so *many* other things that might happen. And I know that it is more likely that one of the *many* things will happen and not one of the few.

D: Daddy, you're just an old bookmaker, backing *all* the other horses against the *one* horse that I want to bet on.

F: That's right, my dear. I get them to bet on what they call the "tidy" way—I know that there are infinitely many muddled ways—so things will always go toward muddle and mixedness.

D: But why didn't you say that at the beginning, Daddy? I could have understood *that* all right.

F: Yes, I suppose so. Anyhow, it's now bedtime.

D: Daddy, why do grownups have wars, instead of just fighting the way children do?

F: No—bedtime. Be off with you. We'll talk about wars another time.

# Metalogue: Why Do Frenchmen?*

Daughter: Daddy, why do Frenchmen wave their arms
about?

Father: What do you mean?

D: I mean when they talk. Why do they wave their arms
and all that?

F: Well—why do you smile? Or why do you stamp your
foot sometimes?

D: But that's not the same thing, Daddy. I don't wave my
arms about like a Frenchman does. I don't believe they
can stop doing it, Daddy. Can they?

F: I don't know—they might find it hard to stop. . . . Can
you stop smiling?

D: But Daddy, I don't smile all the time. It's hard to stop
when I feel like smiling. But I don't feel like it *all* the
time. And then I stop.

F: That's true—but then a Frenchman doesn't wave his
arms in the same way all the time. Sometimes he waves
them in one way and sometimes in another—and sometimes, I think, he stops waving them.

*   *   *

F: What do you think? I mean, what does it make you
think when a Frenchman waves his arms?

*This metalogue is reprinted from *Impulse 1951*, an
annual of contemporary dance, by permission of Impulse
Publications, Inc. It has also appeared in *ETC.: A Review of General Semantics*, Vol. X, 1953.

D:  I think it looks silly, Daddy. But I don't suppose it looks like that to another Frenchman. They cannot all look silly to each other. Because if they did, they would stop it. Wouldn't they?

F:  Perhaps—but that is not a very simple question. What else do they make you think?

D:  Well—they look all excited . . .

F:  All right—"silly" and "excited."

D:  But are they really as excited as they look? If I were as excited as that, I would want to dance or sing or hit somebody on the nose . . . but they just go on waving their arms. They can't be really excited.

F:  Well—are they really as silly as they look to you? And anyhow, why do you sometimes want to dance and sing and punch somebody on the nose?

D:  Oh. Sometimes I just feel like that.

F:  Perhaps a Frenchman just feels "like that" when he waves his arms about.

D:  But he couldn't feel like that *all* the time, Daddy, he just couldn't.

F:  You mean—the Frenchman surely does not feel when he waves his arms exactly as you would feel if you waved yours. And surely you are right.

D:  But, then, how *does* he feel?

F:  Well—let us suppose you are talking to a Frenchman and he is waving his arms about, and then in the middle of the conversation, after something that you have said, he suddenly stops waving his arms, and just talks. What would you think then? That he had just stopped being silly and excited?

D:  No . . . I'd be frightened. I'd think I had said something that hurt his feelings and perhaps he might be really angry.

F:  Yes—and you might be right.

• • •

D:  All right—so they stop waving their arms when they start being angry.

F:  Wait a minute. The question, after all, is what does one Frenchman tell another Frenchman by waving his arms? And we have part of an answer—he tells him something about how he feels about the other guy. He tells him he is not seriously angry—that he is willing and able to be what you call "silly."

D: But—no—that's not sensible. He cannot do all that work so that *later* he will be able to tell the other guy that he *is* angry by just keeping his own arms still. How does he know that he is going to be angry later on?

F: He doesn't know. But, just in case . . .

D: No, Daddy, it doesn't make sense. I don't smile so as to be able to tell you I am angry by not smiling later on.

F: Yes—I think that that *is* part of the reason for smiling. And there are lots of people who smile in order to tell you that they are *not* angry—when they really are.

D: But that's different, Daddy. That's a sort of telling lies with one's face. Like playing poker.

F: Yes.

• • •

F: Now where are we? You don't think it sensible for Frenchmen to work so hard to tell each other that they are not angry or hurt. But after all what is most conversation about? I mean, among Americans?

D: But, Daddy, it's about all sorts of things—baseball and ice cream and gardens and games. And people talk about other people and about themselves and about what they got for Christmas.

F: Yes, yes—but who listens? I mean—all right, so they talk about baseball and gardens. But are they exchanging information? And, if so, *what* information?

D: Sure—when you come in from fishing, and I ask you "did you catch anything?" and you say "nothing," I didn't *know* that you wouldn't catch anything till you told me.

F: Hmm.

• • •

F: All right—so you mention my fishing—a matter about which I am sensitive—and then there is a gap, a silence in the conversation—and that silence tells you that I don't like cracks about how many fish I didn't catch. It's just like the Frenchman who stops waving his arms about when he is hurt.

D: I'm sorry, Daddy, but you did say . . .

F: No—wait a minute—let's not get confused by being

sorry—I shall go out fishing again tomorrow and I shall still know that I am unlikely to catch a fish . . .

D:  But, Daddy, you said all conversation is only telling other people that you are not angry with them . . .

F:  Did I? No—not *all* conversation, but much of it. Sometimes if both people are willing to listen carefully, it is possible to do more than exchange greetings and good wishes. Even to do more than exchange information. The two people may even find out something which neither of them knew before.

*       *       *

F:  Anyhow, most conversations are only about whether people are angry or something. They are busy telling each other that they are friendly—which is sometimes a lie. After all, what happens when they cannot think of anything to say? They all feel uncomfortable.

D:  But wouldn't that be information, Daddy? I mean—information that they are not cross?

F:  Surely, yes. But it's a different sort of information from "the cat is on the mat."

*       *       *

D:  Daddy, why cannot people just *say* "I am not cross at you" and let it go at that?

F:  Ah, now we are getting to the real problem. The point is that the messages which we exchange in gestures are really not the same as any translation of those gestures into words.

D:  I don't understand.

F:  I mean—that no amount of telling somebody in mere words that one is or is not angry is the same as what one might tell them by gesture or tone of voice.

D:  But, Daddy, you cannot have words without some tone of voice, can you? Even if somebody uses as little tone as he can, the other people will hear that he is holding himself back—and that will be a sort of tone, won't it?

F:  Yes—I suppose so. After all that's what I said just now about gestures—that the Frenchman can say something special by *stopping* his gestures.

*       *       *

F:  But then, what do I mean by saying that "mere words"

    can never convey the same message as gestures—if there are no "mere words"?

D: Well, the words might be written.

F: No—that won't let me out of the difficulty. Because written words still have some sort of rhythm and they still have overtones. The point is that *no* mere words exist. There are *only* words with either gesture or tone of voice or something of the sort. But, of course, gestures without words are common enough.

\*   \*   \*

D: Daddy, when they teach us French at school, why don't they teach us to wave our hands?

F: I don't know. I'm sure I don't know. That is probably one of the reasons why people find learning languages so difficult.

\*   \*   \*

F: Anyhow, it is all nonsense. I mean, the notion that language is made of words is all nonsense—and when I said that gestures could not be translated into "mere words," I was talking nonsense, because there is no such thing as "mere words." And all the syntax and grammar and all that stuff is nonsense. It's all based on the idea that "mere" words exist—and there are none.

D: But, Daddy . . .

F: I tell you—we have to start all over again from the beginning and assume that language is first and foremost a system of gestures. Animals after all have *only* gestures and tones of voice—and words were invented later. Much later. And after that they invented school-masters.

D: Daddy?

F: Yes.

D: Would it be a good thing if people gave up words and went back to only using gestures?

F: Hmm. I don't know. Of course we would not be able to have any conversations like this. We could only bark, or mew, and wave our arms about, and laugh and grunt and weep. But it might be fun—it would make life a sort of ballet—with dancers making their own music.

# Metalogue: About Games and Being Serious*

Daughter: Daddy, are these conversations serious?
Father: Certainly they are.
D:  They're not a sort of game that you play with me?
F:  God forbid . . . but they are a sort of game that we play together.
D:  Then they're *not* serious!

* * *

F:  Suppose you tell me what you would understand by the words "serious" and a "game."
D:  Well . . . if you're . . . I don't know.
F:  If I am what?
D:  I mean . . . the conversations are serious for me, but if you are only playing a game . . .
F:  Steady now. Let's look at what is good and what is bad about "playing" and "games." First of all, I don't mind —not much—about winning or losing. When your questions put me in a tight spot, sure, I try a little harder to think straight and to say clearly what I mean. But I don't bluff and I don't set traps. There is no temptation to cheat.
D:  That's just it. It's not serious to you. It's a game. People who cheat just don't know how to *play*. They treat a game as though it were serious.
F:  But it *is* serious.

*This metalogue is reprinted by permission from *ETC.: A Review of General Semantics*, Vol. X, 1953.

D: No, it isn't—not for you it isn't.

F: Because I don't even want to cheat?

D: Yes—partly that.

F: But do you want to cheat and bluff all the time?

D: No—of course not.

F: Well then?

D: Oh—Daddy—you'll *never* understand.

F: I guess I never will.

F: Look, I scored a sort of debating point just now by forcing you to admit that you don't want to cheat— and then I tied onto that admission the conclusion that therefore the conversations are not "serious" for you either. Was that a sort of cheating?

D: Yes—sort of.

F: I agree—I think it was. I'm sorry.

D: You see, Daddy—if I cheated or wanted to cheat, that would mean that I was not serious about the things we talk about. It would mean that I was only playing a game with you.

F: Yes, that makes sense.

* * *

D: But it doesn't make sense, Daddy. It's an awful muddle.

F: Yes—a muddle—but still a sort of sense.

D: How, Daddy?

* * *

F: Wait a minute. This is difficult to say. First of all— I think that we get somewhere with these conversations. I enjoy them very much and I think you do. But also, apart from that, I think that we get some ideas straight and I think that the muddles help. I mean—that if we both spoke logically all the time, we would never get anywhere. We would only parrot all the old clichés that everybody has repeated for hundreds of years.

D: What is a cliché, Daddy?

F: A cliché? It's a French word, and I think it was originally a printer's word. When they print a sentence they have to take the separate letters and put them one by one into a sort of grooved stick to spell out the sentence. But for words and sentences which people use often, the printer keeps little sticks of letters ready made up. And these ready-made sentences are called clichés.

D: But I've forgotten now what you were saying about clichés, Daddy.

F: Yes—it was about the muddles that we get into in these talks and how getting into muddles makes a sort of sense. If we didn't get into muddles, our talks would be like playing rummy without first shuffling the cards.

D: Yes, Daddy—but what about those things—the ready-made sticks of letters?

F: The clichés? Yes—it's the same thing. We all have lots of ready-made phrases and ideas, and the printer has ready-made sticks of letters, all sorted out into phrases. But if the printer wants to print something new—say, something in a new language, he will have to break up all that old sorting of the letters. In the same way, in order to think new thoughts or to say new things, we have to break up all our ready-made ideas and shuffle the pieces.

D: But, Daddy, the printer would not shuffle all the letters? Would he? He wouldn't shake them all up in a bag. He would put them one by one in their places—all the *a*'s in one box and all the *b*'s in another, and all the commas in another, and so on.

F: Yes—that's right. Otherwise he would go mad trying to find an *a* when he wanted it.

* * *

F: What are you thinking?

D: No—it's only that there are so many questions.

F: For example?

D: Well, I see what you mean about our getting into muddles. That that makes us say new sorts of things. But I am thinking about the printer. He has to keep all his little letters sorted out even though he breaks up all the ready-made phrases. And I am wondering about our muddles. Do we have to keep the little pieces of our thought in some sort of order—to keep from going mad?

F: I think so—yes—but I don't know *what* sort of order. That would be a terribly hard question to answer. I don't think we could get an answer to that question today.

* * *

F: You said there were "so many questions." Do you have another?

D: Yes—about games and being serious. That's what we started from, and I don't know how or why that led us to talk about our muddles. The way you confuse everything—it's a sort of cheating.

F: No, absolutely not.

\* \* \*

F: You brought up two questions. And really there are a lot more . . . We started from the question about these conversations—are they serious? Or are they a sort of game? And you felt hurt that I might be playing a game, while you were serious. It looks as though a conversation is a game if a person takes part in it with one set of emotions or ideas—but not a "game" if his ideas or emotions are different.

D: Yes, it's if your ideas about the conversation are different from mine . . .

F: If we *both* had the game idea, it would be all right?

D: Yes—of course.

F: Then it seems to be up to me to make clear what I mean by the game idea. I know that I am serious— whatever that means—about the things that we talk about. We talk about ideas. And I know that I play with the ideas in order to understand them and fit them together. It's "play" in the same sense that a small child "plays" with blocks . . . And a child with building blocks is mostly very serious about his "play."

D: But is it a *game*, Daddy? Do you play *against* me?

F: No. I think of it as you and I playing together against the building blocks—the ideas. Sometimes competing a bit—but competing as to who can get the next idea into place. And sometimes we attack each other's bit of building, or I will try to defend my built-up ideas from your criticism. But always in the end we are working together to build the ideas up so that they will stand.

\* \* \*

D: Daddy, do our talks have *rules*? The difference between a game and just playing is that a game has rules.

F: Yes. Let me think about that. I think we do have a sort of rules . . . and I think a child playing with blocks

has rules. The blocks themselves make a sort of rules.
They will balance in certain positions and they will not
balance in other positions. And it would be a sort of
cheating if the child used glue to make the blocks
stand up in a position from which they would otherwise
fall.

D:  But what rules do *we* have?

F:  Well, the ideas that we play with bring in a sort of rules.
There are rules about how ideas will stand up and support each other. And if they are wrongly put together
the whole building falls down.

D:  No glue, Daddy?

F:  No—no glue. Only logic.

* * *

D:  But you said that if we always talked logically and did
not get into muddles, we could never say anything new.
We could only say ready-made things. What did you
call those things?

F:  Clichés. Yes. Glue is what clichés are stuck together
with.

D:  But you said "logic," Daddy.

F:  Yes, I know. We're in a muddle again. Only I don't see
a way out of this particular muddle.

* * *

D:  How did we get into it, Daddy?

F:  All right, let's see if we can retrace our steps. We were
talking about the "rules" of these conversations. And I
said that the ideas that we play with have rules of
logic . . .

D:  Daddy! Wouldn't it be a good thing if we had a few
more rules and obeyed them more carefully? Then we
might not get into these dreadful muddles.

F:  Yes. But wait. You mean that I get us into these muddles
because I cheat against rules which we don't have. Or
put it this way. That we might have rules which would
stop us from getting into muddles—as long as we obeyed
them.

D:  Yes, Daddy, that's what the rules of a game are for.

F:  Yes, but do you want to turn these conversations into
*that* sort of a game? I'd rather play canasta—which
is fun too.

D: Yes, that's right. We can play canasta whenever we want to. But at the moment I would rather play this game. Only I don't know what sort of a game this is. Nor what sort of rules it has.

F: And yet we have been playing for some time.

D: Yes. And it's been fun.

F: Yes.

• • •

F: Let's go back to the question which you asked and which I said was too difficult to answer today. We were talking about the printer breaking up his clichés, and you said that he would still keep some sort of order among his letters—to keep from going mad. And then you asked "What sort of order should we cling to so that when we get into a muddle we do not go mad?" It seems to me that the "rules" of the game is only another name for that sort of order.

D: Yes—and cheating is what gets us into muddles.

F: In a sense, yes. That's right. Except that the whole point of the game is that we do get into muddles, and do come out on the other side, and if there were no muddles our "game" would be like canasta or chess—and that is not how we want it to be.

D: Is it *you* that make the rules, Daddy? Is that fair?

F: That, daughter, is a dirty crack. And probably an unfair one. But let me accept it at face value. Yes, it is I who make the rules—after all, I do not want us to go mad.

D: All right. But, Daddy, do you also change the rules? Sometimes?

F: Hmm, another dirty crack. Yes, daughter, I change them constantly. Not all of them, but some of them.

D: I wish you'd tell me when you're going to change them!

F: Hmm—yes—again. I wish I could. But it isn't like that. If it were like chess or canasta, I could tell you the rules, and we could, if we wanted to, stop playing and discuss the rules. And then we could start a new game with the new rules. But what rules would hold us between the two games? While we were discussing the rules?

D: I don't understand.

F: Yes. The point is that the purpose of these conversations is to discover the "rules." It's like life—a game whose purpose is to discover the rules, which rules are always changing and always undiscoverable.

D: But I don't call that a *game*, Daddy.

F: Perhaps not. I would call it a game, or at any rate "play." But it certainly is not like chess or canasta. It's more like what kittens and puppies do. Perhaps. I don't know.

* * *

D: Daddy, why do kittens and puppies play?

F: I don't know—I don't know.

# Metalogue: How Much Do You Know?*

Daughter: Daddy, how much do you know?

Father: Me? Hmm—I have about a pound of knowledge.

D:  Don't be silly. Is it a pound sterling or a pound weight? I mean *really* how much do you know?

F:  Well, my brain weighs about two pounds and I suppose I use about a quarter of it—or use it at about a quarter efficiency. So let's say half a pound.

D:  But do you know more than Johnny's daddy? Do you know more than I do?

F:  Hmm—I once knew a little boy in England who asked his father, "Do fathers always know more than sons?" and the father said, "Yes." The next question was, "Daddy, who invented the steam engine?" and the father said, "James Watt." And then the son came back with "—but why didn't James Watt's father invent it?"

* * *

D:  I know. I know more than that boy because I know why James Watt's father didn't. It was because somebody else had to think of something else before *anybody* could make a steam engine. I mean something like—I don't know—but there was somebody else who had to discover oil before anybody could make an engine.

F:  Yes—that makes a difference. I mean, it means that knowledge is all sort of knitted together, or woven, like

*This metalogue is reprinted by permission from *ETC.: A Review of General Semantics*, Vol. X, 1953.*

21

cloth, and each piece of knowledge is only meaningful or useful because of the other pieces—and . . .

D: Do you think we ought to measure it by the yard?

F: No. I don't.

D: But that's how we buy cloth.

F: Yes. But I didn't mean that it *is* cloth. Only it's like it— and certainly would not be flat like cloth—but in three dimensions—perhaps four dimensions.

D: What do you mean, Daddy?

F: I really don't know, my dear. I was just trying to think.

F: I don't think we are doing very well this morning. Suppose we start out on another tack. What we have to think about is how the pieces of knowledge are woven together. How they help each other.

D: How do they?

F: Well—it's as if sometimes two facts get added together and all you have is just two facts. But sometimes instead of just adding they multiply—and you get *four* facts.

D: You cannot multiply one by one and get four. You know you can't.

F: Oh.

* * *

F: But yes I can, too. If the things to be multiplied are pieces of knowledge or facts or something like that. Because every one of them is a double something.

D: I don't understand.

F: Well—at least a double something.

D: Daddy!

F: Yes—take the game of Twenty Questions. You think of something. Say you think of "tomorrow." All right. Now I ask "Is it abstract?" and you say "Yes." Now from your "yes" I have got a double bit of information. I know that it *is* abstract and I know that it isn't concrete. Or say it this way—from your "yes" I can *halve* the number of possibilities of what the thing can be. And that's a multiplying by one over two.

D: Isn't it a division?

F: Yes—it's the same thing. I mean—all right—it's a multiplication by .5. The important thing is that it's not just a subtraction or an addition.

D: How do you *know* it isn't?

F: How do I know it?—Well, suppose I ask another question which will halve the possibilities among the abstractions. And then another. That will have brought down the total possibilities to an eighth of what they were at the beginning. And two times two times two is eight.

D: And two and two and two is only six.

F: That's right.

D: But, Daddy, I don't see—what happens with Twenty Questions?

F: The point is that if I pick my questions properly I can decide between two times two times two times two twenty times over things—$2^{20}$ things. That's over a million things that you might have thought of. One question is enough to decide between two things; and two questions will decide between four things—and so on.

D: I don't like arithmetic, Daddy.

F: Yes, I know. The working it out is dull, but some of the ideas in it are amusing. Anyhow, you wanted to know how to measure knowledge, and if you start measuring things that always leads to arithmetic.

D: We haven't measured any knowledge yet.

F: No. I know. But we have made a step or two toward knowing how we would measure it if we wanted to. And that means we are a little nearer to knowing what knowledge is.

D: That would be a funny sort of knowledge, Daddy. I mean knowing *about* knowledge—would we measure that sort of knowing the same way?

F: Wait a minute—I don't know—that's really the $64 Question on this subject. Because—well, let's go back to the game of Twenty Questions. The point that we never mentioned is that those questions have to be in a certain order. First the wide general question and then the detailed question. And it's only from answers to the wide questions that I know which detailed questions to ask. But we counted them all alike. I don't know. But now you ask me if knowing about knowledge would be measured the same way as other knowledge. And the answer must surely be no. You see, if the early questions in the game tell me what questions to ask later, then they must be partly questions about knowing. They're exploring the business of knowing.

D: Daddy—has anybody ever measured how much anybody knew.

F: Oh yes. Often. But I don't quite know what the answers meant. They do it with examinations and tests and quizzes, but it's like trying to find out how big a piece of paper is by throwing stones at it.

D: How do you mean?

F: I mean—if you throw stones at two pieces of paper from the same distance and you find that you hit one piece more often than the other, then probably the one that you hit most will be bigger than the other. In the same way, in an examination you throw a lot of questions at the students, and if you find that you hit more pieces of knowledge in one student than in the others, then you think that student must know more. That's the idea.

D: But could one measure a piece of paper that way?

F: Surely one could. It might even be quite a good way of doing it. We do measure a lot of things that way. For example, we judge how strong a cup of coffee is by looking to see how black it is—that is, we look to see how much light is stopped. We throw light waves at it instead of stones, it's the same idea.

D: Oh.

* * *

D: But then—why shouldn't we measure knowledge that way?

F: How? By quizzes? No—God forbid. The trouble is that that sort of measuring leaves out your point—that there are different sorts of knowledge—and that there's knowing about knowledge. And ought one to give higher marks to the student who can answer the widest question? Or perhaps there should be a different *sort* of marks for each different sort of question.

D: Well, all right. Let's do that and then add the marks together and then . . .

F: No—we couldn't add them together. We might multiply or divide one sort of marks by another sort but we couldn't add them.

D: Why not, Daddy?

F: Because—because we couldn't. No wonder you don't like arithmetic if they don't tell you that sort of thing at school—What do they tell you? Golly—I wonder what the teachers think arithmetic is about.

D:  What *is* it about, Daddy?

F:  No. Let's stick to the question of how to measure knowledge—Arithmetic is a set of tricks for thinking clearly and the only fun in it is just its clarity. And the first thing about being clear is not to mix up ideas which are really different from each other. The idea of two oranges is really different from the idea of two miles. Because if you add them together you only get fog in your head.

D:  But, Daddy, I can't keep ideas separate. Ought I to do that?

F:  No— No— Of course not. Combine them. But don't add them. That's all. I mean—if the ideas are numbers and you want to combine two different sorts, the thing to do is to multiply them by each other. Or divide them by each other. And then you'll get some new sort of idea, a new sort of quantity. If you have miles in your head, and you have hours in your head, and you divide the miles by the hours, you get "miles per hour"— that's a speed.

D:  Yes, Daddy. What would I get if I multiplied them?

F:  Oh—er—I suppose you'd get mile-hours. Yes. I know what they are. I mean, what a mile-hour is. It's what you pay a taxi driver. His meter measures miles and he has a clock which measures hours, and the meter and the clock work together and multiply the hours by the miles and then it multiplies the mile-hours by something else which makes mile-hours into dollars.

D:  I did an experiment once.

F:  Yes?

D:  I wanted to find out if I could think two thoughts at the same time. So I thought "It's summer" and I thought "It's winter." And then I tried to think the two thoughts together.

F:  Yes?

D:  But I found I wasn't having two thoughts. I was only having one thought *about* having two thoughts.

F:  Sure, that's just it. You can't mix thoughts, you can only combine them. And in the end, that means you can't count them. Because counting is really only adding things together. And you mostly can't do that.

D: Then *really* do we only have one big thought which has lots of branches—lots and lots and lots of branches?

F: Yes. I think so. I don't know. Anyhow I think that is a clearer way of saying it. I mean it's clearer than talking about bits of knowledge and trying to count them.

* * *

D: Daddy, why don't you use the other three-quarters of your brain?

F: Oh, yes—that—you see the trouble is that I had school-teachers too. And they filled up about a quarter of my brain with fog. And then I read newspapers and listened to what other people said, and that filled up another quarter with fog.

D: And the other quarter, Daddy?

F: Oh—that's fog that I made for myself when I was trying to think.

# Metalogue: Why Do Things Have Outlines?*

Daughter: Daddy, why do things have outlines?

Father:  Do they? I don't know. What sort of things do you mean?

D:  I mean when I draw things, why do they have outlines?

F:  Well, what about other sorts of things—a flock of sheep? or a conversation? Do they have outlines?

D:  Don't be silly. I can't draw a conversation. I mean *things.*

F:  Yes—I was trying to find out just what you meant. Do you mean "Why do we give things outlines when we draw them?" or do you mean that the things *have* outlines whether we draw them or not?

D:  I don't know, Daddy. You tell me. Which do I mean?

F:  I don't know, my dear. There was a very angry artist once who scribbled all sorts of things down, and after he was dead they looked in his books and in one place they found he'd written "Wise men see outlines and therefore they draw them" but in another place he'd written "Mad men see outlines and therefore they draw them."

D:  But which does he mean? I don't understand.

F:  Well, William Blake—that was his name—was a great artist and a very angry man. And sometimes he rolled

*Reprinted by permission from *ETC.: A Review of General Semantics*, Vol. XI, 1953.

up his ideas into little spitballs so that he could throw them at people.

D: But what was he mad about, Daddy?

F: But what was he mad about? Oh, I see—you mean "angry." We have to keep those two meanings of "mad" clear if we are going to talk about Blake. Because a lot of people thought he was mad—really mad—crazy. And that was one of the things he was mad-angry about. And then he was mad-angry, too, about some artists who painted pictures as though things didn't have outlines. He called them "the slobbering school."

D: He wasn't very tolerant, was he, Daddy?

F: Tolerant? Oh, God. Yes, I know—that's what they drum into you at school. No, Blake was not very tolerant. He didn't even think tolerance was a good thing. It was just more slobbering. He thought it blurred all the outlines and muddled everything—that it made all cats gray. So that nobody would be able to see anything clearly and sharply.

D: Yes, Daddy.

F: No, that's not the answer. I mean "Yes, Daddy" is not the answer. All that says is that you don't know what your opinion is—and you don't give a damn what I say or what Blake says and that the school has so befuddled you with talk about tolerance that you cannot tell the difference between anything and anything else.

D: (Weeps.)

F: Oh, God. I'm sorry, but I was angry. But not really angry with you. Just angry at the general mushiness of how people act and think—and how they preach muddle and call it tolerance.

D: But, Daddy—

F: Yes?

D: I don't know. I don't seem able to think very well. It's all in a muddle.

F: I'm sorry. I suppose I muddled you by starting to let off steam.

* * *

D: Daddy?

F: Yes?

D: Why is that something to get angry about?

F:  Is what something to get angry about?

D:  I mean—about whether things have outlines. You said
William Blake got angry about it. And then you get
angry about it. Why is that, Daddy?

F:  Yes, in a way I think it is. I think it matters. Perhaps in
a way, is *the* thing that matters. And other things only
matter because they are part of this.

D:  What do you mean, Daddy?

F:  I mean, well, let's talk about tolerance. When Gentiles
want to bully Jews because they killed Christ, I get
intolerant. I think the Gentiles are being muddle-
headed and are blurring all the outlines. Because the
Jews didn't kill Christ, the Italians did it.

D:  Did they, Daddy?

F:  Yes, only the ones who did are called Romans today,
and we have another word for their descendants. We
call them Italians. You see there are two muddles and
I was making the second muddle on purpose so we
could catch it. First there's the muddle of getting the
history wrong and saying the Jews did it, and then
there's the muddle of saying that the descendants
should be responsible for what their ancestors didn't
do. It's all slovenly.

D:  Yes, Daddy.

F:  All right, I'll try not to get angry again. All I'm trying to
say is that muddle is something to get angry about.

D:  Daddy?

F:  Yes?

D:  We were talking about muddle the other day. Are we
really talking about the same thing now?

F:  Yes. Of course we are. That's why it's important—
what we said the other day.

D:  And you said that getting things clear was what Science
was about.

F:  Yes, that's the same thing again.

• • •

D:  I don't seem to understand it all very well. Everything
seems to be everything else, and I get lost in it.

F:  Yes, I know it's difficult. The point is that our conversations do have an outline, somehow—if only one could
see it clearly.

F:   Let's think about a real concrete out-and-out muddle,
     for a change, and see if that will help. Do you remem-
     ber the game of croquet in *Alice in Wonderland?*

D:   Yes—with flamingos?

F:   That's right.

D:   And porcupines for balls?

F:   No, hedgehogs. They were hedgehogs. They don't have
     porcupines in England.

D:   Oh. Was it in England, Daddy? I didn't know.

F:   Of course it was in England. You don't have duchesses
     in America either.

D:   But there's the Duchess of Windsor, Daddy.

F:   Yes, but she doesn't have quills, not like a real porcu-
     pine.

D:   Go on about Alice and don't be silly, Daddy.

F:   Yes, we were talking about flamingos. The point is that
     the man who wrote Alice was thinking about the same
     things that we are. And he amused himself with little
     Alice by imagining a game of croquet that would be all
     muddle, just absolute muddle. So he said they should
     use flamingos as mallets because the flamingos would
     bend their necks so the player wouldn't know even
     whether his mallet would hit the ball or how it would
     hit the ball.

D:   Anyhow the ball might walk away of its own accord
     because it was a hedgehog.

F:   That's right. So that it's all so muddled that nobody can
     tell at all what's going to happen.

D:   And the hoops walked around, too, because they were
     soldiers.

F:   That's right—everything could move and nobody could
     tell how it would move.

D:   Did everything have to be *alive* so as to make a com-
     plete muddle?

F:   No—he could have made it a muddle by . . . no, I
     suppose you're right. That's interesting. Yes, it had to be
     that way. Wait a minute. It's curious but you're
     right. Because if he'd muddled things any other way,
     the players could have learned how to deal with the
     muddling details. I mean, suppose the croquet lawn was
     bumpy, or the balls were a funny shape, or the heads

of the mallets just wobbly instead of being alive, then
the people could still learn and the game would only
be more difficult—it wouldn't be impossible. But once
you bring live things into it, it becomes impossible. I
wouldn't have expected that.

D: Wouldn't you, Daddy? I would have. That seems natural to me.

F: Natural? Sure—natural enough. But I would not have
expected it to work that way.

D: Why not? That's what I would have expected.

F: Yes. But this is the thing that I would not have expected. That animals, which are themselves able to see
things ahead and act on what they think is going to
happen—a cat can catch a mouse by jumping to land
where the mouse will probably be when she has completed her jump—but it's just the fact that animals are
capable of seeing ahead and learning that makes them
the only really unpredictable things in the world. To
think that we try to make laws as though people were
quite regular and predictable.

D: Or do they make the laws just because people are not
predictable, and the people who make the laws wish
the other people were predictable?

F: Yes, I suppose so.

• • •

D: What were we talking about?

F: I don't quite know—not yet. But you started a new
line by asking if the game of croquet could be made
into a real muddle only by having all the things in it
alive. And I went chasing after that question, and I
don't think I've caught up with it yet. There is something funny about that point.

D: What?

F: I don't quite know—not yet. Something about living
things and the difference between them and the things
that are not alive—machines, stones, so on. Horses
don't fit in a world of automobiles. And that's part of
the same point. They're unpredictable, like flamingos
in the game of croquet.

D: What about people, Daddy?

F: What about them?

D: Well, they're alive. Do they fit? I mean on the streets?

F:  No, I suppose they don't really fit—or only by working pretty hard to protect themselves and make themselves fit. Yes, they have to make themselves predictable, because otherwise the machines get angry and kill them.

D:  Don't be silly. If the machines can get angry, then *they* would not be predictable. They'd be like you, Daddy. You can't predict when you're angry, can you?

F:  No, I suppose not.

D:  But, Daddy, I'd rather have you unpredictable—sometimes.

* * *

D:  What did you mean by a conversation having an outline? Has this conversation had an outline?

F:  Oh, surely, yes. But we cannot see it yet because the conversation isn't finished. You cannot ever see it while you're in the middle of it. Because if you could see it, you would be predictable—like the machine. And I would be predictable—and the two of us together would be predictable—

D:  But I don't understand. You say it is important to be clear about things. And you get angry about people who blur the outlines. And yet we think it's better to be unpredictable and not to be like a machine. And you say that we cannot see the outlines of our conversation till it's over. Then it doesn't matter whether we're clear or not. Because we cannot *do* anything about it then.

F:  Yes, I know—and I don't understand it myself. . . . But anyway, who wants to *do* anything about it?

# Metalogue: Why a Swan?*

Daughter: Why a swan?

Father:   Yes—and why a puppet in Petroushka?

D:. No—that's different. After all a puppet is sort of human—and that particular puppet is very human.

F:   More human than the people?

D:   Yes.

F:   But still only *sort of* human? And after all the swan is also sort of human.

D:   Yes.

* * *

D:   But what about the dancer? Is she human? Of course she *really* is, but, on the stage, she seems inhuman or impersonal—perhaps superhuman. I don't know.

F:   You mean—that while the swan is only a *sort of* swan and has no webbing between her toes, the dancer seems only *sort of* human.

D:   I don't know—perhaps it's something like that.

* * *

F:   No—I get confused when I speak of the "swan" and the dancer as two different things. I would rather say that the thing I see on the stage—the swan figure—is both "sort of" human and "sort of" swan.

D:   But then you would be using the word "sort of" in two senses.

*This metalogue appeared in *Impulse 1954* and is reprinted by permission of Impulse Publications, Inc.

33

F:  Yes, that's so. But anyhow, when I say that the swan figure is "sort of" human, I don't mean that it (or she) is a member of that species or sort which we call human.

D:  No, of course not.

F:  Rather that she (or it) is a member of another subdivision of a larger group which would include Petroushka puppets and ballet swans and people.

D:  No, it's not like genera and species. Does your larger group include geese?

•  •  •

F:  All right. Then I evidently do not know what the word "sort of" means. But I do know that the whole of fantasy, poetry, ballet, and art in general owes its meaning and importance to the relationship which I refer to when I say that the swan figure is a "sort of" swan—or a "pretend" swan.

D:  Then we shall never know why the dancer is a swan or a puppet or whatever, and shall never be able to say what art or poetry is until someone says what is really meant by "sort of."

F:  Yes.

•  •  •

F:  But we don't have to avoid puns. In French the phrase *espèce de* (literally "sort of") carries a special sort of punch. If one man calls another "a camel" the insult may be a friendly one. But if he calls him an *espèce de chameau*—a *sort of* camel—that's bad. It's still worse to call a man an *espèce d'espèce*—a sort of a sort.

D:  A sort of a sort of what?

F:  No—just a sort of a sort. On the other hand, if you say of a man that he is a *true* camel, the insult carries a flavor of grudging admiration.

D:  But when a Frenchman calls a man a sort of camel, is he using the phrase *sort of* in anything like the same way as I, when I say the swan is *sort of* human?

•  •  •

F:  It's like—there's a passage in Macbeth. Macbeth is talking to the murderers whom he is sending out to kill Banquo. They claim to be men, and he tells them they are sort of men.

    Ay—in the catalogue ye go for men.

as hounds and greyhounds, mongrels, spaniels, curs,
shoughs, water-rugs and demi-wolves are clept
all by the name of dogs.

(*Macbeth*, Act III, Scene 1)

D: No—that's what you said just now. What was it?
"Another subdivision of a larger group?" I don't think
that's it at all.

F: No, it's not only that. Macbeth, after all, uses dogs in his
simile. And "dogs" means either noble hounds or scav-
engers. It would not be the same if he had used the
domestic varieties of cats—or the subspecies of wild
roses.

D: All right, all right. But what is the answer to my
question? When a Frenchman calls a man a "sort of"
camel, and I say that the swan is "sort of" human, do
we both mean the same thing by "sort of"?

\* \* \*

F: All right, let's try to analyze what "sort of" means. Let's
take a single sentence and examine it. If I say "the
puppet Petroushka is *sort of* human," I state a relationship.

D: Between what and what?

F: Between ideas, I think.

D: Not between a puppet and people?

F: No. Between some ideas that I have about a puppet
and some ideas that I have about people.

D: Oh.

\* \* \*

D: Well then, what sort of a relationship?

F: I don't know. A metaphoric relationship?

\* \* \*

F: And then there is that other relationship which is
emphatically *not* "sort of." Many men have gone to the
stake for the proposition that the bread and wine are
*not* "sort of" the body and blood.

D: But is that the same thing? I mean—is the swan ballet
a sacrament?

F: Yes—I think so—at least for some people. In Protestant
language we might say that the swanlike costume and
movements of the dancer are "outward and visible
signs of some inward and spiritual grace" of woman.

But in Catholic language that would make the ballet into a mere metaphor and not a sacrament.

D: But you said that for some people it is a sacrament. You mean for Protestants?

F: No, no. I mean that if for some people the bread and wine are only a metaphor, while for others—Catholics —the bread and wine are a sacrament; then, if there be some for whom the ballet is a metaphor, there may be others for whom it is emphatically more than a metaphor—but rather a sacrament.

D: In the Catholic sense?

F: Yes.

* * *

F: I mean that if we could say clearly what is meant by the proposition "the bread and wine is *not* 'sort of' the body and blood"; then we should know more about what we mean when we say either that the swan is "sort of" human or that the ballet is a sacrament.

D: Well—how do you tell the difference?

F: Which difference?

D: Between a sacrament and a metaphor.

* * *

F: Wait a minute. We are, after all, talking about the performer or the artist or the poet, or a given member of the audience. You ask me how I tell the difference between a sacrament and a metaphor. But my answer must deal with the person and not the message. You ask me how I would decide whether a certain dance on a certain day is or is not sacramental for the particular dancer.

D: All right—but get on with it.

F: Well—I think it's a sort of a secret.

D: You mean you won't tell me?

F: No—it's not that sort of secret. It's not something that one must not tell. It's something that one *cannot* tell.

D: What do you mean? Why not?

F: Let us suppose I asked the dancer, "Miss X, tell me, that dance which you perform—is it for you a sacrament or a mere metaphor?" And let us imagine that I can make this question intelligible. She will perhaps

put me off by saying, "You saw it—it is for you to decide, if you want to, whether or not it is sacramental for
you." Or she might say, "Sometimes it is and sometimes
it isn't." Or "How was I, last night?" But in any case
she can have no direct control over the matter.

\* \* \*

D: Do you mean that anybody who knew this secret would
have it in their power to be a great dancer or a great
poet?

F: No, no, no. It isn't like that at all. I mean first that great
art and religion and all the rest of it is about this
secret; but knowing the secret in an ordinary conscious
way would not give the knower control.

\* \* \*

D: Daddy, what has happened? We were trying to find
out what "sort of" means when we say that the swan
is "sort of" human. I said that there must be two senses
of "sort of." One in the phrase "the swan figure is a 'sort
of' swan, and another in the phrase "the swan figure is
'sort of' human." And now you are talking about mysterious secrets and control.

F: All right. I'll start again. The swan figure is not a real
swan but a pretend swan. It is also a pretend-not human being. It is also "really" a young lady wearing a
white dress. And a real swan would resemble a young
lady in certain ways.

D: But which of these is sacramental?

F: Oh Lord, here we go again. I can only say this: that it
is not one of these statements but their combination
which constitutes a sacrament. The "pretend" and the
"pretend-not" and the "really" somehow get fused together into a single meaning.

D: But we ought to keep them separate.

F: Yes. That is what the logicians and the scientists try to
do. But they do not create ballets that way—nor sacra-
ments.

# Metalogue: What Is an Instinct?*

Daughter:   Daddy, what is an instinct?

Father:   An instinct, my dear, is a explanatory principle.

D:   But what does it explain?

F:   Anything—almost anything at all. Anything you want it to explain.

D:   Don't be silly. It doesn't explain gravity.

F:   No. But that is because nobody wants "instinct" to explain gravity. If they did, it would explain it. We could simply say that the moon has an instinct whose strength varies inversely as the square of the distance . . .

D:   But that's nonsense, Daddy.

F:   Yes, surely. But it was you who mentioned "instinct," not I.

D:   All right—but then what does explain gravity?

F:   Nothing, my dear, because gravity is an explanatory principle.

D:   Oh.

D:   Do you mean that you cannot use one explanatory principle to explain another? Never?

F:   Hmm . . . hardly ever. That is what Newton meant when he said, "*hypotheses non fingo.*"

D:   And what does that mean? Please.

F:   Well, you know what "hypotheses" are. Any statement

*This metalogue is reprinted by permission of Mouton & Co. from *Approaches to Animal Communication*, edited by Thomas A. Sebeok, 1969.

linking together two descriptive statements is an hypothesis. If you say that there was a full moon on February 1st and another on March 1st; and then you link these two observations together in any way, the statement which links them is an hypothesis.

D: Yes—and I know what *non* means. But what's *fingo?*

F: Well—*fingo* is a late Latin word for "make." It forms a verbal noun *fictio* from which we get the word "fiction."

D: Daddy, do you mean that Sir Isaac Newton thought that all hypotheses were just *made up* like stories?

F: Yes—precisely that.

D: But didn't he discover gravity? With the apple?

F: No, dear. He invented it.

D: Oh. . . . Daddy, who invented instinct?

F: I don't know. Probably biblical.

D: But if the idea of gravity links together two descriptive statements, it must be an hypothesis.

F: That's right.

D: Then Newton did *fingo* an hypothesis after all.

F: Yes—indeed he did. He was a very great scientist.

D: Oh.

D: Daddy, is an explanatory principle the same thing as an hypothesis?

F: Nearly, but not quite. You see, an hypothesis tries to explain some particular something but an explanatory principle—like "gravity" or "instinct"—really explains nothing. It's a sort of conventional agreement between scientists to stop trying to explain things at a certain point.

D: Then is that what Newton meant? If "gravity" explains nothing but is only a sort of full stop at the end of a line of explanation, then inventing gravity was not the same as inventing an hypothesis, and he could say he did not *fingo* any hypotheses.

F: That's right. There's no explanation of an explanatory principle. It's like a black box.

D: Oh.

D: Daddy, what's a black box?

F: A "black box" is a conventional agreement between

　　　　scientists to stop trying to explain things at a certain
　　　　point. I guess it's usually a temporary agreement.

D: But that doesn't sound like a black box.

F: No—but that's what it's called. Things often don't sound
　　like their names.

D: No.

F: It's a word that comes from the engineers. When they
　　draw a diagram of a complicated machine, they use a
　　sort of shorthand. Instead of drawing all the details,
　　they put a box to stand for a whole bunch of parts and
　　label the box with what that bunch of parts is supposed
　　to *do*.

D: So a "black box" is a label for what a bunch of things
　　are supposed to do. . . .

F: That's right. But it's not an explanation of *how* the
　　bunch works.

D: And gravity?

F: Is a label for what gravity is supposed to do. It's not
　　an explanation of how it does it.

D: Oh.


D: Daddy, what is an instinct?

F: It's a label for what a certain black box is supposed to
　　do.

D: But what's it supposed to do?

F: Hm. That is a very difficult question . . .

D: Go on.

F: Well. It's supposed to control—partly control—what an
　　organism does.

D: Do plants have instincts?

F: No. If a botanist used the word "instinct," when talking
　　about plants, he would be accused of zoomorphism.

D: Is that bad?

F: Yes. Very bad for botanists. For a botanist to be guilty
　　of zoomorphism is as bad as for a zoologist to be guilty
　　of anthropomorphism. Very bad, indeed.

D: Oh. I see.


D: What did you mean by "partly control"?

F: Well. If an animal falls down a cliff, its falling is con-
　　trolled by gravity. But if it wiggles while falling, that
　　might be due to instinct.

D: Self-preservative instinct?

F: I suppose so.

D: What is a self, Daddy? Does a dog know it has a self?

F: I don't know. But if the dog does know it has a self, and it wiggles in order to preserve that self, then its wiggling is *rational*, not instinctive.

D: Oh. Then a "self-preservative instinct" is a contradiction.

F: Well, it's a sort of halfway house on the road to anthropomorphism.

D: Oh. That's bad.

F: But the dog might *know* it had a self and not know that that self should be preserved. It would then be rational to *not* wiggle. So if the dog still wiggles, this would be instinctive. But if it *learned* to wiggle, then it would not be instinctive.

D: Oh.

D: What would not be instinctive, Daddy? The learning or the wiggling?

F: No—just the wiggling.

D: And the *learning* would be instinctive?

F: Well . . . yes. Unless the dog had to *learn* to learn.

D: Oh.

D: But, Daddy, what is instinct supposed to explain?

F: I keep trying to avoid that question. You see, instincts were invented before anybody knew anything about genetics, and most of modern genetics was discovered before anybody knew anything about communication theory. So it is doubly difficult to translate "instinct" into modern terms and ideas.

D: Yes, go on.

F: Well, you know that in the chromosomes, there are genes; and that the genes are some sort of messages which have to do with how the organism develops and with how it behaves.

D: Is developing different from behaving, Daddy? What's the difference? And which is learning? Is it "developing" or "behaving?"

F: No! No! Not so fast. Let's avoid those questions by putting developing-learning-behavior all together in one basket. A single spectrum of phenomena. Now let's try to say how instinct contributes to explaining this spectrum.

D: But is it a spectrum?

F: No—that's only a loose way of talking.

D: Oh.

D: But isn't instinct all on the behavior end of that "spectrum"? And isn't learning all determined by environment and not chromosomes?

F: Let's get this clear—that there is no behavior and no anatomy and no learning in the chromosomes themselves.

D: Don't they have their own anatomy?

F: Yes, of course. And their own physiology. But the anatomy and physiology of the genes and chromosomes is *not* the anatomy and physiology of the whole animal.

D: Of course not.

F: But it is *about* the anatomy and physiology of the whole animal.

D: Anatomy *about* anatomy?

F: Yes, just as letters and words have their own forms and shapes and those shapes are parts of words or sentences and so on—which may be *about* anything.

D: Oh.

D: Daddy, is the anatomy of the genes and chromosomes about the anatomy of the whole animal? And the physiology of the genes and chromosomes about the physiology of the whole animal?

F: No, no. There is no reason to expect that. It's not like that. Anatomy and physiology are not separate in that way.

D: Daddy, are you going to put anatomy and physiology together in one basket, like you did developing-learning-behavior?

F: Yes. Certainly.

D: Oh.

D: The *same* basket?

F: Why not? I think *developing* is right in the middle of that basket. Right smack in the middle.

D: Oh.

D: If chromosomes and genes have anatomy and physiology, they must have development.

F: Yes. That follows.

D: Do you think their development could be *about* the development of the whole organism?

F: I don't even know what that question would mean.

D: I do. It means that the chromosomes and genes would be changing or developing somehow while the baby is developing, and the changes in the chromosomes would be *about* the changes in the baby. Controlling them or *partly* controlling them.

F: No. I don't think so.

D: Oh.


D: Do chromosomes *learn?*

F: I don't know.

D: They do sound rather like black boxes.

F: Yes, but if chromosomes or genes can learn, then they are much more complicated black boxes than anybody at present believes. Scientists are always assuming or hoping that things are simple, and then discovering that they are not.

D: Yes, Daddy.


D: Daddy, is that an instinct?

F: Is what an instinct?

D: Assuming that things are simple.

F: No. Of course not. Scientists have to be taught to do that.

D: But I thought no organism could be taught to be wrong *every* time.

F: Young lady, you are being disrespectful and wrong. In the first place, scientists are not wrong every time they assume that things are simple. Quite often they are right or partly right and still more often, they think they are right and tell each other so. And that is enough reinforcement. And, anyhow you are wrong in saying that no organism can be taught to be wrong every time.


D: When people say that something is "instinctive," are they trying to make things simple?

F: Yes, indeed.

D: And are they wrong?

F: I don't know. It depends on what they mean.

D: Oh.

D: *When* do they do it?

F: Yes, that's a better way of asking the question. They do it when they see a creature do something, and they are sure: first, that the creature did not learn how to do that something and, second, that the creature is too stupid to understand why it should do that.

D: Any other time?

F: Yes. When they see that all members of the species do the same things under the same circumstances; and when they see the animal repeating the same action even when the circumstances are changed so that the action fails.

D: So there are four ways of knowing that it's instinctive.

F: No. Four conditions under which scientists talk about instinct.

D: But what if one condition isn't there? An instinct sounds rather like a habit or a custom.

F: But habits are learned.

D: Yes.

D: Are habits always *twice* learned?

F: What do you mean?

D: I mean—when I learn a set of chords on the guitar, first I learn them or find them; and then later when I practice, I get the *habit* of playing them that way. And sometimes I get bad habits.

F: Learning to be wrong *every* time?

D: Oh—all right. But what about that twice-over business? Would *both* parts of learning be not there if guitar playing were instinctive?

F: Yes. If both parts of learning were clearly not there, scientists might say that guitar playing is instinctive.

D: But what if only one part of learning was missing?

F: Then, logically, the missing part could be explained by "instinct."

D: Could *either* part be missing?

F: I don't know. I don't think anybody knows.

D: Oh.

D: Do birds *practice* their songs?

F: Yes. Some birds are said to practice.

D: I guess instinct gives them the first part of singing, but they have to work on the second part.

F: Perhaps.


D: Could *practicing* be instinctive?

F: I suppose it could be—but I am not sure what the word "instinct" is coming to mean in this conversation.

D: It's an explanatory principle, Daddy, just like you said. . . . There's one thing I don't understand.

F: Yes?

D: Is there a whole lot of instinct? Or are there lots of instincts?

F: Yes. That's a good question, and scientists have talked a great deal about it, making lists of separate instincts and then lumping them together again.

D: But what's the answer?

F: Well. It's not quite clear. But one thing is certain: That explanatory principles must be not multiplied beyond necessity.

D: And that means? Please?

F: It's the idea behind monotheism—that the idea of one big God is to be preferred to the idea of two little gods.

D: Is God an explanatory principle?

F: Oh, yes—a very big one. You shouldn't use two black boxes—or two instincts—to explain what one black box would explain . . .

D: If it were big enough.

F: No. It means . . .

D: Are there big instincts and little instincts?

F: Well—as a matter of fact, scientists do talk as if there were. But they call the little instincts by other names —"reflexes," "innate releasing mechanisms," "fixed action patterns," and so on.

D: I see—like having one big God to explain the universe and lots of little "imps" or "goblins" to explain the small things that happen.

F: Well, yes. Rather like that.

D: But, Daddy, how do they lump things together to make the big instincts?

F: Well, for example, they don't say that the dog has one instinct which makes it wiggle when it falls down the cliff and another which makes it run away from fire.

D: You mean those would both be explained by a self-preservative instinct?

F: Something like that. Yes.

D: But if you put those different acts together under one instinct, then you cannot get away from saying that the dog has the use of the notion of "self."

F: No, perhaps not.

D: What would you do about the instinct for the song and the instinct for practicing the song?

F: Well—depending on what the song is used for. Both song and practice might be under a territorial instinct or a sexual instinct.

D: I wouldn't put them together.

F: No?

D: Because what if the bird also practiced picking up seed or something? You'd have to multiply the instincts —what is it?—beyond necessity.

F: What do you mean?

D: I mean a food-getting instinct to explain the practicing picking up seed, and a territory instinct for practicing song. Why not have a *practicing* instinct for both? That saves one black box.

F: But then you would throw away the idea of lumping together under the same instinct actions which have the same purpose.

D: Yes—because if the practicing is for a purpose—I mean, if the *bird* has a purpose—then the practicing is *rational* and not instinctive. Didn't you say something like that?

F: Yes, I did say something like that.

D: Could we do without the idea of "instinct"?

F: How would you explain things then?

D: Well. I'd just look at the little things: When something goes "pop," the dog jumps. When the ground is not under his feet, he wiggles. And so on.

F: You mean—all the imps but no gods?

D: Yes, something like that.

F: Well. There are scientists who try to talk that way, and it's becoming quite fashionable. They say it is more *objective*.

D: And is it?

F: Oh, yes.

D: What does "objective" mean?

F: Well. It means that you look very hard at those things which you choose to look at.

D: That sounds right. But how do the objective people choose which things they will be objective about?

F: Well. They choose those things about which it is easy to be objective.

D: You mean easy for them?

F: Yes.

D: But how do they *know* that those are the easy things?

F: I suppose they try different things and find out by experience.

D: So it's a subjective choice?

F: Oh, yes. All experience is subjective.

D: But it's *human* and subjective. They decide which bits of animal behavior to be objective about by consulting human subjective experience. Didn't you say that anthropomorphism is a bad thing?

F: Yes—but they do try to be not human.

D: Which things do they leave out?

F: What do you mean?

D: I mean—subjective experience shows them which things it is easy to be objective about. So, they go and study those things. But which things does their experience show are difficult? So that they avoid those things. Which are the things they avoid?

F: Well, you mentioned earlier something called "practice." That's a difficult thing to be objective about. And there are other things that are difficult in the same sort of way. *Play*, for example. And *exploration*. It's difficult to be objective about whether a rat is *really* exploring or *really* playing. So they don't investigate those things. And then there's love. And, of course, hate.

D: I see. Those are the sorts of things that I wanted to invent separate instincts for.

F: Yes—those things. And don't forget humor.

D: Daddy—are animals objective?

F: I don't know—probably not. I don't think they are subjective either. I don't think they are split that way.

D: Isn't it true that people have a special difficulty about being objective about the more animal parts of their nature?

F: I guess so. Anyhow Freud said so, and I think he was right. Why do you ask?

D: Because, oh dear, those poor people. They try to study animals. And they specialize in those things that they can study objectively. And they can only be objective about those things in which they themselves are least like animals. It must be difficult for them.

F: No—that does not necessarily follow. It is still possible for people to be objective about *some* things in their animal nature. You haven't shown that the whole of animal behavior is within the set of things that people cannot be objective about.

D: No?

D: What are the really big differences between people and animals?

F: Well—intellect, language, tools. Things like that.

D: And it is easy for people to be intellectually objective in language and about tools?

F: That's right.

D: But that must mean that in people there is a whole set of ideas or whatnot which are all tied together. A sort of second creature within the whole person, and that second creature must have a quite different way of thinking about everything. An objective way.

F: Yes. The royal road to consciousness and objectivity is through language and tools.

D: But what happens when this creature looks at all those parts of the person about which it is difficult for people to be objective? Does it just look? Or does it meddle?

F: It meddles.

D: And what happens?

F: That's a very terrible question.

D: Go on. If we are going to study animals, we must face that question.

F: Well . . . The poets and artists know the answer better than the scientists. Let me read you a piece:

> *Thought* chang'd the infinite to a serpent, that which pitieth
> To a devouring flame; and man fled from its face and hid
> In forests of night: then all the eternal forests were divided
> Into earths rolling in circles of space, that like an ocean rush'd
> And overwhelmed all except this finite wall of flesh.
> Then was the serpent temple form'd, image of infinite
> Shut up in finite revolutions; and man became an Angel,
> Heaven a mighty circle turning, God a tyrant crown'd.*

D: I don't understand it. It sounds terrible, but what does it mean?

F: Well. It's not an objective statement, because it is talking about the *effect* of objectivity—what the poet calls here "thought" upon the whole person or the whole of life. "Thought" should remain a part of the whole but instead spreads itself and meddles with the rest.

D: Go on.

F: Well. It slices everything to bits.

D: I don't understand.

F: Well, the first slice is between the objective thing and the rest. And then *inside* the creature that's made in the model of intellect, language, and tools, it is natural that *purpose* will evolve. Tools are for purposes and anything which blocks purpose is a hindrance. The world of the objective creature gets split into "helpful" things and "hindering" things.

D: Yes. I see that.

F: All right. Then the creature applies that split to the world of the whole person, and "helpful" and "hinder-

---

*Blake, W., 1794, *Europe a Prophecy*, printed and published by the author. (Italics added.)

ing" become Good and Evil, and the world is then split between God and the Serpent. And after that, more and more splits follow because the intellect is always classifying and dividing things up.

D: Multiplying explanatory principles beyond necessity?

F: That's right.

D: So, inevitably, when the objective creature looks at animals, it splits things up and makes the animals look like human beings *after* their intellects have invaded their souls.

F: Exactly. It's a sort of inhuman anthropomorphism.

D: And that is why the objective people study all the little imps instead of the larger things?

F: Yes. It's called S-R psychology. It's easy to be objective about sex but not about love.

D: Daddy, we've talked about two ways of studying animals—the big instinct way and the S-R way, and neither way seemed very sound. What do we do now?

F: I don't know.

D: Didn't you say that the royal road to objectivity and consciousness is language and tools? What's the royal road to the other half?

F: Freud said dreams.

D: Oh.

D: What are dreams? How are they put together?

F: Well—dreams are bits and pieces of the stuff of which we are made. The non-objective stuff.

D: But how are they put together?

F: Look. Aren't we getting rather far from the question of explaining animal behavior?

D: I don't know, but I don't think so. It looks as if we are going to be anthropomorphic in one way or another, whatever we do. And it is obviously wrong to build our anthropomorphism on that side of man's nature in which he is most unlike the animals. So let's try the other side. You say dreams are the royal road to the other side. So . . .

F: I didn't. Freud said it. Or something like it.

D: All right. But how are dreams put together?

F: Do you mean how are two dreams related to each other?

D: No. Because, as you said, they are only bits and pieces. What I mean is: How is a dream put together inside itself? Could animal behavior be put together in the same sort of way?

F: I don't know where to begin.

D: Well. Do dreams go by opposites?

F: Oh Lord! The old folk idea. No. They don't predict the future. Dreams are sort of suspended in time. They don't have any tenses.

D: But if a person is afraid of something which he knows will happen tomorrow, he might dream about it to-night?

F: Certainly. Or about something in his past. Or about both past and present. But the dream contains no label to tell him what it is "about" in this sense. It just is.

D: Do you mean it's as if the dream had no title page?

F: Yes. It's like an old manuscript or a letter that has lost its beginning and end, and the historian has to guess what it's all about and who wrote it and when—from what's *inside* it.

D: Then we're going to have to be objective, too?

F: Yes indeed. But we know that we have to be careful about it. We have to watch that we don't force the concepts of the creature that deals in language and tools upon the dream material.

D: How do you mean?

F: Well. For example: if dreams somehow have not tenses and are somehow suspended in time, then it would be forcing the wrong sort of objectivity to say that a dream "predicts" something. And equally wrong to say it is a statement about the past. It's not history.

D: Only propaganda?

F: What do you mean?

D: I mean—is it like the sort of stories that propagandists write which they say are history but which are really only fables?

F: All right. Yes. Dreams are in many ways like myths and fables. But not consciously made up by a propagandist. Not planned.

D: Does a dream always have a moral?

F: I don't know about *always*. But *often*, yes. But the moral is not stated in the dream. The psychoanalyst tries to get the patient to find the moral. Really the whole dream is the moral.

D: What does that mean?

F: I don't quite know.

D: Well. Do dreams go by opposites? Is the moral the opposite of what the dream seems to say?

F: Oh yes. Often. Dreams often have an ironic or sarcastic twist. A sort of *reductio ad absurdum*.

D: For example?

F: All right. A friend of mine was a fighter pilot in World War II. After the war he became a psychologist and had to sit for his Ph. D. oral exam. He began to be terrified of the oral, but, the night before the exam, he had a nightmare in which he experienced again being in a plane which had been shot down. Next day he went into the examination without fear.

D: Why?

F: Because it was silly for a fighter pilot to be afraid of a bunch of university professors who couldn't *really* shoot him down.

D: But how did he know that? The dream could have been telling him that the professors *would* shoot him down. How did he know it was ironic?

F: Hmm. The answer is he didn't know. The dream doesn't have a label on it to say it is ironic. And when people are being ironic in waking conversation, they often don't tell you they are being ironic.

D: No. That's true. I always think it's sort of cruel.

F: Yes. It often is.

D: Daddy, are animals ever ironic or sarcastic?

F: No. I guess not. But I am not sure that those are quite the words we should use. "Ironic" and "sarcastic" are words for the analysis of message material in language. And animals don't have language. It's perhaps part of the wrong sort of objectivity.

D: All right. Then do animals deal in opposites?

F: Well, yes. As a matter of fact, they do. But I'm not sure it's the same thing . . .

D: Go on. *How* do they? And when?

F: Well. You know how a puppy lies on his back and presents his belly to a bigger dog. That's sort of inviting the bigger dog to attack. But it works in the opposite way. It stops the bigger dog from attacking.

D: Yes. I see. It is a sort of use of opposites. But do they *know* that?

F: You mean does the big dog know that the little dog is saying the opposite of what he means? And does the little dog know that that is the way to stop the big dog?

D: Yes.

F: I don't know. I sometimes think the little dog knows a little more about it than the big dog. Anyhow, the little dog does not give any signals to show that he knows. He obviously couldn't do that.

D: Then it's like the dreams. There's no label to say that the dream is dealing in opposites.

F: That's right.

D: I think we're getting somewhere. Dreams deal in opposites, and animals deal in opposites, and neither carries labels to say when they are dealing in opposites.

F: Hmm.

D: Why do animals fight?

F: Oh, for many reasons. Territory, sex, food . . .

D: Daddy, you're talking like instinct theory. I thought we agreed not to do that.

F: All right. But what sort of an answer do you want to the question, why animals fight?

D: Well. Do they deal in opposites?

F: Oh. Yes. A lot of fighting ends up in some sort of peace-making. And certainly playful fighting is partly a way of affirming friendship. Or discovering or rediscovering friendship.

D: I thought so. . . .

D: But why are the labels missing? Is it for the same reason in both animals and dreams?

F: I don't know. But, you know, dreams do not always deal in opposites.

D:   No—of course not—nor do animals.

F:   All right then.

D:   Let's go back to that dream. Its total effect on the man was the same as if somebody had said to him, " 'you in a fighter plane' is not equal to 'you in an oral exam.' "

F:   Yes. But the dream didn't spell that out. It only says, "you in a fighter plane." It leaves out the "not," and it leaves out the instruction to compare the dream with something else and it doesn't say what he should compare it with.

D:   All right. Let's take the "not" first. Is there any "not" in animal behavior?

F:   How could there be?

D:   I mean can an animal say by its actions, "I will not bite you"?

F:   Well, to begin with. Communication by actions cannot possibly have tenses. They are only possible in language.

D:   Didn't you say that dreams have no tenses?

F:   Hmm. Yes, I did.

D:   Okay. But what about "not". Can the animal say, "I am not biting you"?

F:   That still has a tense in it. But never mind. If the animal *is* not biting the other, he's not biting it, and that's it.

D:   But he might be not doing all sorts of other things, sleeping, eating, running, and so on. How can he say, "It's biting that I'm not doing"?

F:   He can only do that if biting has somehow been mentioned.

D:   Do you mean that he could say, "I am not biting you" by first showing his fangs and *then* not biting?

F:   Yes. Something like that.

D:   But what about *two* animals? They'd both have to show their fangs.

F:   Yes.

D:   And, it seems to me, they might misunderstand each other, and get into a fight.

F:   Yes. There is always that danger when you deal in opposites and do not or cannot say what you are doing, especially when you do not *know* what you are doing.

D:   But the animals would know that they bared their fangs in order to say, "I won't bite you."

F: I doubt whether they would know. Certainly neither animal knows it about the other. The dreamer doesn't know at the beginning of the dream how the dream is going to end.

D: Then it's a sort of experiment. . . .

F: Yes.

D: So they might get into a fight in order to find out whether fighting was what they had to do.

F: Yes—but I'd rather put it less purposively—that the fight shows them what sort of relationship they have, after it. It's not planned.

D: Then "not" is really not there when the animals show their fangs?

F: I guess not. Or often not. Perhaps old friends might engage in playful fighting and know at the beginning what they are doing.

D: All right. Then the "not" is absent in animal behavior because "not" is part of verbal language, and there cannot be any action signal for "not." And because there is no "not," the only way to agree on a negative is to act out the whole *reductio ad absurdum*. You have to act out the battle to prove it isn't one, and then you have to act out the submission to prove that the other won't eat you.

F: Yes.

D: Did the animals have to think that out?

F: No. Because it's all *necessarily* true. And that which is necessarily true will govern what you do regardless of whether you know that it is necessarily true. If you put two apples with three apples you will get five apples— even though you cannot count. It's another way of "explaining" things.

D: Oh.

D: But, then, why does the dream leave out the "not"?

F: I think really for a rather similar reason. Dreams are mostly made of images and feelings, and if you are going to communicate in images and feelings and such, you again are governed by the fact that there is no image for "not."

D: But you could dream of a "Stop" sign with a line through it, which would mean "No Stopping."

F: Yes. But that's halfway toward language. And the deleting line isn't the word "not." It's the word "don't." "Don't" can be conveyed in action language—if the *other* person makes a move to mention what you want to forbid. You can even dream in words, and the word "not" might be among them. But I doubt if you can dream a "not" which is about the dream. I mean a "not" which means "This dream is not to be taken literally." Sometimes, in very light sleep, one knows that one is dreaming.

D: But, Daddy, you still haven't answered the question about how dreams are put together.

F: I think really I have answered it. But let me try again. A dream is a metaphor or a tangle of metaphors. Do you know what a metaphor is?

D: Yes. If I say you are *like* a pig that is a simile. But if I say you *are* a pig, that is a metaphor.

F: Approximately, yes. When a metaphor is *labeled* as a metaphor it becomes a simile.

D: And it's that labeling that a dream leaves out.

F: That's right. A metaphor compares things without spelling out the comparison. It takes what is true of one group of things and applies it to another. When we say a nation "decays," we are using a metaphor, suggesting that some changes in a nation are like changes which bacteria produce in fruit. But we don't stop to mention the fruit or the bacteria.

D: And a dream is like that?

F: No. It's the other way around. The dream would mention the fruit and possibly the bacteria but would not mention the nation. The dream elaborates on the *relationship* but does not identify the things that are related.

D: Daddy, could you make a dream for me?

F: You mean, on this recipe? No. Let's take the piece of verse which I read you just now and turn it into a dream. It's almost dream material the way it stands. For most of it, you have only to substitute images for the words. And the words are vivid enough. But the whole string of metaphors or images is pegged down, which would not be so in a dream.

D: What do you mean by "pegged down"?

F: I mean by the first word: "Thought." That word the writer is using literally, and that one word tells you what all the rest is about.

D: And in a dream?

F: That word, too, would have been metaphoric. Then the whole poem would have been much more difficult.

D: All right—change it then.

F: What about "*Barbara* changed the infinite . . ." and so on.

D: But why? Who is she?

F: Well, she's barbarous, and she's female, and she is the mnemonic name of a syllogistic mood. I thought she would do rather well as a monstrous symbol for "Thought." I can see her now with a pair of calipers, pinching her own brain to change her universe.

D: Stop it.

F: All right. But you see what I mean by saying that in dreams the metaphors are not pegged down.

D: Do animals peg down their metaphors?

F: No. They don't have to. You see, when a grown-up bird makes like a baby bird in approaching a member of the opposite sex, he's using a metaphor taken from the relationship between child and parent. But he doesn't have to peg down whose relationship he is talking *about*. It's obviously the relationship between himself and the other bird. They're both of them present.

D: But don't they ever use metaphors—act out metaphors —about something other than their own relationships?

F: I don't think so. No—not mammals. And I don't think birds do either. Bees—perhaps. And, of course, people.

D: There's one thing I don't understand.

F: Yes?

D: We've found a whole lot of things in common between dreams and animal behavior. They both deal in opposites, and they both have no tenses, and they both have no "not," and they both work by metaphor, and neither of them pegs the metaphors down. But what I don't understand is—why, when the animals do these things, it makes sense. I mean for them to work in opposites. And they don't *have* to peg down their metaphors—but I don't see why dreams should be like that, too.

F: Nor do I.

D: And there's another thing.

F: Yes?

D: You talked about genes and chromosomes carrying messages about development. Do they talk like animals and dreams? I mean in metaphors and with no "nots"? Or do they talk like us?

F: I don't know. But I am sure their message system contains no simple transform of Instinct Theory.

# Part II: Form and Pattern
in Anthropology

# Culture Contact and Schismogenesis*

The Memorandum written by a Committee of the Social
Sciences Research Council (*Man*, 1935, 162) has stimulated
me to put forward a point of view which differs considerably
from theirs; and, though the beginning of this article may
appear to be critical of their Memorandum, I wish to make
it clear from the outset that I regard as a real contribution
any serious attempt to devise categories for the study of culture contact. Moreover, since there are several passages in
the Memorandum (among them the Definition) which I do
not perfectly understand, my criticisms are offered with some
hesitation, and are directed not so much against the Committee as against certain errors prevalent among anthropologists.

(1) *The uses of such systems of categories.* In general
it is unwise to construct systems of this sort until the problems which they are designed to elucidate have been clearly
formulated; and so far as I can see, the categories drawn
up by the Committee have been constructed not in reference
to any specifically defined problems, but to throw a general

*The whole controversy of which this article was a part
has been reprinted in *Beyond the Frontier*, edited by
Paul Bohannon and Fred Plog. But the ripples of this
controversy have long since died down, and the article
is included here only for its positive contributions. It is
reprinted, unchanged, from *Man*, Article 199, Vol.
XXXV, 1935, by permission of the Royal Anthropological Institute of Great Britain and Ireland.

light on "the problem" of acculturation, while the problem itself remains vague.

(2) From this it follows that our immediate need is not so much the construction of a set of categories which will throw a light on all the problems, but rather the schematic formulation of the problems in such a way that they may be separately investigable.

(3) Although the Committee leave their problems undefined, we may from a careful reading of the categories gather roughly what questions they are asking of the material. It seems that the Committee have, as a matter of fact, been influenced by the sort of questions which administrators ask of anthropologists—"Is it a good thing to use force in culture contacts?" "How can we make a given people accept a certain sort of trait?" and so on. In response to this type of question we find in the definition of acculturation an emphasis upon difference in culture between the groups in contact and upon the resulting changes; and such dichotomies as that between "elements forced upon a people or received voluntarily by them"[1] may likewise be regarded as symptomatic of this thinking in terms of administrative problems. The same may be said of the categories V, A, B, and C, "acceptance," "adaptation" and "reaction."

(4) We may agree that answers are badly needed to these questions of administration and, further, that a study of culture contacts is likely to give these answers. But it is almost certain that the scientific formulation of the problems of contact will not follow these lines. It is as if in the construction of categories for the study of criminology we started with a dichotomy of individuals into criminal and noncriminal —and, indeed, that curious science was hampered for a long while by this very attempt to define a "criminal type."

(5) The Memorandum is based upon a fallacy: that we can classify the traits of a culture under such headings as economic, religious, etc. We are asked, for example, to classify traits into three classes, presented respectively because of: (a) economic profit or political dominance; (b) desirability of bringing about conformity to values of donor group; and (c) ethical and religious considerations. This idea, that each trait has either a single function or at least some one

---

[1] In any case it is clear that in a scientific study of processes and natural laws this invocation of free will can have no place.

function which overtops the rest, leads by extension to the idea that a culture can be subdivided into "institutions" where the bundle of traits which make up one institution are alike in their major functions. The weakness of this method of subdividing a culture has been conclusively demonstrated by Malinowski and his pupils, who have shown that almost the *whole* of a culture may be seen variously as a mechanism for modifying and satisfying the sexual needs of the individuals, or for the enforcement of the norms of behavior, or for supplying the individuals with food.[2] From this exhaustive demonstration we must expect that any single trait of a culture will prove on examination to be not simply economic or religious or structural, but to partake of all these qualities according to the point of view from which we look

[2] Cf. Malinowski, *Sexual Life* and *Crime and Custom;* A. I. Richards, *Hunger and Work.* This question of the subdivision of a culture into "institutions" is not quite as simple as I have indicated; and, in spite of their own works, I believe that the London School still adheres to a theory that some such division is practicable. It is likely that confusion arises from the fact that certain native peoples—perhaps all, but in any case those of Western Europe—actually think that their culture is so subdivided. Various cultural phenomena also contribute something toward such a subdivision, *e.g.,* (*a*) the division of labor and differentiation of norms of behavior between different groups of individuals in the same community, and (*b*) an emphasis, present in certain cultures, upon the subdivisions of place and time upon which behavior is ordered. These phenomena lead to the possibility, in such cultures, of dubbing all behavior which, for example, takes place in church between 11.30 and 12.30 on Sundays as "religious." But even in the study of such cultures the anthropologist must look with some suspicion upon his classification of traits into institutions and must expect to find a great deal of overlapping between various institutions.

An analogous fallacy occurs in psychology, and consists in regarding behavior as classifiable according to the impulses which inspire it, *e.g.,* into such categories as self-protective, assertive, sexual, acquisitive, etc. Here, too, confusion results from the fact that not only the psychologist, but also the individual studied, is prone to think in terms of these categories. The psychologists would do well to accept the probability that every bit of behavior is—at least in a well-integrated individual —simultaneously relevant to all these abstractions.

at it. If this be true of a culture seen in synchronic section, then it must also apply to the diachronic processes of culture contact and change; and we must expect that for the offering, acceptance or refusal of every trait that are simultaneous causes of an economic, structural, sexual, and religious nature.

(6) From this it follows that our categories "religious," "economic," etc., are not *real* subdivisions which are present in the cultures which we study, but are merely *abstractions* which we make for our own convenience when we set out to describe cultures in words. They are not phenomena present in culture, but are labels for various points of view which we adopt in our studies. In handling such abstractions we must be careful to avoid Whitehead's "fallacy of misplaced concreteness," a fallacy into which, for example, the Marxian historians fall when they maintain that economic "phenomena" are "primary."

With this preamble, we may now consider an alternative scheme for the study of contact phenomena.

(7) *Scope of the inquiry* I suggest that we should consider under the head of "culture contact" not only those cases in which the contact occurs between two communities with different cultures and results in profound disturbance of the culture of one or both groups; but also cases of contact within a single community. In these cases the contact is between differentiated groups of individuals, *e.g.*, between the sexes, between old and young, between aristocracy and plebs, between clans, etc., groups which live together in approximate equilibrium. I would even extend the idea of "contact" so widely as to include those processes whereby a child is molded and trained to fit the culture into which he was born,[3] but for the present we may confine ourselves to contacts between groups of individuals, with different cultural norms of behavior in each group.

(8) If we consider the possible end of the drastic distur-

---

[3] The present scheme is oriented toward the study of social rather than psychological processes, but a closely analogous scheme might be constructed for the study of psychopathology. Here the idea of "contact" would be studied, especially in the contexts of the molding of the individual, and the processes of schismogenesis would be seen to play an important part not only in accentuating the maladjustments of the deviant, but also in assimilating the normal individual to his group.

bances which follow contacts between profoundly different communities, we see that the changes must theoretically result in one or other of the following patterns:

(a) the complete fusion of the originally different groups

(b) the elimination of one or both groups

(c) the persistence of both groups in dynamic equilibrium within one major community

(9) My purpose in extending the idea of contact to cover the conditions of differentiation inside a single culture is to use our knowledge of these quiescent states to throw light upon the factors which are at work in states of disequilibrium. It may be easy to obtain a knowledge of the factors from their quiet working, but impossible to isolate them when they are violent. The laws of gravity cannot conveniently be studied by observation of houses collapsing in an earthquake.

(10) *Complete fusion* Since this is one of the possible ends of the process we must know what factors are present in a group of individuals with consistent homogeneous patterns of behavior in all members of the group. An approach to such conditions may be found in any community which is in a state of approximate equilibrium but, unfortunately, our own communities in Europe are in a state of such flux that these conditions scarcely occur. Moreover, even in primitive communities the conditions are usually complicated by differentiation, so that we must be content with studies of such homogeneous groups as can be observed within the major differentiated communities.

Our first task will be to ascertain what sorts of unity obtain within such groups, or rather—bearing in mind that we are concerned with *aspects* and not classes of phenomena—what aspects of the unity of the body of traits we must describe in order to get a whole view of the situation. I submit that the material, to be fully understood, *must* be examined in, at least, the following five separable aspects:

(a) *A structural aspect of unity* The behavior of any one individual in any one context is, in some sense, cognitively consistent with the behavior of all the other individuals in all other contexts. Here we must be prepared to find that the inherent logic of one culture differs profoundly from that of others. From this point of view we shall see, for example, that when individual A gives a drink to individual B, that behavior is consistent with other norms of behavior obtaining within the group which contains A and B.

This aspect of the unity of the body of behavior patterns may be restated in terms of a standardization of the cognitive aspects of the personalities of the individuals. We may say that the patterns of thought of the individuals are so standardized that their behavior appears to them *logical.*

(*b*) *Affective aspects of unity* In studying the culture from this point of view, we are concerned to show the emotional setting of all the details of behavior. We shall see the whole body of behavior as a concerted mechanism oriented toward affective satisfaction and dissatisfaction of the individuals.

This aspect of a culture may also be described in terms of a standardization of affective aspects of the personalities of the individuals, which are so modified by their culture that their behavior is to them emotionally consistent.

(*c*) *Economic unity* Here we shall see the whole body of behavior as a mechanism oriented toward the production and distribution of material objects.

(*d*) *Chronological and spatial unity* Here we shall see the behavior patterns as schematically ordered according to time and place. We shall see A as giving the drink to B "because it is Saturday evening in the Blue Boar."

(*e*) *Sociological unity* Here we shall see the behavior of the individuals as oriented toward the integration and disintegration of the major unit, the Group as a whole. We shall see the giving of drinks as a factor which promotes the solidarity of the group.

(11) In addition to studying the behavior of members of the homogeneous group from all these points of view, we must examine a number of such groups to discover the effects of standardization of these various points of view in the people we are studying. We have stated above that every bit of behavior must be regarded as probably relevant to all these viewpoints, but the fact remains that some peoples are more inclined than others to see and phrase their own behavior as "logical" or "for the good of the State."

(12) With this knowledge of the conditions which obtain in homogeneous groups, we shall be in a position to examine the processes of fusion of two diverse groups into one. We may even be able to prescribe measures which will either

promote or retard such fusion, and predict that a trait which fits the five aspects of unity can be added to a culture without other changes. If it does not fit, then we can search for appropriate modifications either of the culture or of the trait.

(13) *The elimination of one or both groups* This end result is perhaps scarcely worth studying, but we should at least examine any material that is available, to determine what sort of effects such hostile activity has upon the culture of the survivors. It is possible, for example, that the patterns of behavior associated with elimination of other groups may be assimilated into their culture so that they are impelled to eliminate more and more.

(14) *Persistence of both groups in dynamic equilibrium* This is probably the most instructive of the possible end results of contact, since the factors active in the dynamic equilibrium are likely to be identical or analogous with those which, in disequilibrium, are active in cultural change. Our first task is to study the relationships obtaining between groups of individuals with differentiated behavior patterns, and later to consider what light these relationships throw upon what are more usually called "contacts." Every anthropologist who has been in the field has had opportunity of studying such differentiated groups.

(15) The possibilities of differentiation of groups are by no means infinite, but fall clearly into two categories (*a*) cases in which the relationship is chiefly symmetrical, *e.g.*, in the differentiation of moieties, clans, villages and the nations of Europe; and (*b*) cases in which the relationship is *complementary*, *e.g.*, in the differentiation of social strata, classes, castes, age grades, and, in some cases, the cultural differentiation between the sexes.[4] Both these types of dif-

---

[4] Cf. Margaret Mead, *Sex and Temperament*, 1935. Of the communities described in this book, the Arapesh and the Mundugumor have a preponderantly symmetrical relationship between the sexes, while the Chambuli have a complementary relationship. Among the Iatmul, a tribe in the same area, which I have studied, the relationship between the sexes is complementary, but on rather different lines from that of the Chambuli. I hope shortly to publish a book on the Iatmul with sketches of their culture from the points of view *a*, *b*, and *e* outlined in paragraph 10. (See Bibliography, items 1936 and 1958 B.)

ferentiation contain dynamic elements, such that when certain restraining factors are removed the differentiation or split between the groups increases progressively toward either breakdown or a new equilibrium.

(16) *Symmetrical differentiation* To this category may be referred all those cases in which the individuals in two groups A and B have the same aspirations and the same behavior patterns, but are differentiated in the orientation of these patterns. Thus members of group A exhibit behavior patterns A,B,C in their dealings with each other, but adopt the patterns X,Y,Z in their dealings with members of group B. Similarly, group B adopt the patterns A,B,C among themselves, but exhibit X,Y,Z in dealing with group A. Thus a position is set up in which the behavior X,Y,Z is the standard reply to X,Y,Z. This position contains elements which may lead to progressive differentiation or *schismogenesis* along the same lines. If, for example, the patterns X,Y,Z include boasting, we shall see that there is a likelihood, if boasting is the reply to boasting, that each group will drive the other into excessive emphasis of the pattern, a process which if not restrained can only lead to more and more extreme rivalry and ultimately to hostility and the breakdown of the whole system.

(17) *Complementary differentiation* To this category we may refer all those cases in which the behavior and aspirations of the members of the two groups are fundamentally different. Thus members of group A treat each other with patterns L,M,N, and exhibit the patterns O,P,Q in dealings with group B. In reply to O,P,Q, the members of group B exhibit the patterns U,V,W, but among themselves they adopt patterns R,S,T. Thus it comes about that O,P,Q is the reply to U,V,W, and vice versa. This differentiation may become progressive. If, for example, the series, O,P,Q includes patterns culturally regarded as assertive, while U,V,W includes cultural submissiveness, it is likely that submissiveness will promote further assertiveness which in turn will promote further submissiveness. This schismogenesis, unless it is restrained, leads to a progressive unilateral distortion of the personalities of the members of both groups, which results in mutual hostility between them and must end in the breakdown of the system.

(18) *Reciprocity* Though relationships between groups

can broadly be classified into two categories, symmetrical and complementary, this subdivision is to some extent blurred by another type of differentiation which we may describe as *reciprocal*. In this type the behavior patterns X and Y are adopted by members of each group in their dealings with the other group, but instead of the symmetrical system whereby X is the reply to X and Y is the reply to Y, we find here that X is the reply to Y. Thus in every single instance the behavior is asymmetrical, but symmetry is regained over a large number of instances since sometimes group A exhibit X to which group B reply with Y, and sometimes group A exhibit Y and group B reply with X. Cases in which group A sometimes sell sago to group B and the latter sometimes sell the same commodity to A, may be regarded as reciprocal; but if group A habitually sell sago to B while the latter habitually sell fish to A, we must, I think, regard the pattern as complementary. The reciprocal pattern, it may be noted, is compensated and balanced within itself and therefore does not tend toward schismogenesis.

(19) *Points for investigation:*

(*a*) We need a proper survey of the types of behavior which can lead to schismogeneses of the symmetrical type. At present it is only possible to point to boasting and commercial rivalry, but no doubt there are many other patterns which will be found to be accompanied by the same type of effect.

(*b*) We need a survey of the types of behavior which are mutually complementary and lead to schismogeneses of the second type. Here we can at present only cite assertiveness versus submissiveness, exhibitionism versus admiration, fostering versus expressions of feebleness and, in addition, the various possible combinations of these pairs.

(*c*) We need verification of the general law assumed above, that when two groups exhibit complementary behavior to each other, the internal behavior between members of group A must necessarily differ from the internal behavior between members of group B.

(*d*) We need a systematic examination of schismogeneses of both types from the various points of view outlined in paragraph 10. At present I have only looked at the matter from the ethological and structural points of view (paragraph 10, aspects *a* and *b*). In addition to this, the Marxian historians have given us a picture of the economic aspect of complementary schismogenesis in Western Europe. It is likely, however, that they themselves have been influenced unduly by the schismogenesis which they studied and have been thereby prompted into exaggeration.

(e) We need to know something about the occurrence of reciprocal behavior in relationships which are preponderantly either symmetrical or complementary.

(20) *Restraining factors* But, more important than any of the problems in the previous paragraph, we need a study of the factors which restrain both types of schismogenesis. At the present moment, the nations of Europe are far advanced in symmetrical schismogenesis and are ready to fly at each other's throats; while within each nation are to be observed growing hostilities between the various social strata, symptoms of complementary schismogenesis. Equally, in the countries ruled by new dictatorships we may observe early stages of complementary schismogenesis, the behavior of his associates pushing the dictator into ever greater pride and assertiveness.

The purpose of the present article is to suggest problems and lines of investigation rather than to state the answers, but, tentatively, suggestions may be offered as to the factors controlling schismogenesis:

(a) It is possible that, actually, no healthy equilibrated relationship between groups is either purely symmetrical or purely complementary, but that every such relationship contains elements of the other type. It is true that it is easy to classify relationships into one or the other category according to their predominant emphases, but it is possible that a very small admixture of complementary behavior in a symmetrical relationship, or a very small admixture of symmetrical behavior in a complementary relationship, may go a long way toward stabilizing the position. Examples of this type of stabilization are perhaps common. The squire is in a predominantly complementary and not always comfortable relationship with his villagers, but if he participate in village cricket (a symmetrical rivalry) but once a year, this may have a curiously disproportionate effect upon his relationship with them.

(b) It is certain that, as in the case quoted above in which group A sell sago to B while the latter sell fish to A, complementary patterns may sometimes have a real stabilizing effect by promoting a mutual dependence between the groups.

(c) It is possible that the presence of a number of truly reciprocal elements in a relationship may tend to stabilize it, preventing the schismogenesis which otherwise might result either from symmetrical or complementary elements. But this would seem to be at best a very weak defense: on the one hand, if we consider the effects of symmetrical schismogenesis upon the reciprocal behavior patterns, we see that the latter tend to be less and less exhibited. Thus, as the individuals composing the nations of Europe become more and more involved in their symmetrical international rivalries, they gradually leave off behaving in a reciprocal manner, deliberately reducing to a minimum their former reciprocal commercial behavior.[5] On the other hand, if we consider the effects of complementary schismogenesis upon the reciprocal behavior patterns, we see that one-half of the reciprocal pattern is liable to lapse. Where formerly both groups exhibited both X and Y, a system gradually evolves in which one of the groups exhibits only X, while the other exhibits only Y. In fact, behavior which was formerly reciprocal is reduced to a typical complementary pattern and is likely after that to contribute to the complementary schismogenesis.

(d) It is certain that either type of schismogenesis between two groups can be checked by factors which unite the two groups either in loyalty or opposition to some outside element. Such an outside element may be either a symbolic individual, an enemy people or some quite impersonal circumstance—the lion will lie down with the lamb if only it rain hard enough. But it must be noted that where the outside element is a person or group of persons, the relationship of the combined groups A and B to the outside group will always be itself a potentially schismogenic relationship of one or the other type. Examination of multiple systems of this kind is badly

[5] In this, as in the other examples given, no attempt is made to consider the schismogenesis from all the points of view outlined in paragraph 10. Thus, inasmuch as the economic aspect of the matter is not here being considered, the effects of the slump upon the schismogenesis are ignored. A complete study would be subdivided into separate sections, each treating one of the aspects of the phenomena.

needed and especially we need to know more about the systems (*e.g.*, military hierarchies) in which the distortion of personality is modified in the middle groups of the hierarchy by permitting the individuals to exhibit respect and submission in dealings with higher groups while they exhibit assertiveness and pride in dealing with the lower.

(*e*) In the case of the European situation, there is one other possibility—a special case of control by diversion of attention to outside circumstances. It is possible that those responsible for the policy of classes and nations might become conscious of the processes with which they are playing and cooperate in an attempt to solve the difficulties. This, however, is not very likely to occur since anthropology and social psychology lack the prestige necessary to advise; and, without such advice, governments will continue to react to each other's reactions rather than pay attention to circumstances.

(21) In conclusion, we may turn to the problems of the administrator faced with a black-white culture contact. His first task is to decide which of the end results outlined in paragraph 8 is desirable and possible of attainment. This decision he must make without hypocrisy. If he chooses fusion, then he must endeavor to contrive every step so as to promote the conditions of consistency which are outlined (as problems for investigation) in paragraph 10. If he chooses that both groups shall persist in some form of dynamic equilibrium, then he must contrive to establish a system in which the possibilities of schismogenesis are properly compensated or balanced against each other. But at every step in the scheme which I have outlined there are problems which must be studied by trained students and which when solved will contribute, not only to applied sociology, but to the very basis of our understanding of human beings in society.

# Experiments in Thinking About Observed

# Ethnological Material*

As I understand it, you have asked me for an honest, introspective—personal—account of how I think about anthropological material, and if I am to be honest and personal about my thinking, then I must be impersonal about the results of that thinking. Even if I can banish both pride and shame for half an hour, honesty will still be difficult.

Let me try to build up a picture of how I think by giving you an autobiographical account of how I have acquired my kit of conceptual tools and intellectual habits. I do not mean an academic biography or a list of what subjects I have studied, but something more significant than that—a list rather of the motifs of thought in various scientific subjects which left so deep an impression on my mind that when I came to work on anthropological material, I naturally used those borrowed motifs to guide my approach to this new material.

I owe the greatest part of this kit of tools to my father, William Bateson, who was a geneticist. In schools and universities they do very little to give one an idea of the basic principles of scientific thinking, and what I learned of this came in very large measure from my father's conversation

*This paper was given at the Seventh Conference on Methods in Philosophy and the Sciences, held at the New School for Social Research, April 28, 1940. It is here reprinted from *Philosophy of Science*, Vol. 8, No. 1, copyright 1941, The Williams & Wilkins Co. Reproduced by permission.

and perhaps especially from the overtones of his talk. He himself was inarticulate about philosophy and mathematics and logic, and he was articulately distrustful of such subjects, but still, in spite of himself, I think, he passed on to me something of these matters.

The attitudes which I got from him were especially those which he had denied in himself. In his early—and as I think he knew—his best work he posed the problems of animal symmetry, segmentation, serial repetition of parts, patterns, etc. Later he turned away from this field into Mendelism, to which he devoted the remainder of his life. But he had always a hankering after the problems of pattern and symmetry, and it was this hankering and the mysticism that inspired it that I picked up and which, for better or worse, I called "science."

I picked up a vague mystical feeling that we must look for the same sort of processes in all fields of natural phenomena—that we might expect to find the same sort of laws at work in the structure of a crystal as in the structure of society, or that the segmentation of an earthworm might really be comparable to the process by which basalt pillars are formed.

I should not preach this mystical faith in quite those terms today but would say rather that I believe that the types of mental operation which are useful in analyzing one field may be equally useful in another—that the framework (the *eidos*) of science, rather than the framework of Nature, is the same in all fields. But the more mystical phrasing of the matter was what I vaguely learnt, and it was of paramount importance. It lent a certain dignity to any scientific investigation, implying that when I was analyzing the patterns of partridges' feathers, I might really get an answer or a bit of an answer to the whole puzzling business of pattern and regularity in nature. And further, this bit of mysticism was important because it gave me freedom to use my scientific background, the ways of thought that I had picked up in biology and elementary physics and chemistry; it encouraged me to expect these ways of thought to fit in with very different fields of observation. It enabled me to regard all my training as potentially useful rather than utterly irrelevant to anthropology.

When I came into anthropology there was a considerable

reaction taking place against the use of loose analogies, especially against the Spencerian analogy between the Organism and Society. Thanks to this mystical belief in the pervading unity of the phenomena of the world, I avoided a great deal of intellectual waste. I never had any doubt that this analogy was fundamentally sound; since to doubt would have been emotionally expensive. Nowadays, of course, the emphasis has shifted. Few would seriously doubt that the ways of analysis which have been found useful in analyzing one complex functioning system are likely to be of use in analyzing any other similar system. But the mystical prop was useful then, though its phrasing was bad.

There is another way, too, in which that mysticism has helped—a way which is especially relevant to my thesis. I want to emphasize that whenever we pride ourselves upon finding a newer, stricter way of thought or exposition; whenever we start insisting too hard upon "operationalism" or symbolic logic or any other of these very essential systems of tramlines, we lose something of the ability to think new thoughts. And equally, of course, whenever we rebel against the sterile rigidity of formal thought and exposition and let our ideas run wild, we likewise lose. As I see it, the advances in scientific thought come from a *combination of loose and strict thinking*, and this combination is the most precious tool of science.

My mystical view of phenomena contributed specifically to build up this double habit of mind—it led me into wild "hunches" and, at the same time, compelled more formal thinking about those hunches. It encouraged looseness of thought and then immediately insisted that that looseness be measured up against a rigid concreteness. The point is that the first hunch from analogy is wild, and then, the moment I begin to work out the analogy, I am brought up against the rigid formulations which have been devised in the field from which I borrow the analogy.

Perhaps it is worth giving an example of this; it was a matter of formulating the social organization of a New Guinea tribe,—the Iatmul. The Iatmul social system differs from ours in one very essential point. Their society completely lacks any sort of chieftainship, and I phrased this matter loosely by saying that the control of the individual was achieved by what I called "lateral" sanctions rather than by "sanctions from above." Going over my material, I found further that in general the subdivisions of the society—the clans, moieties, etc.—had virtually no means of punishing their own members. I had a case in which a ceremonial house owned by a particular junior age grade had been defiled, and though the other members of the grade were very angry with the defiler, they could do nothing about it. I asked whether they would kill one of his pigs or take any of his property, and they replied "No, of course not. *He is a member of their own initiatory grade.*" If the same thing had happened in the big senior ceremonial house which belongs to several grades, then the defiler would be punished. His own grade would defend him but the others would start a brawl.[1]

I then began looking for more concrete cases which could be compared with the contrast between this system and our own. I said, "It's like the difference between the radially symmetrical animals (jellyfish, sea anemones, etc.) and the animals which have transverse segmentation (earthworms, lobsters, man, etc.)."

Now in the field of animal segmentation we know very little about the mechanisms concerned, but at least the problems are more concrete than in the social field. When we compare a social problem with a problem of animal differentiation, we are at once provided with a visual diagram, in terms of which we may be able to talk a little more precisely. And for the transversely segmented animals, at least, we have something more than a merely anatomical diagram. Thanks to the work that has been done on experimental embryology and axial gradients, we have some idea of the dynamics of the system. We know that some sort of asymmetrical relation obtains between the successive segments, that each segment would, if it could (I speak loosely) form a head, but that the next anterior segment prevents this. Further, this dynamic asymmetry in the relations between successive segments is reflected morphologically; we find in most such animals a serial difference—what is called metameric differentiation—between the successive segments.

[1] For details of this and other similar incidents cf. *Naven*, pp. 98–107, Cambridge, Cambridge University Press, 1936.

Their appendages, though they can be shown to conform to a single basic structure, differ one from another as we go down the series. (The legs of the lobster provide a familiar example of the sort of thing I mean.)

In contrast with this, in the radially symmetrical animals, the segments, arranged around the center like sectors of a circle, are usually all alike.

As I say, we do not know much about the segmentation of animals, but at least here was enough for me to take back to the problem of Iatmul social organization. My "hunch" had provided me with a set of stricter words and diagrams, in terms of which I could try to be more precise in my thinking about the Iatmul problem. I could now look again at the Iatmul material to determine whether the relationship between the clans was really in some sense *symmetrical* and to determine whether there was anything that could be compared with the lack of metameric differentiation. I found that the "hunch" worked. I found that so far as opposition, control, etc. between the clans was concerned, the relations between them were reasonably symmetrical, and further, as to the question of differentiation between them, it could be shown that, though there were considerable differences, these followed no serial pattern. Additionally, I found that there was a strong tendency for clans to imitate each other, to steal bits of each other's mythological history and to incorporate these into their own past—a sort of fraudulent heraldry, each clan copying the others so that the whole system tended to diminish the differentiation between them. (The system perhaps also contained tendencies in an opposite direction, but this question I need not discuss now.)

I followed up the analogy in another direction. Impressed by the phenomena of metameric differentiation, I made the point that in our society with its hierarchical systems (comparable to the earthworm or the lobster), when a group secedes from the parent society, it is usual to find that the line of fission, the division between the new group and the old, marks a differentiation of mores. The Pilgrim Fathers wander off in order to be *different*. But among the Iatmul, when two groups in a village quarrel, and one half goes off and founds a new community, the mores of the two groups remain identical. In our society, fission tends to be heretical (a following after other doctrines or mores), but in Iatmul, fission is rather schismatic (a following after other leaders without change of dogma).

You will note that here I overrode my analogy at one point and that this matter is still not perfectly clear. When a transverse fission or a lateral budding occurs in a transversely segmented animal, the products of that bud or fission are *identical,* the posterior half which was held in check by the anterior is relieved of this control and develops into a normal, complete animal. I am therefore not in step with my analogy when I regard the differentiation which accompanies fission in a hierarchical society as comparable with that which exists before fission in a transversely segmented animal. This divergence from the analogy will surely be worth investigation; it will take us into a more precise study of the asymmetrical relations which obtain between the units in the two cases and raise questions about the reactions of the subordinate member to its position in the asymmetry. This aspect of the matter I have not yet examined.

Having got some sort of conceptual frame within which to describe the interrelations between clans, I went on from this to consider the interrelations between the various age grades in terms of this same frame. Here, if anywhere, where age might be expected to provide a basis for serial differentiation, we ought to expect to find some analogue of the transverse segmentation with asymmetrical relations between the successive grades—and to a certain extent the age-grade system fitted this picture. Each grade has its ceremonies and its secrets of initiation into that grade; and in these ceremonies and secrets it was perfectly easy to trace a metameric differentiation. Ceremonies which are fully developed at the top of the system are still recognizable in their basic form in the lower levels—but more rudimentary at each level as we go down the series.

But the initiatory system contains one very interesting element which was brought into sharp relief when my point of view was defined in terms of animal segmentation. The grades *alternate,* so that the whole system consists of two opposed groups, one group made up of grades 3, 5, 7, etc. (the odd numbers), and the other made up of 2, 4, 6, etc.; and these two groups maintain the type of relationship which I had already described as "symmetrical"—each providing sanctions by quarreling with the other when their rights are infringed.

Thus even where we might expect the most definite hierarchy, the Iatmul have substituted for it a headless system in which one side is symmetrically opposed to the other.

From this conclusion my enquiry, influenced by many other types of material, will go on to look at the matter from other points of view—especially the psychological problems of whether a preference for symmetrical rather than asymmetrical relationships can be implanted in the individual, and what the mechanisms of such character formation may be. But we need not go into that now.

Enough has been said to bring out the methodological theme—that a vague "hunch" derived from some other science leads into the precise formulations of that other science in terms of which it is possible to think more fruitfully about our own material.

You will have noticed that the form in which I used the biological findings was really rather different from that in which a zoologist would talk about his material. Where the zoologist might talk of axial gradients, I talked about "asymmetrical relationships between successive segments," and in my phrasing I was prepared to attach to the word "successive" two simultaneous meanings—in referring to the animal material it meant a morphological series in a three-dimensional concrete organism, while in referring to the anthropological material the word "successive" meant some abstracted property of a hierarchy.

I think it would be fair to say that I use the analogies in some curiously abstract form—that, as for "axial gradients" I substitute "asymmetrical relationships," so also I endow the word "successive" with some abstract meaning which makes it applicable to both sorts of cases.

This brings us to another very important motif in my thinking—a habit of constructing abstractions which refer to terms of comparison between entities; and to illustrate this I can clearly remember the first occasion on which I was guilty of such an abstraction. It was in my Zoological Tripos examination at Cambridge, and the examiner had tried to compel me to answer at least one question on each branch of the subject. Comparative anatomy I had always regarded as a waste of time, but I found myself face to face with it in the examination and had not the necessary detailed knowledge. I was asked to compare the urinogenital system of the amphibia with that of the mammalia, and I did not know much about it.

Necessity was the mother of invention. I decided that I ought to be able to defend the position that comparative anatomy was a muddled waste of time, and so I set to work to attack the whole emphasis on homology in zoological theory. As you probably will know, zoologists conventionally deal in two sorts of comparability between organs—*homology* and *analogy*. Organs are said to be "homologous" when it can be shown that they have similar structure or bear similar structural relations to other organs, *e.g.*, the trunk of the elephant is homologous with the nose and lip of a man because it has the same formal relation to other parts—eyes, etc.; but the trunk of an elephant is analogous to the hand of a man because both have the same uses. Fifteen years ago comparative anatomy revolved endlessly around these two sorts of comparability, which incidentally are good examples of what I mean by "abstractions which define the terms of a comparison between entities."

My attack on the system was to suggest that there might be other sorts of comparability and that these would confuse the issue to such a degree that mere morphological analysis would not suffice. I argued that the bilateral fins of a fish would conventionally be regarded as homologous with the bilateral limbs of a mammal, but that the tail of a fish, a median organ, would conventionally be regarded a "different from" or at most only "analogous to" the fins. But what about the double-tailed Japanese goldfish? In this animal the factors causing an anomaly of the tail also cause the same anomaly in the bilateral fins; therefore there was here another sort of comparability, an equivalence in terms of processes and laws of growth. Well, I don't know what mark I got for my answer. I found out much later that, as a matter of fact, the lateral fins of the goldfish are scarcely, if at all, affected by the factors which cause the anomaly in the tail, but I doubt if the examiner caught me in my bluff; and I found also that, curiously, Haekel in 1854 had actually coined the word "homonomy" for the very type of equivalence that I was inventing. The word is, so far as I know, obsolete, and was obsolete when I wrote my answer.

So far as I was concerned, however, the idea was new

and I had thought of it myself. I felt that I had discovered how to think. That was in 1926, and this same old clue— recipe, if you like—has remained with me ever since. I did not realize that I had a recipe; and it was not until ten years later that I fully grasped the significance of this analogy-homology-homonomy business.

Perhaps it will be of interest to recount in some detail my various brushes with these concepts and the recipe which they contained. Soon after the examination to which I have referred, I went into anthropology and for some time stopped thinking—wondering rather what could be made of this subject, but not getting anything clear except a repudiation of most of the conventional approaches which, to me, seemed meaningless. I wrote a little skit on the concept of totemism in 1930, first proving that the totemism of the Iatmul is *true* totemism because it contains a "high percentage" of characteristics of totemism listed in "Notes and Queries on Anthropology" issued more or less ex cathedra by the Royal Anthropological Institute, and then going on to the question, what sort of equivalence we thought we were referring to when we equate some bits of Iatmul culture with the totemism of North America, and dragging in homology-homonomy, etc.

In this discussion of "true" totemism I still had the homonomy-homology abstractions perfectly clear and was using the concepts with a clean (though inarticulate) understanding of what sort of abstractions they were—but it is interesting that I afterwards made some other comparable abstractions for the analysis of Iatmul material and muddled the issues through forgetting this very thing.

I was especially interested in studying what I called the "feel" of culture, and I was bored with the conventional study of the more formal details. I went out to New Guinea with that much vaguely clear—and in one of my first letters home I complained of the hopelessness of putting any sort of salt on the tail of such an imponderable concept as the "feel" of culture. I had been watching a casual group of natives chewing betel, spitting, laughing, joking, etc., and I felt acutely the tantalizing impossibility of what I wanted to do.

A year later, still in New Guinea, I read *Arabia Deserta* and recognized with a thrill that Doughty had in a sense done what I wanted to do. He had put salt on the tail of the very bird that I was hunting. But I realized also—sadly—that he had used the wrong kind of salt. I was not interested in achieving a literary or artistic representation of the "feel" of the culture; I was interested in a scientific analysis of it.

On the whole I think that Doughty was an encouragement to me, and the greatest encouragement I got from him was due to a fallacious bit of thinking which he prompted. It appeared to me that it was impossible to understand the behavior of his Arabs apart from the "feel" of their culture, and from this it seemed to follow that the "feel" of the culture was in some way *causative* in shaping native behavior. This encouraged me to go on thinking that I was trying after something that was important—so far so good. But it also guided me into regarding the "feel" of the culture as much more concrete and causally active than I had any right to do.

This false concreteness was reinforced later by an accident of language. Radcliffe-Brown called to my attention the old word "*ethos*" and told me that that was what I was trying to study. Words are dangerous things, and it so happens that "ethos" is in some ways a very bad word. If I had been compelled to make up my own word for what I wanted to say, I might have done better and saved myself a great deal of confusion. I would, I hope, have put forward something like "ethonomy," which would have reminded me that I was referring to an abstraction of the same order as homology or homonomy. The trouble with the word "ethos" is just this—that it is *too short*. It is a unit word, a single Greek substantive, and as such helped me to go on thinking that it referred to a unit something which I could still regard as *causative*. I handled the word as if it were a category of behavior or a sort of factor which shaped behavior.

We are all familiar with this loose use of words in such phrases as: "the causes of war are economic," "economic behavior," "he was influenced by his emotions," "his symptoms are the result of conflict between his superego and his id." (I am not sure how many of these fallacies are contained in that last example; at a rough count, there seem to be five with a possible sixth, but there may be more. Psychoanalysis has erred sadly in using words that are too short and therefore appear more concrete than they are.) I was guilty of just this sort of shoddy thinking in my handling of the word "ethos," and you must excuse me if I have gathered moral support for this confession by a digression to show that at any rate others have committed the same crime.

Let us examine the stages by which I got into the fallacy and the way in which I got out of it. I think the first step toward an escape from sin was to multiply offenses—and there is a good deal to be said for this method. Vice is after all a dull business whether it be physical or intellectual, and an effective cure can sometimes be achieved by indulgence to the point at which the patient realizes this. It is a way of proving that a given line of thought or conduct will not do, by experimentally extrapolating it to infinity, when its absurdities become evident.

I multiplied my offenses by creating several more concepts of about the same degree of abstraction as "ethos"— I had "eidos," "cultural structure," "sociology"—and all these I handled as though they were concrete entities. I pictured the relations between ethos and cultural structure as being like the relation between a river and its banks—"The river molds the banks and the banks guide the river. Similarly, the ethos molds the cultural structure and is guided by it." I was still looking for physical analogies, but now the position was not quite the same as when I was looking for analogies in order to get concepts which I could use in analyzing observed material. I was looking now for physical analogies which I could use in analyzing my own concepts, and that is a very much less satisfactory business. I do not mean, of course, that the other sciences can give one no help in the attempt to straighten out one's thoughts; they surely can. For example, the theory of Dimensions in physics may be of enormous help in this field. What I mean is that when one is seeking an analogy for the elucidation of material of one sort, it is good to look at the way analogous material has been analyzed. But when one is seeking an elucidation of one's own concepts, then one must look for analogies on an equally abstract level. However, these similes about rivers and their banks seemed pretty to me and I treated them quite seriously.

Here I must digress for a moment to describe a trick of thought and speech, which I have found useful. When I am faced with a vague concept and feel that the time is not yet ripe to bring that concept into strict expression, I coin some loose expression for referring to this concept and do not want to prejudge the issue by giving the concept too meaningful a term. I therefore dub it hastily with some brief concrete colloquial term—generally Anglo-Saxon rather than Latin—I will speak of the "stuff" of culture, or "bits" of culture, or the "feel" of culture. These brief Anglo-Saxon terms have for me a definite feeling-tone which reminds me all the time that the concepts behind them are vague and await analysis. It is a trick like tying a knot in a handkerchief—but has the advantage that it still permits me, if I may so express it, to go on using the handkerchief for other purposes. I can go on using the vague concept in the valuable process of loose thinking—still continually reminded that my thoughts are loose.

But these similes about ethos being the river and the formulations of culture or "cultural structure" being its banks were not Anglo-Saxon reminders that I was leaving something for analysis at a later date. They were, as I thought, the real thing—a real contribution to our understanding of how culture works. I thought that there was one sort of phenomenon which I could call "ethos" and another sort which I could call "cultural structure" and that these two worked together—had mutual effect one on the other. All that remained for me to do was to discriminate clearly between these various sorts of phenomena so that other people could perform the same sort of analysis that I was doing.

This effort of discrimination I postponed, feeling perhaps that the problem was not quite ripe—and I went on with the cultural analysis. And did what I still think was good work. I want to emphasize this last point—that, as a matter of fact, considerable contributions to science can be made with very blunt and crooked concepts. We may joke about the way misplaced concreteness abounds in every word of psychoanalytic writing—but in spite of all the muddled thinking that Freud started, psychoanalysis remains as *the* outstanding contribution, almost the only contribution to our understanding of the family—a monument to the importance and value of loose thinking.

Finally I had completed my book on Iatmul culture, with the exception of the last chapter, the writing of which was to be the final testing and review of my various theoretical concepts and contributions. I planned that this chapter should contain some attempt to discriminate between the sort of thing that I called "ethos" and the sort of thing that I called "eidos," etc.

I was in a state approximating that panic in the examination room which formerly produced the concept of *homonomy*. I was due to sail for my next field trip—my book had to be finished before I sailed—the book could not stand without some clear statement about the interrelations of these concepts of mine.

Here I will quote what finally appeared in the book in this last chapter:

"I began to doubt the validity of my own categories, and performed an experiment. I chose three bits of culture: (*a*) a *wau* (mother's brother) giving food to a *laua* (sister's son); a pragmatic bit, (*b*) a man scolding his wife; an ethological bit, and (*c*) a man marrying his father's sister's daughter; a structural bit. Then I drew a lattice of nine squares on a large piece of paper, three rows of squares with three squares in each row. I labeled the horizontal rows with my bits of culture and the vertical columns with my categories. Then I forced myself to see each bit as conceivably belonging to each category. I found that it could be done.

"I found that I could think of each bit of culture structurally; I could see it as in accordance with a consistent set of rules or formulations. Equally, I could see each bit as 'pragmatic,' either as satisfying the needs of individuals or as contributing to the integration of society. Again, I could see each bit ethologically, as an expression of emotion.

"This experiment may seem puerile, but to me it was very important, and I have recounted it at length because there may be some among my readers who tend to regard such concepts as 'structure' as concrete parts which 'interact' in culture, and who find, as I did, a difficulty in thinking of these concepts as labels merely for points of view adopted either by the scientist or by the natives. It is instructive to perform the same experiment with such concepts as economics, etc."[2]

In fact, "ethos" and the rest were finally reduced to abstractions of the same general order as "homology," "homonomy," etc.; they were labels for points of view voluntarily adopted by the investigator. I was, as you may imagine, enormously excited at getting this tangle straightened out—but I was also worried because I thought I should be compelled to rewrite the whole book. But I found that this was not so. I had to tune up the definitions, check through to see that each time the technical term appeared I could substitute the new definition for it, mark the more egregious pieces of nonsense with footnotes warning the reader that these passages might be taken as a warning of how not to say things—and so on. But the body of the book was sound enough—all that it needed was new castors on its legs.

So far I have spoken of my own personal experiences with strict and loose thinking, but I think actually the story which I have narrated is typical of the whole fluctuating business of the advance of science. In my case, which is a small one and comparatively insignificant in the whole advance of science, you can see both elements of the alternating process—first the loose thinking and the building up of a structure on unsound foundations and then the correction to stricter thinking and the substitution of a new underpinning beneath the already constructed mass. And that, I believe, is a pretty fair picture of how science advances, with this exception, that usually the edifice is larger and the individuals who finally contribute the new underpinning are different people from those who did the initial loose thinking. Sometimes, as in physics, we find centuries between the first building of the edifice and the later correction of the foundations—but the process is basically the same.

And if you ask me for a recipe for speeding up this process, I would say first that we ought to accept and enjoy this dual nature of scientific thought and be willing to value the way in which the two processes work together to give us advances in understanding of the world. We ought not to frown too much on either process, or at least to frown equally on either process when it is unsupplemented by the other. There is, I think, a delay in science when we start to specialize for too long either in strict or in loose thinking. I suspect, for example, that the Freudian edifice has been allowed to grow too big before the corrective of strict thought is applied to it—and now when investigators start rephrasing the Freudian dogmas in new stricter terms there may be a lot of ill feeling, which is wasteful. (At this point I might perhaps throw out a word of comfort to the orthodox in psychoanalysis. When the formulators begin rooting about among the most basic of analytic premises and questioning the concrete reality of such concepts as the "ego" or "wishes" or the "id" or the "libido"—as indeed they are already beginning to root—there is no need to get alarmed and to start having terror dreams of chaos and storms at sea. It is certain that most of the old fabric of analysis will still be left standing after the new underpinning has been inserted. And when the concepts, postulates, and premises have been straightened out, analysts will be able to embark upon a new and still more fruitful orgy of loose thinking, until they reach a stage at which again the results of their thinking must be strictly conceptualized. I think that they ought to enjoy this alternating quality in the progress of science and not delay the progress of science by a refusal to accept this dualism.)

Further than this, besides simply not hindering progress, I think we might do something to hasten matters, and I have suggested two ways in which this might be done. One is to train scientists to look among the older sciences for wild analogies to their own material, so that their wild hunches about their own problems will land them among the strict formulations. The second method is to train them to tie knots in their handkerchiefs whenever they leave some matter unformulated—to be willing to leave the matter so for years, but still leave a warning sign in the very terminology they use, such that these terms will forever stand, not as fences hiding the unknown from future investigators, but rather as signposts which read: "UNEXPLORED BEYOND THIS POINT."

# Morale and National Character*

We shall proceed as follows: (1) We shall examine some of the criticisms which can be urged against our entertaining any concept of "national character." (2) This examination will enable us to state certain conceptual limits within which the phrase "national character" is likely to be valid. (3) We shall then go on, within these limits, to outline what orders of difference we may expect to find among Western nations, trying, by way of illustration, to guess more concretely at some of these differences. (4) Lastly, we shall consider how the problems of morale and international relations are affected by differences of this order.

## Barriers to Any Concept of "National Character"

Scientific enquiry has been diverted from questions of this type by a number of trains of thought which lead scientists to regard all such questions as unprofitable or unsound. Before we hazard any constructive opinion as to the order of differences to be expected among European populations, therefore, these diverting trains of thought must be examined.

*This essay appeared in *Civilian Morale*, edited by Goodwin Watson, copyright 1942 by the Society for the Psychological Study of Social Issues. It is here reprinted by permission of the publisher. Some introductory material has been edited out.

It is, in the first place, argued that not the people but rather the circumstances under which they live differ from one community to another; that we have to deal with differences either in historical background or in current conditions, and that these factors are sufficient to account for all differences in behavior without our invoking any differences of character in the individuals concerned. Essentially this argument is an appeal to Occam's Razor—an assertion that we ought not to multiply entities beyond necessity. The argument is that, where observable differences in circumstance exist, we ought to invoke those rather than mere inferred differences in character, which we cannot observe.

The argument may be met in part by quoting experimental data, such as Lewin's experiments (unpublished material), which showed that there are great differences in the way in which Germans and Americans respond to failure in an experimental setting. The Americans treated failure as a challenge to increase effort; the Germans responded to the same failure with discouragement. But those who argue for the effectiveness of conditions rather than character can still reply that the experimental conditions are not, in fact, the same for both groups; that the stimulus value of any circumstance depends upon how that circumstance stands out against the background of other circumstances in the life of the subject, and that this contrast cannot be the same for both groups.

It is possible, in fact, to argue that since the same circumstances *never* occur for individuals of different cultural background, it is therefore unnecessary to invoke such abstractions as national character. This argument breaks down, I believe, when it is pointed out that, in stressing circumstance rather than character, we would be ignoring the known facts about *learning*. Perhaps the best documented generalization in the field of psychology is that, at any given moment, the behavioral characteristics of any mammal, and especially of man, depend upon the previous experience and behavior of that individual. Thus in presuming that character, as well as circumstance, must be taken into account, we are not multiplying entities beyond necessity; we *know* of the significance of learned character from other types of data, and it is this knowledge which compels us to consider the additional "entity."

A second barrier to any acceptance of the notion of "national character" arises after the first has been negotiated. Those who grant that character must be considered can still doubt whether any uniformity or regularity is likely to obtain within such a sample of human beings as constitutes a nation. Let us grant at once that *uniformity* obviously does not occur, and let us proceed to consider what sorts of *regularity* may be expected.

The criticism which we are trying to meet is likely to take five forms. (1) The critic may point to the occurrence of subcultural differentiation, to differences between the sexes, or between classes, or between occupational groups within the community. (2) He may point to the extreme heterogeneity and confusion of cultural norms which can be observed in "melting-pot" communities. (3) He may point to the accidental deviant, the individual who has undergone some "accidental" traumatic experience, not usual among those in his social environment. (4) He may point to the phenomena of cultural change, and especially to the sort of differentiation which results when one part of the community lags behind some other in rate of change. (5) Lastly, he may point to the arbitrary nature of national boundaries.

These objections are closely interrelated, and the replies to them all derive ultimately from two postulates: first, that the individual, whether from a physiological or a psychological point of view, is a single *organized* entity, such that all its "parts" or "aspects" are mutually modifiable and mutually interacting; and second, that a community is likewise *organized* in this sense.

If we look at social differentiation in a stable community—say, at sex differentiation in a New Guinea tribe[1]—we find that it is not enough to say that the habit system or the character structure of one sex is *different* from that of another. The significant point is that the habit system of each sex cogs into the habit system of the other; that the

---

[1] Cf. M. Mead (*Sex and Temperament in Three Primitive Societies*, New York, Morrow, 1935), especially Part III, for an analysis of sex differentiation among the Chambuli; also G. Bateson (*Naven*, Cambridge, Cambridge University Press, 1936) for an analysis of sex differentiation among adults in Iatmul, New Guinea.

behavior of each promotes the habits of the other.[2] We find, for example, between the sexes, such complementary patterns as spectatorship-exhibitionism, dominance-submission, and succoring-dependence, or mixtures of these. Never do we find mutual irrelevance between such groups.

Although it is unfortunately true that we know very little about the terms of habit differentiation between classes, sexes, occupational groups, etc., in Western nations, there is, I think, no danger in applying this general conclusion to all cases of stable differentiation between groups which are living in mutual contact. It is, to me, inconceivable that two differing groups could exist side by side in a community without some sort of mutual relevance between the special characteristics of one group and those of the other. Such an occurrence would be contrary to the postulate that a community is an organized unit. We shall, therefore, presume that this generalization applies to all stable social differentiation.

Now, all that we know of the mechanics of character formation—especially the processes of projection, reaction formation, compensation, and the like—forces us to regard these bipolar patterns as unitary within the individual. If we know that an individual is trained in overt expression of one-half of one of these patterns, *e.g.*, in dominance behavior, we can predict with certainty (though not in precise language) that the seeds of the other half—submission—are simultaneously sown in his personality. We have to think of the individual, in fact, as trained in dominance-submission, not in either dominance *or* submission. From this it follows that where we are dealing with stable differentiation within a community, we are justified in ascribing common character to the members of that community, provided we take the precaution of describing that common character in terms of the motifs of relationship between the differentiated sections of the community.

The same sort of considerations will guide us in dealing

[2] We are considering here only those cases in which ethological differentiation follows the sex dichotomy. It is also probable that, where the ethos of the two sexes is *not* sharply differentiated, it would still be correct to say that the ethos of each promotes that of the other, *e.g.*, through such mechanisms as competition and mutual imitation. Cf. M. Mead (*op. cit.*).

with our second criticism—the extremes of heterogeneity, such as occur in modern "melting-pot" communities. Suppose we attempted to analyze out all the motifs of relationship between individuals and groups in such a community as New York City; if we did not end in the madhouse long before we had completed our study, we should arrive at a picture of common character that would be almost infinitely complex—certainly that would contain more fine differentiations than the human psyche is capable of resolving within itself. At this point, then, both we and the individuals whom we are studying are forced to take a short cut: to treat heterogeneity as a positive characteristic of the common environment, *sui generis*. When, with such an hypothesis, we begin to look for common motifs of behavior, we note the very clear tendencies toward glorying in heterogeneity for its own sake (as in the Robinson Latouche "Ballad for Americans") and toward regarding the world as made up of an infinity of disconnected quiz-bits (like Ripley's "Believe It or Not").

The third objection, the case of the individual deviant, falls in the same frame of reference as that of the differentiation of stable groups. The boy on whom an English public-school education does not take, even though the original roots of his deviance were laid in some "accidental" traumatic incident, is reacting *to* the public-school system. The behavioral habits which he acquires may not follow the norms which the school intends to implant, but they are acquired in reaction to those very norms. He may (and often does) acquire patterns the exact opposite of the normal; but he cannot conceivably acquire irrelevant patterns. He may become a "bad" public-school Englishman, he may become insane, but still his deviant characteristics will be systematically related to the norms which he is resisting. We may describe his character, indeed, by saying that it is as systematically related to the standard public-school character as the character of Iatmul natives of one sex is systematically related to the character of the other sex. His character is oriented to the motifs and patterns of relationship in the society in which he lives.

The same frame of reference applies to the fourth consideration, that of changing communities and the sort of differentiation which occurs when one section of a community lags behind another in change. Since the direction in which a change occurs will necessarily be conditioned by the *status quo ante*, the new patterns, being reactions to the old, will be systematically related to the old. As long as we confine ourselves to the terms and themes of this systematic relationship, therefore, we are entitled to expect regularity of character in the individuals. Furthermore, the *expectation and experience of change* may, in some cases, be so important as to become a common character-determining factor[3] *sui generis,* in the same sort of way that "heterogeneity" may have positive effects.

Lastly, we may consider cases of shifting national boundaries, our fifth criticism. Here, of course, we cannot expect that a diplomat's signature on a treaty will immediately modify the characters of the individuals whose national allegiance is thereby changed. It may even happen—for example, in cases where a preliterate native population is brought for the first time in contact with Europeans—that, for some time after the shift, the two parties to such a situation will behave in an exploratory or almost random manner, each retaining its own norms and not yet developing any special adjustments to the situation of contact. During this period, we should still not expect any generalizations to apply to both groups. Very soon, however, we know that each side does develop special patterns of behavior to use in its contacts with the other.[4] At this point, it becomes meaningful to ask what systematic terms of relationship will describe the common character of the two groups; and from this point on, the de-

---

[3] For a discussion of the role played by "change" and "heterogeneity" in melting-pot communities, cf. M. Mead ("Educative effects of social environment as disclosed by studies of primitive societies." Paper read at the Symposium on Environment and Education, University of Chicago, September 22, 1941). Also F. Alexander ("Educative influence of personality factors in the environment." Paper read at the Symposium on Environment and Education, University of Chicago, September 22, 1941).

[4] In the South Seas, those special modes of behavior which Europeans adopt toward native peoples, and those other modes of behavior which the native adopts toward Europeans, are very obvious. Apart from analyses of "pidgin" languages, we have, however, no psychological data on these patterns. For a description of the analogous patterns in Negro-white relationships, cf. J. Dollard (*Caste and Class in a Southern Town,* New Haven, Yale University Press, 1937), especially Chapter XII, Accommodation Attitudes of Negroes.

gree of common character structure will increase until the two groups become related to each other just as two classes or two sexes in a stable, differentiated society.[5]

In sum, to those who argue that human communities show too great internal differentiation or contain too great a random element for any notion of common character to apply, our reply would be that we expect such an approach to be useful (*a*) provided we describe common character in terms of the themes of relationship *between* groups and individuals within the community, and (*b*) provided that we allow sufficient time to elapse for the community to reach some degree of equilibrium or to accept either change or heterogeneity as a characteristic of their human environment.

## Differences Which We May Expect Between National Groups

The above examination of "straw men" in the case against "national character" has very stringently limited the scope of this concept. But the conclusions from this examination are by no means simply negative. To limit the scope of a concept is almost synonymous with defining it.

We have added one very important tool to our equipment —the technique of describing the common character (or the "highest common factor" of character) of individuals in a human community in terms of bipolar adjectives. Instead of despairing in face of the fact that nations are highly differentiated, we shall take the dimensions of that differentiation as our clues to the national character. No longer content to say, "Germans are submissive," or "Englishmen are aloof," we shall use such phrases as "dominant-submissive" when relationships of this sort can be shown to occur. Similarly, we shall not refer to "the paranoidal element in German character," unless we can show that by "paranoidal" we mean some bipolar characteristic of German-German or German-foreign relationships. We shall not describe varieties of character by defining a given character in terms of its position on a continuum between extreme dominance and extreme submissiveness, but we shall, instead, try to use for our de-

[5] Cf. G. Bateson, "Culture Contact and Schismogenesis," *Man*, 1935, 8: 199. (Reprinted in this volume.)

scriptions some such continua as "degree of interest in, or orientation toward, dominance-submission."

So far, we have mentioned only a very short list of bipolar characteristics: dominance-submission, succoring-dependence, and exhibitionism-spectatorship. One criticism will certainly be uppermost in the reader's mind, that, in short, all three of these characteristics are clearly present in all Western cultures. Before our method becomes useful, therefore, we must try to expand it to give us sufficient scope and discriminatory power to differentiate one Western culture from another.

As this conceptual frame develops, no doubt, many further expansions and discriminations will be introduced. The present paper will deal with only three such types of expansion.

## Alternatives to Bipolarity

When we invoked bipolarity as a means of handling differentiation within society without foregoing some notion of common character structure, we considered only the possibility of simple bipolar differentiation. Certainly this pattern is very common in Western cultures; take, for instance, Republican-Democrat, political Right-Left, sex differentiation, God and the devil, and so on. These peoples even try to impose a binary pattern upon phenomena which are not dual in nature—youth versus age, labor versus capital, mind versus matter—and, in general, lack the organizational devices for handling triangular systems; the inception of any "third" party is always regarded, for example, as a threat to our political organization. This clear tendency toward dual systems ought not, however, to blind us to the occurrence of other patterns.[6]

> [*] The Balinese social system in the mountain communities is almost entirely devoid of such dualisms. The ethological differentiation of the sexes is rather slight; political factions are completely absent. In the plains, there is a dualism which has resulted from the intrusive Hindoo caste system, those with caste being discriminated from those without caste. At the symbolic level (partly as a result of Hindoo influence) dualisms are much more frequent, however, than they are in the social structure (*e.g.*, Northeast vs. Southwest, Gods vs. demons, symbolic Left vs. Right, symbolic Male vs. Female, etc.).

There is, for example, a very interesting tendency in English communities toward the formation of ternary systems, such as parents-nurse-child, king-ministers-people, officers-N.C.O.'s-privates.[7] While the precise motifs of relationship in these ternary systems remain to be investigated, it is important to note that these systems, to which I refer as "ternary," are neither "simple hierarchies" nor "triangles." By a pure hierarchy, I should mean a serial system in which face-to-face relations do not occur between members when they are separated by some intervening member; in other words, systems in which the only communication between A and C passes through B. By a triangle I should mean a threefold system with no serial properties. The ternary system, parent-nurse-child, on the other hand, is very different from either of these other forms. It contains serial elements, but face-to-face contact does occur between the first and the third members. Essentially, the function of the middle member is to instruct and discipline the third member in the forms of behavior which he should adopt in his contacts with the first. The nurse teaches the child how to behave toward its parents, just as the N.C.O. teaches and disciplines the private in how he should behave toward officers. In psychoanalytic terminology, the process of introjection is done *indirectly*, not by direct impact of the parental personality upon the child.[8] The face-to-face contacts between the first and third members are, however, very important. We may refer, in this connection, to the vital daily ritual in the British Army, in which the officer of the day asks the assembled privates and N.C.O.'s whether there are any complaints.

[7] A fourth instance of this threefold pattern occurs in some great public schools (as in Charterhouse), where the authority is divided between the quieter, more polished, intellectual leaders ("monitors") and the rougher, louder, athletic leaders (captain of football, head of long room, etc.), who have the duty of seeing to it that the "fags" run when the monitor calls.

[8] For a general discussion of cultural variants of the Oedipus situation and the related systems of cultural sanctions, cf. M. Mead ("Social change and cultural surrogates," *Journal of Educ. Sociol.*, 1940, 14: 92–128); also G. Roheim (*The Riddle of the Sphinx*, London, Hogarth Press, 1934).

Certainly, any full discussion of English character ought to allow for ternary, as well as bipolar patterns.

## Symmetrical Motifs

So far, we have considered only what we have called "complementary" patterns of relationship, in which the behavior patterns at one end of the relationship are different from, but fit in with, the behavior patterns at the other end (dominance-submission, etc.). There exists, however, a whole category of human interpersonal behavior which does not conform to this description. In addition to the contrasting complementary patterns, we have to recognize the existence of a series of *symmetrical* patterns, in which people respond to what others are doing by themselves doing something similar. In particular, we have to consider those competitive[9] patterns in which individual or group A is stimulated to *more* of any type of behavior by perceiving more of that same type of behavior (or greater success in that type of behavior) in individual or group B.

There is a very profound contrast between such competitive systems of behavior and complementary dominance-submission systems—a highly significant contrast for any discussion of national character. In complementary striving, the stimulus which prompts A to greater efforts is the relative *weakness* in B; if we want to make A subside or submit, we ought to show him that B is stronger than he is. In fact, the complementary character structure may be summarized by the phrase "bully-coward," implying the combination of these characteristics in the personality. The symmetrical competitive systems, on the other hand, are an almost precise functional opposite of the complementary. Here the stimulus which evokes greater striving in A is the vision of greater

[9] The term "cooperation," which is sometimes used as the opposite of "competition," covers a very wide variety of patterns, some of them symmetrical and others complementary, some bipolar and others in which the cooperating individuals are chiefly oriented to some personal or impersonal goal. We may expect that some careful analysis of these patterns will give us vocabulary for describing other sorts of national characteristics. Such an analysis cannot be attempted in this paper.

*strength* or greater striving in B; and, inversely, if we demonstrate to A that B is really weak, A will relax his efforts.

It is probable that these two contrasting patterns are alike available as potentialities in all human beings; but clearly, any individual who behaves in both ways at once will risk internal confusion and conflict. In the various national groups, consequently, different methods of resolving this discrepancy have developed. In England and in America, where children and adults are subjected to an almost continuous barrage of disapproval whenever they exhibit the complementary patterns, they inevitably come to accept the ethics of "fair play." Responding to the challenge of difficulties, they cannot, without guilt, kick the underdog.[10] For British morale Dunkirk was a stimulus, not a depressant.

In Germany, on the other hand, the same clichés are apparently lacking, and the community is chiefly organized on the basis of a complementary hierarchy in terms of dominance-submission. The dominance behavior is sharply and clearly developed; yet the picture is not perfectly clear and needs further investigation. Whether a pure dominance-submission hierarchy could ever exist as a stable system is doubtful. It seems that in the case of Germany, the submission end of the pattern is masked, so that overt submissive behavior is almost as strongly tabooed as it is in America or England. In place of submission, we find a sort of parade-ground impassivity.

A hint as to the process by which the submissive role is modified and rendered tolerable comes to us out of the interviews in a recently begun study of German life histories.[11] One German subject described how different was the treatment which he, as a boy, received in his South German home, from that which his sister received. He said that much more was demanded of him; that his sister was allowed to evade discipline; that whereas he was always expected to click his

---

[10] It is, however, possible that in certain sections of these nations, complementary patterns occur with some frequency—particularly among groups who have suffered from prolonged insecurity and uncertainty, *e.g.*, racial minorities, depressed areas, the stock exchange, political circles, etc.

[11] G. Bateson, unpublished research for the Council on Human Relations.

heels and obey with precision, his sister was allowed much more freedom. The interviewer at once began to look for intersex sibling jealousy, but the subject declared that it was a greater honor for the boy to obey. "One doesn't expect too much of girls," he said. "What one felt they (boys) should accomplish and do was very serious, because they had to be prepared for life." An interesting inversion of *noblesse oblige*.

## Combinations of Motifs

Among the complementary motifs, we have mentioned only three—dominance-submission, exhibitionism-spectatorship, and succorance-dependence—but these three will suffice to illustrate the sort of verifiable hypotheses at which we can arrive by describing national character in this hyphenated terminology.[12]

Since, clearly, all three of these motifs occur in all Western cultures, the possibilities for international difference are limited to the proportions and ways in which the motifs are combined. The proportions are likely to be very difficult to detect, except where the differences are very large. We may be sure ourselves that Germans are more oriented toward dominance-submission than are Americans, but to demonstrate this certainty is likely to be difficult. To estimate differences in the degree of development of exhibitionism-spectatorship or succorance-dependence in the various nations will, indeed, probably be quite impossible.

If, however, we consider the possible ways in which these motifs may be combined together, we find sharp qualitative differences which are susceptible of easy verification. Let us assume that all three of these motifs are developed in all relationships in all Western cultures, and from this assumption go on to consider *which individual plays which role*.

It is logically possible that in one cultural environment A will be dominant and exhibitionist, while B is submissive and

[12] For a fuller study, we ought to consider such other motifs as aggression-passivity, possessive-possessed, agent-tool, etc. And all of these motifs will require somewhat more critical definition than can be attempted in this paper.

spectator; while in another culture X may be dominant and spectator, while Y is submissive and exhibitionist.

Examples of this sort of contrast rather easily come to mind. Thus we may note that whereas the dominant Nazis preen themselves before the people, the czar of Russia kept his private ballet, and Stalin emerges from seclusion only to review his troops. We might perhaps present the relationship between the Nazi Party and the people thus:

| *Party* | *People* |
|---------|----------|
| Dominance | Submission |
| Exhibitionism | Spectatorship |

While the czar and his ballet would be represented:

| *Czar* | *Ballet* |
|--------|----------|
| Dominance | Submission |
| Spectatorship | Exhibitionism |

Since these European examples are comparatively unproved, it is worthwhile at this point to demonstrate the occurrence of such differences by describing a rather striking ethnographic difference which has been documented more fully. In Europe, where we tend to associate succoring behavior with social superiority, we construct our parent symbols accordingly. Our God, or our king, is the "father" of his people. In Bali, on the other hand, the gods are the "children" of the people, and when a god speaks through the mouth of a person in trance, he addresses anyone who will listen as "father." Similarly, the rajah is *sajanganga* ("spoilt" like a child) by his people. The Balinese, further, are very fond of putting children in the combined roles of god and dancer; in mythology, the perfect prince is polished and narcissistic. Thus the Balinese pattern might be summarized thus:

| *High Status* | *Low Status* |
|---------------|--------------|
| Dependence | Succoring |
| Exhibitionism | Spectatorship |

And this diagram would imply, not only that the Balinese feel dependence and exhibitionism and superior status to go naturally together, but also that a Balinese will not readily combine succoring with exhibitionism (that is, Bali completely lacks the ostentatious gift-giving characteristic of many primitive peoples) or will be embarrassed if forced by the context to attempt such a combination.

Although the analogous diagrams for our Western cultures cannot be drawn with the same certainty, it is worthwhile to attempt them for the parent-child relationships in English, American, and German cultures. One extra complication must, however, be faced; when we look at parent-child relationships instead of at relationships between princes and people, we have to make specific allowance for the changes in the pattern which occur as the child grows older. Succorance-dependence is undoubtedly a dominant motif in early childhood, but various mechanisms later modify this extreme dependence, to bring about some degree of psychological independence.

The English upper- and middle-class system would be represented diagrammatically thus:

| Parents | Children |
|---------|----------|
| Dominance | Submission |
| | (modified by "ternary" nurse system) |
| Succoring | Dependence |
| | (dependence habits broken by separation—children sent to school) |
| Exhibitionism | Spectatorship |
| | (children listen silently at meals) |

In contrast with this, the analogous American pattern seems to be:

| Parents | Children |
|---------|----------|
| Dominance (slight) | Submission (slight) |
| Succoring | Dependence |
| Spectatorship | Exhibitionism |

And this pattern differs from the English not only in the reversal of the spectatorship-exhibitionism roles, but also in the content of what is exhibited. The American child is encouraged by his parents to *show off his independence*. Usually the process of psychological weaning is not accomplished by sending the child away to a boarding school; instead, the child's exhibitionism is played off against his independence, until the latter is neutralized. Later, from this beginning in the exhibition of independence, the individual may sometimes go on in adult life to show off succorance, his wife and family becoming in some degree his "exhibits."

Though the analogous German pattern probably resembles the American in the arrangement of the paired complementary roles, certainly it differs from the American in that the father's dominance is much stronger and much more consistent, and especially in that the content of the boy's exhibitionism is quite different. He is, in fact, dominated into a sort of heel-clicking exhibitionism which takes the place of overt submissive behavior. Thus, while in the American character exhibitionism is encouraged by the parent as a method of psychological weaning, both its function and its content are for the German entirely different.

Differences of this order, which may be expected in all European nations, are probably the basis of many of our naive and often unkind international comments. They may, indeed, be of considerable importance in the mechanics of international relations, in as much as an understanding of them might dispel some of our misunderstandings. To an American eye, the English too often appear "arrogant," whereas to an English eye the American appears to be "boastful." If we could show precisely how much of truth and how much of distortion is present in these impressions, it might be a real contribution to interallied cooperation.

In terms of the diagrams above, the "arrogance" of the Englishman would be due to the combination of dominance and exhibitionism. The Englishman in a performing role (the parent at breakfast, the newspaper editor, the political spokesman, the lecturer, or what not) assumes that he is also in a dominant role—that he can decide in accordance with vague, abstract standards what sort of performance to give —and the audience can "take it or leave it." His own arrogance he sees either as "natural" or as mitigated by his humility in face of the abstract standards. Quite unaware that his behavior could conceivably be regarded as a comment upon his audience, he is, on the contrary, aware only of behaving in the performer's role, as he understands that role. But the American does not see it thus. To him, the "arrogant" behavior of the Englishman appears to be directed *against* the audience, in which case the implicit invocation of some abstract standard appears only to add insult to injury.

Similarly, the behavior which an Englishman interprets as "boastful" in an American is not aggressive, although the Englishman may feel that he is being subjected to some sort of invidious comparison. He does not know that, as a matter of fact, Americans will only behave like this to people whom they rather like and respect. According to the hypothesis above, the "boasting" pattern results from the curious linkage whereby exhibition of self-sufficiency and independence is played off against overdependence. The American, when he boasts, is looking for approval of his upstanding independence; but the naive Englishman interprets this behavior as a bid for some sort of dominance or superiority.

In this sort of way, we may suppose that the whole flavor of one national culture may differ from that of another, and that such differences may be considerable enough to lead to serious misunderstandings. It is probable, however, that these differences are not so complex in their nature as to be beyond the reach of investigation. Hypotheses of the type which we have advanced could be easily tested, and research on these lines is urgently needed.

## National Character and American Morale

Using the motifs of interpersonal and intergroup relationship as our clues to national character, we have been able to indicate certain orders of regular difference which we may expect to find among the peoples who share our Western civilization. Of necessity, our statements have been theoretical rather than empirical; still, from the theoretical structure which we have built up, it is possible to extract certain formulas which may be useful to the builder of morale.

All of these formulas are based upon the general assumption that people will respond most energetically when the context is structured to appeal to their habitual patterns of reaction. It is not sensible to encourage a donkey to go up hill by offering him raw meat, nor will a lion respond to grass.

(1) Since all Western nations tend to think and behave in bipolar terms, we shall do well, in building American morale, to think of our various enemies as a single hostile entity. The distinctions and gradations which intellectuals might prefer are likely to be disturbing.

(2) Since both Americans and English respond most energetically to symmetrical stimuli, we shall be very unwise if we soft-pedal the disasters of war. If our enemies defeat us at any point, that fact ought to be used to the maximum as a challenge and a spur to further effort. When our forces have suffered some reverse, our newspapers ought to be in no hurry to tell us that "enemy advances have been checked." Military progress is always intermittent, and the moment to strike, the moment when maximum morale is needed, occurs when the enemy is solidifying his position and preparing the next blow. At such a moment, it is not sensible to reduce the aggressive energy of our leaders and people by smug reassurance.

(3) There is, however, a superficial discrepancy between the habit of symmetrical motivation and the need for showing self-sufficiency. We have suggested that the American boy learns to stand upon his own feet through those occasions in childhood when his parents are approving spectators of his self-sufficiency. If this diagnosis is correct, it would follow that a certain bubbling up of self-appreciation is normal and healthy in Americans and is perhaps an essential ingredient of American independence and strength.

A too literal following of the formula above, therefore, a too great insistence upon disasters and difficulties, might lead to some loss of energy through the damming up of this spontaneous exuberance. A rather concentrated diet of "blood, sweat, and tears" may be good for the English; but Americans, while no less dependent upon symmetrical motivation, cannot feel their oats when fed on nothing but disaster. Our public spokesmen and newspaper editors should never soft-pedal the fact that we have a man-sized job on our hands, but they will do well to insist also that America is a man-sized nation. Any sort of attempt to reassure Americans by minimizing the strength of the enemy must be avoided, but frank boasts of real success are good.

(4) Because our vision of the peace is a factor in our war-making morale, it is worthwhile to ask at once what light the study of national differences may throw upon the problems of the peace table.

We have to devise a peace treaty (*a*) such that Americans and British will fight to achieve it, and (*b*) such that it will bring out the best rather than the worst characteristics of our enemies. If we approach it scientifically, such a problem is by no means beyond our skill.

The most conspicuous psychological hurdle to be negotiated, in imagining such a peace treaty, is the contrast between British and American symmetrical patterns and the German complementary pattern, with its taboo on overt submissive behavior. The allied nations are not psychologically equipped to enforce a harsh treaty; they might draw up such a treaty, but in six months they would tire of keeping the underdog down. The Germans, on the other hand, if they see their role as "submissive," will not stay down without harsh treatment. We have seen that these considerations applied even to such a mildly punitive treaty as was devised at Versailles; the allies omitted to enforce it, and the Germans refused to accept it. It is, therefore, useless to dream of such a treaty, and worse than useless to repeat such dreams as a way of raising our morale now, when we are angry with Germany. To do that would only obscure the issues in the final settlement.

This incompatibility between complementary and symmetrical motivation means, in fact, that the treaty cannot be organized around simple dominance-submissive motifs; hence we are forced to look for alternative solutions. We must examine, for example, the motif of exhibitionism-spectatorship —what dignified role is each of the various nations best fitted to play?—and that of succoring-dependence—in the starving postwar world, what motivational patterns shall we evoke between those who give and those who receive food? And, alternative to these solutions, we have the possibility of some threefold structure, within which both the allies and Germany would submit, not to each other, but to some abstract principle.

# Bali: The Value System of a Steady State*

## "Ethos" and "Schismogenesis"

It would be an oversimplification—it would even be false—to say that science necessarily advances by the construction and empirical testing of successive working hypotheses. Among the physicists and chemists there may be some who really proceed in this orthodox manner, but among the social scientists there is perhaps not one. Our concepts are loosely defined—a haze of chiaroscuro prefiguring sharper lines still undrawn—and our hypotheses are still so vague that rarely can we imagine any crucial instance whose investigation will test them.

The present paper is an attempt to make more precise an idea which I published in 1936[1] and which has lain fallow since that time. The notion of *ethos* had proved a useful conceptual tool for me, and with it I had been able to get a sharper understanding of Iatmul culture. But this experience by no means proved that this tool would necessarily be useful in other hands or for the analysis of other cultures. The most general conclusion I could draw was of this order: that my

*This essay appeared in *Social Structure: Studies Presented to A. R. Radcliffe-Brown*, edited by Meyer Fortes, 1949. It is reprinted by permission of the Clarendon Press. Preparation of the essay was aided by a Guggenheim Fellowship.

[1] G. Bateson, *Naven*, Cambridge, Cambridge University Press, 1936.

own mental processes had certain characteristics; that the sayings, actions, and organization of the Iatmul had certain characteristics; and that the abstraction, "ethos," performed some role—catalytic, perhaps—in easing the relation between these two specificities, my mind and the data which I myself had collected.

Immediately after completing the manuscript of *Naven*, I went to Bali with the intention of trying upon Balinese data this tool which had been evolved for the analysis of Iatmul. For one reason or another, however, I did not do this, partly because in Bali Margaret Mead and I were engaged in devising other tools—photographic methods of record and description—and partly because I was learning the techniques of applying genetic psychology to cultural data, but more especially because at some inarticulate level I felt that the tool was unsuitable for this new task.

It was not that ethos was in any sense disproved—indeed, a tool or a method can scarcely be proved false. It can only be shown to be not useful, and in this case there was not even a clear demonstration of uselessness. The method remained almost untried, and the most I could say was that, after that surrender to the data which is the first step in all anthropological study, ethological analysis did not seem to be the next thing to do.

It is now possible to show with Balinese data what peculiarities of that culture may have influenced me away from ethological analysis, and this demonstration will lead to a greater generalization of the abstraction, ethos. We shall in the process make certain heuristic advances which may guide us to more rigorous descriptive procedures in dealing with other cultures.

(1) The analysis of Iatmul data led to the definition of ethos as "The expression of *a culturally standardized system of organization of the instincts and emotions of the individuals.*"[2]

(2) Analysis of Iatmul ethos—consisting in the ordering of data so as to make evident certain recurrent "emphases" or "themes"—led to recognition of schismogenesis. It appeared that the working of Iatmul society involved *inter alia*

[a] *Naven*, p. 118.

two classes of regenerative[3] or "vicious" circles. Both of these were sequences of social interaction such that A's acts were stimuli for B's acts, which in turn became stimuli for more intense action on the part of A, and so on, A and B being persons acting either as individuals or as group members.

(3) These schismogenic sequences could be classified into two classes: (*a*) *symmetrical schismogenesis*, where the mutually promoting actions of A and B were essentially similar, *e.g.*, in cases of competition, rivalry, and the like; and (*b*) *complementary schismogenesis*, where the mutually promoting actions are essentially dissimilar but mutually appropriate, *e.g.*, in cases of dominance-submission, succoring-dependence, exhibitionism-spectatorship, and the like.

(4) In 1939 a considerable advance was made in defining the formal relations between the concepts of symmetrical and complementary schismogenesis. This came from an attempt to state schismogenic theory in terms of Richardson's equations for international armaments races.[4] The equations for rivalry evidently gave a first approximation to what I had called "symmetrical schismogenesis." These equations assume that the intensity of A's actions (the rate of his arming, in Richardson's case) is simply proportional to the amount by which B is ahead of A. The stimulus term in fact is $(B - A)$,

---

[3] The terms "regenerative" and "degenerative" are borrowed from communications engineering. A regenerative or "vicious" circle is a chain of variables of the general type: increase in A causes increase in B; increase in B causes increase in C; . . . increase in N causes increase in A. Such a system, if provided with the necessary energy sources and if external factors permit, will clearly operate at a greater and greater rate or intensity. A "degenerative" or "self-corrective" circle differs from a regenerative circle in containing at least one link of the type: "increase in N causes *decrease* in M." The house thermostat or the steam engine with a governor are examples of such self-correcting systems. It will be noted that in many instances the same material circuit may be either regenerative or degenerative according to the amount of loading, frequency of impulses transmitted around the path, and time characteristics of the total path.

[4] L. F. Richardson, "Generalized Foreign Politics," *British Journal of Psychology*, Monograph Supplement xxiii, 1939.

and when this term is positive it is expected that A will engage in efforts to arm. Richardson's second equation makes the same assumption *mutatis mutandis* about B's actions. These equations suggested that other simply rivalrous or competitive phenomena—*e.g.*, boasting—though not subject to such simple measurement as expenditure on armament, might yet when ultimately measured be reducible to a simply analogous set of relations.

The matter was, however, not so clear in the case of complementary schismogenesis. Richardson's equations for "submission" evidently define a phenomenon somewhat different from a progressive complementary relationship, and the form of his equations describes the action of a factor "submissiveness" which slows down and ultimately reverses the sign of warlike effort. What was, however, required to describe complementary schismogenesis was an equational form giving a sharp and discontinuous reversal of sign. Such an equational form is achieved by supposing A's actions in a complementary relationship to be proportional to a stimulus term of the type $(A - B)$. Such a form has also the advantage of automatically defining the actions of one of the participants as negative, and thus gives some mathematical analogue for the apparent psychological relatedness of domination to submission, exhibitionism to spectatorship, succoring to dependence, etc.

Notably this formulation is itself a negative of the formulation for rivalry, the stimulus term being the opposite. It had been observed that symmetrical sequences of actions tend sharply to reduce the strain of excessively complementary relationships between persons or groups.[5] It is tempting to ascribe this effect to some hypothesis which would make the two types of schismogenesis in some degree psychologically incompatible, as is done by the above formulation.

(5) It is of interest to note that all the modes associated with the erogenous zones,[6] though not clearly quantifiable, define themes for *complementary* relationship.

---

[5] *Naven*, p. 173.

[6] E. H. Homburger, "Configurations in Play: Psychological Notes," *Psychoanalytical Quarterly*, 1937, vi: 138–214. This paper, one of the most important in the literature seeking to state psychoanalytic hypotheses in more rigorous terms, deals with the "modes" appropriate to the various erogenous zones—intrusion, incorporation,

(6) The link with erogenous zones suggested in 5, above, indicates that we ought, perhaps, not to think of simple rising exponential curves of intensity limited only by factors analogous to fatigue, such as Richardson's equations would imply; but rather that we should expect our curves to be bounded by phenomena comparable to orgasm—that the achievement of a certain degree of bodily or neural involvement or intensity may be followed by a release of schismogenic tension. Indeed, all that we know about human beings in various sorts of simple contests would seem to indicate that this is the case, and that the conscious or unconscious wish for release of this kind is an important factor which draws the participants on and prevents them from simply withdrawing from contests which would otherwise not commend themselves to "common sense." If there be any basic human characteristic which makes man prone to struggle, it would seem to be this hope of release from tension through total involvement. In the case of war this factor is undoubtedly often potent. (The real truth—that in modern warfare only a very few of the participants achieve this climactic release—seems hardly to stand against the insidious myth of "total" war.)

(7) In 1936 it was suggested that the phenomenon of "falling in love" might be comparable to a schismogenesis with the signs reversed, and even that "if the course of true love ever ran smooth it would follow an exponential curve."[7] Richardson[8] has since, independently, made the same point in more formal terms. Paragraph 6, above, clearly indicates that the "exponential curves" must give place to some type of curve which will not rise indefinitely but will reach a climax and then fall. For the rest, however, the obvious relationship of these interactive phenomena to climax and orgasm very much strengthens the case for regarding schismogenesis and those cumulative sequences of interaction which lead to

retention, and the like—and shows how these modes may be transferred from one zone to another. This leads the writer to a chart of the possible permutations and combinations of such transferred modalities. This chart provides precise means of describing the course of the development of a large variety of different types of character structure (*e.g.*, as met with in different cultures).

[7] *Naven*, p. 197.

[8] *Op. cit.*, 1939.

love as often psychologically equivalent. (Witness the curious confusions between fighting and lovemaking, the symbolic identifications of orgasm with death, the recurrent use by mammals of organs of offense as ornaments of sexual attraction, etc.)

(8) *Schismogenic sequences were not found in Bali.* This negative statement is of such importance and conflicts with so many theories of social opposition and Marxian determinism that, in order to achieve credibility, I must here describe schematically the process of character formation, the resulting Balinese character structure, the exceptional instances in which some sort of cumulative interaction can be recognized, and the methods by which quarrels and status differentiation are handled. (Detailed analysis of the various points and the supporting data cannot here be reproduced, but references will be given to published sources where the data can be examined.)[9]

## Balinese Character

(a) The most important exception to the above generalization occurs in the relationship between adults (especially parents) and children. Typically, the mother will start a small flirtation with the child, pulling its penis or otherwise stimulating it to interpersonal activity. This will excite the child, and for a few moments cumulative interaction will occur. Then just as the child, approaching some small climax, flings its arms around the mother's neck, her attention wanders. At this point the child will typically start an alternative cumulative interaction, building up toward temper tantrum. The mother will either play a spectator's role, enjoying the child's tantrum, or, if the child actually attacks her, will brush off his attack with no show of anger on her part. These sequences can be seen either as an expression of the mother's distaste for this type of personal involvement or as context in which the child acquires a deep distrust of such involvement. The perhaps basically human tendency towards cumu-

[9] See especially G. Bateson and M. Mead, *Balinese Character: A Photographic Analysis.* Since this photographic record is available, no photographs are included in the present paper.

lative personal interaction is thus muted.[10] It is possible that some sort of continuing plateau of intensity is substituted for climax as the child becomes more fully adjusted to Balinese life. This cannot at present be clearly documented for sexual relations, but there are indications that a plateau type of sequence is characteristic for trance and for quarrels (see *d*, below).

(*b*) Similar sequences have the effect of diminishing the child's tendencies toward competitive and rivalrous behavior. The mother will, for example, tease the child by suckling the baby of some other woman and will enjoy her own child's efforts to push the intruder from the breast.[11]

(*c*) In general the lack of climax is characteristic for Balinese music, drama, and other art forms. The music typically has a progression, derived from the logic of its formal structure, and modifications of intensity determined by the duration and progress of the working out of these formal relations. It does not have the sort of rising intensity and climax structure characteristic of modern Occidental music, but rather a formal progression.[12]

(*d*) Balinese culture includes definite techniques for dealing with quarrels. Two men who have quarrelled will go formally to the office of the local representative of the Rajah and will there register their quarrel, agreeing that whichever speaks to the other shall pay a fine or make an offering to the gods. Later, if the quarrel terminates, this contract may be formally nullified. Smaller—but similar—avoidances (*pwik*) are practiced, even by small children in their quarrels. It is significant, perhaps, that this procedure is not an attempt to influence the protagonists away from hostility and toward friendship. Rather, it is a formal recognition of the state of their mutual relationship, and possibly, in some sort, a pegging of the relationship at that state. If this interpretation is correct, this method of dealing with quarrels would correspond to the substitution of a plateau for a climax.

[10] *Balinese Character: A Photographic Analysis*, pl. 47, and pp. 32–6.

[11] *Ibid.*, pls. 49, 52, 53, and 69–72.

[12] See Colin McPhee, "The Absolute Music of Bali," *Modern Music*, 1935; and *A House in Bali*, London, Gollancz, 1947.

(e) In regard to warfare, contemporary comment on the old wars between the Rajahs indicates that in the period when the comments were collected (1936–39) war was thought of as containing large elements of mutual avoidance. The village of Bajoeng Gede was surrounded by an old vallum and foss, and the people explained the functions of these fortifications in the following terms: "If you and I had a quarrel, then you would go and dig a ditch around your house. Later I would come to fight with you, but I would find the ditch and then there would be no fight"—a sort of mutual Maginot Line psychology. Similarly the boundaries between neighboring kingdoms were, in general, a deserted no-man's land inhabited only by vagrants and exiles. (A very different psychology of warfare was no doubt developed when the kingdom of Karangasem embarked on the conquest of the neighboring island of Lombok in the beginning of the eighteenth century. The psychology of this militarism has not been investigated, but there is reason to believe that the time perspective of the Balinese colonists in Lombok is today significantly different from that of Balinese in Bali.)[13]

(f) The formal techniques of social influence—oratory and the like—are almost totally lacking in Balinese culture. To demand the continued attention of an individual or to exert emotional influence upon a group are alike distasteful and virtually impossible; because in such circumstances the attention of the victim rapidly wanders. Even such continued speech as would, in most cultures, be used for the telling of stories does not occur in Bali. The narrator will, typically, pause after a sentence or two, and wait for some member of the audience to ask him a concrete question about some detail of the plot. He will then answer the question and so resume his narration. This procedure apparently breaks the cumulative tension by irrelevant interaction.

(g) The principal hierarchical structures in the society—the caste system and the hierarchy of full citizens who are the village council—are rigid. There are no contexts in which one individual could conceivably compete with another for position in either of these systems. An individual may lose

[13] See G. Bateson, "An Old Temple and a New Myth," *Djawa*, xvii, Batavia, 1937.

his membership in the hierarchy for various acts, but his place in it cannot be altered. Should he later return to orthodoxy and be accepted back, he will return to his original position in relation to the other members.[14]

The foregoing descriptive generalizations are all partial answers to a negative question—"Why is Balinese society nonschismogenic?"—and from the combination of these generalizations we arrive at a picture of a society differing very markedly from our own, from that of the Iatmul, from those systems of social opposition which Radcliffe-Brown has analyzed, and from any social structure postulated by Marxian analysis.

We started with the hypothesis that human beings have a tendency to involve themselves in sequences of cumulative interaction, and this hypothesis is still left virtually intact. Among the Balinese the babies, at least, evidently have such tendencies. But for sociological validity this hypothesis must now be guarded with a parenthetical clause stipulating that these tendencies are operative in the dynamics of society only if the childhood training is not such as to prevent their expression in adult life.

We have made an advance in our knowledge of the scope of human character formation in demonstrating that these tendencies toward cumulative interaction are subject to some sort of modification, deconditioning, or inhibition.[15] And this is an important advance. We know how it is that the Balinese are nonschismogenic and we know how their distaste for schismogenic patterns is expressed in various details of the social organization—the rigid hierarchies, the institutions for the handling of quarrels, etc.—but we still know nothing of the positive dynamics of the society. We have answered only the negative question.

[14] See M. Mead, "Public Opinion Mechanisms among Primitive Peoples," *Public Opinion Quarterly*, 1937, i: 5–16.

[15] As is usual in anthropology, the data are not sufficiently precise to give us any clue as to the nature of the learning processes involved. Anthropology, at best, is only able to *raise* problems of this order. The next step must be left for laboratory experimentation.

### Balinese Ethos

The next step, therefore, is to ask about Balinese ethos. What actually are the motives and the values which accompany the complex and rich cultural activities of the Balinese? What, if not competitive and other types of cumulative interrelationship, causes the Balinese to carry out the elaborate patterns of their lives?

(1) It is immediately clear to any visitor to Bali that the driving force for cultural activity is *not* either acquisitiveness or crude physiological need. The Balinese, especially in the plains, are not hungry or poverty-stricken. They are wasteful of food, and a very considerable part of their activity goes into entirely nonproductive activities of an artistic or ritual nature in which food and wealth are lavishly expended. Essentially, we are dealing with an economy of plenty rather than an economy of scarcity. Some, indeed, are rated "poor" by their fellows, but none of these poor are threatened by starvation, and the suggestion that human beings may actually starve in great Occidental cities was, to the Balinese, unutterably shocking.

(2) In their economic transactions the Balinese show a great deal of carefulness in their small dealings. They are "penny wise." On the other hand, this carefulness is counteracted by occasional "pound foolishness" when they will expend large sums of money upon ceremonials and other forms of lavish consumption. There are very few Balinese who have the idea of steadily maximizing their wealth or property; these few are partly disliked and partly regarded as oddities. For the vast majority the "saving of pennies" is done with a limited time perspective and a limited level of aspiration. They are saving until they have enough to spend largely on some ceremonial. We should not describe Balinese economics in terms of the individual's attempt to maximize value, but rather compare it with the relaxation oscillations of physiology and engineering, realizing that not only is this analogy descriptive of their sequences of transactions, but that they themselves see these sequences as naturally having some such form.

(3) The Balinese are markedly dependent upon spatial orientation. In order to be able to behave they must know their cardinal points, and if a Balinese is taken by motor car over twisting roads so that he loses his sense of direction, he may become severely disorientated and unable to act (*e.g.*, a dancer may become unable to dance) until he has got back his orientation by seeing some important landmark, such as the central mountain of the island around which the cardinal points are structured. There is a comparable dependence upon social orientation, but with this difference: that where the spatial orientation is in a horizontal plane, social orientation is felt to be, in the main, vertical. When two strangers are brought together, it is necessary, before they can converse with any freedom, that their relative caste positions be stated. One will ask the other, "Where do you sit?" and this is a metaphor for caste. It is asking, essentially, "Do you sit high or low?" When each knows the caste of the other, each will then know what etiquette and what linguistic forms he should adopt, and conversation can then proceed. Lacking such orientation, a Balinese is tongue-tied.

(4) It is common to find that activity (other than the "penny wisdom" mentioned above) rather than being purposive, *i.e.*, aimed at some deferred goal, is valued for itself. The artist, the dancer, the musician, and the priest may receive a pecuniary reward for their professional activity, but only in rare cases is this reward adequate to recompense the artist even for his time and materials. The reward is a token of appreciation, it is a definition of the context in which the theatrical company performs, but it is not the economic mainstay of the troupe. The earnings of the troupe may be saved up to enable them to buy new costumes, but when finally the costumes are bought it is usually necessary for every member to make a considerable contribution to the common fund in order to pay for them. Similarly, in regard to the offerings which are taken to every temple feast, there is no purpose in this enormous expenditure of artistic work and real wealth. The god will not bring any benefit because you made a beautiful structure of flowers and fruit for the calendric feast in his temple, nor will he avenge your abstention. Instead of deferred purpose there is an immediate and immanent satisfaction in performing beautifully, with everybody

else, that which it is correct to perform in each particular context.

(5) In general there is evident enjoyment to be had from doing things busily with large crowds of other people.[16] Conversely there is such misfortune inherent in the loss of group membership that the threat of this loss is one of the most serious sanctions in the culture.

(6) It is of great interest to note that many Balinese actions are articulately accounted for in sociological terms rather than in terms of individual goals or values.[17]

This is most conspicuous in regard to all actions related to the village council, the hierarchy which includes all full citizens. This body, in its secular aspects, is referred to as *I Desa* (literally, "Mr. Village"), and numerous rules and procedures are rationalized by reference to this abstract personage. Similarly, in its sacred aspects, the village is deified as *Betara Desa* (God Village), to whom shrines are erected and offerings brought. (We may guess that a Durkheimian analysis would seem to the Balinese to be an obvious and appropriate approach to the understanding of much of their public culture.)

In particular all money transactions which involve the village treasury are governed by the generalization, "The village does not lose" (*Desanne sing dadi potjol*). This generalization applies, for example, in all cases in which a beast is sold from the village herd. Under no circumstances can the village accept a price less than that which it actually or nominally paid. (It is important to note that the rule takes the form of fixing a lower limit and is not an injunction to maximize the village treasury.)

A peculiar awareness of the nature of social processes is evident in such incidents as the following: A poor man was about to undergo one of the important and expensive *rites de passage* which are necessary for persons as they approach the top of the council hierarchy. We asked what would happen if he refused to undertake this expenditure. The first answer was that, if he were too poor, *I Desa* would *lend*

---

[16] Bateson and Mead, *op. cit.*, pl. 5.

[17] Cf. *Naven*, pp. 250 ff., where it was suggested that we must expect to find that some peoples of the world would relate their actions to the sociological frame.

him the money. In response to further pressing as to what would happen if he really refused, we were told that nobody ever had refused, but that if somebody did, nobody would go through the ceremony again. Implicit in this answer and in the fact that nobody ever does refuse is the assumption that the ongoing cultural process is itself to be valued.

(7) Actions which are culturally correct (*patoet*) are acceptable and aesthetically valued. Actions which are permissible (*dadi*) are of more or less neutral value; while actions which are not permissible (*sing dadi*) are to be deprecated and avoided. These generalizations, in their translated form, are no doubt true in many cultures, but it is important to get a clear understanding of what the Balinese mean by *dadi*. The notion is not to be equated with our "etiquette" or "law," since each of these invokes the value judgment of some other person or sociological entity. In Bali there is no feeling that actions have been or are categorized as *dadi* or *sing dadi* by some human or supernatural authority. Rather, the statement that such-and-such an action is *dadi* is an absolute generalization to the effect that under the given circumstances this action is regular.[18] It is wrong for a casteless person to address a prince in other than the "polished language," and it is wrong for a menstruating woman to enter a temple. The prince or the deity may express annoyance, but there is no feeling that either the prince, the deity, or the casteless person made the rules. The offense is felt to be against the order and natural structure of the universe rather than against the actual person offended. The offender, even in such serious matters as incest (for which he may be extruded from the society)[19] is not blamed for anything worse than stupidity and clumsiness. Rather, he is "an unfortunate person" (*anak latjoer*), and misfortune may come to any of us "when it is our turn." Further, it must be stressed that these patterns which define correct and permissible behavior are exceedingly complex (especially the rules of language) and that the indi-

---

[18] The word *dadi* is also used as a copula referring to changes in social status. *I Anoe dadi Koebajan* means "So-and-so has become a village official."

[19] Mead, "Public Opinion Mechanisms among Primitive Peoples," *loc. cit.*, 1937.

vidual Balinese (even to some degree inside his own family) has continual anxiety lest he make an error. Moreover, the rules are not of such a kind that they can be summarized either in a simple recipe or an emotional attitude. Etiquette cannot be deduced from some comprehensive statement about the other person's feelings or from respect for superiors. The details are too complex and too various for this, and so the individual Balinese is forever picking his way, like a tightrope walker, afraid at any moment lest he make some misstep.

(8) The metaphor from postural balance used in the last paragraph is demonstrably applicable in many contexts of Balinese culture:

(*a*) The fear of loss of support is an important theme in Balinese childhood.[20]

(*b*) Elevation (with its attendant problems of physical and metaphorical balance) is the passive complement of respect.[21]

(*c*) The Balinese child is elevated like a superior person or a god.[22]

(*d*) In cases of actual physical elevation[23] the duty of balancing the system falls on the supporting lower person, but control of the direction in which the system will move is in the hands of the elevated. The little girl in the figure standing in trance on a man's shoulders can cause her bearer to go wherever she desires by merely leaning in that direction. He must then move in that direction in order to maintain the balance of the system.

(*e*) A large proportion of our collection of 1200 Balinese carvings shows preoccupation on the part of the artist with problems of balance.[24]

(*f*) The Witch, the personification of fear, frequently uses a gesture called *kapar*, which is described as that of a man

[20] Bateson and Mead, *op. cit.*, pls. 17, 67, and 79.

[21] *Ibid.*, pls. 10–14.

[22] *Ibid.*, pl. 45.

[23] *Ibid.*, pl. 10, fig. 3.

[24] At present it is not possible to make such a statement in sharply defined quantitative terms, the available judgments being subjective and Occidental.

falling from a coconut palm on suddenly seeing a snake. In this gesture the arms are raised sideways to a position somewhat above the head.

(g) The ordinary Balinese term for the period before the coming of the white man is "when the world was steady" (*doegas goemine enteg*).

## Applications of the Von Neumannian Game

Even this very brief listing of some of the elements in Balinese ethos suffices to indicate theoretical problems of prime importance. Let us consider the matter in abstract terms. One of the hypotheses underlying most sociology is that the dynamics of the social mechanism can be described by assuming that the individuals constituting that mechanism are motivated to maximize certain variables. In conventional economic theory it is assumed that the individuals will maximize value, while in schismogenic theory it was tacitly assumed that the individuals would maximize intangible but still simple variables such as prestige, self-esteem, or even submissiveness. The Balinese, however, do not maximize any such simple variables.

In order to define the sort of contrast which exists between the Balinese system and any competitive system, let us start by considering the premisses of a strictly competitive Von Neumannian game and proceed by considering what changes we must make in these premisses in order to approximate more closely to the Balinese system.

(1) The players in a Von Neumannian game are, by hypothesis, motivated only in terms of a single linear (sc. monetary) scale of value. Their strategies are determined: (a) by the rules of the hypothetical game; and (b) by their intelligence, which is, by hypothesis, sufficient to solve all problems presented by the game. Von Neumann shows that, under certain definable circumstances depending upon the number of players and upon the rules, coalitions of various sorts will be formed by the players, and in fact Von Neumann's analysis concentrates mainly upon the structure of these coalitions and the distribution of value among the members. In comparing these games with human societies we

shall regard social organizations as analogous to coalition systems.[25]

(2) Von Neumannian systems differ from human societies in the following respects:

(a) His "players" are from the start completely intelligent, whereas human beings learn. For human beings we must expect that the rules of the game and the conventions associated with any particular set of coalitions will become incorporated into the character structures of the individual players.

(b) The mammalian value scale is not simple and monotone, but may be exceedingly complex. We know, even at a physiological level, that calcium will not replace vitamins, nor will an amino acid replace oxygen. Further, we know that the animal does not strive to maximize its supply of any of these discrepant commodities, but rather is required to maintain the supply of each within tolerable limits. Too much may be as harmful as too little. It is also doubtful whether mammalian preference is always transitive.

(c) In the Von Neumannian system the number of moves in a given "play" of a game is assumed to be finite. The strategic problems of the individuals are soluble because the individual can operate within a limited time perspective. He need only look forward a finite distance to the end of the play when the gains and losses will be paid up and everything will start again from a *tabula rasa*. In human society life

[25] Alternatively, we might handle the analogy in another way. A social system is, as Von Neumann and Morgenstern point out, comparable to a non-zero sum game in which one or more coalitions of people play against each other and against nature. The non-zero sum characteristic is based on the fact that value is continually extracted from the natural environment. Inasmuch as Balinese society exploits nature, the total entity, including both environment and people, is clearly comparable to a game requiring coalition between people. It is possible, however, that that subdivision of the total game comprising the *people only* might be such that the formation of coalitions within it would not be essential—that is, Balinese society may differ from most other societies in that the "rules" of the relationship between people define a "game" of the type Von Neumann would call "nonessential." This possibility is not here examined. (See Von Neumann and Morgenstern, *op. cit.*)

is not punctuated in this way, and each individual faces a vista of unknowable factors whose number increases (probably exponentially) into the future.

(*d*) The Von Neumannian players are, by hypothesis, not susceptible either to economic death or to boredom. The losers can go on losing forever, and no player can withdraw from the game, even though the outcome of every play is definitely predictable in probability terms.

(3) Of these differences between Von Neumannian and human systems, only the differences in value scales and the possibility of "death" concern us here. For the sake of simplicity we shall assume that the other differences, though very profound, can for the moment be ignored.

(4) Curiously, we may note that, although men are mammals and therefore have a primary value system which is multidimensional and nonmaximizing, it is yet possible for these creatures to be put into contexts in which they will strive to maximize one or a few simple variables (money, prestige, power, etc.).

(5) Since the multidimensional value system is apparently primary, the problem presented by, for example, Iatmul social organization is not so much to account for the behavior of Iatmul individuals by invoking (or abstracting) their value system; we should also ask how that value system is imposed on the mammalian individuals by the social organization in which they find themselves. Conventionally in anthropology this question is attacked through genetic psychology. We endeavor to collect data to show how the value system implicit in the social organization is built into the character structure of the individuals in their childhood. There is, however, an alternative approach which would momentarily ignore, as Von Neumann does, the phenomena of learning and consider merely the strategic implications of those contexts which must occur in accordance with the given "rules" and the coalition system. In this connection it is important to note that competitive contexts—provided the individuals can be made to recognize the contexts as competitive—inevitably reduce the complex gamut of values to very simple and even linear and monotone terms.[26] Con-

[26] L. K. Frank, "The Cost of Competition," *Plan Age*, 1940, vi: 314–24.

siderations of this sort, *plus* descriptions of the regularities in the process of character formation, probably suffice to describe how simple value scales are imposed upon mammalian individuals in competitive societies such as that of the Iatmul or twentieth-century America.

(6) In Balinese society, on the other hand, we find an entirely different state of affairs. Neither the individual nor the village is concerned to maximize any simple variable. Rather, they would seem to be concerned to maximize something which we may call stability, using this term perhaps in a highly metaphorical way. (There is, in fact, one simple quantitative variable which does appear to be maximized. This variable is the amount of any fine imposed by the village. When first imposed the fines are mostly very small, but if payment is delayed the amount of the fine is increased very steeply, and if there be any sign that the offender is *refusing* to pay—"opposing the village"—the fine is at once raised to an enormous sum and the offender is deprived of membership in the community until he is willing to give up his opposition. Then a part of the fine may be excused.)

(7) Let us now consider an hypothetical system consisting of a number of identical players, plus an umpire who is concerned with the maintenance of stability among the players. Let us further suppose that the players are liable to economic death, that our umpire is concerned to see that this shall not occur, and that the umpire has power to make certain alterations in the rules of the game or in the probabilities associated with chance moves. Clearly this umpire will be in more or less continual conflict with the players. He is striving to maintain a dynamic equilibrium or steady state, and this we may rephrase as the attempt to maximize the chances *against* the maximization of any single simple variable.

(8) Ashby has pointed out in rigorous terms that the steady state and continued existence of complex interactive systems depend upon preventing the maximization of any variable, and that any continued increase in any variable will inevitably result in, and be limited by, irreversible changes in the system. He has also pointed out that in such systems it is very important to permit certain variables to alter.[27] The steady state of an engine with a governor is

[27] W. R. Ashby, "Effect of Controls on Stability," *Nature*, clv, no. 3930, February 24, 1945, 242–43.

unlikely to be maintained if the position of the balls of the governor is clamped. Similarly a tightrope walker with a balancing pole will not be able to maintain his balance except by *varying* the forces which he exerts upon the pole.

(9) Returning now to the conceptual model suggested in paragraph 7, let us take one further step toward making this model comparable with Balinese society. Let us substitute for the umpire a village council composed of all the players. We now have a system which presents a number of analogies to our balancing acrobat. When they speak as members of the village council, the players by hypothesis are interested in maintaining the steady state of the system—that is, in preventing the maximization of any simple variable the excessive increase of which would produce irreversible change. In their daily life, however, they are still engaged in simple competitive strategies.

(10) The next step toward making our model resemble Balinese society more closely is clearly to postulate in the character structure of the individuals and/or in the contexts of their daily life those factors which will motivate them toward maintenance of the steady state not only when they speak in council, but also in their other interpersonal relations. These factors are in fact recognizable in Bali and have been enumerated above. In our analysis of why Balinese society is nonschismogenic, we noted that the Balinese child learns to avoid cumulative interaction, *i.e.*, the maximization of certain simple variables, and that the social organization and contexts of daily life are so constructed as to preclude competitive interaction. Further, in our analysis of the Balinese ethos, we noted recurrent valuation: (*a*) of the clear and static definition of status and spatial orientation, and (*b*) of balance and such movement as will conduce to balance.

In sum it seems that the Balinese extend to human relationships attitudes based upon bodily balance, and that they generalize the idea that motion is essential to balance. This last point gives us, I believe, a partial answer to the question of why the society not only continues to function but functions rapidly and busily, continually undertaking ceremonial and artistic tasks which are not economically or competitively determined. This steady state is maintained by continual nonprogressive change.

## Schismogenic System versus the Steady State

I have discussed two types of social system in such
schematic outline that it is possible to state clearly a contrast
between them. Both types of system, so far as they are
capable of maintaining themselves without progressive or irreversible change, achieve the steady state. There are, however, profound differences between them in the manner in
which the steady state is regulated.

The Iatmul system, which is here used as a prototype of
schismogenic systems, includes a number of regenerative
causal circuits or vicious circles. Each such circuit consists
of two or more individuals (or groups of individuals) who
participate in potentially cumulative interaction. Each
human individual is an energy source or "relay," such that the
energy used in his responses is not derived from the stimuli
but from his own metabolic processes. It therefore follows
that such a schismogenic system is—unless controlled—
liable to excessive increase of those acts which characterize
the schismogeneses. The anthropologist who attempts even a
qualitative description of such a system must therefore
identify: (1) the individuals and groups involved in schismogenesis and the routes of communication between them; (2)
the categories of acts and contexts characteristic of the
schismogeneses; (3) the processes whereby the individuals
become psychologically apt to perform these acts and/or the
nature of the contexts which force these acts upon them;
and lastly, (4) he must identify the mechanisms or factors
which control the schismogeneses. These controlling factors
may be of at least three distinct types: (*a*) degenerative
causal loops may be superposed upon the schismogeneses so
that when the latter reach a certain intensity some form of
restraint is applied—as occurs in Occidental systems when
a government intervenes to limit economic competition; (*b*)
there may be, in addition to the schismogeneses already considered, other cumulative interactions acting in an opposite
sense and so promoting social integration rather than fission;
(*c*) the increase in schismogenesis may be limited by factors
which are internally or externally environmental to the parts
of the schismogenic circuit. Such factors which have only

small restraining effect at low intensities of schismogenesis may increase with increase of intensity. Friction, fatigue, and limitation of energy supply would be examples of such factors.

In contrast with these schismogenic systems, Balinese society is an entirely different type of mechanism, and in describing it the anthropologist must follow entirely different procedures, for which rules cannot as yet be laid down. Since the class of "nonschismogenic" social systems is defined only in negative terms, we cannot assume that members of the class will have common characteristics. In the analysts of the Balinese system, however, the following steps occurred, and it is possible that some at least of these may be applicable in the analysis of other cultures of this class: (1) it was observed that schismogenic sequences are rare in Bali; (2) the exceptional cases in which such sequences occur were investigated; (3) from this investigation it appeared, (*a*) that in general the contexts which recur in Balinese social life preclude cumulative interaction and (*b*) that childhood experience trains the child away from seeking climax in personal interaction; (4) it was shown that certain positive values—related to balance—recur in the culture and are incorporated into the character structure during childhood, and, further, that these values may be specifically related to the steady state; (5) a more detailed study is now required to arrive at a systematic statement about the self-correcting characteristics of the system. It is evident that the ethos alone is insufficient to maintain the steady state. From time to time the village or some other entity does step in to correct infractions. The nature of these instances of the working of the corrective mechanism must be studied; but it is clear that this intermittent mechanism is very different from the continually acting restraints which must be present in all schismogenic systems.

# Style, Grace, and Information in Primitive Art*

## Introduction

This paper consists of several still-separate attempts to map a theory associated with culture and the nonverbal arts. Since no one of these attempts is completely successful, and since the attempts do not as yet meet in the middle of the territory to be mapped, it may be useful to state, in non-technical language, what it is I am after.

Aldous Huxley used to say that the central problem for humanity is the quest for *grace*. This word he used in what he thought was the sense in which it is used in the New Testament. He explained the word, however, in his own terms. He argued—like Walt Whitman—that the communication and behavior of animals has a naiveté, a simplicity, which man has lost. Man's behavior is corrupted by deceit—even self-deceit—by purpose, and by self-consciousness. As Aldous saw the matter, man has lost the "grace" which animals still have.

In terms of this contrast, Aldous argued that God resembles the animals rather than man: He is ideally unable to deceive and incapable of internal confusions.

In the total scale of beings, therefore, man is as if dis-

*This essay was a position paper for the Wenner-Gren Conference on Primitive Art, 1967. It is here reprinted from *A Study of Primitive Art*, edited by Dr. Anthony Forge, to be published by Oxford University Press, by permission of the publisher.

128

placed sideways and lacks that grace which the animals have and which God has.

I argue that art is a part of man's quest for grace; sometimes his ecstasy in partial success, sometimes his rage and agony at failure.

I argue also that there are many species of grace within the major genus; and also that there are many kinds of failure and frustration and departure from grace. No doubt each culture has its characteristic species of grace toward which its artists strive, and its own species of failure.

Some cultures may foster a negative approach to this difficult integration, an avoidance of complexity by crass preference either for total consciousness or total unconsciousness. Their art is unlikely to be "great."

I shall argue that the problem of grace is fundamentally a problem of integration and that what is to be integrated is the diverse parts of the mind—especially those multiple levels of which one extreme is called "consciousness" and the other the "unconscious." For the attainment of grace, the reasons of the heart must be integrated with the reasons of the reason.

Edmund Leach has confronted us, in this conference, with the question: How is it that the art of one culture can have meaning or validity for critics raised in a different culture? My answer would be that, if art is somehow expressive of something like grace or psychic integration, then the *success* of this expression might well be recognizable across cultural barriers. The physical grace of cats is profoundly different from the physical grace of horses, and yet a man who has the physical grace of neither can evaluate that of both.

And even when the subject matter of art is the frustration of integration, cross-cultural recognition of the products of this frustration is not too surprising.

The central question is: In what form is information about psychic integration contained or coded in the work of art?

## Style and Meaning

They say that "every picture tells a story," and this generalization holds for most of art if we exclude "mere" geometric ornamentation. But I want precisely to avoid analyzing the "story." That aspect of the work of art which can most easily be reduced to words—the *mythology* connected with the subject matter—is not what I want to discuss. I shall not even mention the unconscious mythology of phallic symbolism, except at the end.

I am concerned with what important psychic information is in the art object quite apart from what it may "represent." *"Le style est l'homme même"* ("The style is the man himself") (Buffon). What is implicit in style, materials, composition, rhythm, skill, and so on?

Clearly this subject matter will include geometrical ornamentation along with the composition and stylistic aspects of more representational works.

The lions in Trafalgar Square could have been eagles or bulldogs and still have carried the same (or similar) messages about empire and about the cultural premises of nineteenth-century England. And yet, how different might their message have been had they been made of wood!

But representationalism as such is relevant. The extremely realistic horses and stags of Altamira are surely not about the same cultural premises as the highly conventionalized black outlines of a later period. The *code* whereby perceived objects or persons (or supernaturals) are transformed into wood or paint is a source of information about the artist and his culture.

It is the very rules of transformation that are of interest to me—not the message, but the code.

My goal is not instrumental. I do not want to use the transformation rules when discovered to undo the transformation or to "decode" the message. To translate the art object into mythology and then examine the mythology would be only a neat way of dodging or negating the problem of "what is art?"

I ask, then, not about the meaning of the encoded message but rather about the meaning of the code chosen. But still that most slippery word "meaning" must be defined.

It will be convenient to define meaning in the most general possible way in the first instance.

"Meaning" may be regarded as an approximate synonym of pattern, redundancy, information, and "restraint," within a paradigm of the following sort:

Any aggregate of events or objects (*e.g.*, a sequence of

phonemes, a painting, or a frog, or a culture) shall be said to contain "redundancy" or "pattern" if the aggregate can be divided in any way by a "slash mark," such that an observer perceiving only what is on one side of the slash mark can *guess*, with better than random success, what is on the other side of the slash mark. We may say that what is on one side of the slash contains *information* or has *meaning* about what is on the other side. Or, in engineer's language, the aggregate contains "redundancy." Or, again, from the point of view of a cybernetic observer, the information available on one side of the slash will restrain (*i.e.*, reduce the probability of) wrong guessing. Examples:

The letter T in a given location in a piece of written English prose proposes that the next letter is likely to be an H or an R or a vowel. It is possible to make a better than random guess across a slash which immediately follows the T. English spelling contains redundancy.

From a part of an English sentence, delimited by a slash, it is possible to guess at the syntactic structure of the remainder of the sentence.

From a tree visible above ground, it is possible to guess at the existence of roots below ground. The top provides information about the bottom.

From an arc of a *drawn* circle, it is possible to guess at the position of other parts of the circumference. (From the diameter of an *ideal* circle, it is possible to assert the length of the circumference. But this is a matter of truth within a tautological system.)

From how the boss acted yesterday, it may be possible to guess how he will act today.

From what I say, it may be possible to make predictions about how you will answer. My words contain meaning or information about your reply.

Telegraphist A has a written message on his pad and sends this message over wire to B, so that B now gets the same sequence of letters on his message pad. This transaction (or "language game" in Wittgenstein's phrase) has created a redundant universe for an observer O. If O knows what was on A's pad, he can make a better than random guess at what is on B's pad.

The essence and *raison d'être* of communication is the creation of redundancy, meaning, pattern, predictability, information, and/or the reduction of the random by "restraint."

It is, I believe, of prime importance to have a conceptual system which will force us to see the "message" (*e.g.*, the art object) as *both* itself internally patterned *and* itself a part of a larger patterned universe—the culture or some part of it.

The characteristics of objects of art are believed to be *about*, or to be partly derived from, or determined by, other characteristics of cultural and psychological systems. Our problem might therefore be oversimply represented by the diagram:

[Characteristics of art object/Characteristics of rest of culture]

where square brackets enclose the universe of relevance, and where the oblique stroke represents a slash across which some guessing is possible, in one direction or in both. The problem, then, is to spell out what sorts of relationships, correspondences, etc., cross or transcend this oblique stroke.

Consider the case in which I say to you, "It's raining," and you guess that if you look out the window you will see raindrops. A similar diagram will serve:

[Characteristics of "It's raining"/Perception of raindrops]

Notice, however, that this case is by no means simple. Only if you know the *language* and have some trust in my veracity will you be able to make a guess about the raindrops. In fact, few people in this situation restrain themselves from seemingly duplicating their information by looking out of the window. We like to prove that our guesses are right, and that our friends are honest. Still more important, *we like to test or verify the correctness of our view of our relationship to others*.

This last point is nontrivial. It illustrates the necessarily hierarchic structure of all communicational systems: the fact of conformity or nonconformity (or indeed any other relationship) between parts of a patterned whole may itself be informative as part of some still larger whole. The matter may be diagrammed thus:

[("It's raining"/raindrops)/you–me relationship]

where redundancy across the slash mark within the smaller universe enclosed in round brackets proposes (is a message about) a redundancy in the larger universe enclosed in square brackets.

But the message "It's raining" is itself conventionally coded and internally patterned, so that several slash marks could be drawn across the message indicating patterning within the message itself.

And the same is true of the rain. It, too, is patterned and structured. From the direction of one drop, I could predict the direction of others. And so on.

*But the slash marks across the verbal message "It's raining" will not correspond in any simple way to the slash marks across the raindrops.*

If, instead of a verbal message, I had given you a picture of the rain, some of the slashes on the picture would have corresponded with slashes on the perceived rain.

This difference provides a neat formal criterion to separate the "arbitrary" and digital coding characteristic of the verbal part of language from the *iconic* coding of depiction.

But verbal description is often iconic in its larger structure. A scientist describing an earthworm might start at the head end and work down its length—thus producing a description iconic in its sequence and elongation. Here again we observe a hierarchic structuring, digital or verbal at one level and iconic at another.

## Levels and Logical Types

"Levels" have been mentioned: (*a*) It was noted that the *combination* of the message "It's raining" with the perception of raindrops can itself constitute a message about a universe of personal relations; and (*b*) that when we change our focus of attention from smaller to larger units of message material, we may discover that a larger unit contains iconic coding though the smaller parts of which it was made are verbal: the verbal description of an earthworm may, as a whole, be elongated.

The matter of levels now crops up in another form which is crucial for any epistemology of art:

The word "know" is not merely ambiguous in covering both *connaître* (to know through the senses, to recognize or perceive) and *savoir* (to know in the mind), but varies—

actively shifts—in meaning for basic systemic reasons. That which we know through the senses can *become* knowledge in the mind.

"I know the way to Cambridge" might mean that I have studied the map and can give you directions. It might mean that I can recall details all along the route. It might mean that when driving that route I *recognize* many details even though I could recall only a few. It might mean that when driving to Cambridge I can trust to "habit" to make me turn at the right points, without having to *think* where I am going. And so on.

In all cases, we deal with a redundancy or patterning of a quite complex sort:

[("I know . . ."/my mind)//the road]

and the difficulty is to determine the nature of the patterning within the round brackets, or, to put the matter another way: what *parts* of the mind are redundant with the particular message about "knowing."

Last, there is a special form of "knowing" which is usually regarded as adaptation rather than information. A shark is beautifully shaped for locomotion in water, but the genome of the shark surely does not contain direct information about hydrodynamics. Rather, the genome must be supposed to contain information or instructions which are the *complement* of hydrodynamics. Not hydrodynamics, but what hydrodynamics requires, has been built up in the shark's genome. Similarly, a migratory bird perhaps does not know the way to its destination in any of the senses outlined above, but the bird may contain the complementary instructions necessary to cause it to fly right.

*"Le coeur a ses raisons que la raison ne connaît point"* ("The heart has its reasons which the reason does not at all perceive"). It is this—the complex layering of consciousness and unconsciousness—that creates difficulty when we try to discuss art or ritual or mythology. The matter of *levels* of the mind has been discussed from many points of view, at least four of which must be mentioned and woven into any scientific approach to art:

(1) Samuel Butler's insistence that the better an organism "knows" something, the less conscious it becomes of its knowledge, *i.e.*, there is a process whereby knowledge (or "habit"

—whether of action, perception, or thought) sinks to deeper and deeper levels of the mind. This phenomenon, which is central to Zen discipline (cf. Herrigel, *Zen in the Art of Archery*), is also relevant to all art and all skill.

(2) Adalbert Ames' demonstrations that the conscious, three-dimensional visual images, which we make of that which we see, are made by processes involving mathematical premises of perspective, etc., of the use of which we are totally unconscious. Over these processes, we have no voluntary control. A drawing of a chair with the perspective of van Gogh affronts the conscious expectations and, dimly, reminds the consciousness of what had been (unconsciously) taken for granted.

(3) The Freudian (especially Fenichel's) theory of dreams as metaphors coded according to *primary process*. I shall consider style—neatness, boldness of contrast, etc.— as metaphoric and therefore as linked to those levels of the mind where primary process holds sway.

(4) The Freudian view of the unconscious as the cellar or cupboard to which fearful and painful memories are consigned by a process of repression.

Classical Freudian theory assumed that dreams were a *secondary* product, created by "dream work." Material unacceptable to conscious thought was supposedly translated into the metaphoric idiom of primary process to avoid waking the dreamer. And this may be true of those items of information which are held in the unconscious by the process of repression. As we have seen, however, many other sorts of information are inaccessible to conscious inspection, including most of the premises of mammalian interaction. It would seem to me sensible to think of these items as existing *primarily* in the idiom of primary process, only with difficulty to be translated into "rational" terms. In other words, I believe that much of early Freudian theory was upside down. At that time many thinkers regarded conscious reason as normal and self-explanatory while the unconscious was regarded as mysterious, needing proof, and needing explanation. Repression was the explanation, and the unconscious was filled with thoughts which could have been conscious but which repression and dream work had distorted. Today we think of consciousness as the mysterious, and of the computational methods of the unconscious, *e.g.*, primary process, as continually active, necessary, and all-embracing.

These considerations are especially relevant in any attempt to derive a theory of art or poetry. Poetry is not a sort of distorted and decorated prose, but rather prose is poetry which has been stripped down and pinned to a Procrustean bed of logic. The computer men who would program the translation of languages sometimes forget this fact about the primary nature of language. To try to construct a machine to translate the art of one culture into the art of another would be equally silly.

Allegory, at best a distasteful sort of art, is an inversion of the normal creative process. Typically an abstract relation, *e.g.*, between truth and justice, is first conceived in rational terms. The relationship is then metaphorized and dolled up to look like a product of primary process. The abstractions are personified and made to participate in a pseudomyth, and so on. Much advertising art is allegorical in this sense, that the creative process is inverted.

In the cliché system of Anglo-Saxons, it is commonly assumed that it would be somehow better if what is unconscious were made conscious. Freud, even, is said to have said, "Where id was, there ego shall be," as though such an increase in conscious knowledge and control would be both possible and, of course, an improvement. This view is the product of an almost totally distorted epistemology and a totally distorted view of what sort of thing a man, or any other organism, is.

Of the four sorts of unconsciousness listed above, it is very clear that the first three are necessary. Consciousness, for obvious mechanical reasons,[1] must always be limited to a rather small fraction of mental process. If useful at all, it must therefore be husbanded. The unconsciousness associated with habit is an economy both of thought and of consciousness; and the same is true of the inaccessability of the processes of perception. The conscious organism does not require (for pragmatic purposes) to know *how* it perceives —only to know *what* it perceives. (To suggest that we might

---

[1] Consider the impossibility of constructing a television set which would report upon its screen *all* the workings of its component parts, including especially those parts concerned in this reporting.

operate without a foundation in primary process would be to suggest that the human brain ought to be differently structured.) Of the four types, only the Freudian cupboard for skeletons is perhaps undesirable and could be obviated. But there may still be advantages in keeping the skeleton off the dining room table.

In truth, our life is such that its unconscious components are continuously present in all their multiple forms. It follows that in our relationships we continuously exchange messages about these unconscious materials, and it becomes important also to exchange metamessages by which we tell each other what order and species of unconsciousness (or consciousness) attaches to our messages.

In a merely pragmatic way, this is important because the orders of truth are different for different sorts of messages. Insofar as a message is conscious and voluntary, it could be deceitful. I can tell you that the cat is on the mat when in fact she is not there. I can tell you "I love you" when in fact I do not. But discourse about relationship is commonly accompanied by a mass of semivoluntary kinesic and autonomic signals which provide a more trustworthy comment on the verbal message.

Similarly with skill, the fact of skill indicates the presence of large unconscious components in the performance.

It thus becomes relevant to look at any work of art with the question: What components of this message material had what orders of unconsciousness (or consciousness) for the artist? And this question, I believe, the sensitive critic usually asks, though perhaps not consciously.

Art becomes, in this sense, an exercise in communicating about the species of unconsciousness. Or, if you prefer it, a sort of play behavior whose function is, amongst other things, to practice and make more perfect communication of this kind.

I am indebted to Dr. Anthony Forge for a quotation from Isadora Duncan: "If I could tell you what it meant, there would be no point in dancing it."

Her statement is ambiguous. In terms of the rather vulgar premises of our culture, we would translate the statement to mean: "There would then be no point in dancing it, because I could tell it to you, quicker and with less ambiguity, in words." This interpretation goes along with the silly idea that it would be a good thing to be conscious of everything of which we are unconscious.

But there is another possible meaning of Isadora Duncan's remark: If the message were the sort of message that could be communicated in words, there would be no point in dancing it, but it is not that sort of message. It is, in fact, precisely the sort of message which would be falsified if communicated in words, because the use of words (other than poetry) would imply that this is a fully conscious and voluntary message, and this would be simply untrue.

I believe that what Isadora Duncan or any artist is trying to communicate is more like: "This is a particular sort of partly unconscious message. Let us engage in this particular sort of partly unconscious communication." Or perhaps: "This is a message about the interface between conscious and unconscious."

The message of *skill* of any sort must always be of this kind. The sensations and qualities of skill can never be put in words, and yet the fact of skill is conscious.

The artist's dilemma is of a peculiar sort. He must practice in order to perform the craft components of his job. But to practice has always a double effect. It makes him, on the one hand, more able to do whatever it is he is attempting; and, on the other hand, by the phenomenon of habit formation, it makes him less aware of how he does it.

If his attempt is to communicate about the unconscious components of his performance, then it follows that he is on a sort of moving stairway (or escalator) about whose position he is trying to communicate but whose movement is itself a function of his efforts to communicate.

Clearly, his task is impossible, but, as has been remarked, some people do it very prettily.

## Primary Process

"The heart has its *reasons* which the reason does not at all perceive." Among Anglo-Saxons, it is rather usual to think of the "reasons" of the heart or of the unconscious as inchoate forces or pushes or heavings—what Freud called *Trieben*. To Pascal, a Frenchman, the matter was rather different, and he no doubt thought of the reasons of the heart as a body of logic or computation as precise and complex as the reasons of consciousness.

(I have noticed that Anglo-Saxon anthropologists sometimes misunderstand the writings of Claude Lévi-Strauss for precisely this reason. They say he emphasizes too much the intellect and ignores the "feelings." The truth is that he assumes that the heart has precise algorithms.)

These algorithms of the heart, or, as they say, of the unconscious, are, however, coded and organized in a manner totally different from the algorithms of language. And since a great deal of conscious thought is structured in terms of the logics of language, the algorithms of the unconscious are doubly inaccessible. It is not only that the conscious mind has poor access to this material, but also the fact that when such access is achieved, *e.g.*, in dreams, art, poetry, religion, intoxication, and the like, there is still a formidable problem of translation.

This is usually expressed in Freudian language by saying that the operations of the unconscious are structured in terms of *primary process*, while the thoughts of consciousness (especially verbalized thoughts) are expressed in *secondary process*.

Nobody, to my knowledge, knows anything about secondary process. But it is ordinarily assumed that everybody knows all about it, so I shall not attempt to describe secondary process in any detail, assuming that you know as much about it as I.

Primary process is characterized (*e.g.*, by Fenichel) as lacking negatives, lacking tense, lacking in any identification of linguistic mood (*i.e.*, no identification of indicative, subjunctive, optative, etc.) and metaphoric. These characterizations are based upon the experience of psychoanalysts, who must interpret dreams and the patterns of free association.

It is also true that the subject matter of primary-process discourse is different from the subject matter of language and consciousness. Consciousness talks about things or persons, and attaches predicates to the specific things or persons which have been mentioned. In primary process the things or persons are usually not identified, and the focus of the discourse is upon the *relationships* which are asserted to obtain between them. This is really only another way of saying that the discourse of primary process is metaphoric. A metaphor retains unchanged the relationship which it "illustrates" while substituting other things or persons for the relata. In a simile, the fact that a metaphor is being used is marked by the insertion of the words "as if" or "like." In primary process (as in art) there are no markers to indicate to the conscious mind that the message material is metaphoric.

(For a schizophrenic, it is a major step towards a more conventional sanity when he can frame his schizophrenic utterances or the comments of his voices in an "as if" terminology.)

The focus of "relationship" is, however, somewhat more narrow than would be indicated merely by saying that primary-process material is metaphoric and does not identify the specific relata. The subject matter of dream and other primary-process material is, in fact, relationship in the more narrow sense of relationship between self and other persons or between self and the environment.

Anglo-Saxons who are uncomfortable with the idea that feelings and emotions are the outward signs of precise and complex algorithms usually have to be told that these matters, the relationship between self and others, and the relationship between self and environment, are, in fact, the subject matter of what are called "feelings"—love, hate, fear, confidence, anxiety, hostility, etc. It is unfortunate that these abstractions referring to *patterns* of relationship have received names, which are usually handled in ways that assume that the "feelings" are mainly characterized by quantity rather than by precise pattern. This is one of the nonsensical contributions of psychology to a distorted epistemology.

Be all that as it may, for our present purposes it is important to note that the characteristics of primary process as described above are the inevitable characteristics of any communicational system between organisms who must use only iconic communication. This same limitation is characteristic of the artist and of the dreamer and of the prehuman mammal or bird. (The communication of insects is, perhaps, another matter.)

In iconic communication, there is no tense, no simple negative, no modal marker.

The absence of simple negatives is of especial interest because it often forces organisms *into saying the opposite of what they mean in order to get across the proposition that they mean the opposite of what they say.*

Two dogs approach each other and need to exchange the message: "We are *not* going to fight." But the only way in which fight can be mentioned in iconic communication is by the showing of fangs. It is then necessary for the dogs to discover that this mention of fight was, in fact, only exploratory. They must, therefore, explore what the showing of fangs means. They therefore engage in a brawl; discover that neither ultimately intends to kill the other; and, after that, they can be friends.

(Consider the peace-making ceremonials of the Andaman Islanders. Consider also the functions of inverted statement or sarcasm, and other sorts of humor in dream, art, and mythology.)

In general, the discourse of animals is concerned with relationship either between self and other or self and environment. In neither case is it necessary to identify the relata. Animal A tells B about his relationship with B and he tells C about his relationship with C. Animal A does not have to tell animal C about his relationship with B. Always the relata are perceptibly present to illustrate the discourse, and always the discourse is iconic in the sense of being composed of part actions ("intention movements") which mention the whole action which is being mentioned. Even when the cat asks you for milk, she cannot mention the object which she wants (unless it be perceptibly present). She says, "Mama, mama," and you are supposed from this invocation of dependency to guess that it is milk that she requires.

All this indicates that primary-process thoughts and the communication of such thoughts to others are, in an evolutionary sense, more archaic than the more conscious operations of language, etc. This has implications for the whole economics and dynamic structure of the mind. Samuel Butler was perhaps first to point out that that which we know best is that of which we are least conscious, *i.e.*, that the process of habit formation is a sinking of knowledge down to less conscious and more archaic levels. The unconscious contains not only the painful matters which consciousness prefers to not inspect, but also many matters which are so familiar that we do not need to inspect them. Habit, therefore, is a major economy of conscious thought. We can do things without consciously thinking about them. The skill of an artist, or rather his demonstration of a skill, becomes a message *about* these parts of his unconsciousness. (But not perhaps a message *from* the unconscious.)

But the matter is not quite so simple. Some types of knowledge can conveniently be sunk to unconscious levels, but other types must be kept on the surface. Broadly, we can afford to sink those sorts of knowledge which continue to be true regardless of changes in the environment, but we must maintain in an accessible place all those controls of behavior which must be modified for every instance. The lion can sink into his unconscious the proposition that zebras are his natural prey, but in dealing with any particular zebra he must be able to modify the movements of his attack to fit with the particular terrain and the particular evasive tactics of the particular zebra.

The economics of the system, in fact, pushes organisms toward sinking into the unconscious those generalities of relationship which remain permanently true and toward keeping within the conscious the pragmatics of particular instances.

The premises may, economically, be sunk, but particular conclusions must be conscious. But the "sinking," though economical, is still done at a price—the price of inaccessibility. Since the level to which things are sunk is characterized by iconic algorithms and metaphor, it becomes difficult for the organism to examine the matrix out of which his conscious conclusions spring. Conversely, we may note that what is *common* to a particular statement and a corresponding metaphor is of a generality appropriate for sinking.

## Quantitative Limits of Consciousness

A very brief consideration of the problem shows that it is not conceivably possible for any system to be totally conscious. Suppose that on the screen of consciousness there are reports from many parts of the total mind, and consider the addition to consciousness of those reports necessary to cover what is, at a given stage of evolution, not already covered. This addition will involve a very great increase in the circuit structure of the brain but still will not achieve total coverage. The next step will be to cover the processes and events occurring in the circuit structure which we have just added. And so on.

Clearly, the problem is insoluble, and every next step in the approach to total consciousness will involve a great increase in the circuitry required.

It follows that all organisms must be content with rather little consciousness, and that if consciousness has any useful functions whatever (which has never been demonstrated but is probably true), then *economy* in consciousness will be of the first importance. No organism can afford to be conscious of matters with which it could deal at unconscious levels.

This is the economy achieved by habit formation.

## Qualitative Limits of Consciousness

It is, of course, true for the TV set that a satisfactory picture on the screen is an indication that many parts of the machine are working as they should; and similar considerations apply to the "screen" of consciousness. But what is provided is only a very indirect report of the working of all those parts. If the TV suffers from a blown tube, or the man from a stroke, *effects* of this pathology may be evident enough on the screen or to consciousness, but diagnosis must still be done by an expert.

This matter has bearings upon the nature of art. The TV which gives a distorted or otherwise imperfect picture is, in a sense, communicating about its unconscious pathologies— exhibiting its symptoms; and one may ask whether some artists are not doing something similar. But this still won't do.

It is sometimes said that the distortions of art (say, van Gogh's "Chair") are directly representative of what the artist *"sees."* If such statements refer to "seeing" in the simplest physical sense (*e.g.*, remediable with spectacles), I presume that they are nonsense. If van Gogh could only see the chair in that wild way, his eyes would not serve properly to guide him in the very accurate placing of paint on canvas. And, conversely, a photographically accurate representation of the chair on the canvas would also be seen by van Gogh in the wild way. He would see no need to distort the painting.

But suppose we say that the artist is painting today what he saw yesterday—or that he is painting what he somehow knows that he *might* see. "I see as well as you do—but do you realize that this other way of seeing a chair exists as a human potentiality? And that that potentiality is always in you and in me?" Is he exhibiting symptoms which he *might* have, because the whole spectrum of psychopathology is possible for us all?

Intoxication by alcohol or drugs may help us to see a distorted world, and these distortions may be fascinating in that we recognize the distortions as *ours*. *In vino pars veritatis*. We can be humbled or aggrandized by realizing that this, too, is a *part* of the human self, a *part* of Truth. But intoxication does not increase skill—at best it may release skill previously acquired.

Without skill is no art.

Consider the case of the man who goes to the blackboard —or to the side of his cave—and draws, freehand, a perfect reindeer in its posture of threat. He cannot *tell* you about the drawing of the reindeer ("If he could, there would be no point in drawing it"). "Do you know that his perfect way of seeing—and drawing—a reindeer exists as a human potentiality?" The consummate skill of the draftsman validates the artist's message about his relationship to the animal—his empathy.

(They say the Altamira things were made for sympathetic hunting magic. But magic only needs the crudest sort of representations. The scrawled arrows which deface the beautiful reindeer may have been magical—perhaps a vulgar attempt to murder the artist, like moustaches scrawled on the Mona Lisa.)

## The Corrective Nature of Art

It was noted above that consciousness is necessarily selective and partial, *i.e.*, that the content of consciousness is, at best, a small part of truth about the self. But if this part be *selected* in any systematic manner, it is certain that the partial truths of consciousness will be, in aggregate, a distortion of the truth of some larger whole.

In the case of an iceberg, we may guess, from what is above surface, what sort of stuff is below; but we cannot make the same sort of extrapolation from the content of consciousness. It is not merely the selectivity of preference, whereby the skeletons accumulate in the Freudian unconscious, that makes such extrapolation unsound. Such a selection by preference would only promote optimism.

What is serious is the crosscutting of the circuitry of the mind. If, as we must believe, the total mind is an integrated network (of propositions, images, processes, neural pathology, or what have you—according to what scientific language you prefer to use), and if the content of consciousness is only a sampling of different parts and localities in this network; then, inevitably, the conscious view of the network as a whole is a monstrous denial of the *integration* of that whole. From the cutting of consciousness, what appears above the surface is *arcs* of circuits instead of either the complete circuits or the larger complete circuits of circuits.

What the unaided consciousness (unaided by art, dreams, and the like) can never appreciate is the *systemic* nature of mind.

This notion can conveniently be illustrated by an analogy: the living human body is a complex, cybernetically integrated system. This system has been studied by scientists—mostly medical men—for many years. What they now know about the body may aptly be compared with what the unaided consciousness knows about the mind. Being doctors, they had purposes: to cure this and that. Their research efforts were therefore focused (as attention focuses the consciousness) upon those short trains of causality which they could manipulate, by means of drugs or other intervention, to correct more or less specific and identifiable states or symptoms. Whenever they discovered an effective "cure" for something, research in that area ceased and attention was directed elsewhere. We can now prevent polio, but nobody knows much more about the systemic aspects of that fascinating disease. Research on it has ceased or is, at best, confined to improving the vaccines.

But a bag of tricks for curing or preventing a list of specified diseases provides no overall *wisdom*. The ecology and population dynamics of the species has been disrupted; parasites have been made immune to antibiotics; the relationship between mother and neonate has been almost destroyed; and so on.

Characteristically, errors occur wherever the altered causal chain is part of some large or small circuit structure of system. And the remainder of our technology (of which medical science is only a part) bids fair to disrupt the rest of our ecology.

The point, however, which I am trying to make in this paper is not an attack on medical science but a demonstration of an inevitable fact: that mere purposive rationality unaided by such phenomena as art, religion, dream, and the like, is necessarily pathogenic and destructive of life; and that its virulence springs specifically from the circumstance that life depends upon interlocking *circuits* of contingency, while consciousness can see only such short arcs of such circuits as human purpose may direct.

In a word, the unaided consciousness must always involve man in the sort of stupidity of which evolution was guilty when she urged upon the dinosaurs the common-sense values of an armaments race. She inevitably realized her mistake a million years later and wiped them out.

Unaided consciousness must always tend toward hate; not only because it is good common sense to exterminate the other fellow, but for the more profound reason that, seeing only arcs of circuits, the individual is continually surprised and necessarily angered when his hardheaded policies return to plague the inventor.

If you use DDT to kill insects, you may succeed in reducing the insect population so far that the insectivores will starve. You will then have to use more DDT than before to kill the insects which the birds no longer eat. More probably, you will kill off the birds in the first round when they eat the poisoned insects. If the DDT kills off the dogs, you will have to have more police to keep down the burglars. The burglars will become better armed and more cunning . . . and so on.

That is the sort of world we live in—a world of circuit structures—and love can survive only if wisdom (*i.e.*, a sense or recognition of the fact of circuitry) has an effective voice.

What has been said so far proposes questions about any particular work of art somewhat different from those which have been conventionally asked by anthropologists. The "culture and personality school," for example, has traditionally used pieces of art or ritual as samples or probes to reveal particular psychological themes or states.

The question has been: Does the art tell us about what sort of person made it? But if art, as suggested above, has a positive function in maintaining what I called "wisdom," *i.e.*, in correcting a too purposive view of life and making the view more systemic, then the question to be asked of the given work of art becomes: What sorts of correction in the direction of wisdom would be achieved by creating or viewing this work of art?

The question becomes dynamic rather than static.

## Analysis of Balinese Painting

Turning now from the consideration of epistemology to a specific art style, we note first what is most general and most obvious.

With almost no exceptions, the behaviors called art or their products (also called art) have two characteristics: they require or exhibit *skill*, and they contain redundancy or pattern.

But those two characteristics are not separate: the skill is first in maintaining and then in modulating the redundancies.

The matter is perhaps most clear where the skill is that of the journeyman and the redundancy is of comparatively low order. For example, in the Balinese painting by Ida Bagus Djati Sura of the village of Batuan, 1937 and in almost all painting of the Batuan school, skill of a certain elementary but highly disciplined sort was exercised or practiced in the background of foliage. The redundancies to be achieved involve rather uniform and rhythmical repetition of leaf forms, but this redundancy is, so to speak, fragile. It would be broken or interrupted by smudges or irregularities of size or tone in the painting of the successive leaves.

When a Batuan artist looks at the work of another, one of the first things he examines is the technique of the leafy background. The leaves are first drawn, in free outline in pencil; then each outline is tightly redefined with pen and black ink. When this has been done for all the leaves, the artist begins to paint with brush and Chinese ink. Each leaf is covered with a pale wash. When these washes are dry, each leaf receives a smaller concentric wash and after this another still smaller, and so on. The final result is a leaf with an almost white rim inside the inked outline, and successive steps of darker and darker color toward the center of the leaf.

A "good" picture has up to five or six such successive washes on every leaf. (This particular painting is not very "good" in this sense. The leaves are done in only three or four steps.)

The skill and the patterning so far discussed depend upon muscular rote and muscular accuracy—achieving the perhaps not negligible artistic level of a well-laid out field of turnips.

I was watching a very gifted American carpenter-architect at work on the woodwork of a house he had designed. I commented on the sureness and accuracy of each step. He said, "Oh, that. That's only like using a typewriter. You have to be able to do that without thinking."

But on top of this level of redundancy is another. The uniformity of the lower-level redundancy must be modulated to give higher orders of redundancy. The leaves in one area must be *different* from the leaves in another area, and these *differences* must be in some way mutually redundant: they must be part of a larger pattern.

Indeed, the function and necessity of the first-level control is precisely to make the second level possible. The perceiver of the work of art must receive information that the artist *can* paint a uniform area of leaves because without this information he will not be able to accept as significant the variations in that uniformity.

Only the violinist who can control the quality of his notes can use variations of that quality for musical purposes.

This principle is basic and accounts, I suggest, for the almost universal linkage in aesthetics between skill and pattern. The exceptions—*e.g.*, the cult of natural landscapes, "found objects," inkblots, scattergrams, and the works of Jackson Pollock—seem to exemplify the same rule in reverse. In these cases, a larger patterning seems to propose the illusion that the details must have been controlled. Intermediate cases also occur: *e.g.*, in Balinese carving, the natural grain of the wood is rather frequently used to suggest details of the form or surface of the subject. In these cases, the skill lies not in the draftsmanship of the details, but in the artist's placement of his design within the three-dimensional structure of the wood. A special "effect" is achieved, not by the mere representationalism, but by the perceiver's partial awareness that a physical system *other* than that of draftsmanship has contributed to determine his perception.

We now turn to more complex matters, still concentrating attention upon the most obvious and elementary.

## Composition

(1) The delineation of leaves and other forms does not reach to the edge of the picture but shades off into darkness so that almost all around the rectangle there is a band of undifferentiated dark pigment. In other words, the picture is framed within its own fade-out. We are allowed to feel that the matter is in some sense "out of this world"; and this in spite of the fact that the scene depicted is familiar— the starting out of a cremation procession.

(2) The picture is *filled*. The composition leaves no open spaces. Not only is none of the paper left unpainted, but no considerable area is left in uniform wash. The largest such areas are the very dark patches at the bottom between the legs of the men.

To Occidental eyes, this gives an effect of "fussiness." To psychiatric eyes, the effect is of "anxiety" or "compulsivity." We are all familiar with the strange look of those letters from cranks, who feel that they must fill the page.

(3) But before trying too fast to diagnose or evaluate, we have to note that the composition of the lower half of the picture, apart from this filling of background space, is turbulent. Not merely a depiction of active figures, but a swirling composition mounting upwards and closed off by the contrasting direction of the gestures of the men at the top of the pyramid.

The upper half of the picture, in contrast, is serene. Indeed, the effect of the perfectly balanced women with offerings on their heads is so serene that, at first glance, it appears that the men with musical instruments must surely be sitting. (They are supposed to be moving in procession.)

But this compositional structure is the reverse of the usual Occidental. We expect the lower part of a picture to be the more stable and expect to see action and movement in the upper part—if anywhere.

(4) At this point, it is appropriate to examine the picture as a sexual pun and, in this connection, the internal evidence for sexual reference is at least as strong as it is in the case of the Tangaroa figure discussed by Leach. All you have to do is to set your mind in the correct posture and you will see an enormous phallic object (the cremation tower) with two elephants' heads at the base. This object must pass through a narrow entrance into a serene courtyard and thence onward and upward through a still more narrow passageway. Around the base of the phallic object you see a turbulent mass of homunculi, a crowd in which

> Was none who would be foremost
> To lead such dire attack;
> But those behind cried "Forward!"
> And those before cried "Back!"

And if you are so minded, you will find that Macaulay's poem about how Horatius kept the bridge is no less sexual than the present picture. The game of sexual interpretation is easy if you want to play it. No doubt the snake in the tree to the left of the picture could also be woven into the sexual story.

It is still possible, however, that something is added to our understanding of a work of art by the hypothesis that the subject matter is double: that the picture represents both the start of a cremation procession and a phallus with vagina. With a little imagination, we could also see the picture as a symbolic representation of Balinese social organization in which the smooth relations of etiquette and gaiety metaphorically cover the turbulence of passion. And, of course, "Horatius" is very evidently an idealized myth of nineteenth-century imperial England.

It is probably an error to think of dream, myth, and art as being about any one matter other than relationship. As was mentioned earlier, dream is metaphoric and is not particularly about the relata mentioned in the dream. In the conventional interpretation of dream, another set of relata, often sexual, is substituted for the set in the dream. But perhaps by doing this we only create another dream. There indeed is no a priori reason for supposing that the sexual relata are any more primary or basic than any other set.

In general, artists are very unwilling to accept interpretations of this sort, and it is not clear that their objection is to the sexual nature of the interpretation. Rather, it seems that rigid focusing upon any single set of relata destroys for the artist the more profound significance of the work. If the picture were *only* about sex or *only* about social organization, it would be trivial. It is nontrivial or profound precisely because it is about sex and social organization and cremation, and other things. In a word, it is only about relationship and not about *any* identifiable relata.

(5) It is appropriate then to ask how the artist has handled the identification of his subject matter within the picture. We note first that the cremation tower which occupies almost one-third of the picture is almost invisible. It does not stand out against its background as it should if the artist wanted to assert unequivocally "this is a cremation." Notably also, the coffin, which might be expected to be a focal point, is appropriately placed just below the center but even so does not catch the eye. In fact, the artist has inserted details which label the picture as a cremation scene but these details become almost whimsical asides, like the snake and the little birds in the trees. The women are carrying the ritually correct offerings on their heads, and two men appropriately bring bamboo containers of palm toddy, but these details, too, are only whimsically added. The artist plays down the subject identification and thereby gives major stress to the contrast between the turbulent and the serene mentioned in 3, above.

(6) In sum, it is my opinion that the crux of the picture is the interwoven contrast between the serene and the turbulent. And a similar contrast or combination was also present, as we have seen, in the painting of the leaves. There, too, an exuberant freedom was overlaid by precision.

In terms of this conclusion, I can now attempt an answer to the question posed above: What sorts of correction, in the direction of systemic wisdom, could be achieved by creating or viewing this work of art? In final analysis, the picture can be seen as an affirmation that to choose either turbulence or serenity as a human purpose would be a vulgar error. The conceiving and creating of the picture must have provided an experience which exposed this error. The unity and integration of the picture assert that neither of these contrasting poles can be chosen to the exclusion of the other, because the poles are mutually dependent. This profound and general truth is simultaneously asserted for the fields of sex, social organization, and death.

# Comment on Part II

Since World War II, it has been fashionable to engage in "interdisciplinary" research, and this usually means, for example, that an ecologist will need a geologist to tell him about the rocks and soils of the particular terrain which he is investigating. But there is another sense in which scientific work may claim to be interdisciplinary.

The man who studies the arrangement of leaves and branches in the growth of a flowering plant may note an analogy between the formal relations between stems, leaves, and buds, and the formal relations that obtain between different sorts of words in a sentence. He will think of a "leaf" not as something flat and green but as something related in a particular way to the stem from which it grows and to the secondary stem (or bud) which is formed in the angle between leaf and primary stem. Similarly the modern linguist thinks of a "noun" not as the "name of a person, place, or thing," but as a member of a class of words defined by their *relationship* in sentence structure to "verbs" and other parts.

Those who think first of the "things" which are related (the "relata") will dismiss any analogy between grammar and the anatomy of plants as far-fetched. After all, a leaf and a noun do not at all resemble each other in outward appearance. But if we think first of the relationships and consider the relata as defined solely by their relationships, then we begin to wonder. Is there a profound analogy between grammar and anatomy? Is there an interdisciplinary science which should concern itself with such analogies? What would such a science claim as its subject matter? And why should we expect such far-flung analogies to have significance?

In dealing with any analogy, it is important to define exactly what is claimed when we say that the analogy is meaningful. In the present example, it is not claimed that a noun should look like a leaf. It is not even claimed that the relation between leaf and stem is the same as the relation between noun and verb. What is claimed is, first, that in both anatomy and grammar the parts are to be classified according to the relations between them. In both fields, the *relations* are to be thought of as somehow primary, the relata as secondary. Beyond this, it is claimed that the relations are of the sort generated by processes of information exchange.

In other words, the mysterious and polymorphic relation between *context* and *content* obtains in both anatomy and linguistics; and evolutionists of the nineteenth century, preoccupied with what were called "homologies," were, in fact, studying precisely the contextual structures of biological development.

All of this speculation becomes almost platitude when we realize that both grammar and biological structure are products of communicational and organizational process. The anatomy of the plant is a complex transform of genotypic instructions, and the "language" of the genes, like any other language, must of necessity have contextual structure. Moreover, in all communication, there must be a relevance between the contextual structure of the message and some structuring of the recipient. The tissues of the plant could not "read" the genotypic instructions carried in the chromosomes of every cell unless cell and tissue exist, at that given moment, in a contextual structure.

What has been said above will serve as sufficient definition of what is here meant by "form and pattern." The focus of discussion was upon form rather than content, upon context rather than upon what occurs "in" the given context, upon relationship rather than upon the related persons or phenomena.

The essays included range from a discussion of "schismogenesis" (1935) to two essays written after the birth of cybernetics.

In 1935, I certainly had not clearly grasped the central importance of "context." I thought that the processes of schismogenesis were important and nontrivial because in them I seemed to see evolution at work: if interaction between persons could undergo progressive qualitative change as intensity increased, then surely this could be the very stuff of cultural evolution. It followed that all directional change, even in biological evolution and phylogeny, might—or must —be due to progressive interaction between organisms. Under natural selection, such change in relationships would favor progressive change in anatomy and physiology.

The progressive increase in size and armament of the dinosaurs was, as I saw it, simply an interactive armaments race—a schismogenic process. But I could not then see that the evolution of the horse from *Eohippus* was not a one-sided adjustment to life on grassy plains. Surely the grassy plains themselves were evolved *pari passu* with the evolution of the teeth and hooves of the horses and other ungulates. Turf was the evolving response of the vegetation to the evolution of the horse. It is the *context* which evolves.

The classification of schismogenic process into "symmetrical" and "complementary" was already a classification of contexts of behavior; and, already in this essay, there is a proposal to examine the possible combinations of themes in complementary behavior. By 1942, I had completely forgotten this old proposal, but I attempted to do precisely what I had proposed seven years previously. In 1942 many of us were interested in "national character" and the contrast between England and America fortunately brought into focus the fact that "spectatorship" is in England a filial characteristic, linked with dependency and submission, while in America spectatorship is a parental characteristic linked with dominance and succoring.

This hypothesis, which I called "end-linkage," marked a turning point in my thinking. From that time on, I have consciously focused upon the qualitative structure of contexts rather than upon intensity of interaction. Above all, the phenomena of end-linkage showed that contextual structures could themselves be *messages*—an important point which is not made in the 1942 article. An Englishman when he is applauding another is indicating or signaling potential submission and/or dependency; when he shows off or demands spectatorship, he is signaling dominance or superiority; and so on. Every Englishman who writes a book must be guilty of this. For the American, the converse must hold. His boasting is but a bid for quasiparental approval.

The notion of context reappears in the essay "Style, Grace, and Information in Primitive Art," but here the idea of context has evolved to meet the related ideas of "redundancy," "pattern," and "meaning."

# Part III: Form and Pathology in Relationship

# Social Planning and the Concept of
# Deutero-Learning*

Let me take as focus for this comment the last item[1] in Dr. Mead's summary of her paper. To the layman who has not occupied himself with the comparative study of human cultures, this recommendation may appear strange; it may appear to be an ethical or philosophical paradox, a suggestion that we discard purpose in order to achieve

*This article was my comment on Margaret Mead's article "The Comparative Study of Culture and the Purposive Cultivation of Democratic Values," published as Chapter IV of *Science, Philosophy and Religion, Second Symposium*, copyright 1942 by the Conference on Science, Philosophy and Religion, New York. It is here reprinted by permission of the Conference and of Harper & Row, Inc.

I have italicized a parenthesis in footnote 5 which prefigures the concept of the "double bind."

[1] Dr. Mead writes: ". . . those students who have devoted themselves to studying cultures as wholes, as systems of dynamic equilibrium, can make the following contributions: . . .

"4. Implement plans for altering our present culture by recognizing the importance of including the social scientist *within* his experimental material, and by recognizing that by working toward defined *ends* we commit ourselves to the manipulation of persons, and therefore to the negation of democracy. Only by working in terms of values which are limited to defining a *direction* is it possible for us to use scientific methods in the control of the process without the negation of the moral autonomy of the human spirit." (Italics hers.)

159

our purpose; it may even call to mind some of the basic aphorisms of Christianity and Taoism. Such aphorisms are familiar enough; but the layman will be a little surprised to find them coming from a scientist and dressed in all the paraphernalia of analytic thought. To other anthropologists and social scientists, Dr. Mead's recommendations will be even more surprising, and perhaps more meaningless, because instrumentality and "blueprints" are an essential ingredient in the whole structure of life as science sees it. Likewise, to those in political life, Dr. Mead's recommendation will be strange, since they see decisions as classifiable into policy-making decisions versus executive decisions. The governors and the scientists alike (not to mention the commercial world) see human affairs as patterned upon purpose, means and ends, connation and satisfaction.

If anybody doubts that we tend to regard purpose and instrumentality as distinctively human, let him consider the old quip about eating and living. The creature who "eats to live" is the highest human; he who "lives to eat" is coarser-grained, but still human; but if he just "eats *and* lives," without attributing instrumentality or a spurious priority in time sequence to either process, he is rated only among the animals, and some, less kind, will regard him as vegetable.

Dr. Mead's contribution consists in this—that she, fortified by comparative study of other cultures, has been able to transcend the habits of thought current in her own culture and has been able to say virtually this: "Before we apply social science to our own national affairs, we must re-examine and change our habits of thought on the subject of means and ends. We have learnt, in our cultural setting, to classify behavior into 'means' and 'ends' and if we go on defining ends as separate from means *and* apply the social sciences as crudely instrumental means, using the recipes of science to manipulate people, we shall arrive at a totalitarian rather than a democratic system of life." The solution which she offers is that we look for the "direction," and "values" implicit in the means, rather than looking ahead to a blueprinted goal and thinking of this goal as justifying or not justifying manipulative means. We have to find the value of a planned act implicit in and simultaneous with the act itself, not separate from it in the sense

that the act would derive its value from reference to a
future end or goal. Dr. Mead's paper is, in fact, not a
direct preachment about ends and means; she does not say
that ends either do or do not justify the means. She is
talking not directly about ends and means, but about the
way we tend to think about ways and means, and about
the dangers inherent in our habit of thought.

It is specifically at this level that the anthropologist has
most to contribute to our problems. It is his task to see
the highest common factor implicit in a vast variety of
human phenomena, or inversely, to decide whether phenomena which appear to be similar are not intrinsically different. He may go to one South Sea community, such as
the Manus, and there find that though everything that the
natives do is concretely different from our own behavior,
yet the underlying system of motives is rather closely comparable with our own love of caution and wealth accumulation; or again he may go to another society such as Bali
and there find that, while the outward appearance of the
native religion is closely comparable with our own—kneel-
ing to pray, incense, intoned utterances punctuated by a
bell, etc.—the basic emotional attitudes are fundamentally
different. In Balinese religion we find an approval accorded
to rote, nonemotional performance of certain acts instead
of the insistence upon correct emotional attitude, characteristic of Christian churches.

In every case the anthropologist is concerned not with
mere description but with a slightly higher degree of abstraction, a wider degree of generalization. His first task
is the meticulous collection of masses of concrete observations of native life—but the next step is not a mere sum-
marizing of these data; it is rather to interpret the data in
an abstract language which shall transcend and comprehend
the vocabulary and notions explicit and implicit in our own
culture. It is not possible to give a scientific description of
a native culture in English words; the anthropologist must
devise a more abstract vocabulary in terms of which both
our own and the native culture can be described.

This then is the type of discipline which has enabled Dr.
Mead to point out that a discrepancy—a basic and fundamental discrepancy—exists between "social engineering,"

manipulating people in order to achieve a planned blue-print society, and the ideals of democracy, the "supreme worth and moral responsibility of the individual human person." The two conflicting motifs have long been implicit in our culture, science has had instrumental leanings since before the Industrial Revolution, and emphasis upon individual worth and responsibility is even older. The threat of conflict between the two motifs has only come recently, with increasing consciousness of, and emphasis upon, the democratic motif and simultaneous spread of the instrumental motif. Finally, the conflict is now a life-or-death struggle over the role which the social sciences shall play in the ordering of human relationships. It is hardly an exaggeration to say that this war is ideologically about just this—the role of the social sciences. Are we to reserve the techniques and the right to manipulate people as the privilege of a few planning, goal-oriented, and power-hungry individuals, to whom the instrumentality of science makes a natural appeal? Now that we have the techniques, are we, in cold blood, going to treat people as things? Or what are we going to do with these techniques?

The problem is one of very great difficulty as well as urgency, and it is doubly difficult because we, as scientists, are deeply soaked in habits of instrumental thought—those of us, at least, for whom science is a part of life, as well as a beautiful and dignified abstraction. Let us try to surmount this additional source of difficulty by turning the tools of science upon this habit of instrumental thought and upon the new habit which Dr. Mead envisages—the habit which looks for "direction" and "value" in the chosen act, rather than in defined goals. Clearly, both of these habits are ways of looking at time sequences. In the old jargon of psychology, they represent different ways of apperceiving sequences of behavior, or in the newer jargon of gestalt psychology, they might both be described as habits of looking for one or another sort of contextual frame for behavior. The problem which Dr. Mead—who advocates a change in such habits—raises is the problem of how habits of this abstract order are learned.

This is not the simple type of question which is posed in most psychological laboratories, "Under what circumstances will a dog learn to salivate in response to a bell?" or, "What variables govern success in rote learning?" Our question is one degree more abstract, and, in a sense, bridges the gap between the experimental work on simple learning and the approach of the gestalt psychologists. We are asking, "How does the dog acquire a habit of punctuating or apperceiving the infinitely complex stream of events (including his own behavior) so that this stream appears to be made up of one type of short sequences rather than another?" Or, substituting the scientist for the dog, we might ask, "What circumstances determine that a given scientist will punctuate the stream of events so as to conclude that all is predetermined, while another will see the stream of events as so regular as to be susceptible of control?" Or, again, on the same level of abstraction let us ask—and this question is very relevant to the promotion of democracy— "What circumstances promote that specific habitual phrasing of the universe which we call 'free will' and those others which we call 'responsibility,' 'constructiveness,' 'energy,' 'passivity,' 'dominance,' and the rest?" For all these abstract qualities, the essential stock-in-trade of the educators, can be seen as various habits of punctuating the stream of experience so that it takes on one or another sort of coherence and sense. They are abstractions which begin to assume some operational meaning when we see them take their place on a conceptual level between the statements of simple learning and those of gestalt psychology.

We can, for example, put our finger very simply on the process which leads to tragedy and disillusion whenever men decide that the "end justifies the means" in their efforts to achieve either a Christian or a blueprinted heaven-on-earth. They ignore the fact that in social manipulation, the tools are not hammers and screwdrivers. A screwdriver is not seriously affected when, in an emergency, we use it as a wedge; and a hammer's outlook on life is not affected because we sometimes use its handle as a simple lever. But in social manipulation our tools are people, and people learn, and they acquire habits which are more subtle and pervasive than the tricks which the blueprinter teaches them. With the best intentions in the world, he may train children to spy upon their parents in order to eradicate some tendency prejudicial to the success of his blueprint, but because the children are people they will do more than learn this simple trick—they will build this experience into their whole philosophy of life; it will color all their future attitudes toward authority. Whenever they meet certain sorts of context, they will tend to see these contexts as structured on an earlier familiar pattern. The blueprinter may derive an initial advantage from the children's tricks; but the ultimate success of his blueprint may be destroyed by the habits of mind which were learned with the trick. (Unfortunately, there is no reason to believe that the Nazi blueprint will break down for these reasons. It is probable that the unpleasant attitudes here referred to are envisaged as basic *both* to the plan itself and to the means of achieving it. The road to hell can also be paved with bad intentions, though well-intentioned people find this hard to believe.)

We are dealing, apparently, with a sort of habit which is a by-product of the learning process. When Dr. Mead tells us that we should leave off thinking in terms of blue-prints and should instead evaluate our planned acts in terms of their immediate implicit value, she is saying that in the upbringing and education of children, we ought to try to inculcate a sort of by-product habit rather different from that which we acquired and which we daily reinforce in ourselves in our contacts with science, politics, newspapers, and so on.

She states perfectly clearly that this new shift in the emphasis or gestalt of our thinking will be a setting forth into uncharted waters. We cannot know what manner of human beings will result from such a course, nor can we be sure that we ourselves would feel at home in the world of 1980. Dr. Mead can only tell us that if we proceed on the course which would seem most natural, planning our applications of social science as a means of attaining a defined goal, we shall surely hit a rock. She has charted the rock for us, and advises that we embark on a course in a direction where the rock is not; but in a new, still uncharted direction. Her paper raises the question of how we are to chart this new direction.

Actually, science can give us something approaching a chart. I indicated above that we might see a mixed bunch of abstract terms—free will, predestination, responsibility, constructiveness, passivity, dominance, etc.—as all of them descriptive of apperceptive habits, habitual ways of looking at the stream of events of which our own behavior is a part, and further that these habits might all be, in some sense, by-products of the learning process. Our next task, if we are to achieve some sort of chart, is clearly to get something better than a random list of these possible habits. We must reduce this list to a classification which shall show how each of these habits is systematically related to the others.

We meet in common agreement that a sense of individual autonomy, a habit of mind somehow related to what I have called "free will," is an essential of democracy, but we are still not perfectly clear as to how this autonomy should be defined operationally. What, for example, is the relation between "autonomy" and compulsive negativism? The gas stations which refuse to conform to the curfew—are they or are they not showing a fine democratic spirit? This sort of "negativism" is undoubtedly of the same degree of abstraction as "free will" or "determinism"; like them it is an habitual way of apperceiving contexts, event sequences and own behavior; but it is not clear whether this negativism is a "subspecies" of individual autonomy; or is it rather some entirely different habit? Similarly, we need to know how the new habit of thought which Dr. Mead advocates is related to the others.

Evidently our need is for something better than a random list of these habits of mind. We need some systematic framework or classification which shall show how each of these habits is related to the others, and such a classification might provide us with something approaching the chart we lack. Dr. Mead tells us to sail into as yet uncharted waters, adopting a new habit of thought; but if we knew how this habit is related to others, we might be able to judge of the benefits and dangers, the possible pitfalls of such a course. Such a chart might provide us with the answers to some of the questions which Dr. Mead raises—as to how we are to judge of the "direction" and value implicit in our planned acts.

You must not expect the social scientist to produce such a chart or classification at a moment's notice, like a rabbit out of a hat, but I think we can take a first step in this direction; we can suggest some of the basic themes—the cardinal points, if you like—upon which the final classification must be built.

We have noted that the sorts of habit with which we are concerned are, in some sense, by-products of the learning processes, and it is therefore natural that we look first to the phenomena of simple learning as likely to provide us with a clue. We are raising questions one degree more abstract than those chiefly studied by the experimental psychologists, but it is still to their laboratories that we must look for our answers.

Now it so happens that in the psychological laboratories there is a common phenomenon of a somewhat higher degree of abstraction or generality than those which the experiments are planned to elucidate. It is a commonplace that the experimental subject—whether animal or man, becomes a better subject after repeated experiments. He not only learns to salivate at the appropriate moments, or to recite the appropriate nonsense syllables; he also, in some way, *learns to learn*. He not only solves the problems set him by the experimenter, where each solving is a piece of simple learning; but, more than this, he becomes more and more skilled in the solving of problems.

In semigestalt or semianthropomorphic phraseology, we might say that the subject is learning to orient himself to certain types of contexts, or is acquiring "insight" into the contexts of problem solving. In the jargon of this paper, we may say that the subject has acquired a habit of looking for contexts and sequences of one type rather than another, a habit of "punctuating" the stream of events to give repetitions of a certain type of meaningful sequence.

The line of argument which we have followed has brought us to a point at which statements about simple learning meet statements about gestalt and contextual structure, and we have reached the hypothesis that "learning to learn" is a synonym for the acquisition of that class of abstract habits of thought with which this paper is concerned; that the states of mind which we call "free will," instrumental thinking, dominance, passivity, etc., are acquired by a process which we may equate with "learning to learn."

This hypothesis is to some extent new[2] to psychologists

[2] Psychological papers bearing upon this problem of the relationship between gestalt and simple learning are very numerous, if we include all who have worked on the

as well as to laymen, and therefore I must digress at this point to supply technical readers with a more precise statement of my meaning. I must demonstrate at least my willingness to state this bridge between simple learning and gestalt in operational terms.

Let us coin two words, "proto-learning" and "deutero-learning," to avoid the labor of defining operationally all the other terms in the field (transfer of learning, generalization, etc., etc.). Let us say that there are two sorts of gradient discernible in all continued learning. The gradient at any point on a simple learning curve (*e.g.*, a curve of rote learning) we will say chiefly represents rate of proto-learning. If, however, we inflict a series of similar learning experiments on the same subject, we shall find that in each successive experiment the subject has a somewhat steeper proto-learning gradient, that he learns somewhat more rapidly. This progessive change in rate of proto-learning we will call "deutero-learning."

From this point we can easily go on to represent deutero-learning graphically with a curve whose gradient shall represent rate of deutero-learning. Such a representation might be obtained, for example, by intersecting the series of proto-learning curves at some arbitarily chosen number of trials, and noting what proportion of successful responses occurred in each experiment at this point. The curve of deutero-learning

---

concepts of transfer of learning, generalization, irradiation, reaction threshold (Hull), insight, and the like. Historically, one of the first to pose these questions was Mr. Frank (L. K. Frank, "The Problems of Learning," *Psych. Review*, 1926, 33: 329–51; and Professor Maier has recently introduced a concept of "direction" which is closely related to the notion of "deutero-learning." He says: "direction . . . is the force which integrates memories in a particular manner without being a memory itself." (N. R. F. Maier, "The Behavior Mechanisms Concerned with Problem Solving," *Psych. Review*, 1940, 47: 43–58.) If for "force" we substitute "habit," and for "memory" we substitute "experience of the stream of events," the concept of deutero-learning can be seen as almost synonymous with Professor Maier's concept of "direction."

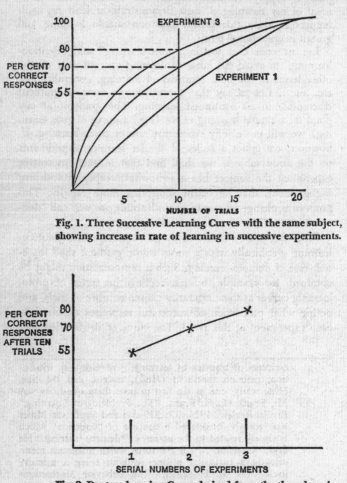

Fig. 1. Three Successive Learning Curves with the same subject, showing increase in rate of learning in successive experiments.

Fig. 2. Deutero-learning Curve derived from the three learning experiments in Fig. 1.

would then be obtained by plotting these numbers against the serial numbers of the experiments.[3]

In this definition of proto- and deutero-learning, one phrase remains conspicuously vague, the phrase "a series of similar experiments." For purposes of illustration, I imagined a series of experiments in rote learning, each experiment similar to the last, except for the substitution of a new series of nonsense syllables in place of those already learned. In this example, the curve of deutero-learning represented increasing proficiency in the business of rote learning, and, as an experimental fact, such increase in rote proficiency can be demonstrated.[4]

Apart from rote learning, it is much more difficult to define what we mean by saying that one learning context is "similar" to another, unless we are content to refer the matter back to the experimentalists by saying that learning contexts shall be considered to be "similar" one to another whenever it can be shown experimentally that experience of learning in one context does, as a matter of fact, promote speed of learning in another, and asking the experimentalists to find out for us what sort of classification they can build up by use of this criterion. We may hope that they will do this; but we cannot hope for immediate answers to our questions, because there are very serious difficulties in the way of such experimentation. Experiments in simple learning are already difficult enough to control and to perform with critical exactness, and experiments in deutero-learning are likely to prove almost impossible.

There is, however, an alternative course open to us. When we equated "learning to learn" with acquiring apperceptive habits, this did not exclude the possibility that such

[3] It will be noted that the operational definition of deutero-learning is necessarily somewhat easier than that of proto-learning. Actually, no simple learning curve represents proto-learning alone. Even within the duration of the single learning experiment we must suppose that some deutero-learning will occur, and this will make the gradient at any point somewhat steeper than the hypothetical gradient of "pure" proto-learning.

[4] C. Hull, *Mathematico-Deductive Theory of Rote Learning*, New Haven, Yale University Press, 1940.

habits might be acquired in other ways. To suggest that the only method of acquiring one of these habits is through repeated experience of learning contexts of a given kind would be logically analogous to saying that the only way to roast pig is by burning the house down. It is obvious that in human education such habits are acquired in very various ways. We are not concerned with a hypothetical isolated individual in contact with an impersonal events stream, but rather with real individuals who have complex emotional patterns of relationship with other individuals. In such a real world, the individual will be led to acquire or reject apperceptive habits by the very complex phenomena of personal example, tone of voice, hostility, love, etc. Many such habits, too, will be conveyed to him, not through his own naked experience of the stream of events, for no human beings (not even scientists) are naked in this sense. The events stream is mediated to them through language, art, technology, and other cultural media which are structured at every point by tramlines of apperceptive habit.

It therefore follows that the psychological laboratory is not the only possible source of knowledge about these habits; we may turn instead to the contrasting patterns implicit and explicit in the various cultures of the world studied by the anthropologists. We can amplify our list of these obscure habits by adding those which have been developed in cultures other than our own.

Most profitably, I believe, we can combine the insights of the experimental psychologists with those of the anthropologists, taking the contexts of experimental learning in the laboratory and asking of each what sort of apperceptive habit we should expect to find associated with it; then looking around the world for human cultures in which this habit has been developed. Inversely, we may be able to get a more definite—more operational—definition of such habits as "free will" if we ask about each, "What sort of experimental learning context would we devise in order to inculcate this habit?" "How would we rig the maze or problem-box so that the anthropomorphic rat shall obtain a repeated and reinforced impression of his own free will?"

The classification of contexts of experimental learning is as yet very incomplete, but certain definite advances have been made.[5] It is possible to classify the principal contexts of positive learning (as distinct from negative learning or inhibition, learning *not* to do things) under four heads, as follows:

(1) Classical Pavlovian contexts

These are characterized by a rigid time sequence in which the conditioned stimulus (*e.g.*, buzzer) always precedes the unconditioned stimulus (*e.g.*, meat powder) by a fixed interval of time. This rigid sequence of events is not altered by anything that the animal may do. In these contexts, the animal learns to respond to the conditioned stimulus with behavior (*e.g.*, salivation) which was formerly evoked only by the unconditioned stimulus.

(2) Contexts of instrumental reward or escape

These are characterized by a sequence which depends upon the animal's behavior. The unconditioned stimulus in these contexts is usually vague (*e.g.*, the whole sum of circumstances in which the animal is put, the problem-box) and may be internal to the animal (*e.g.*, hunger). If and when, under these circumstances, the animal performs some act within its behavioral repertoire and previously selected

---

[5] Various classifications have been devised for purposes of exposition. Here I follow that of Hilgard and Marquis (E. R. Hilgard and D. G. Marquis, *Conditioning and Learning,* New York, Appleton Century Co., 1940). These authors subject their own classification to a brilliant critical analysis, and to this analysis I am indebted for one of the formative ideas upon which this paper is based. They insist that any learning context can be described in terms of any theory of learning, if we are willing to stretch and overemphasize certain aspects of the context to fit onto the Procrustean bed of the theory. I have taken this notion as a cornerstone of my thinking, substituting "apperceptive habits" for "theories of learning," and arguing that almost any sequence of events can be stretched and warped and punctuated to fit in with any type of apperceptive habit. (*We may suppose that experimental neurosis is what happens when the subject fails to achieve this assimilation.*)

I am also indebted to Lewin's topological analysis of the contexts of reward and punishment. (K. Lewin, *A Dynamic Theory of Personality,* New York, McGraw-Hill Book Co., 1936.)

by the experimenter (e.g., lifts its leg), it is immediately rewarded.

(3) Contexts of instrumental avoidance

These are also characterized by a conditional sequence. The unconditioned stimulus is usually definite (e.g., a warning buzzer) and this is followed by an unpleasant experience (e.g., electric shock) *unless* in the interval the animal performs some selected act (e.g., lifts leg).

(4) Contexts of serial and rote learning

These are characterized by the predominant conditioned stimulus being an act of the subject. He learns, for example, always to give the conditioned response (nonsense syllable B) after he has himself uttered the conditioned stimulus (nonsense syllable A).

This small beginning of a classification[6] will be sufficient to

---

[6] Many people feel that the contexts of experimental learning are so oversimplified as to have no bearing upon the phenomena of the real world. Actually, expansion of this classification will give means of defining systematically many hundreds of possible contexts of learning with their associated apperceptive habits. The scheme may be expanded in the following ways:

a. Inclusion of contexts of negative learning (inhibition).

b. Inclusion of mixed types (e.g., cases in which salivation, with its physiological relevance to meat powder, is also instrumental in obtaining the meat powder).

c. Inclusion of the cases in which the subject is able to deduce some sort of relevance (other than the physiological) between some two or more elements in the sequence. For this to be true, the subject must have experience of contexts differing systematically one from another, e.g., contexts in which some type of change in one element is constantly accompanied by a constant type of change in another element. These cases can be spread out on a lattice of possibilities, according to which pair of elements the subject sees as interrelated. There are only five elements (conditioned stimulus, conditioned response, reward or punishment, and two time intervals), but any pair of these may be interrelated, and of the interrelated pair, either may be seen by the subject as determining the other. These possibilities, multiplied for our four basic contexts, give forty-eight types.

d. The list of basic types may be extended by including those cases (not as yet investigated in learning ex-

illustrate the principles with which we are concerned and we can now go on to ask about the occurrence of the appropriate apperceptive habits among men of various cultures. Of greatest interest—because least familiar—are the Pavlovian patterns and the patterns of rote. It is a little hard for members of Western civilization to believe that whole systems of behavior can be built on premises other than our own mixture of instrumental reward and instrumental avoidance. The Trobriand Islanders, however, appear to live a life whose coherence and sense is based upon looking at events through Pavlovian spectacles, only slightly tinted with the hope of instrumental reward, while the life of the Balinese is sensible if we accept premises based upon combining rote with instrumental avoidance.

Clearly, to the "pure" Pavlovian, only a very limited fatalism would be possible. He would see all events as preordained and he would see himself as fated only to search for omens, not able to influence the course of events—able, at most, from his reading of the omens, to put himself in the properly receptive state, *e.g.*, by salivation, before the inevitable occurred. Trobriand culture is not so purely Pavlovian as this, but Dr. Lee,[7] analyzing Professor Malinowski's rich observations, has shown that Trobriand phrasings of purpose, cause, and effect are profoundly different from our own; and though Dr. Lee does not use the sort of classification here proposed, it appears from Trobriand magic that these people continually exhibit a habit of thinking that to act as if a thing were so will make it so. In this sense, we may describe them as semi-Pavlovians who have decided that "salivation" is instrumental to obtaining "meat powder."

---

periments but common in interpersonal relationships) in which the roles of subject and experimenter are reversed. In these, the learning partner provides the initial and final elements, while some other person (or circumstance) provides the middle term. In these types, we see the buzzer and the meat powder as the behavior of a person and ask: "What does this person learn?" A great part of the gamut of apperceptive habits associated with authority and parenthood is based on contexts of this general type.

[7] Dorothy Lee, "A Primitive System of Values," *Journal Philos. of Science*, 1940, 7: 355–78.

Malinowski, for example, gives us a dramatic description of the almost physiological extremes of rage[8] which the Trobriand black magician practices in his incantations, and we may take this as an illustration of the semi-Pavlovian frame of mind in contrast with the very various types of magical procedure in other parts of the world, where, for example, the efficacy of a spell may be associated not with the intensity but with the extreme rote accuracy of the recitation.

Among the Balinese[9] we find another pattern which contrasts sharply both with our own and with that of the Trobrianders. The treatment of children is such that they learn not to see life as composed of connative sequences ending in satisfaction, but rather to see it as composed of rote sequences inherently satisfying in themselves—a pattern which is to some extent related to that pattern which Dr. Mead has recommended, of looking for value in the act itself rather than regarding the act as a means to an end. There is, however, one very important difference between the Balinese pattern and that recommended by Dr. Mead. The Balinese pattern is essentially derivative from contexts of instrumental avoidance; they see the world as dangerous, and themselves as avoiding, by the endless rote behavior of ritual and courtesy, the ever-present risk of *faux pas*. Their life is built upon fear, albeit that in general they enjoy fear. The positive value with which they endow their immediate acts, not looking for a goal, is somehow associated with this enjoyment of fear. It is the acrobat's enjoyment both of the thrill and of his own virtuosity in avoiding disaster.

[8] It is possible that semi-Pavlovian phrasings of the stream of events tend, like the experiments which are their prototypes, to hinge particularly upon autonomic reactions—that those who see events in these terms tend to see these reactions, which are only partially subject to voluntary control, as peculiarly effective and powerful causes of outside events. There may be some ironical logic in Pavlovian fatalism which predisposes us to believe that we can alter the course of events *only* by means of those behaviors which we are least able to control.

[9] The Balinese material collected by Dr. Mead and myself has not yet been published *in extenso*, but a brief outline of the theory here suggested is available—cf. G. Bateson, "The Frustration-Aggression Hypothesis and Culture," *Psychological Review*, 1941, 48: 350-55.

We are now, after a somewhat long and technical excursion into psychological laboratories and foreign cultures, in a position to examine Dr. Mead's proposal in somewhat more concrete terms. She advises that when we apply the social sciences we look for "direction" and "value" in our very acts, rather than orient ourselves to some blueprinted goal. She is not telling us that we ought to be like the Balinese, except in our time orientation, and she would be the first to disparage any suggestion that fear (even enjoyed fear) should be our basis for assigning value to our acts. Rather, as I understand it, this basis should be some sort of hope—not looking to some far-off future, but still some sort of hope or optimism. In fact, we might summarize the recommended attitude by saying that it ought to be formally related to instrumental reward, as the Balinese attitude is related to instrumental avoidance.

Such an attitude is, I believe, feasible. The Balinese attitude might be defined as a habit of rote sequences inspired by a thrilling sense of ever-imminent but indefinite danger, and I think that what Dr. Mead is urging us toward might be defined in like terms, as a habit of rote sequences inspired by a thrilling sense of ever-imminent but undefined reward.

As to the rote component, which is almost certainly a necessary concomitant of the peculiar time orientation advocated by Dr. Mead, I, personally, would welcome it, and I believe that it would be infinitely preferable to the compulsive type of accuracy after which we strive. Anxious taking-care and automatic, rote caution are alternative habits which perform the same function. We can either have the habit of automatically looking before we cross the street, or the habit of carefully remembering to look. Of the two I prefer the automatic, and I think that, if Dr. Mead's recommendation implies an increase in rote automatism, we ought to accept it. Already, indeed, our schools are inculcating more and more automatism in such processes as reading, writing, arithmetic, and languages.

As to the reward component, this, too, should not be beyond our reach. If the Balinese is kept busy and happy by a nameless, shapeless fear, not located in space or time, we might be kept on our toes by a nameless, shapeless, unlocated hope of enormous achievement. For such a hope to be effective, the achievement need scarcely be defined.

All we need to be sure of is that, at any moment, achievement may be just around the corner, and, true or false, this can never be tested. We have got to be like those few artists and scientists who work with this urgent sort of inspiration, the urgency that comes from feeling that great discovery, the answer to all our problems, or great creation, the perfect sonnet, is always only just beyond our reach, or like the mother of a child who feels that, provided she pay constant enough attention, there is a real hope that her child may be that infinitely rare phenomenon, a great and happy person.

# A Theory of Play and Fantasy*

This research was planned and started with an hypothesis to guide our investigations, the task of the investigators being to collect relevant observational data and, in the process, to amplify and modify the hypothesis.

The hypothesis will here be described as it has grown in our thinking.

Earlier fundamental work of Whitehead, Russell,[1] Wittgenstein,[2] Carnap,[3] Whorf,[4] etc., as well as my own attempt[5] to use this earlier thinking as an epistemological base for psychiatric theory, led to a series of generalizations:

(1) That human verbal communication can operate and always does operate at many contrasting levels of abstrac-

---

*This essay was read (by Jay Haley) at the A.P.A. Regional Research Conference in Mexico City, March 11, 1954. It is here reprinted from *A.P.A. Psychiatric Research Reports*, II, 1955, by permission of the American Psychiatric Association.

[1] A. N. Whitehead and B. Russell, *Principia Mathematica*, 3 vols., 2nd ed., Cambridge, Cambridge University Press, 1910–13.

[2] L. Wittgenstein, *Tractatus Logico-Philosophicus*, London, Harcourt Brace, 1922.

[3] R. Carnap, *The Logical Syntax of Language*, New York, Harcourt Brace, 1937.

[4] B. L. Whorf, "Science and Linguistics," *Technology Review*, 1940, 44: 229–48.

[5] J. Ruesch and G. Bateson, *Communication: The Social Matrix of Psychiatry*, New York, Norton, 1951.

tion. These range in two directions from the seemingly simple denotative level ("The cat is on the mat"). One range or set of these more abstract levels includes those explicit or implicit messages where the subject of discourse is the language. We will call these metalinguistic (for example, "The verbal sound 'cat' stands for any member of such and such class of objects," or "The word, 'cat,' has no fur and cannot scratch"). The other set of levels of abstraction we will call metacommunicative (*e.g.*, "My telling you where to find the cat was friendly," or "This is play"). In these, the subject of discourse is the relationship between the speakers.

It will be noted that the vast majority of both metalinguistic and metacommunicative messages remain implicit; and also that, especially in the psychiatric interview, there occurs a further class of implicit messages about how metacommunicative messages of friendship and hostility are to be interpreted.

(2) If we speculate about the evolution of communication, it is evident that a very important stage in this evolution occurs when the organism gradually ceases to respond quite "automatically" to the mood-signs of another and becomes able to recognize the sign as a signal: that is, to recognize that the other individual's and its own signals are only signals, which can be trusted, distrusted, falsified, denied, amplified, corrected, and so forth.

Clearly this realization that signals are signals is by no means complete even among the human species. We all too often respond automatically to newspaper headlines as though these stimuli were direct object-indications of events in our environment instead of signals concocted and transmitted by creatures as complexly motivated as ourselves. The nonhuman mammal is automatically excited by the sexual odor of another; and rightly so, inasmuch as the secretion of that sign is an "involuntary" mood-sign; *i.e.*, an outwardly perceptible event which is a part of the physiological process which we have called a mood. In the human species a more complex state of affairs begins to be the rule. Deodorants mask the involuntary olfactory signs, and in their place the cosmetic industry provides the individual with perfumes which are not involuntary signs but voluntary signals, recognizable as such. Many a man has been thrown off balance by a whiff of perfume, and if we are to believe the advertisers, it seems that these signals, voluntarily worn, have sometimes an automatic and autosuggestive effect even upon the voluntary wearer.

Be that as it may, this brief digression will serve to illustrate a stage of evolution—the drama precipitated when organisms, having eaten of the fruit of the Tree of Knowledge, discover that their signals are signals. Not only the characteristically human invention of language can then follow, but also all the complexities of empathy, identification, projection, and so on. And with these comes the possibility of communicating at the multiplicity of levels of abstraction mentioned above.

(3) The first definite step in the formulation of the hypothesis guiding this research occurred in January, 1952, when I went to the Fleishhacker Zoo in San Francisco to look for behavioral criteria which would indicate whether any given organism is or is not able to recognize that the signs emitted by itself and other members of the species are signals. In theory, I had thought out what such criteria might look like—that the occurrence of metacommunicative signs (or signals) in the stream of interaction between the animals would indicate that the animals have at least some awareness (conscious or unconscious) that the signs about which they metacommunicate are signals.

I knew, of course, that there was no likelihood of finding denotative messages among nonhuman mammals, but I was still not aware that the animal data would require an almost total revision of my thinking. What I encountered at the zoo was a phenomenon well known to everybody: I saw two young monkeys *playing*, *i.e.*, engaged in an interactive sequence of which the unit actions or signals were similar to but not the same as those of combat. It was evident, even to the human observer, that the sequence as a whole was not combat, and evident to the human observer that to the participant monkeys this was "not combat."

Now, this phenomenon, play, could only occur if the participant organisms were capable of some degree of metacommunication, *i.e.*, of exchanging signals which would carry the message "this is play."

(4) The next step was the examination of the message "This is play," and the realization that this message contains those elements which necessarily generate a paradox of the

Russellian or Epimenides type—a negative statement containing an implicit negative metastatement. Expanded, the statement "This is play" looks something like this: "These actions in which we now engage do not denote what those actions *for which they stand* would denote."

We now ask about the italicized words, "*for which they stand.*" We say the word "cat" stands for any member of a certain class. That is, the phrase "stands for" is a near synonym of "denotes." If we now substitute "which they denote" for the words "for which they stand" in the expanded definition of play, the result is: "These actions, in which we now engage, do not denote what would be denoted by those actions which these actions denote." The playful nip denotes the bite, but it does not denote what would be denoted by the bite.

According to the Theory of Logical Types such a message is of course inadmissable, because the word "denote" is being used in two degrees of abstraction, and these two uses are treated as synonymous. But all that we learn from such a criticism is that it would be bad natural history to expect the mental processes and communicative habits of mammals to conform to the logician's ideal. Indeed, if human thought and communication always conformed to the ideal, Russell would not—in fact could not—have formulated the ideal.

(5) A related problem in the evolution of communication concerns the origin of what Korzybski[6] has called the map-territory relation: the fact that a message, of whatever kind, does not consist of those objects which it denotes ("The word 'cat' cannot scratch us"). Rather, language bears to the objects which it denotes a relationship comparable to that which a map bears to a territory. Denotative communication as it occurs at the human level is only possible *after* the evolution of a complex set of metalinguistic (but not verbalized)[7] rules which govern how words and sentences shall be related to objects and events. It is therefore appropriate to look for the evolution of such metalinguistic and/or metacommunicative rules at a prehuman and preverbal level.

---

[6] A. Korzybski, *Science and Sanity*, New York, Science Press, 1941.

[7] The verbalization of these metalinguistic rules is a much later achievement which can only occur after the evolution of a nonverbalized meta-metalinguistics.

It appears from what is said above that play is a phenomenon in which the actions of "play" are related to, or denote, other actions of "not play." We therefore meet in play with an instance of signals standing for other events, and it appears, therefore, that the evolution of play may have been an important step in the evolution of communication.

(6) *Threat* is another phenomenon which resembles play in that actions denote, but are different from, other actions. The clenched fist of threat is different from the punch, but it refers to a possible future (but at present nonexistent) punch. And threat also is commonly recognizable among non-human mammals. Indeed it has lately been argued that a great part of what appears to be combat among members of a single species is rather to be regarded as threat (Tinbergen,[8] Lorenz[9]).

(7) Histrionic behavior and deceit are other examples of the primitive occurrence of map-territory differentiation. And there is evidence that dramatization occurs among birds: a jackdaw may imitate her own mood-signs (Lorenz[10]), and deceit has been observed among howler monkeys (Carpenter[11]).

(8) We might expect threat, play, and histrionics to be three independent phenomena all contributing to the evolution of the discrimination between map and territory. But it seems that this would be wrong, at least so far as mammalian communication is concerned. Very brief analysis of childhood behavior shows that such combinations as histrionic play, bluff, playful threat, teasing play in response to threat, histrionic threat, and so on form together a single total complex of phenomena. And such adult phenomena as gambling and playing with risk have their roots in the combination of threat and play. It is evident also that not only threat but the reciprocal of threat—the behavior of the threatened in-

[8] N. Tinbergen, *Social Behavior in Animals with Special Reference to Vertebrates*, London, Methuen, 1953.

[9] K. Z. Lorenz, *King Solomon's Ring*, New York, Crowell, 1952.

[10] *Ibid.*

[11] C. R. Carpenter, "A Field Study of the Behavior and Social Relations of Howling Monkeys," *Comp. Psychol. Monogr.*, 1934, 10: 1–168.

dividual—are a part of this complex. It is probable that not only histrionics but also spectatorship should be included within this field. It is also appropriate to mention self-pity.

(9) A further extension of this thinking leads us to include ritual within this general field in which the discrimination is drawn, but not completely, between denotative action and that which is to be denoted. Anthropological studies of peace-making ceremonies, to cite only one example, support this conclusion.

In the Andaman Islands, peace is concluded after each side has been given ceremonial freedom to strike the other. This example, however, also illustrates the labile nature of the frame "This is play," or "This is ritual." The discrimination between map and territory is always liable to break down, and the ritual blows of peace-making are always liable to be mistaken f r the "real" blows of combat. In this event, the peace-making ceremony becomes a battle (Radcliffe-Brown[12]).

(10) But this leads us to recognition of a more complex form of play; the game which is constructed not upon the premise "This is play" but rather around the question "Is this play?" And this type of interaction also has its ritual forms. *e.g.,* in the hazing of initiation.

(11) Paradox is doubly present in the signals which are exchanged within the context of play, fantasy, threat, etc. Not only does the playful nip not denote what would be denoted by the bite for which it stands, but, in addition, the bite itself is fictional. Not only do the playing animals not quite mean what they are saying but, also, they are usually communicating about something which does not exist. At the human level, this leads to a vast variety of complications and inversions in the fields of play, fantasy, and art. Conjurers and painters of the *trompe l'oeil* school concentrate upon acquiring a virtuosity whose only reward is reached after the viewer detects that he has been deceived and is forced to smile or marvel at the skill of the deceiver. Hollywood film-makers spend millions of dollars to increase the realism of a shadow. Other artists, perhaps more realistically, insist that art be nonrepresentational; and poker play-

[12] A. R. Radcliffe-Brown, *The Andaman Islanders,* Cambridge, Cambridge University Press, 1922.

ers achieve a strange addictive realism by equating the chips for which they play with dollars. They still insist, however, that the loser accept his loss as part of the game.

Finally, in the dim region where art, magic, and religion meet and overlap, human beings have evolved the "metaphor that is meant," the flag which men will die to save, and the sacrament that is felt to be more than "an outward and visible sign, given unto us." Here we can recognize an attempt to deny the difference between map and territory, and to get back to the absolute innocence of communication by means of pure mood-signs.

(12) We face then two peculiarities of play: (*a*) that the messages or signals exchanged in play are in a certain sense untrue or not meant; and (*b*) that that which is denoted by these signals is nonexistent. These two peculiarities sometimes combine strangely to a reverse a conclusion reached above. It was stated (4) that the playful nip denotes the bite, but does not denote that which would be denoted by the bite. But there are other instances where an opposite phenomenon occurs. A man experiences the full intensity of subjective terror when a spear is flung at him out of the 3D screen or when he falls headlong from some peak created in his own mind in the intensity of nightmare. At the moment of terror there was no questioning of "reality," but still there was no spear in the movie house and no cliff in the bedroom. The images did not denote that which they seemed to denote, but these same images did really evoke that terror which would have been evoked by a real spear or a real precipice. By a similar trick of self-contradiction, the film-makers of Hollywood are free to offer to a puritanical public a vast range of pseudosexual fantasy which otherwise would not be tolerated. In *David and Bathsheba*, Bathsheba can be a Troilistic link between David and Uriah. And in *Hans Christian Andersen*, the hero starts out accompanied by a boy. He tries to get a woman, but when he is defeated in this attempt, he returns to the boy. In all of this, there is, of course, no homosexuality, but the choice of these symbolisms is associated in these fantasies with certain characteristic ideas, *e.g.*, about the hopelessness of the heterosexual masculine position when faced with certain sorts of women or with certain sorts of male authority. In sum, the

pseudohomosexuality of the fantasy does not stand for any real homosexuality, but does stand for and express attitudes which might accompany a real homosexuality or feed its etiological roots. The symbols do not denote homosexuality, but do denote ideas for which homosexuality is an appropriate symbol. Evidently it is necessary to re-examine the precise semantic validity of the interpretations which the psychiatrist offers to a patient, and, as preliminary to this analysis, it will be necessary to examine the nature of the frame in which these interpretations are offered.

(13) What has previously been said about play can be used as an introductory example for the discussion of frames and contexts. In sum, it is our hypothesis that the message "This is play" establishes a paradoxical frame comparable to Epimenides' paradox. This frame may be diagrammed thus:

> All statements within this
> frame are untrue.
>
> I love you.
>
> I hate you.

The first statement within this frame is a self-contradictory proposition about itself. If this first statement is true, then it must be false. If it be false, then it must be true. But this first statement carries with it all the other statements in the frame. So, if the first statement be true, then all the others must be false; and vice versa, if the first statement be untrue then all the others must be true.

(14) The logically minded will notice a *non-sequitur*. It could be urged that even if the first staement is false, there remains a logical possibility that some of the other statements in the frame are untrue. It is, however, a characteristic of unconscious or "primary-process" thinking that the thinker is unable to discriminate between "some" and "all," and unable to discriminate between "not all" and "none." It seems that the achievement of these discriminations is performed by higher or more conscious mental processes which serve in the nonpsychotic individual to correct the black-and-white thinking of the lower levels. We assume, and this seems to be an orthodox assumption, that primary process is continual-

ly operating, and that the psychological validity of the paradoxical play frame depends upon this part of the mind.

(15) But, conversely, while it is necessary to invoke the
primary process as an explanatory principle in order to delete
the notion of "some" from between "all" and "none," this
does not mean that play is simply a primary-process phenomenon. The discrimination between "play" and "nonplay,"
like the discrimination between fantasy and nonfantasy, is
certainly a function of secondary process, or "ego." Within
the dream the dreamer is usually unaware that he is dreaming, and within "play" he must often be reminded that "This
is play."

Similarly, within dream or fantasy the dreamer does not
operate with the concept "untrue." He operates with all sorts
of statements but with a curious inability to achieve meta-
statements. He cannot, unless close to waking, dream a statement referring to (*i.e.*, framing) his dream.

It therefore follows that the play frame as here used as
an explanatory principle implies a special combination of
primary and secondary processes. This, however, is related
to what was said earlier, when it was argued that play
marks a step forward in the evolution of communication—
the crucial step in the discovery of map-territory relations.
In primary process, map and territory are equated; in secondary process, they can be discriminated. In play, they are
both equated and discriminated.

(16) Another logical anomaly in this system must be mentioned: that the relationship between two propositions which
is commonly described by the word "premise" has become
intransitive. In general, all asymmetrical relationships are
transitive. The relationship "greater than" is typical in this
respect; it is conventional to argue that if A is greater than
B, and B is greater than C, then A is greater than C. But
in psychological processes the transitivity of asymmetrical relations is not observed. The proposition P may be a premise
for Q; Q may be a premise for R; and R may be a premise
for P. Specifically, in the system which we are considering,
the circle is still more contracted. The message, "All statements within this frame are untrue" is itself to be taken as a
premise in evaluating its own truth or untruth. (Cf. the in-
transitivity of psychological preference discussed by McCul-

loch.[13] The paradigm for all paradoxes of this general type is Russell's[14] "class of classes which are not members of themselves." Here Russell demonstrates that paradox is generated by treating the relationship, "is a member of," as an intransitive.) With this caveat, that the "premise" relation in psychology is likely to be intransitive, we shall use the word "premise" to denote a dependency of one idea or message upon another comparable to the dependency of one proposition upon another which is referred to in logic by saying that the proposition P is a premise for Q.

(17) All this, however, leaves unclear what is meant by "frame" and the related notion of "context." To clarify these, it is necessary to insist first that these are psychological concepts. We use two sorts of analogy to discuss these notions: the physical analogy of the picture frame and the more abstract, but still not psychological, analogy of the mathematical set. In set theory the mathematicians have developed axioms and theorems to discuss with rigor the logical implications of membership in overlapping categories or "sets." The relationships between sets are commonly illustrated by diagrams in which the items or members of a larger universe are represented by dots, and the smaller sets are delimited by imaginary lines enclosing the members of each set. Such diagrams then illustrate a topological approach to the logic of classification. The first step in defining a psychological frame might be to say that it is (or delimits) a class or set of messages (or meaningful actions). The play of two individuals on a certain occasion would then be defined as the set of all messages exchanged by them within a limited period of time and modified by the paradoxical premise system which we have described. In a set-theoretical diagram these messages might be represented by dots, and the "set" enclosed by a line which would separate these from other dots representing nonplay messages. The mathematical analogy breaks down, however, because the psychological frame is not satisfactorily represented by an imaginary line. We assume that the psychological frame has some degree of real existence. In many instances, the frame is consciously

[13] W. S. McCulloch, "A Heterarchy of Values, etc.," *Bulletin of Math. Biophys.*, 1945, 7: 89–93.

[14] Whitehead and Russell, *op. cit.*

recognized and even represented in vocabulary ("play," "movie," "interview," "job," "language," etc.). In other cases, there may be no explicit verbal reference to the frame, and the subject may have no consciousness of it. The analyst, however, finds that his own thinking is simplified if he uses the notion of an unconscious frame as an explanatory principle; usually he goes further than this and infers its existence in the subject's unconscious.

But while the analogy of the mathematical set is perhaps over abstract, the analogy of the picture frame is excessively concrete. The psychological concept which we are trying to define is neither physical nor logical. Rather, the actual physical frame is, we believe, added by human beings to physical pictures because these human beings operate more easily in a universe in which some of their psychological characteristics are externalized. It is these characteristics which we are trying to discuss, using the externalization as an illustrative device.

(18) The common functions and uses of psychological frames may now be listed and illustrated by reference to the analogies whose limitations have been indicated in the previous paragraph:

(*a*) Psychological frames are exclusive, *i.e.*, by including certain messages (or meaningful actions) within a frame, certain other messages are excluded.

(*b*) Psychological frames are inclusive, *i.e.*, by excluding certain messages certain others are included. From the point of view of set theory these two functions are synonymous, but from the point of view of psychology it is necessary to list them separately. The frame around a picture, if we consider this frame as a message intended to order or organize the perception of the viewer, says, "Attend to what is within and do not attend to what is outside." Figure and ground, as these terms are used by gestalt psychologists, are not symmetrically related as are the set and nonset of set theory. Perception of the ground must be positively inhibited and perception of the figure (in this case the picture) must be positively enhanced.

(*c*) Psychological frames are related to what we have called "premises." The picture frame tells the viewer that he is not to use the same sort of thinking in interpreting the picture that he might use in interpreting the wallpaper outside the frame. Or, in terms of the analogy from set theory, the messages enclosed within the imaginary line are defined as members of a class by virtue of their sharing common premises or mutual relevance. The frame itself thus becomes a part of the premise system. Either, as in the case of the play frame, the frame is involved in the evaluation of the messages which it contains, or the frame merely assists the mind in understanding the contained messages by reminding the thinker that these messages are mutually relevant and the messages outside the frame may be ignored.

(*d*) In the sense of the previous paragraph, a frame is metacommunicative. Any message, which either explicitly or implicitly defines a frame, *ipso facto* gives the receiver instructions or aids in his attempt to understand the messages included within the frame.

(*e*) The converse of (*d*) is also true. Every metacommunicative or metalinguistic message defines, either explicitly or implicitly, the set of messages about which it communicates, *i.e.*, every metacommunicative message is or defines a psychological frame. This, for example, is very evident in regard to such small metacommunicative signals as punctuation marks in a printed message, but applies equally to such complex metacommunicative messages as the psychiatrist's definition of his own curative role in terms of which his contributions to the whole mass of messages in psychotherapy are to be understood.

(*f*) The relation between psychological frame and perceptual gestalt needs to be considered, and here the analogy of the picture frame is useful. In a painting by Roualt or Blake, the human figures and other objects represented are outlined. "Wise men see outlines and therefore they draw them." But outside these lines, which delimit the perceptual gestalt or "figure," there is a background or "ground" which in turn is limited by the picture frame. Similarly, in set-theoretical diagrams, the larger universe within which the smaller sets are drawn is itself enclosed in a frame. This double framing is, we believe, not merely a matter of "frames within frames" but an indication that mental processes resemble logic in *needing* an outer frame to delimit the ground against which the figures are to be perceived. This need is often unsatisfied, as when we see a piece of sculpture in a junk shop window, but this is uncomfortable. We suggest that the need for this outer limit to the ground is related to a preference for avoiding the paradoxes of abstraction. When a logical class or set of items is defined—for example, the class of matchboxes—it is necessary to delimit the set of items which are to be excluded, in this case, all those things which are not matchboxes. But the items to be included in the background set must be of the same degree of abstraction, *i.e.*, of the same "logical type" as those within the set itself. Specifically, if paradox is to be avoided, the "class of matchboxes" and the "class of nonmatchboxes" (even though both these items are clearly not matchboxes) must not be regarded as members of the class of nonmatchboxes. No class can be a member of itself. The picture frame then, because it delimits a background, is here regarded as an external representation of a very special and important type of psychological frame—namely a frame whose function is to delimit a logical type. This, in fact, is what was indicated above when it was said that the picture frame is an instruction to the viewer that he should not extend the premises which obtain between the figures within the picture to the wall paper behind it.

But, it is precisely this sort of frame that precipitates paradox. The rule for avoiding paradoxes insists that the items outside any enclosing line be of the same logical type as those within, but the picture frame, as analyzed above, is a line dividing items of one logical type from those of another. In passing, it is interesting to note that Russell's rule cannot be stated without breaking the rule. Russell insists that all items of inappropriate logical type be exluded (*i.e.*, by an imaginary line) from the background of any class, *i.e.*, he insists upon the drawing of an imaginary line of precisely the sort which he prohibits.

(19) This whole matter of frames and paradoxes may be illustrated in terms of animal behavior, where three types of message may be recognized or deduced: (*a*) Messages of the sort which we here call mood-signs; (*b*) messages which simulate mood-signs (in play, threat, histrionics, etc.); and (*c*) messages which enable the receiver to discriminate between mood-signs and those other signs which resemble them. The message "This is play" is of this third type. It tells the receiver that certain nips and other meaningful actions are not messages of the first type.

The message "This is play" thus sets a frame of the sort which is likely to precipitate paradox: it is an attempt to discriminate between, or to draw a line between, categories of different logical types.

(20) This discussion of play and psychological frames establishes a type of triadic constellation (or system of relationships) between messages. One instance of this constellation is analyzed in paragraph 19, but it is evident that constellations of this sort occur not only at the nonhuman level but also in the much more complex communication of human beings. A fantasy or myth may simulate a denotative narrative, and, to discriminate between these types of discourse, people use messages of the frame-setting type, and so on.

(21) In conclusion, we arrive at the complex task of applying this theoretical approach to the particular phenomena of psychotherapy. Here the lines of our thinking may most briefly be summarized by presenting and partially answering these questions:

(*a*) Is there any indication that certain forms of psychopathology are specifically characterized by abnormalities in the patient's handling of frames and paradoxes?

(*b*) Is there any indication that the techniques of psychotherapy necessarily depend upon the manipulation of frames and paradoxes?

(*c*) Is it possible to describe the process of a given psychotherapy in terms of the interaction between the patient's abnormal use of frames and the therapist's manipulation of them?

(22) In reply to the first question, it seems that the "word salad" of schizophrenia can be described in terms of the patient's failure to recognize the metaphoric nature of his fantasies. In what should be triadic constellations of messages, the frame-setting message (*e.g.*, the phrase "as if") is omitted, and the metaphor or fantasy is narrated and acted upon in a manner which would be appropriate if the fantasy were a message of the more direct kind. The absence of metacommunicative framing which was noted in the case of dreams (15) is characteristic of the waking communications of the schizophrenic. With the loss of the ability to set metacommunicative frames, there is also a loss of ability to achieve the more primary or primitive message. The meta-

phor is treated directly as a message of the more primary type. (This matter is discussed at greater length in the paper given by Jay Haley at this Conference.)

(23) The dependence of psychotherapy upon the manipulation of frames follows from the fact that therapy is an attempt to change the patient's metacommunicative habits. Before therapy, the patient thinks and operates in terms of a certain set of rules for the making and understanding of messages. After successful therapy, he operates in terms of a different set of such rules. (Rules of this sort are in general, unverbalized, and unconscious both before and after.) It follows that, in the process of therapy, there must have been communication at a level *meta* to these rules. There must have been communication about a *change* in rules.

But such a communication about change could not conceivably occur in messages of the type permitted by the patient's metacommunicative rules as they existed either before or after therapy.

It was suggested above that the paradoxes of play are characteristic of an evolutionary step. Here we suggest that similar paradoxes are a necessary ingredient in that process of change which we call psychotherapy.

The resemblance between the process of therapy and the phenomenon of play is, in fact, profound. Both occur within a delimited psychological frame, a spatial and temporal bounding of a set of interactive messages. In both play and therapy, the messages have a special and peculiar relationship to a more concrete or basic reality. Just as the pseudocombat of play is not real combat, so also the pseudolove and pseudohate of therapy are not real love and hate. The "transfer" is discriminated from real love and hate by signals invoking the psychological frame; and indeed it is this frame which permits the transfer to reach its full intensity and to be discussed between patient and therapist.

The formal characteristics of the therapeutic process may be illustrated by building up a model in stages. Imagine first two players who engage in a game of canasta according to a standard set of rules. So long as these rules govern and are unquestioned by both players, the game is unchanging, *i.e.*, no therapeutic change will occur. (Indeed many attempts at psychotherapy fail for this reason.) We may imagine, however, that at a certain moment the two canasta players cease to play canasta and start a discussion of the rules. Their discourse is now of a different logical type from that of their play. At the end of this discussion, we can imagine that they return to playing but with modified rules.

This sequence of events is, however, still an imperfect model of therapeutic interaction, though it illustrates our contention that therapy necessarily involves a combination of discrepant logical types of discourse. Our imaginary players avoided paradox by separating their discussion of the rules from their play, and it is precisely this separation that is impossible in psychotherapy. As we see it, the process of psychotherapy is a framed interaction between two persons, in which the rules are implicit but subject to change. Such change can only be proposed by experimental action, but every such experimental action, in which a proposal to change the rules is implicit, is itself a part of the ongoing game. It is this combination of logical types within the single meaningful act that gives to therapy the character not of a rigid game like canasta but, instead, that of an evolving system of interaction. The play of kittens or otters has this character.

(24) In regard to the specific relationship between the way in which the patient handles frames and the way in which the therapist manipulates them, very little can at present be said. It is, however, suggestive to observe that the psychological frame of therapy is an analogue of the frame-setting message which the schizophrenic is unable to achieve. To talk in "word salad" within the psychological frame of therapy is, in a sense, not pathological. Indeed the neurotic is specifically encouraged to do precisely this, narrating his dreams and free associations so that patient and therapist may achieve an understanding of this material. By the process of interpretation, the neurotic is driven to insert an "as if" clause into the productions of his primary process thinking, which productions he had previously deprecated or repressed. He must learn that fantasy contains truth.

For the schizophrenic the problem is somewhat different. His error is in treating the metaphors of primary process with the full intensity of literal truth. Through the discovery of what these metaphors stand for he must discover that they are only metaphors.

(25) From the point of view of the project, however, psychotherapy constitutes only one of the many fields which

we are attempting to investigate. Our central thesis may be summed up as a statement of the necessity of the paradoxes of abstraction. It is not merely bad natural history to suggest that people might or should obey the Theory of Logical Types in their communications; their failure to do this is not due to mere carelessness or ignorance. Rather, we believe that the paradoxes of abstraction must make their appearance in all communication more complex than that of mood-signals, and that without these paradoxes the evolution of communication would be at an end. Life would then be an endless interchange of stylized messages, a game with rigid rules, unrelieved by change or humor.

# Epidemiology of a Schizophrenia*

If we are to discuss the epidemiology of mental conditions, *i.e.*, conditions partly induced by experience, our first task is to pinpoint a defect of an ideational system sufficiently so that we can go on from that pinpointing to postulate what sort of contexts of learning might induce this formal defect.

It is conventionally said that schizophrenics have "ego weakness." I now define ego weakness as trouble in identifying and interpreting those signals which should tell the individual what sort of a message a message is, *i.e.*, trouble with the signals of the same logical type as the signal "This is play." For example, a patient comes into the hospital canteen and the girl behind the counter says, "What can I do for you?" The patient is in doubt as to what sort of a message this is—is it a message about doing him in? Is it an indication that she wants him to go to bed with her? Or is it an offer of a cup of coffee? He hears the message and does not know what sort or order of a message it is. He is unable to pick up the more abstract labels which we are

*This is an edited version of a talk, "How the Deviant Sees His Society," given in May, 1955, at a conference on "The Epidemiology of Mental Health" held at Brighton, Utah, sponsored by the Departments of Psychiatry and Psychology of the University of Utah, and the Veterans Administration Hospital, Fort Douglas Division, of Salt Lake City, Utah. A rough transcript of the talks at this conference was mimeographed and circulated by the organizers.

194

most of us able to use conventionally but are most of us unable to identify in the sense that we don't know what told us what sort of a message it was. It is as if we somehow make a correct guess. We are actuallly quite unconscious of receiving these messages which tell us what sorts of message we receive.

Difficulty with signals of this sort seems to be the center of a syndrome which is characteristic for a group of schizophrenics, so therefore we can reasonably look for an etiology starting from this symptomatology as formally defined.

When you begin thinking in this way, a great deal of what the schizophrenic says falls into place as a description of his experience. That is, we have a second lead toward the theory of etiology or transmission. The first lead is from the symptom. We ask, "How does a human individual acquire an imperfect ability to discriminate these specific signals?" and when we look at his speeches, we find that, in that peculiar language which is schizophrenic salad, he is describing a traumatic situation which involves a metacommunicative tangle.

A patient, for example, has a central notion that "something moved in space," and that that is why he cracked up. I somehow, from the way he spoke about "space," got an idea that space is his mother and said so. He said, "No, space is *the* mother." I suggested to him that she might be in some way a cause of his troubles. He said, "I never condemned her." At a certain point he got angry, and he said—this is verbatim—"If we say she had movement in her because of what she caused, we are only condemning ourselves." Something moved in space that made him crack up. Space is not his mother, it is *the* mother. But now we focus upon his mother whom he says he never condemned. And he now says, "If we say that she had movement in her because of what she caused, we are only condemning ourselves."

Look very carefully at the logical structure of that last quotation. It is circular. It implies a way of interaction and chronic cross-purposes with the mother such that for the child to make those moves which might straighten out the misunderstanding was also prohibited.

On another occasion he had skipped his therapy session in the morning, and I went over to the dining hall at supper time to see him and assure him that he would see me next day. He refused to look at me. He looked away. I made some remark about 9.30 the next morning—no answer. Then, with great difficulty, he said, "The judge disapproves." Before I left him, I said, "You need a defense attorney," and when I found him on the grounds next morning I said, "Here is your defense attorney," and we went into session together. I started out by saying, "Am I right in supposing that the judge not only disapproves of your talking to me but also disapproves of your telling me that he disapproves?" He said, "Yes!" That is, we are dealing with two levels here. The "judge" disapproves of the attempt to straighten out the confusions and disapproves of communicating the fact of his (the judge's) disapproval.

We have to look for an etiology involving multiple levels of trauma.

I am not talking at all about the content of these traumatic sequences, whether they be sexual, or oral. Nor am I talking about the age of the subject at the time of trauma, nor about which parent is involved. That is all episodic as far as I'm concerned. I'm only building up toward the statement that the trauma must have had *formal* structure in the sense that multiple logical types were played against each other to generate this particular pathology in this individual.

Now, if you look at our conventional communication with one another, what you find is that we weave these logical types with incredible complexity and quite surprising facility. We even make jokes, and these may be difficult for a foreigner to understand. Most jokes, both canned and spontaneous, and nearly anywhere, are weavings of multiple logical types. Kidding and hazing similarly depend upon the unresolved question whether the kid-ee can identify that this is kidding. In any culture, the individuals acquire quite extraordinary skill in handling not only the flat identification of what sort of a message a message is but in dealing in multiple identifications of what sort of a message a message is. When we meet these multiple identifications we laugh, and we make new psychological discoveries about what goes on inside ourselves, which is perhaps the reward of real humor.

But there are people who have the utmost difficulty with this problem of multiple levels, and it seems to me that this unequal distribution of ability is a phenomenon which we can approach with the questions and terms of epidemiology. What is needed for a child to acquire, or to not acquire, a skill in the ways of interpreting these signals?

There is not only the miracle that any of them acquire the skills—and a lot of them do—there is also the other side, that a great many people have difficulty. There are people, for example, who, when Big Sister in the soap opera suffers from a cold, will send a bottle of aspirin to the radio station or recommend a cure for Big Sister's cold, in spite of the fact that Big Sister is a fictitious character within a radio soap opera. These particular members of the audience are apparently a little bit askew in their identification of what sort of a communication this is that is coming from their radio.

We all make errors of that kind at various times. I'm not sure that I've ever met anybody that doesn't suffer from "schizophrenia P" more or less. We all have some difficulty in deciding sometimes whether a dream was a dream or not, and it would not be very easy for most of us to say *how* we know that a piece of our own fantasy is fantasy and not experience. The ability to place an experience in time is one of the important cues, and referring it to a sense organ is another.

When you look at the mothers and fathers of patients for an answer to this etiological question, you meet with several sorts of answers.

First of all there are answers connected with what we may call the intensifying factors. Any disease is made worse or more probable by various circumstances, such as fatigue, cold, the number of days of combat, the presence of other diseases, etc. These seem to have a quantitative effect upon the incidence of almost any pathology. Then there are those factors which I mentioned—the hereditary characteristics and potentialities. To get confused about the logical types, one presumably has to be intelligent enough to know that there is something wrong, and not so intelligent as to be able to see what it is that is wrong. I presume that these characteristics are hereditarily determined.

But the nub of the problem, it seems to me, is to identify what real circumstances lead to the specific pathology. I acknowledge that the bacteria are not really by any means the sole determinant of a bacterial disease, and grant also therefore that the occurrence of such traumatic sequences or contexts is not by any means the sole determinant of mental illness. But still it seems to me that the identification of those contexts is the nub of understanding the disease, as identifying the bacteria is essential to understanding a bacterial disease.

I have met the mother of the patient whom I mentioned earlier. The family is not badly off. They live in a nice tract house. I went there with the patient, and when we arrived nobody was home. The newspaper boy had tossed the evening paper out in the middle of the lawn, and my patient wanted to get that paper from the middle of that perfect lawn. He came to the edge of the lawn and started to tremble.

The house looks like what is called a "model" home— a house which has been furnished by the real estate people in order to sell other houses to the public. Not a house furnished to live in, but rather furnished to look like a furnished house.

I discussed his mother with him one day, and suggested that perhaps she was a rather frightened person. He said, "Yes." I said, "What is she frightened of?" He said, "The appeariential securities."

There is a beautiful, perfectly centered mass of artificial, plastic vegetation on the middle of the mantle. A china pheasant here and a china pheasant there, symmetrically arranged. The wall-to-wall carpet is exactly as it should be.

After his mother arrived, I felt a little uncomfortable, intruding in this house. He had not visited there for about five years, but things seemed to be going all right, so I decided to leave him there and to come back when it was time to go back to the hospital. That gave me an hour in the streets with absolutely nothing to do, and I began to think what I would like to do to this setup. What and how could I communicate? I decided that I would like to put into it something that was both beautiful and untidy. In trying to implement that decision, I decided that flowers were the answer, so I bought some gladioluses. I took the gladioluses, and, when I went to get him, I presented them to the mother with a speech that I wanted her to have in her house something that was "both beautiful and untidy." "Oh!" she said, "Those are not untidy flowers. As each one withers, you can snip it off."

Now, as I see it, what is interesting is not so much the castrative statement in that speech, but the putting me in the position of having apologized when in fact I had not. That is, she took my message and reclassified it. She changed the label which indicated what sort of a message it was, and that is, I believe, what she does all the time. An endless taking of the other person's message and replying to it as if it were either a statement of weakness on the part of the speaker or an attack on her which should be turned into a weakness on the part of the speaker; and so on.

What the patient is up against today—and was up against in childhood—is the false interpretation of his messages. If he says, "The cat is on the table," she replies with some reply which makes out that his message is not the sort of message that he thought it was when he gave it. His own message identifier is obscured or distorted by her when the message comes back. And her own message identifier she continually contradicts. She laughs when she is saying that which is least funny to her, and so on.

Now there is a regular maternal dominance picture in this family, but I am not concerned at the moment to say that this is the necessary form of the trauma. I am only concerned with the purely formal aspects of this traumatic constellation; and I presume the constellation could be made up with father taking certain parts of it, mother taking certain other parts of it, and so forth.

I am trying to make only one point: that there is here a probability of trauma which will contain certain formal characteristics. It will propagate a specific syndrome in the patient because the trauma itself has impact upon a certain element in the communicational process. That which is attacked is the use of what I have called the "message-identifying signals"—those signals without which the "ego" dare not discriminate fact from fantasy or the literal from the metaphoric.

What I tried to do was pinpoint a group of syndromata, namely those syndromata related to an inability to know what sort of a message a message is. At one end of the classification of those, there will be more or less hebephrenic individuals for whom no message is of any particular definite type but who live in a sort of chronic shaggy-dog story. At the other end are those who try to overidentify, to make an overly rigid identification of what sort of a message every message is. This will give a much more paranoid type of picture. Withdrawal is another possibility.

Finally, it seems to me that with a hypothesis of this kind, one could look for the determinants in a population which might lead to the occurrence of that sort of constellation. This would seem to me an appropriate matter for epidemiological study.

# Toward a Theory of Schizophrenia*

Schizophrenia—its nature, etiology, and the kind of therapy to use for it—remains one of the most puzzling of the mental illnesses. The theory of schizophrenia presented here is based on communications analysis, and specifically on the Theory of Logical Types. From this theory and from observations of schizophrenic patients is derived a description, and the necessary conditions for, a situation called the "double bind"—a situation in which no matter what a person does, he "can't win." It is hypothesized that a person caught in the double bind may develop schizophrenic symptoms. How and why the double bind may arise in a family situation is discussed, together with illustrations from clinical and experimental data.

This is a report[1] on a research project which has been formulating and testing a broad, systematic view of the nature, etiology, and therapy of schizophrenia. Our research

*This paper by Gregory Bateson, Don D. Jackson, Jay Haley, and John H. Weakland is here reproduced from *Behavioral Science*, Vol. I, No. 4, 1956, by permission of *Behavioral Science*.

[1] This paper derives from hypotheses first developed in a research project financed by the Rockfeller Foundation from 1952–54, administered by the Department of Sociology and Anthropology at Stanford University and directed by Gregory Bateson. Since 1954 the project has

in this field has proceeded by discussion of a varied body of data and ideas, with all of us contributing according to our varied experience in anthropology, communications analysis, psychotherapy, psychiatry, and psychoanalysis. We have now reached common agreement on the broad outlines of a communicational theory of the origin and nature of schizophrenia; this paper is a preliminary report on our continuing research.

## The Base in Communications Theory

Our approach is based on that part of communications theory which Russell has called the Theory of Logical Types.[2] The central thesis of this theory is that there is a discontinuity between a class and its members. The class cannot be a member of itself nor can one of the members *be* the class, since the term used for the class is of a *different level of abstraction*—a different Logical Type—from terms used for members. Although in formal logic there is an attempt to maintain this discontinuity between a class and its members, we argue that in the psychology of real communications this discontinuity is continually and inevitably breached,[3] and that a priori we must expect a pathology to occur in the human organism when certain formal patterns of the breaching occur in the communication between

---

continued, financed by the Josiah Macy, Jr. Foundation. To Jay Haley is due credit for recognizing that the symptoms of schizophrenia are suggestive of an inability to discriminate the Logical Types, and this was amplified by Bateson, who added the notion that the symptoms and etiology could be formally described in terms of a double bind hypothesis. The hypothesis was communicated to D. D. Jackson and found to fit closely with his ideas of family homeostasis. Since then Dr. Jackson has worked closely with the project. The study of the formal analogies between hypnosis and schizophrenia has been the work of John H. Weakland and Jay Haley.

[2] A. N. Whitehead and B. Russell, *Principia Mathematica*, Cambridge, Cambridge University Press, 1910.

[3] G. Bateson, "A Theory of Play and Fantasy," *Psychiatric Research Reports*, 1955, 2: 39–51.

mother and child. We shall argue that this pathology at its extreme will have symptoms whose formal characteristics would lead the pathology to be classified as a schizophrenia.

Illustrations of how human beings handle communication involving multiple Logical Types can be derived from the following fields:

1. *The use of various communicational modes in human communication.* Examples are play, nonplay, fantasy, sacrament, metaphor, etc. Even among the lower mammals there appears to be an exchange of signals which identify certain meaningful behavior as "play," etc.[4] These signals are evidently of higher Logical Type than the messages they classify. Among human beings this framing and labeling of messages and meaningful actions reaches considerable complexity, with the peculiarity that our vocabulary for such discrimination is still very poorly developed, and we rely preponderantly upon nonverbal media of posture, gesture, facial expression, intonation, and the context for the communication of these highly abstract, but vitally important, labels.

2. *Humor.* This seems to be a method of exploring the implicit themes in thought or in a relationship. The method of exploration involves the use of messages which are characterized by a condensation of Logical Types or communicational modes. A discovery, for example, occurs when it suddenly becomes plain that a message was not only metaphoric but also more literal, or vice versa. That is to say, the explosive moment in humor is the moment when the labeling of the mode undergoes a dissolution and resynthesis. Commonly, the punch line compels a re-evaluation of earlier signals which ascribed to certain messages a particular mode (*e.g.*, literalness or fantasy). This has the peculiar effect of attributing *mode* to those signals which had previously the status of that higher Logical Type which classifies the modes.

3. *The falsification of mode-identifying signals.* Among human beings mode identifiers can be falsified, and we have the artificial laugh, the manipulative simulation of friendliness, the confidence trick, kidding, and the like. Similar falsifica-

---

[4] A film prepared by this project, "The Nature of Play; Part I, River Otters," is available.

tions have been recorded among mammals.[5] Among human beings we meet with a strange phenomenon—the unconscious falsification of these signals. This may occur within the self—the subject may conceal from himself his own real hostility under the guise of metaphoric play—or it may occur as an unconscious falsification of the subject's understanding of the other person's mode-identifying signals. He may mistake shyness for contempt, etc. Indeed most of the errors of self-reference fall under this head.

4. *Learning.* The simplest level of this phenomenon is exemplified by a situation in which a subject receives a message and acts appropriately on it: "I heard the clock strike and knew it was time for lunch. So I went to the table." In learning experiments the analogue of this sequence of events is observed by the experimenter and commonly treated as a single message of a higher type. When the dog salivates between buzzer and meat powder, this sequence is accepted by the experimenter as a message indicating that "The dog has *learned* that buzzer means meat powder." But this is not the end of the hierarchy of types involved. The experimental subject may become more skilled in learning. He may *learn to learn,*[6] and it is not inconceivable that still higher orders of learning may occur in human beings.

5. *Multiple levels of learning and the Logical Typing of signals.* These are two inseparable sets of phenomena—inseparable because the ability to handle the multiple types of signals is itself a *learned* skill and therefore a function of the multiple levels of learning.

[5] C. R. Carpenter, "A Field Study of the Behavior and Social Relations of Howling Monkeys," *Comp. Psychol. Monogr.*, 1934, 10: 1–168; also K. Z. Lorenz, *King Solomon's Ring*, New York, Crowell, 1952.

[6] G. Bateson, "Social Planning and the Concept of Deutero-Learning," *Conference on Science, Philosophy and Religion, Second Symposium*, New York, Harper, 1942. (See above, p. 159); also H. F. Harlow, "The Formation of Learning Sets," *Psychol. Review*, 1949, 56: 51–65; also C. L. Hull, *et al.*, *Mathematico-deductive Theory of Rote Learning*, New Haven, Yale University Press, 1940.

According to our hypothesis, the term "ego function" (as this term is used when a schizophrenic is described as having "weak ego function") is precisely *the process of discriminating communicational modes either within the self or between the self and others*. The schizophrenic exhibits weakness in three areas of such function: (*a*) He has difficulty in assigning the correct communicational mode to the messages he receives from other persons. (*b*) He has difficulty in assigning the correct communicational mode to those messages which he himself utters or emits nonverbally. (*c*) He has difficulty in assigning the correct communicational mode to his own thoughts, sensations, and percepts.

At this point it is appropriate to compare what was said in the previous paragraph with von Domarus'[7] approach to the systematic description of schizophrenic utterance. He suggests that the messages (and thought) of the schizophrenic are deviant in syllogistic structure. In place of structures which derive from the syllogism, Barbara, the schizophrenic, according to this theory, uses structures which identify predicates. An example of such a distorted syllogism is:

> Men die.
> Grass dies.
> Men are grass.

But as we see it, von Domarus' formulation is only a more precise—and therefore valuable—way of saying that schizophrenic utterance is rich in metaphor. With that generalization we agree. But metaphor is an indispensable tool of thought and expression—a characteristic of all human communication, even of that of the scientist. The conceptual models of cybernetics and the energy theories of psychoanalysis are, after all, only labeled metaphors. The peculiarity of the schizophrenic is not that he uses metaphors, but that he uses *unlabeled* metaphors. He has special difficulty in handling signals of that class whose members assign Logical Types to other signals.

If our formal summary of the symptomatology is correct

[7] E. von Domarus, "The Specific Laws of Logic in Schizophrenia," *Language and Thought in Schizophrenia*, J. S. Kasanin, ed., Berkeley, University of California Press, 1944.

and if the schizophrenia of our hypothesis is essentially a result of family interaction, it should be possible to arrive a priori at a formal description of these sequences of experience which would induce such a symptomatology. What is known of learning theory combines with the evident fact that human beings use *context* as a guide for mode discrimination. Therefore, we must look not for some specific traumatic experience in the infantile etiology but rather for characteristic sequential patterns. The specificity for which we search is to be at an abstract or formal level. The sequences must have this characteristic: that from them the patient will acquire the mental habits which are exemplified in schizophrenic communication. That is to say, *he must live in a universe where the sequences of events are such that his unconventional communicational habits will be in some sense appropriate*. The hypothesis which we offer is that sequences of this kind in the external experience of the patient are responsible for the inner conflicts of Logical Typing. For such unresolvable sequences of experiences, we use the term "double bind."

## The Double Bind

The necessary ingredients for a double bind situation, as we see it, are:

1. *Two or more persons*. Of these, we designate one, for purposes of our definition, as the "victim." We do not assume that the double bind is inflicted by the mother alone, but that it may be done either by mother alone or by some combination of mother, father, and/or siblings.

2. *Repeated experience*. We assume that the double bind is a recurrent theme in the experience of the victim. Our hypothesis does not invoke a single traumatic experience, but such repeated experience that the double bind structure comes to be an habitual expectation.

3. *A primary negative injunction*. This may have either of two forms: (*a*) "Do not do so and so, or I will punish you," or (*b*) "If you do not do so and so, I will punish you." Here we select a context of learning based on avoidance of punishment rather than a context of reward seeking. There is perhaps no formal reason for this selection. We assume that the punishment may be either the withdrawal

of love or the expression of hate or anger—or most devastating—the kind of abandonment that results from the parent's expression of extreme helplessness.[8]

4. *A secondary injunction conflicting with the first at a more abstract level, and like the first enforced by punishments or signals which threaten survival.* This secondary injunction is more difficult to describe than the primary for two reasons. First, the secondary injunction is commonly communicated to the child by nonverbal means. Posture, gesture, tone of voice, meaningful action, and the implications concealed in verbal comment may all be used to convey this more abstract message. Second, the secondary injunction may impinge upon any element of the primary prohibition. Verbalization of the secondary injunction may, therefore, include a wide variety of forms; for example, "Do not see this as punishment"; "Do not see me as the punishing agent"; "Do not submit to my prohibitions"; "Do not think of what you must not do"; "Do not question my love of which the primary prohibition is (or is not) an example"; and so on. Other examples become possible when the double bind is inflicted not by one individual but by two. For example, one parent may negate at a more abstract level the injunctions of the other.

5. *A tertiary negative injunction prohibiting the victim from escaping from the field.* In a formal sense it is perhaps unnecessary to list this injunction as a separate item since the reinforcement at the other two levels involves a threat to survival, and if the double binds are imposed during infancy, escape is naturally impossible. However, it seems that in some cases the escape from the field is made impossible by certain devices which are not purely negative, *e.g.*, capricious promises of love, and the like.

6. Finally, the complete set of ingredients is no longer necessary when the victim has learned to perceive his universe in double bind patterns. Almost any part of a double bind sequence may then be sufficient to precipitate panic or rage.

[8] Our concept of punishment is being refined at present. It appears to us to involve perceptual experience in a way that cannot be encompassed by the notion of "trauma."

The pattern of conflicting injunctions may even be taken over by hallucinatory voices.[9]

## The Effect of the Double Bind

In the Eastern religion, Zen Buddhism, the goal is to achieve enlightenment. The Zen master attempts to bring about enlightenment in his pupil in various ways. One of the things he does is to hold a stick over the pupil's head and say fiercely, "If you say this stick is real, I will strike you with it. If you say this stick is not real, I will strike you with it. If you don't say anything, I will strike you with it." We feel that the schizophrenic finds himself continually in the same situation as the pupil, but he achieves something like disorientation rather than enlightenment. The Zen pupil might reach up and take the stick away from the master—who might accept this response, but the schizophrenic has no such choice since with him there is no not caring about the relationship, and his mother's aims and awareness are not like the master's.

We hypothesize that there will be a breakdown in any individual's ability to discriminate between Logical Types whenever a double bind situation occurs. The general characteristics of this situation are the following:

(1) When the individual is involved in an intense relationship; that is, a relationship in which he feels it is vitally important that he discriminate accurately what sort of message is being communicated so that he may respond appropriately.

(2) And, the individual is caught in a situation in which the other person in the relationship is expressing two orders of message and one of these denies the other.

(3) And, the individual is unable to comment on the messages being expressed to correct his discrimination of what order of message to respond to, *i.e.*, he cannot make a metacommunicative statement.

We have suggested that this is the sort of situation which

[9] J. Perceval, *A Narrative of the Treatment Experienced by a Gentleman During a State of Mental Derangement, Designed to Explain the Causes and Nature of Insanity,* etc., London, Effingham Wilson, 1836 and 1840. (See bibliographic item, 1961 a.)

occurs between the preschizophrenic and his mother, but it also occurs in normal relationships. When a person is caught in a double bind situation, he will respond defensively in a manner similar to the schizophrenic. An individual will take a metaphorical statement literally when he is in a situation where he must respond, where he is faced with contradictory messages, and when he is unable to comment on the contradictions. For example, one day an employee went home during office hours. A fellow employee called him at his home, and said lightly, "Well, how did you get *there?*" The employee replied, "By automobile." He responded literally because he was faced with a message which asked him what he was doing at home when he should have been at the office, but which denied that this question was being asked by the way it was phrased. (Since the speaker felt it wasn't really his business, he spoke metaphorically.) The relationship was intense enough so that the victim was in doubt how the information would be used, and he therefore responded literally. This is characteristic of anyone who feels "on the spot," as demonstrated by the careful literal replies of a witness on the stand in a court trial. The schizophrenic feels so terribly on the spot at all times that he habitually responds with a defensive insistence on the literal level when it is quite inappropriate, *e.g.*, when someone is joking.

Schizophrenics also confuse the literal and metaphoric in their own utterance when they feel themselves caught in a double bind. For example, a patient may wish to criticize his therapist for being late for an appointment, but he may be unsure what sort of a message that act of being late was—particularly if the therapist has anticipated the patient's reaction and apologized for the event. The patient cannot say, "Why were you late? Is it because you don't want to see me today?" This would be an accusation, and so he shifts to a metaphorical statement. He may then say, "I knew a fellow once who missed a boat, his name was Sam and the boat almost sunk, . . . etc.," Thus he develops a metaphorical story and the therapist may or may not discover in it a comment on his being late. The convenient thing about a metaphor is that it leaves it up to the therapist (or mother) to see an accusation in the statement if he chooses, or to ignore it if he chooses. Should the therapist accept the accusation in the metaphor, then the patient can accept the statement he has made about Sam as metaphorical. If the therapist points out that this doesn't sound like a true statement about Sam, as a way of avoiding the accusation in the story, the patient can argue that there really was a man named Sam. As an answer to the double bind situation, a shift to a metaphorical statement brings safety. However, it also prevents the patient from making the accusation he wants to make. But instead of getting over his accusation by indicating that this is a metaphor, the schizophrenic patient seems to try to get over the fact that it is a metaphor by making it more fantastic. If the therapist should ignore the accusation in the story about Sam, the schizophrenic may then tell a story about going to Mars in a rocket ship as a way of putting over his accusation. The indication that it is a metaphorical statement lies in the fantastic aspect of the metaphor, not in the signals which usually accompany metaphors to tell the listener that a metaphor is being used.

It is not only safer for the victim of a double bind to shift to a metaphorical order of message, but in an impossible situation it is better to shift and become somebody else, or shift and insist that he is somewhere else. Then the double bind cannot work on the victim, because it isn't he and besides he is in a different place. In other words, the statements which show that a patient is disoriented can be interpreted as ways of defending himself against the situation he is in. The pathology enters when the victim himself either does not know that his responses are metaphorical or cannot say so. To recognize that he was speaking metaphorically he would need to be aware that he was defending himself and therefore was afraid of the other person. To him such an awareness would be an indictment of the other person and therefore provoke disaster.

If an individual has spent his life in the kind of double bind relationship described here, his way of relating to people after a psychotic break would have a systematic pattern. First, he would not share with normal people those signals which accompany messages to indicate what a person means. His metacommunicative system—the communications about communication—would have broken down, and he would not know what kind of message a message was. If a person said to him, "What would you like to do today?" he would be unable to judge accurately by the context or by the tone of voice or gesture whether he was being condemned for what he did yesterday, or being offered a sexual invitation, or just what was meant. Given this inability to judge accurately what a person really means and an excessive concern with what is really meant, an individual might defend himself by choosing one or more of several alternatives. He might, for example, assume that behind every statement there is a concealed meaning which is detrimental to his welfare. He would then be excessively concerned with hidden meanings and determined to demonstrate that he could not be deceived—as he had been all his life. If he chooses this alternative, he will be continually searching for meanings behind what people say and behind chance occurrences in the environment, and he will be characteristically suspicious and defiant.

He might choose another alternative, and tend to accept literally everything people say to him; when their tone or gesture or context contradicted what they said, he might establish a pattern of laughing off these metacommunicative signals. He would give up trying to discriminate between levels of message and treat all messages as unimportant or to be laughed at.

If he didn't become suspicious of metacommunicative messages or attempt to laugh them off, he might choose to try to ignore them. Then he would find it necessary to see and hear less and less of what went on around him, and do his utmost to avoid provoking a response in his environment. He would try to detach his interest from the external world and concentrate on his own internal processes and, therefore, give the appearance of being a withdrawn, perhaps mute, individual.

This is another way of saying that if an individual doesn't know what sort of message a message is, he may defend himself in ways which have been described as paranoid, hebephrenic, or catatonic. These three alternatives are not the only ones. The point is that he cannot choose the one alternative which would help him to discover what people mean; he cannot, without considerable help, discuss the messages of others. Without being able to do that, the human being is like any self-correcting system which has lost its governor; it spirals into never-ending, but always systematic, distortions.

## A Description of the Family Situation

The theoretical possibility of double bind situations stimulated us to look for such communication sequences in the schizophrenic patient and in his family situation. Toward this end we have studied the written and verbal reports of psychotherapists who have treated such patients intensively; we have studied tape recordings of psychotherapeutic interviews, both of our own patients and others; we have interviewed and taped parents of schizophrenics; we have had two mothers and one father participate in intensive psychotherapy; and we have interviewed and taped parents and patients seen conjointly.

On the basis of these data we have developed a hypothesis about the family situation which ultimately leads to an individual suffering from schizophrenia. This hypothesis has not been statistically tested; it selects and emphasizes a rather simple set of interactional phenomena and does not attempt to describe comprehensively the extraordinary complexity of a family relationship.

We hypothesize that the family situation of the schizophrenic has the following general characteristics:

(1) A child whose mother becomes anxious and withdraws if the child responds to her as a loving mother. That is, the child's very existence has a special meaning to the mother which arouses her anxiety and hostility when she is in danger of intimate contact with the child.

(2) A mother to whom feelings of anxiety and hostility toward the child are not acceptable, and whose way of denying them is to express overt loving behavior to persuade the child to respond to her as a loving mother and to withdraw from him if he does not. "Loving behavior" does not necessarily imply "affection"; it can, for example, be set in a framework of doing the proper thing, instilling "goodness," and the like.

(3) The absence of anyone in the family, such as a strong and insightful father, who can intervene in the rela-

tionship between the mother and child and support the child in the face of the contradictions involved.

Since this is a formal description we are not specifically concerned with why the mother feels this way about the child, but we suggest that she could feel this way for various reasons. It may be that merely having a child arouses anxiety about herself and her relationships to her own family; or it may be important to her that the child is a boy or a girl, or that the child was born on the anniversary of one of her own siblings,[10] or the child may be in the same sibling position in the family that she was, or the child may be special to her for other reasons related to her own emotional problems.

Given a situation with these characteristics, we hypothesize that the mother of a schizophrenic will be simultaneously expressing at least two orders of message. (For simplicity in this presentation we shall confine ourselves to two orders.) These orders of message can be roughly characterized as (*a*) hostile or withdrawing behavior which is aroused whenever the child approaches her, and (*b*) simulated loving or approaching behavior which is aroused when the child responds to her hostile and withdrawing behavior, as a way of denying that she is withdrawing. Her problem is to control her anxiety by controlling the closeness and distance between herself and her child. To put this another way, if the mother begins to feel affectionate and close to her child, she begins to feel endangered and must withdraw from him; but she cannot accept this hostile act and to deny it must simulate affection and closeness with her child. The important point is that her loving behavior is then a comment on (since it is compensatory for) her hostile behavior and consequently it is of a different *order* of message than the hostile behavior—it is a message about a sequence of messages. Yet by its nature it denies the existence of those messages which it is about, *i.e.*, the hostile withdrawal.

The mother uses the child's responses to affirm that her behavior is loving, and since the loving behavior is simulated, the child is placed in a position where he must not accurately interpret her communication if he is to maintain his relationship with her. In other words, he must not discriminate accurately between orders of message, in this case the difference between the expression of simulated feelings (one Logical Type) and real feelings (another Logical Type). As a result the child must systematically distort his perception of metacommunicative signals. For example, if mother begins to feel hostile (or affectionate) toward her child and also feels compelled to withdraw from him, she might say, "Go to bed, you're very tired and I want you to get your sleep." This overtly loving statement is intended to deny a feeling which could be verbalized as "Get out of my sight because I'm sick of you." If the child correctly discriminates her metacommunicative signals, he would have to face the fact that she both doesn't want him and is deceiving him by her loving behavior. He would be "punished" for learning to discriminate orders of messages accurately. He therefore would tend to accept the idea that he is tired rather than recognize his mother's deception. This means that he must deceive himself about his own internal state in order to support mother in her deception. To survive with her he must falsely discriminate his own internal messages as well as falsely discriminate the messages of others.

The problem is compounded for the child because the mother is "benevolently" defining for him how he feels; she is expressing overt maternal concern over the fact that he is tired. To put it another way, the mother is controlling the child's definitions of his own messages, as well as the definition of his responses to her (*e.g.*, by saying, "You don't really mean to say that," if he should criticize her) by insisting that she is not concerned about herself but only about him. Consequently, the easiest path for the child is to accept mother's simulated loving behavior as real, and his desires to interpret what is going on are undermined. Yet the result is that the mother is withdrawing from him and defining this withdrawal as the way a loving relationship should be.

However, accepting mother's simulated loving behavior as real also is no solution for the child. Should he make this false discrimination, he would approach her; this move toward closeness would provoke in her feelings of fear and helplessness, and she would be compelled to withdraw. But if he then withdrew from her, she would take his withdrawal as a statement that she was not a loving mother and would either punish him for withdrawing or approach him to bring him closer. If he then approached, she would respond by putting him at a distance. *The child is punished for discriminating accurately what she is expressing, and he is punished for discriminating inaccurately—he is caught in a double bind.*

The child might try various means of escaping from this situation. He might, for example, try to lean on his father or some other member of the family. However, from our preliminary observations we think it is likely that the fathers of schizophrenics are not substantial enough to lean on. They are also in the awkward position where if they agreed with the child about the nature of mother's deceptions, they would need to recognize the nature of their own relationships to the mother, which they could not do and remain attached to her in the *modus operandi* they have worked out.

The need of the mother to be wanted and loved also prevents the child from gaining support from some other person in the environment, a teacher, for example. A mother with these characteristics would feel threatened by any other attachment of the child and would break it up and bring the child back closer to her with consequent anxiety when the child became dependent on her.

The only way the child can really escape from the situation is to comment on the contradictory position his mother has put him in. However, if he did so, the mother would take this as an accusation that she is unloving and both punish him and insist that his perception of the situation is distorted. By preventing the child from talking about the situation, the mother forbids him using the metacommunicative level—the level we use to correct our perception of communicative behavior. The ability to communicate about communication, to comment upon the meaningful actions of oneself and others, is essential for successful social intercourse. In any normal relationship there is a constant interchange of metacommunicative messages such as "What do you mean?" or "Why did you do that?" or "Are you kidding me?" and so on. To discriminate accurately what people are really expressing, we must be able to comment directly or indirectly on that expression. This metacommunicative level the schizophrenic seems unable to use successfully.[11] Given these characteristics of the mother, it is apparent why. If she is denying one order of message, then any statement about her statements endangers her and she must forbid it. Therefore, the child grows up unskilled in his ability to communicate about communication and, as a result, unskilled in determining what people really mean and unskilled in expressing what he really means, which is essential for normal relationships.

In summary, then, we suggest that the double bind nature of the family situation of a schizophrenic results in placing the child in a position where, if he responds to his mother's simulated affection, her anxiety will be aroused and she will punish him (or insist, to protect herself, that *his* overtures are simulated, thus confusing him about the nature of his own messages) to defend herself from closeness with him. Thus the child is blocked off from intimate and secure associations with his mother. However, if he does not make overtures of affection, she will feel that this means she is not a loving mother and her anxiety will be aroused. Therefore, she will either punish him for withdrawing or make overtures toward the child to insist that he demonstrate that he loves her. If he then responds and shows her affection, she will not only feel endangered again, but she may resent the fact that she had to force him to respond. In either case in a relationship, the most important in his life and the model for all others, he is punished if he indicates love and affection and punished if he does not; and his escape routes from the situation, such as gaining support from others, are cut off. This is the basic nature of the double bind relationship between mother and child. This description has not depicted, of course, the more complicated interlocking gestalt that is the "family" of which the "mother" is one important part.[12]

[11] G. Bateson, ". . . Play and Fantasy," *op. cit.*

[12] D. D. Jackson, "The Question of Family Homeostasis," presented at the American Psychiatric Association Meeting, St. Louis, May 7, 1954; also Jackson, "Some Factors Influencing the Oedipus Complex," *Psychoanalytic Quarterly*, 1954, 23: 566–81.

## Illustrations from Clinical Data

An analysis of an incident occurring between a schizophrenic patient and his mother illustrates the double bind situation. A young man who had fairly well recovered from an acute schizophrenic episode was visited in the hospital by his mother. He was glad to see her and impulsively put his arm around her shoulders, whereupon she stiffened. He withdrew his arm and she asked, "Don't you love me any more?" He then blushed, and she said, "Dear, you must not be so easily embarrassed and afraid of your feelings." The patient was able to stay with her only a few minutes more and following her departure he assaulted an aide and was put in the tubs.

Obviously, this result could have been avoided if the young man had been able to say, "Mother, it is obvious that you become uncomfortable when I put my arm around you, and that you have difficulty accepting a gesture of affection from me." However, the schizophrenic patient doesn't have this possibility open to him. His intense dependency and training prevents him from commenting upon his mother's communicative behavior, though she comments on his and forces him to accept and to attempt to deal with the complicated sequence. The complications for the patient include the following:

(1) The mother's reaction of not accepting her son's affectionate gesture is masterfully covered up by her condemnation of him for withdrawing, and the patient denies his perception of the situation by accepting her condemnation.

(2) The statement "Don't you love me any more" in this context seems to imply:

(a) "I am lovable."

(b) "You should love me and if you don't you are bad or at fault."

(c) "Whereas you did love me previously you don't any longer," and thus focus is shifted from his expressing affection to his inability to be affectionate. Since the patient has also hated her, she is on good ground here, and he responds appropriately with guilt, which she then attacks.

(d) "What you just expressed *was not* affection," and

in order to accept this statement, the patient must deny what she and the culture have taught him about how one expresses affection. He must also question the times with her, and with others, when he thought he was experiencing affection and when they *seemed* to treat the situation as if he had. He experiences here loss-of-support phenomena and is put in doubt about the reliability of past experience.

(3) The statement, "You must not be so easily embarrassed and afraid of your feelings," seems to imply:

(*a*) "You are not like me and are different from other nice or normal people because we express our feelings."

(*b*) "The feelings you express are all right, it's only that *you* can't accept them." However, if the stiffening on her part had indicated "These are unacceptable feelings," then the boy is told that he should not be embarrassed by unacceptable feelings. Since he has had a long training in what is and is not acceptable to both her and society, he again comes into conflict with the past. If he is unafraid of his own feelings (which mother implies is good), he should be unafraid of his affection and would then notice it was she who was afraid, but he must not notice that because her whole approach is aimed at covering up this shortcoming in herself.

The impossible dilemma thus becomes: "If I am to keep my tie to mother, I must not show her that I love her, but if I do not show her that I love her, then I will lose her."

The importance to the mother of her special method of control is strikingly illustrated by the interfamily situation of a young woman schizophrenic who greeted the therapist on their first meeting with the remark, "Mother had to get married and now I'm here." This statement meant to the therapist that:

(1) The patient was the result of an illegitimate pregnancy.

(2) This fact was related to her present psychosis (in her opinion).

(3) "Here" referred to the psychiatrist's office and to the patient's presence on earth for which she had to be eternally indebted to her mother, especially since her mother had sinned and suffered in order to bring her into the world.

(4) "Had to get married" referred to the shotgun nature of mother's wedding and to the mother's response to pressure that she must marry, and the reciprocal, that she resented the forced nature of the situation and blamed the patient for it.

Actually, all these suppositions subsequently proved to be factually correct and were corroborated by the mother during an abortive attempt at psychotherapy. The flavor of the mother's communications to the patient seemed essentially this: "I am lovable, loving, and satisfied with myself. You are lovable when you are like me and when you do what I say." At the same time the mother indicated to the daughter both by words and behavior: "You are physically delicate, unintelligent, and different from me ('not normal'). You need me and me alone because of these handicaps, and I will take care of you and love you." Thus the patient's life was a series of beginnings, of attempts at experience, which would result in failure and withdrawal back to the maternal hearth and bosom because of the collusion between her and her mother.

It was noted in collaborative therapy that certain areas important to the mother's self-esteem were especially conflictual situations for the patient. For example, the mother needed the fiction that she was close to her family and that a deep love existed between her and her own mother. By analogy the relationship to the grandmother served as the prototype for the mother's relationship to her own daughter. On one occasion when the daughter was seven or eight years old, the grandmother in a rage threw a knife which barely missed the little girl. The mother said nothing to the grandmother but hurried the little girl from the room with the words, "Grandmommy really loves you." It is significant that the grandmother took the attitude toward the patient that she was not well enough controlled, and she used to chide her daughter for being too easy on the child. The grandmother was living in the house during one of the patient's psychotic episodes, and the girl took great delight in throwing various objects at the mother and grandmother while they cowered in fear.

Mother felt herself very attractive as a girl, and she felt that her daughter resembled her rather closely, although by damning with faint praise, it was obvious that she felt the daughter definitely ran second. One of the daughter's first acts during a psychotic period was to announce to her mother that she was going to cut off all her hair. She proceeded to do this while the mother pleaded with her to stop. Subsequently the mother would show a picture of *herself* as a girl and explain to people how the patient would look if she only had her beautiful hair.

The mother, apparently without awareness of the significance of what she was doing, would equate the daughter's illness with not being very bright and with some sort of organic brain difficulty. She would invariably contrast this with her own intelligence as demonstrated by her *own* scholastic record. She treated her daughter with a completely patronizing and placating manner which was insincere. For example, in the psychiatrist's presence she promised her daughter that she would not allow her to have further shock treatments, and as soon as the girl was out of the room she asked the doctor if he didn't feel she should be hospitalized and given electric shock treatments. One clue to this deceptive behavior arose during the mother's therapy. Although the daughter had had three previous hospitalizations, the mother had never mentioned to the doctors that she herself had had a psychotic episode when she discovered that she was pregnant. The family whisked her away to a small sanitarium in a nearby town, and she was, according to her own statement, strapped to a bed for six weeks. Her family did not visit her during this time, and no one except her parents and her sister knew that she was hospitalized.

There were two times during therapy when the mother showed intense emotion. One was in relating her own psychotic experience; the other was on the occasion of her last visit when she accused the therapist of trying to drive her crazy by forcing her to choose between her daughter and her husband. Against medical advice, she took her daughter out of therapy.

The father was as involved in the homeostatic aspects of the intrafamily situation as the mother. For example, he stated that he had to quit his position as an important attorney in order to bring his daughter to an area where competent psychiatric help was available. Subsequently, acting on cues from the patient (*e.g.*, she frequently referred to a character named "Nervous Ned"), the therapist was able to elicit from him that he had hated his job and for years had been trying to "get out from under." However, the daughter was made to feel that the move was initiated for her.

On the basis of our examination of the clinical data, we have been impressed by a number of observations including:

(1) The helplessness, fear, exasperation, and rage which a double bind situation provokes in the patient, but which the mother may serenely and un-understandingly pass over. We have noted reactions in the father that both create double bind situations, or extend and amplify those created by the mother, and we have seen the father, passive and outraged, but helpless, become ensnared in a similar manner to the patient.

(2) The psychosis seems, in part, a way of dealing with double bind situations to overcome their inhibiting and controlling effect. The psychotic patient may make astute, pithy, often metaphorical remarks that reveal an insight into the forces binding him. Contrariwise, he may become rather expert in setting double bind situations himself.

(3) According to our theory, the communication situation described is essential to the mother's security, and by inference to the family homeostasis. If this be so, then when psychotherapy of the patient helps him become less vulnerable to mother's attempts at control, anxiety will be produced in the mother. Similarly, if the therapist interprets to the mother the dynamics of the situation she is setting up with the patient, this should produce an anxiety response in her. Our impression is that when there is a perduring contact between patient and family (especially when the patient lives at home during psychotherapy), this leads to a disturbance (often severe) in the mother and sometimes in both mother and father and other siblings.[13]

[13] D. D. Jackson, "An Episode of Sleepwalking," *Journal of the American Psychoanalytic Association,* 1954, 2: 503–508; also Jackson, "Some Factors . . . ," *Psychoanalytic Quarterly,* 1954, 23: 566–581.

## Current Position and Future Prospects

Many writers have treated schizophrenia in terms of the most extreme contrast with any other form of human thinking and behavior. While it is an isolable phenomenon, so much emphasis on the differences from the normal—rather like the fearful physical segregation of psychotics—does not help in understanding the problems. In our approach we assume that schizophrenia involves general principles which are important in all communication and therefore many informative similarities can be found in "normal" communication situations.

We have been particularly interested in various sorts of communication which involve both emotional significance and the necessity of discriminating between orders of message. Such situations include play, humor, ritual, poetry, and fiction. Play, especially among animals, we have studied at some length.[14] It is a situation which strikingly illustrates the occurrence of metamessages whose correct discrimination is vital to the cooperation of the individuals involved; for example, false discrimination could easily lead to combat. Rather closely related to play is humor, a continuing subject of our research. It involves sudden shifts in Logical Types as well as discrimination of those shifts. Ritual is a field in which unusually real or literal ascriptions of Logical Type are made and defended as vigorously as the schizophrenic defends the "reality" of his delusions. Poetry exemplifies the communicative power of metaphor—even very unusual metaphor—when labeled as such by various signs, as contrasted to the obscurity of unlabeled schizophrenic metaphor. The entire field of fictional communication, defined as the narration or depiction of a series of events with more or less of a label of actuality, is most relevant to the investigation of schizophrenia. We are not so much concerned with the content interpretation of fiction—although analysis of oral and destructive themes is illuminating to the student of schizophrenia—as with the formal problems involved in simultaneous existence of multiple levels of message in

[14] Bateson, "A Theory of Play . . ." *op. cit.*

the fictional presentation of "reality." The drama is especially interesting in this respect, with both performers and spectators responding to messages about both the actual and the theatrical reality.

We are giving extensive attention to hypnosis. A great array of phenomena that occur as schizophrenic symptoms—hallucinations, delusions, alterations of personality, amnesias, and so on—can be produced temporarily in normal subjects with hypnosis. These need not be directly suggested as specific phenomena, but can be the "spontaneous" result of an arranged communication sequence. For example, Erickson[15] will produce a hallucination by first inducing catalepsy in a subject's hand and then saying, "There is no conceivable way in which your hand can move, yet when I give the signal, it must move." That is, he tells the subject his hand will remain in place, yet it will move, and in no way the subject can consciously conceive. When Erickson gives the signal, the subject hallucinates the hand moved, or hallucinates himself in a different place and therefore the hand was moved. This use of hallucination to resolve a problem posed by contradictory commands which cannot be discussed seems to us to illustrate the solution of a double bind situation via a shift in Logical Types. Hypnotic responses to direct suggestions or statements also commonly involve shifts in type, as in accepting the words "Here's a glass of water" or "You feel tired" as external or internal reality, or in literal response to metaphorical statements, much like schizophrenics. We hope that further study of hypnotic induction, phenomena, and waking will, in this controllable situation, help sharpen our view of the essential communicational sequences which produce phenomena like those of schizophrenia.

Another Erickson experiment seems to isolate a double bind communicational sequence without the specific use of hypnosis. Erickson arranged a seminar so as to have a young chain smoker sit next to him and to be without cigarettes; other participants were briefed on what to do. All was ordered so that Erickson repeatedly turned to offer the young man a cigarette, but was always interrupted by a question from someone so that he turned away, "inadver-

---

[15] M. H. Erickson, Personal communication, 1955.

tently" withdrawing the cigarettes from the young man's reach. Later another participant asked this young man if he had received the cigarette from Dr. Erickson. He replied, "What cigarette?", showed clearly that he had forgotten the whole sequence, and even refused a cigarette offered by another member, saying that he was too interested in the seminar discussion to smoke. This young man seems to us to be in an experimental situation paralleling the schizophrenic's double bind situation with mother: an important relationship, contradictory messages (here of giving and taking away), and comment blocked—because there was a seminar going on, and anyway it was all "inadvertent." And note the similar outcome: amnesia for the double bind sequence and reversal from "He doesn't give" to "I don't want."

Although we have been led into these collateral areas, our main field of observation has been schizophrenia itself. All of us have worked directly with schizophrenic patients and much of this case material has been recorded on tape for detailed study. In addition, we are recording interviews held jointly with patients and their families, and we are taking sound motion pictures of mothers and disturbed, presumably preschizophrenic, children. Our hope is that these operations will provide a clearly evident record of the continuing, repetitive double binding which we hypothesize goes on steadily from infantile beginnings in the family situation of individuals who become schizophrenic. This basic family situation, and the overtly communicational characteristics of schizophrenia, have been the major focus of this paper. However, we expect our concepts and some of these data will also be useful in future work on other problems of schizophrenia, such as the variety of other symptoms, the character of the "adjusted state" before schizophrenia becomes manifest, and the nature and circumstances of the psychotic break.

### Therapeutic Implications of this Hypothesis

Psychotherapy itself is a context of multilevel communication, with exploration of the ambiguous lines between the literal and metaphoric, or reality and fantasy, and indeed, various forms of play, drama, and hypnosis have been used extensively in therapy. We have been interested in therapy, and in addition to our own data we have been collecting and examining recordings, verbatim transcripts, and personal accounts of therapy from other therapists. In this we prefer exact records since we believe that how a schizophrenic talks depends greatly, though often subtly, on how another person talks to him; it is most difficult to estimate what was really occurring in a therapeutic interview if one has only a description of it, especially if the description is already in theoretical terms.

Except for a few general remarks and some speculation, however, we are not yet prepared to comment on the relation of the double bind to psychotherapy. At present we can only note:

(1) Double bind situations are created by and within the psychotherapeutic setting and the hospital milieu. From the point of view of this hypothesis, we wonder about the effect of medical "benevolence" on the schizophrenic patient. Since hospitals exist for the benefit of personnel as well as—as much as—more than—for the patient's benefit, there will be contradictions at times in sequences where actions are taken "benevolently" for the patient when actually they are intended to keep the staff more comfortable. We would assume that whenever the system is organized for hospital purposes and it is announced to the patient that the actions are for *his* benefit, then the schizophrenogenic situation is being perpetuated. This kind of deception will provoke the patient to respond to it as a double bind situation, and his response will be "schizophrenic" in the sense that it will be indirect and the patient will be unable to comment on the fact that he feels that he is being deceived. One vignette, fortunately amusing, illustrates such a response. On a ward with a dedicated and "benevolent" physician in charge there was a sign on the physician's door which said "Doctor's Office. Please Knock." The doctor was driven to distraction and finally capitulation by the obedient patient who carefully knocked every time he passed the door.

(2) The understanding of the double bind and its communicative aspects may lead to innovations in therapeutic technique. Just what these innovations may be is difficult to say, but on the basis of our investigation we are assuming that double bind situations occur consistently in psycho-

therapy. At times these are inadvertent in the sense that the therapist is imposing a double bind situation similar to that in the patient's history, or the patient is imposing a double bind situation on the therapist. At other times therapists seem to impose double binds, either deliberately or intuitively, which force the patient to respond differently than he has in the past.

An incident from the experience of a gifted psychotherapist illustrates the intuitive understanding of a double bind communicational sequence. Dr. Frieda Fromm-Reichmann[16] was treating a young woman who from the age of seven had built a highly complex religion of her own replete with powerful gods. She was very schizophrenic and quite hesitant about entering into a therapeutic situation. At the beginning of the treatment she said, "God R says I shouldn't talk with you." Dr. Fromm-Reichmann replied, "Look, let's get something into the record. To me God R doesn't exist, and that whole world of yours doesn't exist. To you it does, and far be it from me to think that I can take that away from you, I have no idea what it means. So I'm willing to talk with you in terms of that world, if only you know I do it so that we have an understanding that it doesn't exist for me. Now go to God R and tell him that we have to talk and he should give you permission. Also you must tell him that I am a doctor and that you have lived with him in his kingdom now from seven to sixteen—that's nine years —and he hasn't helped you. So now he must permit me to try and see whether you and I can do that job. Tell him that I am a doctor and this is what I want to try."

The therapist has her patient in a "therapeutic double bind." If the patient is rendered doubtful about her belief in her god, then she is agreeing with Dr. Fromm-Reichmann, and is admitting her attachment to therapy. If she insists that God R is real, then she must tell him that Dr. Fromm-Reichmann is "more powerful" than he—again admitting her involvement with the therapist.

The difference between the therapeutic bind and the original double bind situation is in part the fact that the therapist is not involved in a life and death struggle him-

¹⁶ F. Fromm-Reichmann, Personal communication, 1956.

self. He can therefore set up relatively benevolent binds and gradually aid the patient in his emancipation from them. Many of the uniquely appropriate therapeutic gambits arranged by therapists seem to be intuitive. We share the goal of most psychotherapists who strive toward the day when such strokes of genius will be well enough understood to be systematic and commonplace.

## Additional References

J. Haley, "Paradoxes in Play, Fantasy, and Psychotherapy," *Psychiatric Research Reports*, 1955, 2: 52–8.

J. Ruesch and G. Bateson, *Communication: The Social Matrix of Psychiatry*, New York, Norton, 1951.

# The Group Dynamics of Schizophrenia*

First, I intend to attach very specific meaning to the title of this paper. An essential notion attached to the word "group" as I shall use it is the idea of relatedness between members. Our concern is not with the sort of phenomena which occur in experimentally formed groups of graduate students who have no previously determined habits of communication—no habitual differentiations of role. The group to which I mostly refer is the family; in general, those families in which the parents maintain an adjustment to the world around them without being recognized as grossly deviant, while one or more of their offspring differ conspicuously from the normal population in the frequency and obvious nature of their responses. I shall also be thinking of other groups analogous to these, *i.e.*, ward organizations, which work in such a way as to promote schizophrenic or schizophrenoid behavior in some of the members.

The word "dynamics" is loosely and conventionally used for all studies of personal interaction and especially when

*The ideas in this lecture represent the combined thinking of the staff of The Project for the Study of Schizophrenic Communication. The staff consisted of Gregory Bateson, Jay Haley, John H. Weakland, Don D. Jackson, M.D., and William F. Fry, M.D.

The article is reprinted from *Chronic Schizophrenia: Explorations in Theory and Treatment,* edited by L. Appleby, J. M. Scher, and J. Cumming, The Free Press, Glencoe, Illinois, 1960; reprinted by permission.

they stress change or learning exhibited by the subjects. Despite our following its conventional use, this word is a misnomer. It evokes analogies with physics which are totally false.

"Dynamics" is principally a language devised by physicists and mathematicians for the description of certain events. In this strict sense, the impact of one billiard ball upon another is subject matter for dynamics, but it would be an error of language to say that billiard balls "behave." Dynamics appropriately describe those events whose descriptions can be checked by asking whether they contravene the First Law of Thermodynamics, the Law of the Conservation of Energy. When one billiard ball strikes another, the motion of the second is energized by the impact of the first, and such transferences of energy are the central subject matter of dynamics. We, however, are not concerned with event sequences which have this characteristic. If I kick a stone, the movement of the stone is energized by the act, but if I kick a dog, the behavior of the dog may indeed be partly conservative—he may travel along a Newtonian trajectory if kicked hard enough, but this is mere physics. What is important is that he may exhibit responses which are energized not by the kick but by his metabolism; he may turn and bite.

This, I think, is what people mean by magic. The realm of phenomena in which we are interested is always characterized by the fact that "ideas" may influence events. To the physicist, this is a grossly magical hypothesis. It is one which cannot be tested by asking questions about the conservation of energy.

All this, however, has been better and more rigorously said by Bertalanffy, which makes it easier for me to further explore this realm of phenomena in which *communication* occurs. We shall settle for the conventional term "dynamics" provided it is clearly understood that we are not talking about dynamics in the physical sense.

Robert Louis Stevenson[1] in "The Poor Thing" has achieved perhaps the most vivid characterization of this magical realm:

<hr>

[1] R. L. Stevenson, "The Poor Thing," *Novels and Tales of Robert Louis Stevenson*, Vol. 20, New York, Scribners, 1918, pp. 496–502.

"In my thought one thing is as good as another in this world; and a shoe of a horse will do." The word "yes" or a whole performance of *Hamlet,* or an injection of epinephrine in the right place on the surface of the brain may be interchangeable objects. Any one of them may, according to the conventions of communication established at that moment, be an affirmative (or a negative) answer to any question. In the famous message, "One if by land; two if by sea," the objects actually used were lamps, but from the point of view of communications theory, they could have been anything from aardvarks to zygomatic arches.

It might well be sufficiently confusing to be told that, according to the conventions of communication in use at the moment, anything can stand for anything else. But this realm of magic is not that simple. Not only can the shoe of a horse stand for anything else according to the conventions of communication, it can also and simultaneously be a signal which will alter the conventions of communication. My fingers crossed behind my back may alter the whole tone and implication of everything. I recall a schizophrenic patient who, like many other schizophrenics, had difficulty with the first person pronoun; in particular, he did not like to sign his name. He had a number of aliases, alternative named aspects of self. The ward organization, of which he was a part, required that he sign his name to obtain a pass, and for one or two weekends he did not receive a pass because he insisted on signing one of his aliases. One day he remarked that he was going out the next weekend. I said, "Oh, did you sign?" He said, "Yes," with an odd grin. His real name, we will say, was Edward W. Jones. What he had actually signed was "W. Edward Jones." The ward officials did not notice the difference. It appeared to them that they had won a battle and had succeeded in forcing him to act sanely. But to himself the message was, "He (the real me) did not sign." He had won the battle. It was as if his fingers were crossed behind his back.

All communication has this characteristic—it can be magically modified by accompanying communication. In this conference, we have been discussing various ways of interacting with patients, describing what we do and what our strategy seems to us to be. It would have been more difficult to discuss our actions from the patients' point of view. How do we qualify our communications to the patients, so that the experience which they receive will be therapeutic?

Appleby, for example, described a set of procedures on his ward, and if I were a schizophrenic listening to him, I would have been tempted to say, "It all sounds like occupational therapy to me." He tells us very convincingly and with figures that his program is successful, and in documenting his success he is no doubt telling the truth. If this is so, then his description of the program must necessarily be incomplete. The experiences which the program provides for the patients must be something a little more alive than the dry bones of the program which he has described. The whole series of therapeutic procedures must have been qualified, possibly with enthusiasm or with humor, with some set of signals which altered the mathematical sign—plus or minus—of what was being done. Appleby has told us only about the shoe of the horse, not about the multitude of realities which determined for what that horseshoe stood.

It is as if he had related that a given musical composition was set in the key of C major, and asked us to believe that this skeletal statement was a sufficient description to enable us to understand why this particular composition altered the mood of the listener in a particular way. What is omitted in all such descriptions is the enormous complexity of modulation of communication. It is this modulation which is music.

Let me shift from a musical to a wide biological analogy in order to examine further this magical realm of communication. All organisms are partially determined by genetics, *i.e.*, by complex constellations of messages carried principally in the chromosomes. We are products of a communicational process, modified and qualified in various ways by environmental impact. It follows, therefore, that the differences between related organisms, say, a crab and a lobster, or between a tall pea and a short pea, must always be the sort of differences that can be created by changes and modulations in a constellation of messages. Sometimes these changes in the message system will be relatively concrete— a shift from "yes" to "no" in the answer to some question governing a relatively superficial detail of the anatomy. The total picture of the animal may be altered by as little as one spot in the whole halftone block, or the change may be one which modifies or modulates the whole system of genetic messages, so that every message in the system takes on a different look while retaining its former relationship to all neighboring messages. It is, I believe, this stability of the relationship between messages under the impact of the change in one part of the constellation that provides a basis for the French aphorism *"Plus ça change, plus c'est la même chose."* It is a recognized fact that the skulls of the various anthropoids can be drawn upon diversely skewed coordinates to demonstrate the fundamental similarity of relations and the systematic nature of the transformation from one species to another.[2]

My father was a geneticist, and he used to say, "It's all vibrations,"[3] and to illustrate this he would point out that the striping of the common zebra is an octave higher than that of Grevy's zebra. While it is true that in this particular case the "frequency" is doubled, I don't think that it is entirely a matter of vibrations as he endeavored to explain it. Rather, he was trying to say that it is all a matter of the sort of modifications which could be expected among systems whose determinants are not a matter of physics in the crude sense, but a matter of messages and modulated systems of messages.

It is worth noting, too, that perhaps organic forms are beautiful to us and the systematic biologist can find aesthetic satisfaction in the *differences* between related organisms simply because the differences are due to modulations of communication, while we ourselves are both organisms who communicate and whose forms are determined by constellations of genetic messages. This is not the place, however, for such a revision of aesthetic theory. An expert in the theory of mathematical groups could make a major contribution in this field.

All messages and parts of messages are like phrases or segments of equations which a mathematician puts in brackets. Outside the brackets there may always be a qualifier or multiplier which will alter the whole tenor of the phrase. Moreover, these qualifiers can always be added, even years later.

[2] D. W. Thompson, *On Growth and Form,* Vol. 2, Oxford, Oxford University Press, 1952.

[3] Beatrice C. Bateson, *William Bateson, Naturalist,* Cambridge, Cambridge University Press, 1928.

They do not have to precede the phrase inside the brackets. Otherwise, there could be no psychotherapy. The patient would be entitled and even compelled to argue, "My mother slapped me down in such and such ways, and, therefore, I am now sick; and because those traumata occured in the past they cannot be altered, and I, therefore, cannot get well." In the realm of communication, the *events* of the past constitute a chain of old horseshoes so that the meaning of that chain can be changed and is continually being changed. What exists today are only messages about the past which we call memories, and these messages can always be framed and modulated from moment to moment.

Up to this point the realm of communication appears to be more and more complex, more flexible, and less amenable to analysis. Now the introduction of the group concept— the consideration of many persons—suddenly simplifies this confused realm of slipping and sliding meanings. If we shake up a number of irregular stones in a bag, or subject them to an almost random beating by the waves on the seashore, even at the crudely physical level, there will be a gradual simplification of the system—the stones will resemble each other. In the end, they will all become spherical, but in practice we usually encounter them as partly rounded pebbles. Certain forms of homogenization result from multiple impact even at the crude physical level, and when the impacting entities are organisms capable of complex learning and communication, the total system operates rapidly toward either uniformity or toward systematic differentiation—an increase of simplicity—which we call organization. If there are differences between the impacting entities, these differences will undergo change, either in the direction of reducing the difference, or in the direction of achieving a mutual fitting or complementarity. Among groups of people, whether the direction of change is toward homogeneity or toward complementarity, the achievement is a sharing of premises regarding the meaning and appropriateness of messages and other acts in the context of the relationship.

I shall not go into the complex problems of learning involved in this process but shall proceed to the problem of schizophrenia. An individual, *i.e.*, the identified patient, exists within a family setting, but when we view him singularly, certain pecularities of his communicational habits are noted.

These peculiarities may be partly determined by genetics or physiological accident, but it is still reasonable to question the function of these peculiarities within the communicational system of which they are a part—the family. A number of living creatures have been, in a sense, shaken up together and one of them has come out apparently different from the rest; we have to ask not only about differences in the material of which this particular individual may be made, but also how his particular characteristics were developed in this family system. Can the peculiarities of the identified patient be seen as *appropriate*, i.e., as either homogeneous with, or complementary to, the characteristics of the other members of the group? We do not doubt that a large part of schizophrenic symptomatology is, in some sense, learned or determined by experience, but an organism can learn only that which it is taught by the circumstances of living and the experiences of exchanging messages with those around him. He cannot learn at random, but only to be like or unlike those around him. We have, therefore, the necessary task of looking at the experiential setting of schizophrenia.

We shall outline briefly what we have been calling the double bind hypothesis, which has been more fully described elsewhere.[4] This hypothesis contains two parts; a formal

[4] G. Bateson, D. D. Jackson, J. Haley, and J. H. Weakland, "Toward a Theory of Schizophrenia," *Behavioral Science*, 1956, 1: 251–64; also G. Bateson, "Language and Psychotherapy, Frieda Fromm-Reichmann's Last Project," *Psychiatry*, 1958, 21: 96–100; also G. Bateson (moderator), "Schizophrenic Distortions of Communication," *Psychotherapy of Chronic Schizophrenic Patients*, C. A. Whitacker, ed., Boston and Toronto, Little, Brown and Co., 1958, pp. 31–56; also G. Bateson, "Analysis of Group Therapy in an Admission Ward, United States Naval Hospital, Oakland, California," *Social Psychiatry in Action*, H. A. Wilmer, Springfield, Ill., Charles C. Thomas, 1958, pp. 334–49; also J. Haley, "The Art of Psychoanalysis," *etc.*, 1958, 15: 190–200; also J. Haley, "An Interactional Explanation of Hypnosis," *American Journal of Clinical Hypnosis*, 1958, 1: 41–57; also J. H. Weakland and D. D. Jackson, "Patient and Therapist Observations on the Circumstances of a Schizophrenic Episode," *AMA Archives of Neurological Psychiatry*, 1958, 79: 554–74.

description of the communicational habits of the schizophrenic, and a formal description of the sequences of experience which would understandably train the individual in his peculiar distortions of communication. Empirically we find that one description of the symptoms is, on the whole, satisfactory, and that the families of schizophrenics are characterized by the behavioral sequences which are predicted by the hypothesis.

Typically, the schizophrenic will eliminate from his messages everything that refers explicitly or implicitly to the relationship between himself and the person he is addressing. Schizophrenics commonly avoid the first and second person pronouns. They avoid telling you what sort of a message they are transmitting—whether it be literal or metaphoric, ironic or direct—and they are likely to have difficulty with all messages and meaningful acts which imply intimate contact between the self and some other. To receive food may be almost impossible, but so also may be the repudiation of food.

When leaving for the A.P.A. meetings in Honolulu, I told my patient that I would be away and where I was going. He looked out the window and said, "That plane flies awfully slowly." He could not say, "I shall miss you," because he would thus be identifying himself in a relationship to me, or me in relationship to himself. To say, "I shall miss you" would be to assert a basic premise about our mutual relationship by defining the sorts of messages which should be characteristic of that relationship.

Observably, the schizophrenic avoids or distorts anything which might seem to identify either himself or the person whom he is addressing. He may eliminate anything which implies that his message refers to, and is a part of, a relationship between two identifiable people, with certain styles and premises governing their behavior in that relationship. He may avoid anything which might enable the other to interpret what he says. He may obscure the fact that he is speaking in metaphor or in some special code, and he is likely to distort or omit all reference to time and place. If we use a Western Union telegram form as an analogy, we might say that he omits what would be put on the procedural parts of the telegraph form and will modify the text of his message to distort or omit any indication of these metacommunicative elements in the total normal message. What remains is likely to be a metaphoric statement unlabelled as to context. Or, in extreme cases, there may be nothing left but a stolid acting out of the message, "There is no relationship between us."

This much is observable and may be summarized by saying that the schizophrenic communicates *as if* he expected to be punished every time he indicates that he is right in his view of the context of his own message.

The "double bind," which is central to the etiological half of our hypothesis, may now simply be summarized by saying that it is an experience of being punished precisely for being right in one's own view of the context. Our hypothesis assumes that repeated experience of punishment in sequences of this kind will lead the individual to behave habitually as if he expected such punishment.

The mother of one of our patients poured out blame upon her husband for refusing for fifteen years to hand over control of the family finances to her. The father of the patient said, "I admit that it was a great mistake of me not to let you handle it, I admit that. I have corrected that. My reasons for thinking it was a mistake are entirely different from yours, but I admit that it was a very serious error on my part."

*Mother:* Now, you're just being facetious.

*Father:* No, I am not being facetious.

*Mother:* Well, anyway I don't care because when you come right down to it the debts were incurred, still there is no reason why a person would not be told of them. I think the woman should be told.

*Father:* It may be the same reason why when Joe (their psychotic son) comes home from school and he has had trouble he doesn't tell you.

*Mother:* Well, that's a good dodge.

The pattern of such a sequence is simply the successive disqualification of each of the father's contributions to the relationship. He is continuously being told that the messages are not valid. They are received as if they were in some way different from that which he thought he intended. We may say that he is penalized either for being right about his views of his own intentions, or he is penalized whenever his reply is appropriate to what she said.

But, per contra, from her viewpoint, it seems that he is endlessly misinterpreting her, and this is one of the most peculiar characteristics of the dynamic system which surrounds—or *is*—schizophrenia. Every therapist who has dealt with schizophrenics will recognize the recurrent trap. The patient endeavors to put the therapist in the wrong by his interpretation of what the therapist said, and the patient does this because he expects the therapist to misinterpret what he (the patient) said. The bind becomes mutual. A stage is reached in the relationship in which neither person can afford to receive or emit metacommunicative messages without distortion.

There is, however, usually, an asymmetry in such relationships. This mutual doublebinding is a type of struggle and commonly one or the other has the upper hand. We have deliberately chosen to work with families where one of the offspring is the identified patient, and, partly for this reason, in our data, it is the supposedly normal parents who have the upper hand over an identifiably psychotic younger member of the group. In such cases, the asymmetry takes the curious form that the identified patient sacrifices himself to maintain the sacred illusion that what the parent says makes sense. To be close to that parent, he must sacrifice his right to indicate that he sees any metacommunicative incongruencies, even when his perception of these incongruencies is correct. There is, therefore, a curious disparity in the distribution of awareness of what is happening. The patient may know but must not tell, and thereby enables the parent to not know what he or she is doing. The patient is an accomplice in the parent's unconscious hypocrisy. The result may be very great unhappiness and very gross, but always systematic, distortions of communication.

Moreover, these distortions are always precisely those which would seem appropriate when the victims are faced with a trap to avoid which would be to destroy the very nature of the self. This paradigm is neatly illustrated by a passage which is worth quoting in full from Festing Jones' life of Samuel Butler.[5]

[5] H. F. Jones, *Samuel Butler: A Memoir*, Vol. 1, London, Macmillan, 1919.

Butler went to dinner at Mr. Seebohm's where he met Skertchley, who told them about a rat-trap invented by Mr. Tylor's coachman.

## DUNKETT'S RAT-TRAP

Mr. Dunkett found all his traps fail one after another, and was in such despair at the way the corn got eaten that he resolved to invent a rat-trap. He began by putting himself as nearly as possible in the rat's place.

"Is there anything," he asked himself, "in which, if I were a rat, I should have such complete confidence that I could not suspect it without suspecting everything in the world and being unable henceforth to move fearlessly in any direction?"

He pondered for a while and had no answer, till one night the room seemed to become full of light and he hears a voice from heaven saying:

"Drain-pipes."

Then he saw his way. To suspect a common drain-pipe would be to cease to be a rat. Here Skertchley enlarged a little, explaining that a spring was to be concealed inside, but that the pipe was to be open at both ends; if the pipe were closed at one end, a rat would naturally not like going into it, for he would not feel sure of being able to get out again; on which I [Butler] interrupted and said:

"Ah, it was just this which stopped me from going into the Church."

When he [Butler] told me this I [Jones] knew what was in his mind, and that, if he had not been in such respectable company, he would have said: "It was just this which stopped me from getting married."

Notice that Dunkett could only invent this double bind for rats by way of an hallucinatory experience, and that both Butler and Jones immediately regarded the trap as a paradigm for human relations. Indeed, this sort of dilemma is not rare and is not confined to the contexts of schizophrenia.

The question which we must face, therefore, is why these sequences are either specially frequent or specially destructive in those families which contain schizophrenics. I do not have the statistics to assert this; however, from limited but intense observation of a few of these families, I can offer an hypothesis about the group dynamics which would determine a system of interaction, such that double bind experiences must recur *ad nauseam*. The problem is to construct a model which will necessarily *cycle* to recreate these patterned sequences over and over again.

Such a model is provided in Von Neumann's and Morgenstern's[6] theory of games, presented here not, indeed, with its full mathematical rigor, but at least in terms somewhat technical.

Von Neumann was concerned with mathematical study of the formal conditions under which entities, with total intelligence and a preference for gain, would form coalitions among themselves in order to maximize the profits which coalition members might receive at the expense of the nonmembers. He imagined these entities as engaged in something like a game and proceeded to ask about the formal characteristics of the rules which would compel the totally intelligent but gain-oriented players to form coalitions. A very curious conclusion emerged, and it is this conclusion which I would propose as a model.

Evidently, coalition between players can only emerge when there are at least three of them. Any two may then get together to exploit the third, and if such a game be symmetrically devised, it evidently has three solutions which we may represent as

$$AB \text{ vs. } C$$
$$BC \text{ vs. } A$$
$$AC \text{ vs. } B$$

For this three-person system, Von Neumann demonstrates that once formed, any one of these coalitions will be stable. If $A$ and $B$ are in alliance, there is nothing $C$ can do about it. And, interestingly enough, $A$ and $B$ will necessarily develop conventions (supplementary to the rules) which will, for example, forbid them from listening to $C$'s approaches.

[6] J. Von Neumann and O. Morgenstern, *Theory of Games and Economic Behavior*, Princeton, Princeton University Press, 1944.

In the five-person game, the position becomes quite different; there will be a variety of possibilities. It may be that four players contemplate a combination against one, illustrated in the following five patterns:

*A* vs. *BCDE*
*B* vs. *ACDE*
*C* vs. *ABDE*
*D* vs. *ABCE*
*E* vs. *ABCD*

But none of these would be stable. The four players within the coalition must, necessarily, engage in a subgame in which they maneuver against each other to achieve an unequal division of the gains which the coalition could squeeze out of the fifth player. This must lead to a coalition pattern which we may describe as 2 vs. 2 vs. 1, *i.e.*, *BC* vs. *DE* vs. *A*. In such a situation, it would become possible for *A* to approach and join one of these pairs, so that the coalition system will become 3 vs. 2.

But in the system 3 vs. 2, it would be advantageous for the three to recruit over to their side one of the two, in order to make their gains more certain. Now we are back to a 4 vs. 1 system—not necessarily the particular line-up that we started from but at any rate a system having the same general properties. It, in turn, must break down into 2 vs. 2 vs. 1, and so on.

In other words, for every possible pattern of coalitions, there is at least one other pattern which will "dominate" it—to use Von Neumann's term—and the relationship of domination between solutions is *intransitive*. There will always be a circular list of alternative solutions so that the system will never cease from passing on from solution to solution, always selecting another solution which is preferable to that which preceded it. This means, in fact, that the robots (owing to their total intelligence) will be unable to decide upon a single "play" of the game.

I offer this model as being reminiscent of what happens in schizophrenic families. No two members seem able to get together in a coalition stable enough to be decisive at the given moment. Some other member or members of the family will always intervene. Or, lacking such intervention, the two members who contemplate a coalition will feel guilty vis-à-vis what the third might do or say, and will draw back from the coalition.

Notice that it takes five hypothetical entities with total intelligence to achieve this particular sort of instability or oscillation in a Von Neumannian game. But *three* human beings seem to be enough. Perhaps they are not totally intelligent or perhaps they are systematically inconsistent regarding the sort of "gain" in terms of which they are motivated.

I want to stress that in such a system, the experience of each separate individual will be of this kind: every move which he makes is the common-sense move in the situation as he correctly sees it at that moment, but his every move is subsequently demonstrated to have been wrong by the moves which other members of the system make in response to his "right" move. The individual is thus caught in a perpetual sequence of what we have called double bind experiences.

I do not know how valid this model may be, but I offer it for two reasons. First, it is proposed as a sample of trying to talk about the larger system—the family—instead of talking, as we habitually do, about the individual. If we are to understand the dynamics of schizophrenia, we must devise a language adequate to the phenomena which are emergent in this larger system. Even if my model is inappropriate, it is still worthwhile to try to talk in the sort of language which we shall need for describing these emergent phenomena. Secondly, conceptual models, even when incorrect, are useful to the extent that criticism of the model may point to new theoretical developments.

Let me, therefore, point out one criticism of this model, and consider to what ideas it will lead. There is no theorem in Von Neumann's book which would indicate that his entities or robots, engaged in this infinite dance of changing coalitions, would ever become schizophrenic. According to the abstract theory, the entities simply remain totally intelligent *ad infinitum.*

Now, the major difference between people and von Neumann's robots lies in the fact of learning. To be infinitely intelligent implies to be infinitely flexible, and the players in the dance which I have described could never *experience* the pain which human beings would feel if continually proven wrong whenever they had been wise. Human beings have a commitment to the solutions which they discover, and it is this psychological commitment that makes it possible for them to be hurt in the way members of a schizophrenic family are hurt.

It appears then, from consideration of the model, that the double bind hypothesis, to be explanatory of schizophrenia, must depend upon certain psychological assumptions about the nature of the human individual as a learning organism. For the individual to be prone to schizophrenia, individuation must comprise *two* contrasting psychological mechanisms. The first is a mechanism of adaptation to demands of the personal environment; and the second, a process or mechanism whereby the individual becomes either briefly or enduringly committed to the adaptations which the first process has discovered.

I think that what I am calling a brief commitment to an adaptation is what Bertalanffy called the *immanent state of action;* and that the more enduring commitment to adaptation is simply what we usually call "habit."

What is a person? What do I mean when I say "I?" Perhaps what each of us means by the "self" is in fact an aggregate of habits of perception and adaptive action *plus,* from moment to moment, our "immanent states of action." If somebody attacks the habits and immanent states which characterize me at the given moment of dealing with that somebody—that is, if they attack the very habits and immanent states which have been called into being as part of my relationship to them at that moment—they are negating me. If I care deeply about that other person, the negation of me will be still more painful.

What we have said so far is enough to indicate the sorts of strategy—or perhaps we should say symptoms—which are to be expected in that strange institution, the schizophrenic family. But it is still surprising to observe how these strategies may be continually and habitually practiced without friends and neighbors noticing that something is wrong. From theory we may predict that every participant member of such an institution must be defensive of his or her own immanent states of action and enduring adaptive habits; protective, that is, of the self.

To illustrate with one example: a colleague had been

working for some weeks with one of these families, particularly with the father, the mother, and their adult schizophrenic son. His meetings were on the conjoint pattern—the members of the family being present together. This apparently provoked some anxiety in the mother and she requested face-to-face interviews with me. This move was discussed at the next conjoint meeting and in due course she came to her first session. Upon arrival she made a couple of conversational remarks, and then opened her purse and from it handed me a piece of paper, saying, "It seems my husband wrote this." I unfolded the paper and found it to be a single sheet of single-spaced typescript, starting with the words, "My husband and I much appreciate the opportunity of discussing our problems with you," etc. The document then went on to outline certain specific questions which "I would like to raise."

It appeared that the husband had, in fact, sat down at his typewriter the night before and had written this letter to me as though it were written by his wife, and in it he outlined the questions for her to discuss with me.

In normal daily life this sort of thing is common enough; it passes muster. When attention is focused upon the characteristic strategies, however, these self-protecting and self-destroying maneuvers become conspicuous. One suddenly discovers that in such families these strategies seem to predominate over all others. It becomes hardly surprising that the identified patient exhibits behavior which is almost a caricature of that loss of identity which is characteristic of all the family members.

I believe that this is the essence of the matter, that the schizophrenic family is an organization with great ongoing stability whose dynamics and inner workings are such that each member is continually undergoing the experience of negation of self.

# Minimal Requirements for a Theory of

# Schizophrenia*

Every science, like every person, has a duty toward its neighbors, not perhaps to love them as itself, but still to lend them its tools, to borrow tools from them, and, generally, to keep the neighboring sciences straight. We may perhaps judge of the importance of an advance in any one science in terms of the changes which this advance compels the neighboring sciences to make in their methods and in their thinking. But always there is the rule of parsimony. The changes which we in the behavioral sciences may ask for in genetics, or in philosophy, or in information theory must always be minimal. The unity of science as a whole is achieved by this system of minimal demands imposed by each science upon its neighbors, and—not a little—by the lending of conceptual tools and patterns which occurs among the various sciences.

My purpose, therefore, in the present lecture is not so much to discuss the particular theory of schizophrenia which we have been developing at Palo Alto. Rather, I want to indicate to you that this theory and others like it have impact upon ideas about the very nature of explanation. I have used the title "Minimal Requirements for a Theory of Schizo-

* Second Annual Albert D. Lasker Memorial Lecture, delivered at the Institute for Psychosomatic and Psychiatric Research and Training of the Michael Reese Hospital, Chicago, April 7, 1959. This lecture is here reprinted by permission of the *A.M.A. Archives of General Psychiatry* where it appeared in 1960, Vol. 2, pp. 477–491.

phrenia," and what I had in mind in choosing this title was a discussion of the implications of the double bind theory for the wider field of behavioral science and even, beyond that, its effect upon evolutionary theory and biological epistemology. What minimal changes does this theory demand in related sciences?

I want to deal with questions about the impact of an experiential theory of schizophrenia upon that triad of related sciences, learning theory, genetics, and evolution.

The hypothesis may first be briefly described. In its essentials, the idea appeals only to everyday experience, and elementary common sense. The first proposition from which the hypothesis is derived is that learning occurs always in some context which has formal characteristics. You may think, if you will, of the formal characteristics of an instrumental avoidance sequence, or of the formal characteristics of a Pavlovian experiment. To learn to lift a paw in a Pavlovian context is different from learning the same action in a context of instrumental reward.

Further, the hypothesis depends upon the idea that this structured context also occurs within a wider context—a metacontext if you will—and that this sequence of contexts is an open, and conceivably infinite, series.

The hypothesis also assumes that what occurs within the narrow context (*e.g.*, instrumental avoidance) will be affected by the wider context within which this smaller one has its being. There may be incongruence or conflict between context and metacontext. A context of Pavlovian learning may, for example, be set within a metacontext which would punish learning of this kind, perhaps by insisting upon insight. The organism is then faced with the dilemma either of being wrong in the primary context or of being right for the wrong reasons or in a wrong way. This is the so-called double bind. We are investigating the hypothesis that schizophrenic communication is learned and becomes habitual as a result of continual traumata of this kind.

That is all there is to it.

But even these "common-sense" assumptions break away from the classical rules of scientific epistemology. We have learned from the paradigm of the freely falling body—and from many similar paradigms in many other sciences—to approach scientific problems in a peculiar way: the problems are to be simplified by ignoring—or postponing consideration of—the possibility that the larger context may influence the smaller. Our hypothesis runs counter to this rule, and is focused precisely upon the determining relations between larger and smaller contexts.

Even more shocking is the fact that our hypothesis suggests —but does not stand or fall with the suggestion—that there may be an infinite regress of such relevant contexts.

In all of this, the hypothesis requires and reinforces that revision in scientific thought which has been occurring in many fields, from physics to biology. The observer must be included within the focus of observation, and what can be studied is always a relationship or an infinite regress of relationships. Never a "thing."

An example will make clear the relevance of the larger contexts. Let us consider the larger context within which a learning experiment might be conducted using a schizophrenic as a subject. The schizophrenic is what is called a patient, vis-à-vis a member of a superior and unloved organization, the hospital staff. If the patient were a good pragmatic Newtonian, he would be able to say to himself: "The cigarettes which I can get by doing what this fellow expects me to do are after all only cigarettes, and as an applied scientist I will go ahead and do what he wants me to do. I will solve the experimental problem and obtain the cigarettes." But human beings, and especially schizophrenics, do not always see the matter this way. They are affected by the circumstance that the experiment is being conducted by somebody whom they would rather not please. They may even feel that there would be a certain shamelessness about seeking to please some one whom they dislike. It thus comes about that the *sign* of the signal which the experimenter emits, giving or withholding cigarettes, is reversed. What the experimenter thought was a reward turns out to be a message of partial indignity, and what the experimenter thought was a punishment becomes in part a source of satisfaction.

Consider the acute *pain* of the mental patient in a large hospital who is momentarily treated as a human being by a member of the staff.

To explain the observed phenomena we *always* have to consider the wider context of the learning experiment, and *every* transaction between persons is a context of learning.

The double bind hypothesis, then, depends upon attributing certain characteristics to the learning process. If this
hypothesis is even approximately true, room must be made
for it within the theory of learning. In particular, learning
theory must be made discontinuous so as to accommodate the
discontinuities of the hierarchy of the contexts of learning to
which I have referred.

Moreover, these discontinuities are of a peculiar nature. I
have said that the larger context may change the sign of the
reinforcement proposed by a given message, and evidently
the larger context may also change the mode—may place
the message in the category of humor, metaphor, etc. The
setting may make the message inappropriate. The message
may be out of tune with the larger context, and so on. But
there are limits to these modifications. The context may tell
the recipient anything *about* the message, but it cannot ever
destroy or directly contradict the latter. "I was lying when
I said 'The cat is on the mat'" tells the vis-à-vis nothing
about the location of the cat. It tells him only something
about the reliability of his previous information. There is a
gulf between context and message (or between metamessage
and message) which is of the same nature as the gulf between a thing and the word or sign which stands for it, or
between the members of a class and the name of the class.
The context (or metamessage) *classifies* the message, but
can never meet it on equal terms.

In order to fit these discontinuities into learning theory, it
is necessary to enlarge the scope of what is to be included
within the concept of *learning*. What the experimenters have
described as "learning" are in general changes in what an
organism does in response to a given signal. The experimenter observes, for example, that at first the buzzer evokes
no regular response, but that after repeated trials in which
the buzzer has been followed by meat powder, the animal
will begin to salivate whenever it hears the buzzer. We may
say loosely that the animal has begun to attach significance
or meaning to the buzzer.

A change has occurred. In order to construct a hierarchic
series, we pick on the word "change." Series such as we are
interested in are in general built in two ways. Within the
field of pure communications theory, the steps of an hierarchic
series may be constructed by successive use of the word

"about," or "meta." Our hierarchic series will then consist of message, metamessage, meta-metamessage, and so on. Where we deal with phenomena marginal to communications theory, similar hierarchies may be constructed by the piling up of "change" upon "change." In classical physics, the sequence: position; velocity (*i.e.*, change in position); acceleration (*i.e.*, change in velocity or change in change of position); change of acceleration, etc., is an example of such a hierarchy.

Further complications are added—rarely in classical physics but commonly in human communication—by noting that messages may be about (or "meta" to) the relationship between messages of different levels. The smell of the experimental harness may tell the dog that the buzzer will mean meat powder. We will then say that the message of the harness is meta to the message of the buzzer. But in human relations another sort of complexity may be generated; *e.g.*, messages may be emitted forbidding the subject to make the meta connection. An alcoholic parent may punish a child for showing that he knows that he should look out for storms whenever the parent gets the bottle out of the cupboard. The hierarchy of messages and contexts thus becomes a complex branching structure.

So we can construct a similar hierarchic classification within learning theory in substantially the same way as the physicists. What the experimenters have investigated is *change* in the receipt of a signal. But, clearly, to receive a signal already denotes *change*—a change of a simpler or lower order than that which the experimenters have investigated. This gives us the two first steps in a hierarchy of learning, and above these an infinite series can be imagined. This hierarchy[1] can now be laid out as follows:

(1) *The Receipt of a Signal*  I am working at my desk on which there is a paper bag, containing my lunch. I hear the hospital whistle, and from this I know that it is twelve o'clock. I reach out and take my lunch. The whistle may be

[1] 1971. In my final version of this hierarchy of orders of learning, published in this volume as "The Logical Categories of Learning and Communication," (see p. 283) I have used a different system of numbering. The receipt of a signal is there called "Zero Learning"; changes in Zero Learning are called Learning I; "deutero-learning" is called Learning II, etc.

regarded as an answer to a question laid down in my mind by previous learning of the second order; but the single event—the receiving of this piece of information—is a piece of learning, and is demonstrated to be so by the fact that having received it, I am now changed and respond in a special way to the paper bag.

(2) *Those Learnings Which Are Changes in* (1) These are exemplified by the classical learning experiments of various kinds: Pavlovian, instrumental reward, instrumental avoidance, rote, and so on.

(3) *Those Learnings Which Constitute Changes in Second-Order Learning* I have in the past, unfortunately, called these phenomena "deutero-learning," and have translated this as "learning to learn." It would have been more correct to coin the word trito-learning and to translate it as "learning to learn to receive signals." These are the phenomena in which the psychiatrist is preponderantly interested, namely, the changes whereby an individual comes to expect his world to be structured in one way rather than another. These are the phenomena which underlie "transference"—the expectation on a patient's part that the relationship with the therapist will contain the same sorts of contexts of learning that the patient has previously met with in dealing with his parents.

(4) *Changes in Those Processes of Change Referred to in* (3) Whether learning of this fourth order occurs in human beings is unknown. What the psychotherapist attempts to produce in his patient is usually a third-order learning, but it is possible, and certainly conceivable, that some of the slow and unconscious changes may be shifts in sign of some higher derivative in the learning process.

At this point it is necessary to compare three types of hierarchy with which we are faced: (*a*) the hierarchy of *orders* of learning; (*b*) the hierarchy of contexts of learning, and (*c*) hierarchies of circuit structure which we may—indeed, must—expect to find in a telencephalized brain.

It is my contention that (*a*) and (*b*) are synonymous in the sense that all statements made in terms of contexts of learning could be translated (without loss or gain) into statements in terms of orders of learning, and, further, that the classification or hierarchy of contexts must be isomorphic with the classification or hierarchy of orders of learning. Beyond this, I believe that we should look forward to a classification or hierarchy of neurophysiological structures which will be isomorphic with the other two classifications.

This synonymy between statements about context and statements about orders of learning seems to me to be self-evident, but experience shows that it must be spelled out. "The truth cannot be said so as to be understood, and not be believed," but, conversely, it cannot be believed *until* it is said so as to be understood.

It is necessary first to insist that in the world of communication the only relevant entities or "realities" are messages, including in this term parts of messages, relations between messages, significant gaps in messages, and so on. The *perception* of an event or object or relation is real. It is a neurophysiological message. But the event itself or the object itself cannot enter this world and is, therefore, irrelevant and, to that extent, unreal. Conversely, a message has no reality or relevance qua message, in the Newtonian world: it there is reduced to sound waves or printer's ink.

By the same token, the "contexts" and "contexts of contexts" upon which I am insisting are only real or relevant insofar as they are communicationally effective, *i.e.*, function as messages or modifiers of messages.

The difference between the Newtonian world and the world of communication is simply this: that the Newtonian world ascribes reality to objects and achieves its simplicity by excluding the context of the context—excluding indeed all metarelationships—a fortiori excluding an infinite regress of such relations. In contrast, the theorist of communication insists upon examining the metarelationships while achieving its simplicity by excluding all objects.

This world, of communication, is a Berkeleyan world, but the good bishop was guilty of understatement. Relevance or reality must be denied not only to the sound of the tree which falls unheard in the forest but also to this chair which I can see and on which I am sitting. My perception of the chair is communicationally real, and that on which I sit is, for me, only an idea, a message in which I put my trust.

"In my *thought*, one thing is as good as another in this world, and the shoe of a horse will do," because in thought and in experience there are no things, but only messages and the like.

In this world, indeed, I, as a material object, have no relevance and, in this sense, no reality. "I," however, exist in the communicational world as an essential element in the syntax of my experience and in the experience of others, and the communications of others may damage my identity, even to the point of breaking up the organization of my experience.

Perhaps one day, an ultimate synthesis will be achieved to combine the Newtonian and the communicational worlds. But that is not the purpose of the present discussion. Here I am concerned to make clear the relation between the contexts and the orders of learning, and to do this it was first necessary to bring into focus the difference between Newtonian and communicational discourse.

With this introductory statement, however, it becomes clear that the separation between contexts and orders of learning is only an artifact of the contrast between these two sorts of discourse. The separation is only maintained by saying that the contexts have location outside the physical individual, while the orders of learning are located inside. But in the communicational world, this dichotomy is irrelevant and meaningless. The contexts have communicational reality only insofar as they are effective as messages, *i.e.*, insofar as they are represented or reflected (correctly or with distortion) in *multiple* parts of the communicational system which we are studying; and this system is not the physical individual but a wide network of pathways of messages. Some of these pathways *happen* to be located outside the physical individual, others inside; but the characteristics of the *system* are in no way dependent upon any boundary lines which we may superpose upon the communicational map. It is not communicationally meaningful to ask whether the blind man's stick or the scientist's microscope are "parts" of the man who uses them. Both stick and microscope are important pathways of communication and, as such, are parts of the network in which we are interested; but no boundary line—*e.g.*, halfway up the stick—can be relevant in a description of the topology of this net.

However, this discarding of the boundary of the physical individual does not imply (as some might fear) that communicational discourse is necessarily chaotic. On the contrary, the proposed hierarchic classification of learning and/

or context is an ordering of what to the Newtonian looks like chaos, and it is this ordering that is demanded by the double-bind hypothesis.

Man must be the sort of animal whose learning is characterized by hierarchic discontinuities of this sort, else he could not become schizophrenic under the frustrations of the double bind.

On the evidential side, there is beginning to be a body of experiment demonstrating the reality of third-order learning[2]; but on the precise point of *discontinuity* between these orders of learning there is, so far as I know, very little evidence. The experiments of John Stroud are worth quoting. These were tracking experiments. The subject is faced with a screen on which a spot moves to represent a moving target. A second spot, representing the aim of a gun, can be controlled by the subject, who operates a pair of knobs. The subject is challenged to maintain coincidence between the target spot and the spot over which he has control. In such an experiment the target can be given various sorts of motion, characterized by second-, third-, or higher-order derivatives. Stroud showed that, as there is a discontinuity in the orders of the equations which a mathematician might use to describe the movements of the target spot, so also there is a discontinuity in the learning of the experimental subject. It is as if a new learning process were involved with each step to a higher order of complexity in the movement of the target.

It is to me fascinating to find that what one had supposed was a pure artifact of mathematical description is also apparently an inbuilt characteristic of the human brain, in spite of the fact that this brain certainly does not operate by means of mathematical equations in such a task.

There is also evidence of a more general nature which would support the notion of discontinuity between the orders of learning. There is, for example, the curious fact that psychologists have not habitually regarded what I call learn-

[2] C. L. Hull, *et al.*, *Mathematico-deductive Theory of Rote Learning: A Study in Scientific Methodology*, (Yale University Institute of Human Relations), New Haven, Yale University Press, 1940; also H. F. Harlow, "The Formation of Learning Sets," *Psychol. Review*, 1949, 56: 51–65.

ing of the first order, the receipt of a meaningful signal, as learning at all; and the other curious fact, that psychologists have until recently shown very little appreciation of that third order of learning, in which the psychiatrist is predominantly interested. There is a formidable gulf between the thinking of the experimental psychologist and the thinking of the psychiatrist or anthropologist. This gulf I believe to be due to the discontinuity in the hierarchic structure.

## Learning, Genetics, and Evolution

Before we consider the impact of the double bind hypothesis upon genetics and evolutionary theory, it is necessary to examine the relationship between theories of learning and these two other bodies of knowledge. I referred earlier to the three subjects together as a triad. The structure of this triad we must now consider.

Genetics, which covers the communicational phenomena of variation, differentiation, growth, and heredity, is commonly recognized as the very stuff of which evolutionary theory is made. The Darwinian theory, when purged of Lamarckian ideas, consisted of a genetics in which variation was presumed to be random, combined with a theory of natural selection would impart adaptive direction to the accumulation of changes. But the relation between learning and this theory has been a matter of violent controversy which has raged over the so-called "inheritance of acquired characteristics."

Darwin's position was acutely challenged by Samuel Butler, who argued that heredity should be compared with—even identified with—memory. Butler proceeded from this premise to argue that the processes of evolutionary change, and especially adaptation, should be regarded as the achievements of a deep cunning in the ongoing flow of life, not as fortuitous bonuses conferred by luck. He drew a close analogy between the phenomena of invention and the phenomena of evolutionary adaptation, and was perhaps the first to point out the existence of residual organs in machines. The curious homology whereby the engine is located in the front of an automobile, where the horse used to be, would have delighted him. He also argued very cogently that there

is a process whereby the newer inventions of adaptive behavior are sunk deeper into the biological system of the
organism. From planned and conscious actions they become
habits, and the habits become less and less conscious and
less and less subject to voluntary control. He assumed, without evidence, that this habitualization, or sinking process,
could go so deep as to contribute to the body of memories,
which we would call the genotype, and which determine
the characteristics of the next generation.

The controversy about the inheritance of acquired characteristics has two facets. On the one hand, it appears to be
an argument which could be settled by factual material.
One good case of such inheritance might settle the matter
for the Lamarckian side. But the case against such inheritance, being negative, can never be proved by evidence and
must rely upon an appeal to theory. Usually those who take
the negative view argue from the separation between germ
plasm and somatic tissue, urging that there can be no systematic communication from the soma to the germ plasm in
the light of which the genotype might revise itself.

The difficulty looks like this: conceivably a biceps muscle
modified by use or disuse might secrete specific metabolites
into the circulation, and these might conceivably serve as
chemical messengers from muscle to gonad. But (a) it is
difficult to believe that the chemistry of biceps is so different from that of, say, triceps that the message could be
specific, and (b) it is difficult to believe that the gonad
tissue could be equipped to be appropriately affected by
such messages. After all, the receiver of any message must
know the code of the sender, so that if the germ cells are
able to receive the messages from the somatic tissue, they
must already be carrying some version of the somatic code.
The directions which evolutionary change could take with
the aid of such messages from the soma would have to be
*pre*figured in the germ plasm.

The case against the inheritance of acquired characteristics thus rests upon a separation, and the difference between the schools of thought crystallizes around philosophic
reactions to such a separation. Those who are willing to
think of the world as organized upon multiple and separable
principles will accept the notion that somatic changes induced by environment may be covered by an explanation

which could be totally separate from the explanation of evolutionary change. But those who prefer to see a unity in nature will hope that these two bodies of explanation can somehow be interrelated.

Moreover, the whole relationship between learning and evolution has undergone a curious change since the days when Butler maintained that evolution was a matter of cunning rather than luck, and the change which has taken place is certainly one which neither Darwin nor Butler could have foreseen. What has happened is that many theorists now assume learning to be fundamentally a stochastic or probabilistic affair, and indeed, apart from nonparsimonious theories which would postulate some entelechy at the console of the mind, the stochastic approach is perhaps the only organized theory of the nature of learning. The notion is that random changes occur, in the brain or elsewhere, and that the results of such random change are selected for survival by processes of reinforcement and extinction. In basic theory, creative thought has come to resemble the evolutionary process in its fundamentally stochastic nature. Reinforcement is seen as giving direction to the accumulation of random changes of the neural system, just as natural selection is seen as giving direction to the accumulation of random changes of variation.

In both the theory of evolution and the theory of learning, however, the word "random" is conspicuously undefined, and the word is not an easy one to define. In both fields, it is assumed that while change may be dependent upon probabilistic phenomena, the probability of a given change is determined by something different from probability. Underlying both the stochastic theory of evolution and that of learning, there are unstated theories regarding the determinants of the probabilities in question.[3] If, however, we ask about change in these determinants, we shall again be given stochastic answers, so that the word "random," upon which all of these explanations turn, appears to be a word whose meaning is hierarchically structured, like the meaning of the word "learning," which was discussed in the first part of this lecture.

> [3] In this sense, of course, all the theories of change assume that the *next* change is in some degree prefigured in the system which is to undergo that change.

Lastly, the question of the evolutionary function of acquired characteristics has been reopened by Waddington's work on phenocopies in *Drosophila*. At the very least, this work indicates that the changes of phenotype which can be achieved by the organism under environmental stress are a very important part of the machinery by which the species or hereditary line maintains its place in a stressful and competitive environment, pending the later appearance of some mutation or other genetic change which may make the species or line better able to deal with the ongoing stress. In this sense at least, the acquired characteristics have important evolutionary function. However, the actual experimental story indicates something more than this and is worth reproducing briefly.

What Waddington works with is a phenocopy of the phenotype brought about by the gene bithorax. This gene has very profound effects upon the adult phenotype. In its presence the third segment of the thorax is modified to resemble the second, and the little balancing organs, or halteres, on this third segment become wings. The result is a four-winged fly. This four-winged characteristic can be produced artificially in flies which do not carry the gene bithorax by subjecting the pupae to a period of intoxication with ethyl ether. Waddington works with large populations of *Drosophila* flies derived from a wild strain believed to be free of the gene bithorax. He subjects the pupae of this population in successive generations to the ether treatment, and from the resulting adults selects for breeding those which show the best approximation to bithorax. He has continued this experiment over many generations, and already in the twenty-seventh generation he finds that the bithorax appearance is achieved by a limited number of flies whose pupae were withdrawn from the experimental treatment and not subjected to ether. Upon breeding from these, it turns out that their bithorax appearance is not due to the presence of the specific gene, bithorax, but is due to a constellation of genes which work together to give this effect.

These very striking results can be read in various ways. We can say that in selecting the best phenocopies, Waddington was in fact selecting for a genetic potentiality for achieving this phenotype. Or we can say that he was selecting to reduce the threshold of ether stress necessary to produce this result.

Let me suggest a possible model for the description of these phenomena. Let us suppose that the acquired characteristic is achieved by some process of fundamentally stochastic nature—perhaps some sort of somatic learning—and the mere fact that Waddington is able to select the "best" phenocopies would lend support to this assumption. Now, it is evident that any such process is, in the nature of the case, wasteful. To achieve a result by trial and error which could have been achieved in any more direct way necessarily consumes time and effort in some sense of these words. Insofar as we think of adaptability as achieved by stochastic process, we let in the notion of an economics of adaptability.

In the field of mental process, we are very familiar with this sort of economics, and in fact a major and necessary saving is achieved by the familiar process of habit formation. We may, in the first instance, solve a given problem by trial and error; but when similar problems recur later, we tend to deal with them more and more economically by taking them out of the range of stochastic operation and handing over the solutions to a deeper and less flexible mechanism, which we call "habit." It is, therefore, perfectly conceivable that some analogous phenomenon may obtain in regard to the production of bithorax characteristics. It may be more economical to produce these by the rigid mechanism of genetic determination rather than by the more wasteful, more flexible (and perhaps less predictable) method of somatic change.

This would mean that in Waddington's population of flies there would be a selective benefit for any hereditary line of flies which might contain appropriate genes for the whole—or for some part—of the bithorax phenotype. It is also possible that such flies would have an extra advantage in that their somatic adaptive machinery might then be available for dealing with stresses of other kinds. It would appear that in learning, when the solution of the given problem has been passed on to habit, the stochastic or exploratory mechanisms are set free for the solution of other problems, and it is quite conceivable that a similar advantage is achieved by passing on the business of determining a somatic characteristic to the gene-script.[4]

It may be noted that such a model would be characterized by *two* stochastic mechanisms: first, the more superficial mechanism by which the changes are achieved at the somatic level, and, second, the stochastic mechanism of mutation (or the shuffling of gene constellations) at the chromosomal level. These two stochastic systems will, in the long run *under selective conditions*, be compelled to work together, even though no message can pass from the more superficial somatic system to the germ plasm. Samuel Butler's hunch that something like "habit" might be crucial in evolution was perhaps not too wide of the mark.

With this introduction we can now proceed to look at the problems which a double bind theory of schizophrenia would pose for the geneticist.

## Genetic Problems Posed by Double Bind Theory

If schizophrenia be a modification or distortion of the learning process, then when we ask about the genetics of schizophrenia, we cannot be content just with genealogies upon which we discriminate some individuals who have been committed to hospitals, and others who have not. There is no a priori expectation that these distortions of the learning process, which are highly formal and abstract in their nature, will necessarily appear with that appropriate content which would result in hospital commitment. Our task as geneticists will not be the simple one upon which the Mendelians concentrated, assuming a one-to-one relation between phenotype and genotype. We cannot simply assume that the hos-

[4] These considerations alter somewhat the old problem of the evolutionary effect of use and disuse. Orthodox theory could only suggest that a mutation reducing the (potential) size of a disused organ had survival value in terms of the resulting economy of tissue. The present theory would suggest that atrophy of an organ, occurring at the somatic level, may constitute a drain upon the total available adaptability of the organism, and that this waste of adaptability might be saved if reduction of the organ could be achieved more directly by genetic determinants.

pitalized members carry a gene for schizophrenia and that the others do not. Rather, we have to expect that several genes or constellations of genes will alter patterns and potentialities in the learning process, and that certain of the resultant patterns, when confronted by appropriate forms of environmental stress, will lead to overt schizophrenia.

In the most general terms, any learning, be it the absorption of one bit of information or a basic change in the character structure of the whole organism, is, from the point of view of genetics, the acquisition of an "acquired characteristic." It is a change in the phenotype, of which that phenotype was capable thanks to a whole chain of physiologic and embryologic processes which lead back to the genotype. Every step in this backward leading series may (conceivably) be modified or interrupted by environmental impacts; but, of course, many of the steps will be rigid in the sense that environmental impact at that point would destroy the organism. We are concerned only with those points in the hierarchy at which environment can take effect and the organism still be viable. How many such points there may be we are far from knowing. And ultimately, when we reach the genotype, we are concerned to know whether the genotypic elements in which we are interested are or are not variable. Do differences occur from genotype to genotype which will affect the modifiability of the processes leading to the phenotypic behaviors which we observe?

In the case of schizophrenia we deal evidently with a relatively long and complex hierarchy; and the natural history of the disease indicates that the hierarchy is not merely a chain of causes and effects from gene-script to phenotype, which chain becomes at certain points conditional upon environmental factors. Rather, it seems that in schizophrenia the enviromental factors themselves are likely to be modified by the subject's behavior whenever behavior related to schizophrenia starts to appear.

To illustrate these complexities, it is perhaps worthwhile to consider for a moment the genetic problems presented by other forms of communicational behavior—humor, mathematical skill, or musical composition. Perhaps in all these cases, there are considerable genetic differences between individuals in those factors which make for an ability to acquire the appropriate skills. But the skills themselves and their particular expression also depend largely upon environmental circumstances and even upon specific training. In addition, however, to these two components of the situation, there is the fact that the individual who shows ability, *e.g.*, in musical composition, is likely to mold his environment in a direction which will favor his developing his ability, and that he will, in turn, create an environment for others which will favor their development in the same direction.

In the case of humor, the situation may even be one degree more complicated. It is not clear that in this case the relationship between humorist and his human environment will necessarily be symmetrical. Granted that in some cases the humorist promotes humor in others, in many other cases there occurs the well-known complementary relationship between humorist and "straight" man. Indeed, the humorist, insofar as he hogs the center of the stage, may reduce others to the position of receiving humor but not themselves contributing.

These considerations can be applied unchanged to the problem of schizophrenia. Anybody watching the transactions which occur between the members of a family containing an identified schizophrenic will perceive immediately that the symptomatic behavior of the identified patient fits with this environment and, indeed, promotes in the other members those characteristics which evoke the schizophrenic behavior. Thus, in addition to the two stochastic mechanisms outlined in the previous section, we now face a third, namely the mechanism of those changes whereby the family, perhaps gradually, becomes organized (*i.e.*, limits the behaviors of the component individuals) in such a way as to fit the schizophrenia.

A question which is frequently asked is this: "If this family is schizophrenogenic, how does it happen that all of the siblings are not diagnosable as schizophrenic patients?" Here it is necessary to insist that the family, like any other organization, creates and depends upon differentiation among its members. As in many organizations, there is room only for one boss, in spite of the fact that the organization operates upon those premises which would induce administrative skill and ambition in its members; so also in the schizophrenogenic family there may be room for only one schizophrenic. The case of the humorist is quite comparable. The organization of the Marx family, which could create four professional humorists, must have been quite exceptional. More usually one such individual would suffice to reduce the others to more commonplace behavioral roles. Genetics may play a role in deciding which of several siblings shall be the schizophrenic—or which shall be the clown—but it is by no means clear that such hereditary factors could completely determine the evolution or roles within the family organization.

A second question—to which we have no final answer—concerns the degree of schizophrenia (genetic and/or acquired) which must be assigned to the schizophrenogenic parent. Let me, for purposes of the present inquiry, define two degrees of schizophrenic symptomatology, and note that the so-called "psychotic break" sometimes divides these two degrees.

The more serious and conspicuous degree of symptomatology is what is conventionally called schizophrenia. I will call it "overt schizophrenia." The persons so afflicted behave in ways which are grossly deviant from the cultural environment. In particular, their behavior seems characterized by conspicuous or exaggerated errors and distortions regarding the nature and typing of their own messages (internal and external), and of the messages which they receive from others. Imagination is seemingly confused with perception. The literal is confused with the metaphoric. Internal messages are confused with external. The trivial is confused with the vital. The originator of the message is confused with the recipient and the perceiver with the thing perceived. And so on. In general, these distortions boil down to this: that the patient behaves in such a way that he shall be responsible for no metacommunicative aspect of his messages. He does this, moreover, in a manner which makes his condition conspicuous: in some cases, flooding the environment with messages whose logical typing is either totally obscure or misleading; in other cases, overtly withdrawing to such a point that he commits himself to no overt message.

In the "covert" case the behavior of the identified patient is similarly but less conspicuously characterized by a continual changing of the logical typing of his or her messages, and a tendency to respond to the messages of others (especially to those of other family members) as though these were of logical type, different from that which the speaker intended. In this system of behavior the messages of the vis-à-vis are continually disqualified, either by indicating that they are inappropriate replies to what the covert schizophrenic has said or by indicating that they are the product of some fault in the character or motivation of the speaker. Moreover, this destructive behavior is in general maintained in such a way as to be undetected. So long as the covert schizophrenic can succeed in putting the other in the wrong, his or her pathology is obscured and the blame falls elsewhere. There is some evidence that these persons fear collapse into overt schizophrenia when faced by circumstances which would force them to recognize the pattern of their operations. They will even use the threat, "You are driving me crazy," as a defense of their position.

What I am here calling covert schizophrenia is characteristic of the parents of schizophrenics in the families which we have studied. This behavior, when it occurs in the mother, has been extensively caricatured; so I shall use here an example of which the central figure is the father. Mr. and Mrs. P. had been married some eighteen years and have a near-hebephrenic son of sixteen. Their marriage is difficult and is characterized by almost continual hostility. However, she is a keen gardener, and on a certain Sunday afternoon they worked together planting roses in what was to be her rose garden. She recalls that this was an unusually pleasant occasion. On Monday morning, the husband went to work as usual, and while he was gone Mrs. P. received a phone call from a complete stranger inquiring, rather apologetically, when Mrs. P. was going to leave the house. This came as somewhat of a surprise. She did not know that from her husband's point of view the messages of shared work on the rose garden were framed within the larger context of his having agreed during the previous week to sell the house.

In some cases, it almost looks as though the overt schizophrenic were a caricature of the covert.

If we assume that both the grossly schizophrenic symptoms of the identified patient and the "covert schizophrenia" of the parents are in part determined by genetic factors, *i.e.*, that, given the appropriate experiential setting, genetics in some degree renders the patient more liable to develop these particular patterns of behavior, then we have to ask how these two degrees of pathology might be related in a genetic theory.

Certainly, no answer to this question is at present available, but it is clearly possible we here face two quite distinct problems. In the case of the overt schizophrenic, the geneticist will have to identify those formal characteristics of the patient which will render him more likely to be driven to a psychotic break by the covertly inconsistent behavior of his parents (or by this in conjunction and contrast with the more consistent behavior of people outside the family). It is too early to make a specific guess at these characteristics, but we may reasonably assume that they would include some sort of rigidity. Perhaps the person prone to overt schizophrenia would be characterized by some extra strength of psychological commitment to the *status quo* as he at the moment sees it, which commitment would be hurt or frustrated by the parents' rapid shifts of frame and context. Or perhaps this patient might be characterized by the high value of some parameter determining the relationship between problem solving and habit formation. Perhaps it is the person who too readily hands over the solutions to habit who is hurt by those changes in context which invalidate his solutions just at the moment when he has incorporated them into his habit structure.

In the case of covert schizophrenia, the problem for the geneticist will be different. He will have to identify those formal characteristics which we observe in the parents of the schizophrenic. Here what is required would seem to be a flexibility rather than a rigidity. But, having had some experience in dealing with these people, I must confess to feeling that they are rigidly committed to their patterns of inconsistency.

Whether the two questions which the geneticist must answer can simply be lumped together by regarding the covert patterns as merely a milder version of the overt, or can be brought under a single head by suggesting that in some sense the same rigidity operates at different levels in the two cases, I do not know.

Be that as it may, the difficulties which we here face are entirely characteristic of any attempt to find a genetic base for any behavioral characteristic. Notoriously, the *sign* of any message or behavior is subject to reversal, and this generalization is one of the most important contributions of psychoanalysis, to our thinking. If we find that a sexual exhibitionist is the child of a prudish parent, are we justified in going to the geneticist to ask him to trace out the genetics of some basic characteristic which will find its phenotypic expression both in the prudishness of the parent and in the exhibitionism of the offspring? The phenomena of suppression and overcompensation lead continually to the difficulty that an excess of something at one level (*e.g.*, in the genotype) may lead to a deficiency of the direct expression of that something at some more superficial level (*e.g.*, in the phenotype). And conversely.

We are very far, then, from being able to pose specific questions for the geneticist; but I believe that the wider implications of what I have been saying modify somewhat the philosophy of genetics. Our approach to the problems of schizophrenia by way of a theory of levels or logical types has disclosed first that the problems of adaptation and learning and their pathologies must be considered in terms of a hierarchic system in which stochastic change occurs at the boundary points between the segments of the hierarchy. We have considered three such regions of stochastic change —the level of genetic mutation, the level of learning, and the level of change in family organization. We have disclosed the possibility of a relationship of these levels which orthodox genetics would deny, and we have disclosed that at least in human societies the evolutionary system consists not merely in the selective survival of those persons who happen to select appropriate environments but also in the modification of family environment in a direction which might enhance the phenotypic and genotypic characteristics of the individual members.

## What Is Man?

If I had been asked fifteen years ago what I understood by the word materialism, I think I should have said that materialism is a theory about the nature of the universe, and I would have accepted as a matter of course the notion that this theory is in some sense nonmoral. I would have agreed that the scientist is an expert who can provide himself and others with insights and techniques, but that science could have nothing to say about whether these techniques *should* be used. In this, I would have been following the general trend of scientific philosophy associated with such names at Democritus, Galileo, Newton,[5] Lavoisier, and Darwin. I would have been discarding the less respectable views of such men as Heraclitus, the alchemists, William Blake, Lamarck, and Samuel Butler. For these, the motive for scientific inquiry was the desire to build a comprehensive view of the universe which should show what Man is and how he is related to the rest of the universe. The picture which these men were trying to build was ethical and aesthetic.

There is this much connection certainly between scientific truth, on the one hand, and beauty and morality, on the other: that if a man entertain false opinions regarding his own nature, he will be led thereby to courses of action which will be in some profound sense immoral or ugly.

Today, if asked the same question regarding the meaning of materialism, I would say that this word stands in my thinking for a collection of rules about what questions should be asked regarding the nature of the universe. But I would not suppose that this set of rules has any claim to be uniquely right.

The mystic "sees the world in a grain of sand," and the world which he sees is either moral or aesthetic, or both. The Newtonian scientist sees a regularity in the behavior of falling bodies and claims to draw from this regularity no normative conclusions whatsoever. But his claim ceases to be consistent at the moment when he preaches that this is the right way to view the universe. To preach is possible only in terms of normative conclusions.

I have touched upon several matters in the course of this

[5]The *name* of Newton certainly belongs in this list. But the man himself was of a different kidney. His mystical preoccupation with alchemy and apocalyptic writings, and his secret theological monism indicate that he was not the first objective scientist but, rather, the "last of the magicians" (see J. M. Keynes, "Newton, the Man," Tercentenary Celebrations, London, Cambridge University Press, 1947, pp. 27–34). Newton and Blake were alike in devoting much time and thought to the mystical works of Jacob Boehme.

lecture which have been foci of controversy in the long battle between a nonmoral materialism and a more romantic view of the universe. The battle between Darwin and Samuel Butler may have owed some of its bitterness to what looked like personal affronts, but behind all this the argument concerned a question which had religious status. The battle was really about "vitalism." It was a question of how much *life* and what order of life could be assigned to organisms; and Darwin's victory amounted to this, that while he had not succeeded in detracting from the mysterious liveliness of the individual organism, he had at least demonstrated that the evolutionary picture could be reduced to natural "law."

It was, therefore, very important to demonstrate that the as yet unconquered territory—the life of the individual organism—could not contain anything which would recapture this evolutionary territory. It was still mysterious that living organisms could achieve adaptive change during their individual lives, and at all costs these adaptive changes, the famous acquired characteristics, must not have influence upon the evolutionary tree. The "inheritance of acquired characteristics" threatened always to recapture the field of evolution for the vitalist side. One part of biology must be separate from the other. The objective scientists claimed, of course, to believe in a unity in nature—that ultimately the whole of natural phenomena would prove susceptible to their analysis, but for about a hundred years it was convenient to set up an impermeable screen between the biology of the individual and the theory of evolution. Samuel Butler's "inherited memory" was an attack upon this screen.

The question with which I am concerned in this concluding section of the lecture could be put in various ways. Is the battle between nonmoral materialism and the more mystical view of the universe affected by a change in the function assigned to the "acquired characteristics?" Does the older materialist thesis really depend upon the premise that contexts are isolable? Or is our view of the world changed when we admit an infinite regress of contexts, linked to each other in a complex network of metarelations? Does the possibility that the separate levels of stochastic change (in phenotype and genotype) may be connected in the larger context of the ecological system alter our allegiance in the battle?

In breaking away from the premise that contexts are always conceptually isolable, I have let in the notion of a universe much more unified—and in that sense much more mystical—than the conventional universe of nonmoral materialism. Does the new position so achieved give us new grounds for hope that science might answer moral or aesthetic questions?

I believe that the position is significantly changed, and perhaps I can best make this clear by considering a matter which you as psychiatrists have thought about many times. I mean the matter of "control" and the whole related complex suggested by such words as manipulation, spontaneity, free will, and technique. I think you will agree with me that there is no area in which false premises regarding the nature of the self and its relation to others can be so surely productive of destruction and ugliness as this area of ideas about control. A human being in relation with another has very limited control over what happens in that relationship. He is a *part* of a two-person unit, and the control which any part can have over any whole is strictly limited.

The infinite regress of contexts which I have talked about is only another example of the same phenomenon. What I have contributed to this discussion is the notion that the contrast between part and whole, whenever this contrast appears in the realm of communication, is simply a contrast in logical typing. The whole is always in a metarelationship with its parts. As in logic the proposition can never determine the meta proposition, so also in matters of control the smaller context can never determine the larger. I have remarked (*e.g.*, when discussing the phenomena of phenotypic compensation) that in hierarchies of logical typing there is often some sort of change of sign at each level, when the levels are related to each other in such a way as to create a self-corrective system. This appears in a simple diagrammatic form in the initiatory hierarchy which I studied in a New Guinea tribe. The initiators are the natural enemies of the novices, because it is their task to bully the novices into shape. The men who initiated the present initiators now have a role of criticizing what is now being done in the initiation ceremonies, and this makes them the natural allies of the present novices. And so on. Something of the same sort also occurs in American college fraternities, where juniors tend to be allied with freshmen and seniors with sophomores.

This gives us a view of the world which is still almost unexplored. But some of its complexities may be suggested by a very crude and imperfect analogy. I think that the functioning of such hierarchies may be compared with the business of trying to back a truck to which one or more trailers are attached. Each segmentation of such a system denotes a reversal of sign, and each added segment denotes a drastic decrease in the amount of control that can be exerted by the driver of the truck. If the system is parallel to the right-hand side of the road, and he wants the trailer immediately behind him to approach the right-hand side, he must turn his front wheels to the left. This will guide the rear of the truck away from the right-hand side of the road so that the front of the trailer is pulled over to its left. This will now cause the rear of the trailer to point toward the right. And so on.

As anybody who has attempted this will know, the amount of available control falls off rapidly. To back a truck with one trailer is already difficult because there is only a limited range of angles within which the control can be exerted. If the trailer is in line, or almost in line, with the truck, the control is easy, but as the angle between trailer and truck diminishes, a point is reached at which control is lost and the attempt to exert it only results in jackknifing of the system. When we consider the problem of controlling a second trailer, the threshold for jackknifing is drastically reduced, and control becomes, therefore, almost negligible.

As I see it, the world is made up of a very complex network (rather than a chain) of entities which have this sort of relationship to each other, but with this difference, that many of the entities have their own supplies of energy and perhaps even their own ideas of where they would like to go.

In such a world the problems of control become more akin to art than to science, not merely because we tend to think of the difficult and the unpredictable as contexts for art but also because the results of error are likely to be ugliness.

Let me then conclude with a warning that we social scientists would do well to hold back our eagerness to control that world which we so imperfectly understand. The fact of our imperfect understanding should not be allowed to feed our anxiety and so increase the need to control. Rather, our studies could be inspired by a more ancient, but today less honored, motive: a curiosity about the world of which we are part. The rewards of such work are not power but beauty.

It is a strange fact that every great scientific advance— not least the advances which Newton achieved—has been elegant.

## Additional References

W. R. Ashby, *Design for a Brain*, New York, John Wiley & Sons, Inc., 1952.

————, *Introduction to Cybernetics*, New York and London, John Wiley & Sons, Inc., 1956.

G. Bateson, D. D. Jackson, J. Haley, and J. H. Weakland, "Toward a Theory of Schizophrenia," *Behavioral Science*, 1956, 1: 251–64.

G. Bateson, "Cultural Problems Posed by a Study of Schizophrenic Process," *Symposium on Schizophrenia, an Integrated Approach*, by Alfred Auerback, M. D., ed., American Psychiatric Association, Symposium of the Hawaiian Divisional Meeting, 1958, New York, Ronald Press, 1959.

————, "The New Conceptual Frames for Behavioral Research," *Proceedings of the Sixth Annual Psychiatric Conference at the New Jersey Neuro-Psychiatric Institute*, Princeton, 1958, pp. 54–71.

————, "The Group Dynamics of Schizophrenia," *Chronic Schizophrenia*, L. Appleby, J. M. Scher, and J. H. Cummings, eds., Glencoe, Ill., The Free Press, 1960.

————, "Social Planning and the Concept of Deutero-Learning," *Relation to the Democratic Way of Life*, Conference on Science, Philosophy and Religion, Second Symposium, led by L. Bryson and L. Finkelstein, New York, Harper & Bros., 1942.

————, *Naven, a Survey of Problems Suggested by a*

*Composite Picture of Culture of a New Guinea Tribe Drawn from Three Points of View,* Ed. 2, Stanford, Calif., Stanford University Press, 1958.

S. Butler, *Thought and Language,* 1890, published in the Shrewsbury Edition of the works of Samuel Butler, 1925, vol. xix.

―――, *Luck or Cunning as the Main Means of Organic Modification,* London, Trubner, 1887.

C. D. Darlington, "The Origins of Darwinism," *Scientific American,* 1959, 200: 60–65.

C. Darwin, *On the Origin of Species, by Means of Natural Selection,* London, Murray, 1859.

C. C. Gillispie, "Lamarck and Darwin in the History of Science," *American Scientist,* 1958, 46: 388–409.

J. Stroud, "Psychological Moment in Perception-Discussion," *Cybernetics: Circular Causal and Feedback Mechanisms in Biological and Social Systems,* Transactions of the Sixth Conference, H. Von Foerster, *et al.,* eds., New York, Josiah Macy, Jr. Foundation, 1949, pp. 27–63.

C. H. Waddington, *The Strategy of the Genes,* London, George Allen & Unwin, Ltd., 1957.

―――, "The Integration of Gene-Controlled Processes and Its Bearing on Evolution," *Caryologia,* Supplement, 1954, pp. 232–45.

―――, "Genetic Assimilation of an Acquired Character," *Evolution,* 1953, 7: 118–26.

A. Weismann, *Essays upon Heredity,* authorized translation, E. B. Poulton, *et al.,* eds., Oxford, Clarendon Press, 1889.

# Double Bind, 1969*

Double bind theory was, for me, an exemplification of how to think about such matters and, in this aspect at least, the whole business is worth some re-examination.

Sometimes—often in science and always in art—one does not know what the problems were till after they have been solved. So perhaps it will be useful to state retrospectively what problems were solved for me by double bind theory.

First there was the problem of reification.

Clearly there are in the mind no objects or events—no pigs, no coconut palms, and no mothers. The mind contains only transforms, percepts, images, etc., and rules for making these transforms, percepts, etc. In what form these rules exist we do not know, but presumably they are embodied in the very machinery which creates the transforms. The rules are certainly not commonly explicit as conscious "thoughts."

In any case, it is nonsense to say that a man was frightened by a lion, because a lion is not an idea. The man makes an *idea* of the lion.

The explanatory world of *substance* can invoke no differences and no ideas but only forces and impacts. And, per contra, the world of *form* and communication invokes no things, forces, or impacts but only differences and ideas. (A

*This paper was given in August, 1969, at a Symposium on the Double Bind; Chairman, Dr. Robert Ryder; sponsored by the American Psychological Association. It was prepared under Career Development Award (MH-21,931) of the National Institute of Mental Health.

271

difference which makes a difference *is* an idea. It is a "bit," a unit of information.)

But these things I learned only later—was enabled to learn them by double bind theory. And yet, of course, they are implicit in the theory which could hardly have been created without them.

Our original paper on the double bind contains numerous errors due simply to our having not yet articulately examined the reification problem. We talk in that paper as though a double bind were a something and as though such some-things could be counted.

Of course that's all nonsense. You cannot count the bats in an inkblot because there are none. And yet a man—if he be "bat-minded"—may "see" several.

But are there double binds in the mind? The question is not trivial. As there are in the mind no coconuts but only percepts and transforms of coconuts, so also, when I perceive (consciously or unconsciously) a double bind in my boss' behavior, I acquire in my mind no double bind but only a percept or transform of a double bind. And *that* is not what the theory is about.

We are talking then about some sort of tangle in the rules for making the transforms and about the acquisition or cultivation of such tangles. Double bind theory asserts that there is an experiential component in the determination or etiology of schizophrenic symptoms and related behavioral patterns, such as humor, art, poetry, etc. Notably the theory does not distinguish between these subspecies. Within its terms there is nothing to determine whether a given individual shall become a clown, a poet, a schizophrenic, or some combination of these. We deal not with a single syndrome but with a genus of syndromes, most of which are not conventionally regarded as pathological.

Let me coin the word "transcontextual" as a general term for this genus of syndromes.

It seems that both those whose life is enriched by transcontextual gifts and those who are impoverished by transcontextual confusions are alike in one respect: for them there is always or often a "double take." A falling leaf, the greeting of a friend, or a "primrose by the river's brim" is not "just that and nothing more." Exogenous experience may be framed in the contexts of dream, and internal thought may be projected into the contexts of the external world. And so on. For all this, we seek a partial explanation in learning and experience.

There must, of course, also be genetic components in the etiology of the transcontextual syndromes. These would expectably operate at levels more abstract than the experiential. For example, genetic components might determine skill in learning to be transcontextual or (more abstractly) the potentialities for acquiring this skill. Or, conversely, the genome might determine skills in resisting transcontextual pathways, or the potentiality for acquiring this latter skill. (Geneticists have paid very little attention to the necessity of defining the logical typing of messages carried by DNA.)

In any case, the meeting point where the genetic determination meets the experiential is surely quite abstract, and this must be true even though the embodiment of the genetic message be a single gene. (A single *bit* of information—a single difference—may be the yes-or-no answer to a question of any degree of complexity, at any level of abstraction.)

Current theories which propose (for "schizophrenia") a single dominant gene of "low penetrance" seem to leave the field open for any experiential theory which would indicate what class of experiences might cause the latent potentiality to appear in the phenotype.

I must confess however that these theories seem to me of little interest until the proponents try to specify what components of the complex process of determining "schizophrenia" are provided by the hypothetical gene. To identify these components must be a *subtractive* process. Where the contribution of environment is large, the genetics cannot be investigated until the environmental effect has been identified and can be controlled.

But sauce for the goose is also sauce for the gander, and what is said above about geneticists places an obligation upon me to make clear what components of transcontextual process could be provided by double bind experience. It is appropriate therefore to re-examine the theory of deuterolearning upon which double bind theory is based.

All biological systems (organisms and social or ecological organizations of organisms) are capable of adaptive change. But adaptive change takes many forms, such as response, learning, ecological succession, biological evolution, cultural evolution, etc., according to the size and complexity of the system which we choose to consider.

Whatever the system, adaptive change depends upon *feedback loops*, be it those provided by natural selection or those of individual reinforcement. In all cases, then, there must be a process of *trial and error* and a mechanism of *comparison*.

But trial and error must always involve error, and error is always biologically and/or psychically expensive. It follows therefore that adaptive change must always be *hierarchic*.

There is needed not only that first-order change which suits the immediate environmental (or physiological) demand but also second-order changes which will reduce the amount of trial and error needed to achieve the first-order change. And so on. By superposing and interconnecting many feedback loops, we (and all other biological systems) not only solve particular problems but also form *habits* which we apply to the solution of *classes* of problems.

We act as though a whole class of problems could be solved in terms of assumptions or premises, fewer in number than the members of the class of problems. In other words, we (organisms) *learn to learn*, or in the more technical phrase, we deutero-learn.

But habits are notoriously rigid and their rigidity follows as a necessary corollary of their status in the hierarchy of adaptation. The very economy of trial and error which is achieved by habit formation is only possible because habits are comparatively "hard programmed," in the engineers' phrase. The economy consists precisely in *not* re-examining or rediscovering the premises of habit every time the habit is used. We may say that these premises are partly "unconscious", or—if you please—that a *habit* of not examining them is developed.

Moreover, it is important to note that the premises of habit are almost necessarily abstract. Every problem is in some degree different from every other and its description or representation in the mind will therefore contain unique propositions. Clearly to sink these unique propositions to the level of premises of habit would be an error. Habit can deal successfully only with propositions which have general or repetitive truth, and these are commonly of a relatively high order of abstraction.[1]

Now the particular propositions which I believe to be important in the determination of the transcontextual syndromes are those formal abstractions which describe and determine interpersonal relationship.

I say "describe and determine," but even this is inadequate. Better would be to say that the relationship *is* the exchange of these messages; or that the relationship is immanent in these messages.

Psychologists commonly speak as if the abstractions of relationship ("dependency," "hostility," "love," etc.) were real things which are to be described or "expressed" by messages. This is epistemology backwards: in truth, the messages constitute the relationship, and words like "dependency" are verbally coded descriptions of patterns immanent in the combination of exchanged messages.

As has already been mentioned, there are no "things" in the mind—not even "dependency."

We are so befuddled by language that we cannot think straight, and it is convenient, sometimes, to remember that we are really mammals. The epistemology of the "heart" is that of any nonhuman mammal. The cat does not say "milk"; she simply acts out (or *is*) her end of an interchange, the pattern of which we in language would call "dependency."

But to act or be one end of a pattern of interaction is to propose the other end. A *context* is set for a certain class of response.

This weaving of contexts and of messages which propose context—but which, like all messages whatsoever, have

---

[1] What is important, however, is that the proposition be constantly true, rather than that it be abstract. It just so happens—coincidentally—that abstractions, if well chosen, have a constancy of truth. For human beings it is rather constantly true that air is present around the nose; the reflexes which control respiration can therefore be hard-programmed in the medulla. For the porpoise, the proposition "air around the blowhole" is only intermittently true, and therefore respiration must be controlled in a more flexible manner from some higher center.

"meaning" only by virtue of context—is the subject matter of the so-called double bind theory.

The matter may be illustrated by a famous and formally correct[2] botanical analogy. Goethe pointed out 150 years ago that there is a sort of syntax or grammar in the anatomy of flowering plants. A "stem" is that which bears "leaves"; a "leaf" is that which has a bud in its axil; a bud is a stem which originates in the axil of a leaf; etc. The formal (*i.e.*, the communicational) nature of each organ is determined by its contextual status—the context in which it occurs and the context which it sets for other parts.

I said above that double bind theory is concerned with the experiential component in the genesis of tangles in the rules or premises of habit. I now go on to assert that experienced breaches in the weave of contextual structure are in fact "double binds" and must necessarily (if they contribute at all to the hierarchic processes of learning and adaptation) promote what I am calling transcontextual syndromes.

Consider a very simple paradigm: a female porpoise (*Steno bredanensis*) is trained to accept the sound of the trainer's whistle as a "secondary reinforcement." The whistle is expectably followed by food, and if she later repeats what she was doing when the whistle blew, she will expectably again hear the whistle and receive food.

This porpoise is now used by the trainers to demonstrate "operant conditioning" to the public. When she enters the exhibition tank, she raises her head above surface, hears the whistle and is fed. She then raises her head again and is again reinforced. Three repetitions of this sequence is enough for the demonstration and the porpoise is then sent off-stage to wait for the next performance two hours later. She has learned some simple rules which relate her actions, the whistle, the exhibition tank, and the trainer into a pattern— a contextual structure, a set of rules for how to put the information together.

But this pattern is fitted only for a single episode in the exhibition tank. She must break that pattern to deal with the

---

[2] Formally correct because morphogenesis, like behavior, is surely a matter of messages in contexts. (See G. Bateson, "A Re-examination of 'Bateson's Rule,'" *Journal of Genetics*, in press.)

*class* of such episodes. There is a larger *context of contexts* which will put her in the wrong.

At the next performance, the trainer again wants to demonstrate "operant conditioning," but to do this she must pick on a different piece of conspicuous behavior.

When the porpoise comes on stage, she again raises her head. But she gets no whistle. The trainer waits for the next piece of conspicuous behavior—likely a tail flap, which is a common expression of annoyance. This behavior is then reinforced and repeated.

But the tail flap was, of course, not rewarded in the third performance.

Finally the porpoise learned to deal with the context of contexts—by offering a different or *new* piece of conspicuous behavior whenever she came on stage.

All this had happened in the free natural history of the relationship between porpoise and trainer and audience. The sequence was then repeated experimentally with a new porpoise and carefully recorded.[3]

Two points from this experimental repeat of the sequence must be added:

First, that it was necessary (in the trainer's judgment) to break the rules of the experiment many times. The experience of being in the wrong was so disturbing to the porpoise that in order to preserve the relationship between porpoise and trainer (*i.e.*, the context of context of context) it was necessary to give many reinforcements to which the porpoise was not entitled.

Second, that each of the first fourteen sessions was characterized by many futile repetitions of whatever behavior had been reinforced in the immediately previous session. Seemingly only by "accident" did the animal provide a piece of different behavior. In the time-out between the fourteenth and fifteenth sessions, the porpoise appeared to be much excited, and when she came on stage for the fifteenth session she put on an elaborate performance including eight conspicuous pieces of behavior of which four were entirely new—never before observed in this species of animal.

[3] K. Pryor, R. Haag, and J. O'Rielly, "Deutero-Learning in a Roughtooth Porpoise (*Steno bredanensis*)," U. S. Naval Ordinance Test Station, China Lake, NOTS TP 4270.

The story illustrates, I believe, two aspects of the genesis of a transcontextual syndrome:

First, that severe pain and maladjustment can be induced by putting a mammal in the wrong regarding its rules for making sense of an important relationship with another mammal.

And second, that if this pathology can be warded off or resisted, the total experience may promote *creativity*.

## Bibliography

G. Bateson, "Social Planning and the Concept of Deutero-Learning," *Science, Philosophy and Religion; Second Symposium*, L. Bryson and L. Finkelstein, eds., New York, Conference on Science, Philosophy and Religion in their Relation to the Democratic Way of Life, Inc., 1942.

————, "Minimal Requirements for a Theory of Schizophrenia," *A.M.A. Archives of General Psychiatry*, 1960, 2: 477–91.

————, *Perceval's Narrative, A Patient's Account of his Psychosis, 1830–1832*, edited and with an introduction by Gregory Bateson, Stanford, Calif., Stanford University Press, 1961.

————, "Exchange of Information about Patterns of Human Behavior," *Information Storage and Neural Control; Tenth Annual Scientific Meeting of the Houston Neurological Society*, W. S. Fields and W. Abbott, eds., Springfield, Ill., Charles C. Thomas, 1963.

————, "The Role of Somatic Change in Evolution," *Evolution*, 1963, 17: 529–39.

# The Logical Categories of
# Learning and Communication*

All species of behavioral scientists are concerned with "learning" in one sense or another of that word. Moreover, since "learning" is a communicational phenomenon, all are affected by that cybernetic revolution in thought which has occurred in the last twenty-five years. This revolution was triggered by the engineers and communication theorists but has older roots in the physiological work of Cannon and Claude Bernard, in the physics of Clarke Maxwell, and in the mathematical philosophy of Russell and Whitehead. Insofar as behavioral scientists still ignore the problems of *Principia Mathematica*,[1] they can claim approximately sixty years of obsolescence.

It appears, however, that the barriers of misunderstanding which divide the various species of behavioral scientists can be illuminated (but not eliminated) by an application of Russell's Theory of Logical Types to the concept of "learning"

* This essay was written in 1964 while the author was employed by the Communications Research Institute, under a Career Development Award (K3-NH-21, 931) from the National Institute of Mental Health. It was submitted as a position paper to the "Conference on World Views" sponsored by the Wenner-Gren Foundation, August 2–11, 1968. The section on "Learning III" was added in 1971.

[1] A. N. Whitehead and B. Russell, *Principia Mathematica*, 3 vols., 2nd ed., Cambridge, Cambridge University Press, 1910–13.

279

with which all are concerned. To attempt this illumination will be a purpose of the present essay.

## The Theory of Logical Types

First, it is appropriate to indicate the subject matter of the Theory of Logical Types: the theory asserts that no class can, in formal logical or mathematical discourse, be a member of itself; that a class of classes cannot be one of the classes which are its members; that a name is not the thing named; that "John Bateson" is the class of which that boy is the unique member; and so forth. These assertions may seem trivial and even obvious, but we shall see later that it is not at all unusual for the theorists of behavioral science to commit errors which are precisely analogous to the error of classifying the name with the thing named—or eating the menu card instead of the dinner—an error of *logical typing*.

Somewhat less obvious is the further assertion of the theory: that a class cannot be one of those items which are correctly classified as its nonmembers. If we classify chairs together to constitute the class of chairs, we can go on to note that tables and lamp shades are members of a large class of "nonchairs," but we shall commit an error in formal discourse if we count the *class of chairs* among the items within the class of nonchairs.

Inasmuch as no class can be a member of itself, the class of nonchairs clearly cannot be a nonchair. Simple considerations of symmetry may suffice to convince the nonmathematical reader: (*a*) that the class of chairs is of the same order of abstraction (*i.e.*, the same logical type) as the class of nonchairs; and further, (*b*) that if the class of chairs is not a chair, then, correspondingly, the class of nonchairs is not a nonchair.

Lastly, the theory asserts that if these simple rules of formal discourse are contravened, paradox will be generated and the discourse vitiated.

The theory, then, deals with highly abstract matters and was first derived within the abstract world of logic. In that world, when a train of propositions can be shown to generate a paradox, the entire structure of axioms, theorems, etc., involved in generating that paradox is thereby negated and reduced to nothing. It is as if it had never been. But in the real world (or at least in our descriptions of it), there is always *time*, and nothing which has been can ever be totally negated in this way. The computer which encounters a paradox (due to faulty programming) does not vanish away.

The "if . . . then . . ." of logic contains no time. But in the computer, cause and effect are used to *simulate* the "if . . . then . . ." of logic; and all sequences of cause and effect necessarily involve time. (Conversely, we may say that in scientific explanations the "if . . . then . . ." of logic is used to simulate the "if . . . then . . ." of cause and effect.)

The computer never truly encounters logical paradox, but only the simulation of paradox in trains of cause and effect. The computer therefore does not fade away. It merely oscillates.

In fact, there are important differences between the world of logic and the world of phenomena, and these differences must be allowed for whenever we base our arguments upon the partial but important analogy which exists between them.

It is the thesis of the present essay that this partial analogy can provide an important guide for behavioral scientists in their classification of phenomena related to learning. Precisely in the field of animal and mechanical communication something like the theory of types must apply.

Questions of this sort, however, are not often discussed in zoological laboratories, anthropological field camps, or psychiatric conventions, and it is necessary therefore to demonstrate that these abstract considerations are important to behavioral scientists.

Consider the following syllogism:

(*a*) Changes in frequency of items of mammalian behavior can be described and predicted in terms of various "laws" of reinforcement.

(*b*) "Exploration" as observed in rats is a category, or class, of mammalian behavior.

(*c*) Therefore, changes in frequency of "exploration" should be describable in terms of the same "laws" of reinforcement.

Be it said at once: first, that empirical data show that the conclusion (c) is untrue; and second, that if the conclusion (c) were demonstrably true, then either (a) or (b) would be untrue.[2]

Logic and natural history would be better served by an expanded and corrected version of the conclusion (c) somewhat as follows:

> (c) If, as asserted in (b), "exploration" is not an *item* of mammalian behavior but is a *category* of such items, then no descriptive statement which is true of *items* of behavior can be true of "exploration." If, however, descriptive statements which are true of items of behavior are also true of "exploration," then "exploration" is an item and not a category of items.

The whole matter turns on whether the distinction between a *class* and its *members* is an ordering principle in the behavioral phenomena which we study.

In less formal language: you can reinforce a rat (positively or negatively) when he investigates a particular strange object, and he will appropriately learn to approach or avoid it. But the very purpose of exploration is to get information about which objects should be approached and which avoided. The discovery that a given object is dangerous is therefore a *success* in the business of getting information. The success will not discourage the rat from future exploration of other strange objects.

A priori it can be argued that all perception and all response, all behavior and all classes of behavior, all learning and all genetics, all neurophysiology and endocrinology, all organization and all evolution—one entire subject matter—

---

[2] It is conceivable that the same *words* might be used in describing both a class and its members and be true in both cases. The word "wave" is the name of a class of movements of particles. We can also say that the wave itself "moves," but we shall be referring to a movement of a class of movements. Under friction, this metamovement will not lose velocity as would the movement of a particle.

must be regarded as communicational in nature, and therefore subject to the great generalizations or "laws" which apply to communicative phenomena. We therefore are warned to expect to find in our data those principles of order which fundamental communication theory would propose. The Theory of Logical Types, Information Theory, and so forth, are expectably to be our guides.

## The "Learning" of Computers, Rats, and Men

The word "learning" undoubtedly denotes *change* of some kind. To say *what kind* of change is a delicate matter.

However, from the gross common denominator, "change," we can deduce that our descriptions of "learning" will have to make the same sort of allowance for the varieties of logical type which has been routine in physical science since the days of Newton. The simplest and most familiar form of change is *motion*, and even if we work at that very simple physical level we must structure our descriptions in terms of "position or zero motion," "constant velocity," "acceleration," "rate of change of acceleration," and so on.[3]

Change denotes process. But processes are themselves subject to "change." The process may accelerate, it may slow down, or it may undergo other types of change such that we shall say that it is now a "different" process.

These considerations suggest that we should begin the ordering of our ideas about "learning" at the very simplest level.

Let us consider the case of specificity of response, or *zero learning*. This is the case in which an entity shows minimal change in its response to a repeated item of sensory input. Phenomena which approach this degree of simplicity occur in various contexts:

[3] The Newtonian equations which describe the motions of a "particle" stop at the level of "acceleration." *Change of acceleration* can only happen with deformation of the moving body, but the Newtonian "particle" was not made up of "parts" and was therefore (logically) incapable of deformation or any other internal change. It was therefore not subject to rate of change of acceleration.

(a) In experimental settings, when "learning" is complete and the animal gives approximately 100 per cent correct responses to the repeated stimulus.

(b) In cases of habituation, where the animal has ceased to give overt response to what was formerly a disturbing stimulus.

(c) In cases where the pattern of the response is minimally determined by experience and maximally determined by genetic factors.

(d) In cases where the response is now highly stereotyped.

(e) In simple electronic circuits, where *the circuit structure is not itself subject to change resulting from the passage of impulses within the circuit— i.e.,* where the causal links between "stimulus" and "response" are as the engineers say "soldered in."

In ordinary, nontechnical parlance, the word "learn" is often applied to what is here called "zero learning," *i.e.,* to the simple receipt of information from an external event, in such a way that a similar event at a later (and appropriate) time will convey the same information: I "learn" from the factory whistle that it is twelve o'clock.

It is also interesting to note that within the frame of our definition many very simple mechanical devices show at least the phenomenon of zero learning. The question is not, "Can machines learn?" but what level or order of learning does a given machine achieve? It is worth looking at an extreme, if hypothetical, case:

The "player" of a Von Neumannian game is a mathematical fiction, comparable to the Euclidean straight line in geometry or the Newtonian particle in physics. By definition, the "player" is capable of all computations necessary to solve whatever problems the events of the game may present; he is incapable of not performing these computations whenever they are appropriate; he always obeys the findings of his computations. Such a "player" receives information from the events of the game and acts appropriately upon that information. But his learning is limited to what is here called zero learning.

An examination of this formal fiction will contribute to our definition of zero learning.

(1) The "player" may receive, from the events of the game, information of higher or lower logical type, and he may use this information to make decisions of higher or lower type. That is, his decisions may be either strategic or tactical, and he can identify and respond to indications of both the tactics and the strategy of his opponent. It is, however, true that in Von Neumann's formal definition of a "game," all problems which the game may present are conceived as computable, *i.e.*, while the game may contain problems and information of many different logical types, the hierarchy of these types is strictly finite.

It appears then that a definition of zero learning will not depend upon the logical typing of the information received by the organism nor upon the logical typing of the adaptive decisions which the organism may make. A very high (but finite) order of complexity may characterize adaptive behavior based on nothing higher than zero learning.

(2) The "player" may compute the value of information which would benefit him and may compute that it will pay him to acquire this information by engaging in "exploratory" moves. Alternatively, he may make delaying or tentative moves while he waits for needed information.

It follows then that a rat engaging in exploratory behavior might do so upon a basis of zero learning.

(3) The "player" may compute that it will pay him to make random moves. In the game of matching pennies, he will compute that if he selects "heads" or "tails" at random, he will have an even chance of winning. If he uses any plan or pattern, this will appear as a pattern or redundancy in the sequence of his moves and his opponent will thereby receive information. The "player" will therefore elect to play in a random manner.

(4) The "player" is incapable of "error." He may, for good reason, elect to make random moves or exploratory moves, but he is by definition incapable of "learning by trial and error."

If we assume that, in the name of this learning process, the word "error" means what we meant it to mean when we said that the "player" is incapable of error, then "trial and error" is excluded from the repertoire of the Von Neumannian player. In fact, the Von Neumannian "player" forces us to a very careful examination of what we mean by "trial and error" learning, and indeed what is meant by "learning" of any kind. The assumption regarding the meaning of the word "error" is not trivial and must now be examined.

There is a sense in which the "player" can be wrong. For example, he may base a decision upon probabilistic considerations and then make that move which, in the light of the limited available information, was most probably right. When more information becomes available, he may discover that that move was wrong. But *this discovery can contribute nothing to his future skill.* By definition, the player used correctly all the *available* information. He estimated the probabilities correctly and made the move which was most probably correct. The discovery that he was wrong in the particular instance can have no bearing upon future instances. When the same problem returns at a later time, he will *correctly* go through the same computations and reach the same decision. Moreover, the set of alternatives among which he makes his choice will be the same set—and correctly so.

In contrast, an organism is capable of being wrong in a number of ways of which the "player" is incapable. These wrong choices are appropriately called "error" when they are of such a kind that they would provide information to the organism which might contribute to his future skill. These will all be cases in which some of the available information was either ignored or incorrectly used. Various species of such profitable error can be classified.

Suppose that the external event system contains details which might tell the organism: (*a*) from what set of alternatives he should choose his next move; and (*b*) which member of that set he should choose. Such a situation permits two *orders* of error:

(1) The organism may use correctly the information which tells him from what set of alternatives he should choose, but choose the wrong alternative within this set; or

(2) He may choose from the wrong set of alternatives. (There is also an interesting class of cases in which the sets of alternatives contain common members. It is then possible for the organism to be "right" but for the wrong reasons. This form of error is inevitably self-reinforcing.)

If now we accept the overall notion that all learning (other than zero learning) is in some degree stochastic (*i.e.*, contains components of "trial and error"), it follows that an ordering of the processes of learning can be built upon an hierarchic classification of the types of error which are to be corrected in the various learning processes. Zero learning will then be the label for the immediate base of all those acts (simple and complex) which are not subject to correction by trial and error. Learning I will be an appropriate label for the revision of choice within an unchanged set of alternatives; Learning II will be the label for the revision of the *set* from which the choice is to be made; and so on.

## Learning I

Following the formal analogy provided by the "laws" of motion (*i.e.*, the "rules" for describing motion), we now look for the class of phenomena which are appropriately described as *changes* in zero learning (as "motion" describes change of position). These are the cases in which an entity gives at Time 2 a different response from what it gave at Time 1, and again we encounter a variety of cases variously related to experience, physiology, genetics, and mechanical process:

(*a*) There is the phenomenon of habituation—the change from responding to each occurrence of a repeated event to not overtly responding. There is also the extinction or loss of habituation, which may occur as a result of a more or less long gap or other interruption in the sequence of repetitions of the stimulus event. (Habituation is of especial interest. Specificity of response, which we are calling zero learning, is characteristic of all protoplasm, but it is interesting to note that "habituation" is perhaps the only form of Learning I which living things can achieve without a neural circuit.)

(*b*) The most familiar and perhaps most studied case is that of the classical Pavlovian conditioning. At Time 2 the dog salivates in response to the buzzer; he did not do this at Time 1.

(*c*) There is the "learning" which occurs in contexts of instrumental reward and instrumental avoidance.

(d) There is the phenomenon of rote learning, in which an item in the behavior of the organism becomes a stimulus for another item of behavior.

(e) There is the disruption, extinction, or inhibition of "completed" learning which may follow change or absence of reinforcement.

In a word, the list of Learning I contains those items which are most commonly called "learning" in the psychological laboratory.

Note that in all cases of Learning I, there is in our description an assumption about the "context." This assumption must be made explicit. The definition of Learning I assumes that the buzzer (the stimulus) is somehow the "same" at Time 1 and at Time 2. And this assumption of "sameness" must also delimit the "context," which must (theoretically) be the same at both times. It follows that the events which occurred at Time 1 are not, in our description, included in our definition of the context at Time 2, because to include them would at once create a gross difference between "context at Time 1" and "context at Time 2." (To paraphrase Heraclitus: "No man can go to bed with the same girl for the first time twice.")

The conventional assumption that context can be repeated, at least in some cases, is one which the writer adopts in this essay as a cornerstone of the thesis that the study of behavior must be ordered according to the Theory of Logical Types. *Without* the assumption of repeatable context (and the hypothesis that *for the organisms* which we study the sequence of experience is really somehow punctuated in this manner), it would follow that all "learning" would be of one type: namely, all would be zero learning. Of the Pavlovian experiment, we would simply say that the dog's neural circuits contain "soldered in" from the beginning such characteristics that in Context A at Time 1 he will not salivate, and that in the totally different Context B at Time 2 he will salivate. What previously we called "learning" we would now describe as "discrimination" between the events of Time 1 and the events of Time 1 *plus* Time 2. It would then follow logically that all questions of the type, "Is this behavior 'learned' or 'innate'?" should be answered in favor of genetics.

We would argue that without the assumption of repeatable context, our thesis falls to the ground, together with the whole general concept of "learning." If, on the other hand, the assumption of repeatable context is accepted as somehow true of the organisms which we study, then the case for logical typing of the phenomena of learning necessarily stands, because the notion "context" is itself subject to logical typing.

Either we must discard the notion of "context," or we retain this notion and, with it, accept the hierarchic series—stimulus, context of stimulus, context of context of stimulus, etc. This series can be spelled out in the form of a hierarchy of logical types as follows:

Stimulus is an elementary signal, internal or external.

Context of stimulus is a *meta*message which *classifies* the elementary signal.

Context of context of stimulus is a meta-metamessage which classifies the metamessage.

And so on.

The same hierarchy could have been built up from the notion of "response" or the notion of "reinforcement."

Alternatively, following up the hierarchic classification of errors to be corrected by stochastic process or "trial and error," we may regard "context" as a collective term for all those events which tell the organism among what *set* of alternatives he must make his next choice.

At this point it is convenient to introduce the term "context marker." An organism responds to the "same" stimulus differently in differing contexts, and we must therefore ask about the source of the organisms's information. From what percept does he know that Context A is different from Context B?

In many instances, there may be no specific *signal* or label which will classify and differentiate the two contexts, and the organism will be forced to get his information from the actual congeries of events that make up the context in each case. But, certainly in human life and probably in that of many other organisms, there occur signals whose major function is to *classify* contexts. It is not unreasonable to suppose that when the harness is placed upon the dog, who has had prolonged training in the psychological laboratory, he knows from this that he is now embarking upon a series of contexts of a certain sort. Such a source of information we shall call a "context marker," and note immediately that, at least at the human level, there are also "markers of contexts of contexts." For example: an audience is watching *Hamlet* on the stage, and hears the hero discuss suicide in the context of his relationship with his dead father, Ophelia, and the rest. The audience members do not immediately telephone for the police because they have received information about the context of Hamlet's context. They know that it is a "play" and have received this information from many "markers of context of context"—the playbills, the seating arrangements, the curtain, etc., etc. The "King," on the other hand, when he lets his conscience be pricked by the play within the play, is ignoring many "markers of context of context."

At the human level, a very diverse set of events falls within the category of "context markers." A few examples are here listed:

(a) The Pope's throne from which he makes announcements *ex cathedra*, which announcements are thereby endowed with a special order of validity.

(b) The placebo, by which the doctor sets the stage for a change in the patient's subjective experience.

(c) The shining object used by some hypnotists in "inducing trance."

(d) The air raid siren and the "all clear."

(e) The handshake of boxers before the fight.

(f) The observances of etiquette.

These, however, are examples from the social life of a highly complex organism, and it is more profitable at this stage to ask about the analogous phenomena at the preverbal level.

A dog may see the leash in his master's hand and act as if he knows that this indicates a walk; or he may get information from the sound of the word "walk" that this type of context or sequence is coming.

When a rat starts a sequence of exploratory activities, does he do so in response to a "stimulus?" Or in response to a context? Or in response to a context marker?

These questions bring to the surface formal problems about the Theory of Logical Types which must be discussed. The theory in its original form deals only with rigorously digital communication, and it is doubtful how far it may be applied to analogue or iconic systems. What we are here calling "context markers" may be digital (*e.g.*, the word "walk" mentioned above); or they may be analogue signals —a briskness in the master's movements may indicate that a walk is pending; or some *part* of the coming context may serve as a marker (the leash as a part of the walk); or in the extreme case, the walk itself in all its complexity may stand for itself, with no label or marker between the dog and the experience. The perceived event itself may communicate its own occurrence. In this case, of course, there can be no error of the "menu card" type. Moreover, no paradox can be generated because in purely analogue or iconic communication there is no signal for "not."

There is, in fact, almost no formal theory dealing with analogue communication and, in particular, no equivalent of Information Theory or Logical Type Theory. This gap in formal knowledge is inconvenient when we leave the rarified world of logic and mathematics and come face to face with the phenomena of natural history. In the natural world, communication is rarely either purely digital or purely analogic. Often discrete digital pips are combined together to make analogic pictures as in the printer's halftone block; and sometimes, as in the matter of context markers, there is a continuous gradation from the ostensive through the iconic to the purely digital. At the digital end of this scale all the theorems of information theory have their full force, but at the ostensive and analogic end they are meaningless.

It seems also that while much of the behavioral communication of even higher mammals remains ostensive or analogic, the internal mechanism of these creatures has become digitalized at least at the neuronal level. It would seem that analogic communication is in some sense more primitive than digital and that there is a broad evolutionary trend toward the substitution of digital for analogic mechanisms. This trend seems to operate faster in the evolution of internal mechanisms than in the evolution of external behavior.

Recapitulating and extending what was said above:

(*a*) The notion of repeatable context is a necessary premise for any theory which defines "learning" as *change*.

(*b*) This notion is not a mere tool of our description but contains the implicit hypothesis that for the organisms which we study, the sequence of life experience, action, etc., is somehow segmented or punctuated into subsequences or "contexts" which may be equated or differentiated by the organism.

(*c*) The distinction which is commonly drawn between perception and action, afferent and efferent, input and output, is for higher organisms in complex situations not valid. On the one hand, almost every item of action may be reported either by external sense or endoceptive mechanism to the C.N.S., and in this case the report of this item becomes an input. And, on the other hand, in higher organisms, perception is not by any means a process of mere passive receptivity but is at least partly determined by efferent control from higher centers. Perception, notoriously, can be changed by experience. In principle, we must allow both for the possibility that every item of action or output may create an item of input; and that percepts may in some cases partake of the nature of output. It is no accident that almost all sense organs are used for the emission of signals between organisms. Ants communicate by their antennae; dogs by the pricking of their ears; and so on.

(*d*) In principle, even in zero learning, any item of experience or behavior may be regarded as either "stimulus" or "response" or as both, according to how the total sequence is punctuated. When the scientist says that the buzzer is the "stimulus" in a given sequence, his utterance implies an hypothesis about how the organism punctuates that sequence. In Learning I, every item of perception or behavior may be stimulus or response or *reinforcement* according to how the total sequence of interaction is punctuated.

## Learning II

What has been said above has cleared the ground for the consideration of the next level or logical type of "learning" which we shall here call Learning II. Various terms have been proposed in the literature for various phenomena of this order. "Deutero-learning,"[4] "set learning,"[5] "learning to learn," and "transfer of learning" may be mentioned.

We recapitulate and extend the definitions so far given:

*Zero learning* is characterized by *specificity of response,* which—right or wrong—is not subject to correction.

*Learning I* is *change in specificity of response* by correction of errors of choice within a set of alternatives.

*Learning II* is *change in the process of Learning I, e.g.,* a corrective change in the set of alternatives from which choice is made, or it is a change in how the sequence of experience is punctuated.

*Learning III* is *change in the process of Learning II, e.g.,* a corrective change in the system of *sets* of alternatives from which choice is made. (We shall see later that to demand this level of performance of some men and some mammals is sometimes pathogenic.)

*Learning IV* would be *change in Learning III,* but probably does not occur in any adult living organism on this earth. Evolutionary process has, however, created organisms whose ontogeny brings them to Level III. The combination of phylogenesis with ontogenesis, in fact, achieves Level IV.

Our immediate task is to give substance to the definition of Learning II as "change in Learning I," and it is for this that the ground has been prepared. Briefly, I believe that the phenomena of Learning II can all be included under the rubric of changes in the manner in which the stream of action and experience is segmented or punctuated into contexts together with changes in the use of context markers.

The list of phenomena classified under Learning I includes a considerable (but not exhaustive) set of differently structured contexts. In classical Pavlovian contexts, the contingency pattern which describes the relation between "stimulus" (CS), animal's action (CR), and reinforcement (UCS) is profoundly different from the contingency pattern characteristic of instrumental contexts of learning.

---

[4] G. Bateson, "Social Planning and the Concept of Deutero-Learning," *Conference on Science, Philosophy and Religion, Second Symposium,* New York, Harper, 1942.

[5] H. E. Harlow, "The Formation of Learning Sets," *Psychol. Review,* 1949, 56: 51–65.

In the Pavlovian case: *If* stimulus and a certain lapse of time: *then* reinforcement.

In the Instrumental Reward case: *If* stimulus and a particular item of behavior: *then* reinforcement.

In the Pavlovian case, the reinforcement is not contingent upon the animal's behavior, whereas in the instrumental case, it is. Using this contrast as an example, we say that Learning II has occurred if it can be shown that experience of one or more contexts of the Pavlovian type results in the animal's acting in some later context as though this, too, had the Pavlovian contingency pattern. Similarly, if past experience of instrumental sequences leads an animal to act in some later context as though expecting this also to be an instrumental context, we shall again say that Learning II has occurred.

When so defined, Learning II is adaptive only if the animal happens to be right in its expectation of a given contingency pattern, and in such a case we shall expect to see a measurable *learning to learn*. It should require fewer trials in the new context to establish "correct" behavior. If, on the other hand, the animal is wrong in his identification of the later contingency pattern, then we shall expect a delay of Learning I in the new context. The animal who has had prolonged experience of Pavlovian contexts might never get around to the particular sort of trial-and-error behavior necessary to discover a correct instrumental response.

There are at least four fields of experimentation where Learning II has been carefully recorded:

(*a*) In human rote learning. Hull[6] carried out very careful quantitative studies which revealed this phenomenon, and constructed a mathematical model which would simulate or explain the curves of Learning I which he recorded. He also observed a second-order phenomenon which we may call "learning to rote learn" and published the curves for this phenomenon in the Appendix to his book. These curves were separated from the main body of the book because, as he states, his mathematical model (of Rote Learning I) did not cover this aspect of the data.

[6] E. L. Hull, *et al.*, *Mathematico-deductive Theory of Rote Learning*, New Haven, Yale University, Institute of Human Relations, 1940.

It is a corollary of the theoretical position which we here take that no amount of rigorous discourse of a given logical type can "explain" phenomena of a higher type. Hull's model acts as a touchstone of logical typing, automatically excluding from explanation phenomena beyond its logical scope. That this was so—and that Hull perceived it—is testimonial both to his rigor and to his perspicacity.

What the data show is that for any given subject, there is an improvement in rote learning with successive sessions, asymptotically approaching a degree of skill which varied from subject to subject.

The context for this rote learning was quite complex and no doubt appeared subjectively different to each learner. Some may have been more motivated by fear of being wrong, while others looked rather for the satisfactions of being right. Some would be more influenced to put up a good record as compared with the other subjects; others would be fascinated to compete in each session with their own previous showing, and so on. All must have had ideas (correct or incorrect) about the nature of the experimental setting, all must have had "levels of aspiration," and all must have had previous experience of memorizing various sorts of material. Not one of Hull's subjects could have come into the learning context uninfluenced by previous Learning II.

In spite of all this previous Learning II, and in spite of genetic differences which might operate at this level, all showed improvement over several sessions. This improvement cannot have been due to Learning I because any recall of the specific sequence of syllables learned in the previous session would not be of use in dealing with the new sequence. Such recall would more probably be a hindrance. I submit, therefore, that the improvement from session to session can only be accounted for by some sort of adaptation to the *context* which Hull provided for rote learning.

It is also worth noting that educators have strong opinions about the value (positive or negative) of training in rote learning. "Progressive" educators insist on training in "insight," while the more conservative insist on rote and drilled recall.

(*b*) The second type of Learning II which has been experimentally studied is called "set learning." The concept and term are derived from Harlow and apply to a rather special case of Learning II. Broadly, what Harlow did was to present rhesus monkeys with more or less complex *gestalten* or "problems." These the monkey had to solve to get a food reward. Harlow showed that if these problems were of similar "set," *i.e.*, contained similar types of logical complexity, there was a carry-over of learning from one problem to the next. There were, in fact, two orders of contingency patterns involved in Harlow's experiments: first the overall pattern of instrumentalism (*if* the monkey solves the problem, *then* reinforcement); and second, the contingency patterns of logic within the specific problems.

(*c*) Bitterman and others have recently set a fashion in experimentation with "reversal learning." Typically in these experiments the subject is first taught a binary discrimination. When this has been learned to criterion, the meaning of the stimuli is reversed. If $X$ initially "meant" $R_1$, and $Y$ initially meant $R_2$, then after reversal $X$ comes to mean $R_2$, and $Y$ comes to mean $R_1$. Again the trials are run to criterion when again the meanings are reversed. In these experiments, the crucial question is: Does the subject learn about the reversal? *I.e.*, after a series of reversals, does the subject reach criterion in fewer trials than he did at the beginning of the series?

In these experiments, it is conspicuously clear that the question asked is of logical type higher than that of questions about simple learning. If simple learning is based upon a *set* of trials, then reversal learning is based upon a set of such sets. The parallelism between this relation and Russell's relation between "class" and "class of classes" is direct.

(*d*) Learning II is also exemplified in the well-known phenomena of "experimental neurosis." Typically an animal is trained, either in a Pavlovian or instrumental learning context, to discriminate between some $X$ and some $Y$; *e.g.*, between an ellipse and a circle. When this discrimination has been learned, the task is made more difficult: the ellipse is made progressively fatter and the circle is flattened. Finally a stage is reached at which discrimination is impossible. At this stage the animal starts to show symptoms of severe disturbance.

Notably, (*a*) a naive animal, presented with a situation in which some $X$ may (on some random basis) mean either $A$ or $B$, does not show disturbance; and (*b*) the disturbance does not occur in absence of the many context markers characteristic of the laboratory situation.[7]

It appears, then, that Learning II is a necessary preparation for the behavioral disturbance. The information, "This is a context for discrimination," is communicated at the beginning of the sequence and *underlined* in the series of stages in which discrimination is made progressively more difficult. But when discrimination becomes impossible, the structure of the context is totally changed. The context markers (*e.g.*, the smell of the laboratory and the experimental harness) now become misleading because the animal is in a situation which demands guesswork or gambling, *not* discrimination. The entire experimental sequence is, in fact, a procedure for putting the animal in the wrong at the level of Learning II.

In my phrase, the animal is placed in a typical "double bind," which is expectably schizophrenogenic.[8]

In the strange world outside the psychological laboratory, phenomena which belong to the category Learning II are a major preoccupation of anthropologists, educators, psychiatrists, animal trainers, human parents, and children. All who think about the processes which determine the character of the individual or the processes of change in human (or animal) relationship must use in their thinking a variety of assumptions about Learning II. From time to time, these people call in the laboratory psychologist as a consultant, and then are confronted with a linguistic barrier. Such barriers must always result when, for example, the psychiatrist is talking about Learning II, the psychologist is talking about Learning I, and neither recognizes the logical structure of the difference.

Of the multitudinous ways in which Learning II emerges in human affairs, only three will be discussed in this essay:

(*a*) In describing individual human beings, both the scientist and the layman commonly resort to adjectives descriptive of "character." It is said that Mr. Jones is dependent, hostile, fey, finicky, anxious, exhibitionistic, narcissistic,

[7] H. S. Liddell, "Reflex Method and Experimental Neurosis," *Personality and Behavior Disorders*, New York, Ronald Press, 1944.

[8] G. Bateson, *et al.*, "Toward a Theory of Schizophrenia," *Behavioral Science*, 1956, 1: 251–64.

passive, competitive, energetic, bold, cowardly, fatalistic, humorous, playful, canny, optimistic, perfectionist, careless, careful, casual, etc. In the light of what has already been said, the reader will be able to assign all these adjectives to their appropriate logical type. All are descriptive of (possible) results of Learning II, and if we would define these words more carefully, our definition will consist in laying down the contingency pattern of that context of Learning I which would expectably bring about that Learning II which would make the adjective applicable.

We might say of the "fatalistic" man that the pattern of his transactions with the environment is such as he might have acquired by prolonged or repeated experience as subject of Pavlovian experiment; and note that this definition of "fatalism" is specific and precise. There are many other forms of "fatalism" besides that which is defined in terms of this particular context of learning. There is, for example, the more complex type characteristic of classical Greek tragedy where a man's own action is felt to aid the inevitable working of fate.

(*b*) In the punctuation of human interaction. The critical reader will have observed that the adjectives above which purport to describe individual character are really not strictly applicable to the individual but rather describe *transactions* between the individual and his material and human environment. No man is "resourceful" or "dependent" or "fatalistic" in a vacuum. His characteristic, whatever it be, is not his but is rather a characteristic of what goes on between him and something (or somebody) else.

This being so, it is natural to look into what goes on between people, there to find contexts of Learning I which are likely to lend their shape to processes of Learning II. In such systems, involving two or more persons, where most of the important events are postures, actions, or utterances of the living creatures, we note immediately that the stream of events is commonly punctuated into contexts of learning by a tacit agreement between the persons regarding the nature of their relationship—or by context markers and tacit agreement that these context markers shall "mean" the same for both parties. It is instructive to attempt analysis of an ongoing interchange between A and B. We ask about any particular item of A's behavior: Is this item a stimulus for B? Or is it a response of A to something B said earlier? Or is it a reinforcement of some item provided by B? Or is A, in this item, consummating a reinforcement for himself? Etc.

Such questions will reveal at once that for many items of A's behavior the answer is often quite unclear. Or if there be a clear answer, the clarity is due only to a tacit (rarely fully explicit) agreement between A and B as to the nature of their mutual roles, *i.e.*, as to the nature of the contextual structure which they will expect of each other.

If we look at such an exchange in the abstract: . . . . . . $a_1b_1a_2b_2a_3b_3a_4b_4a_5b_5$ . . . . . . ., where the $a$'s refer to items of A's behavior, and the $b$'s to items of B's behavior, we can take any $a_1$ and construct around it three simple contexts of learning. These will be:

i. $(a_1\ b_1\ a_{1+1})$, in which $a_1$ is the stimulus for $b_1$.

ii. $(b_{1-1}\ a_1\ b_1)$, in which $a_1$ is the response to $b_{1-1}$, which response B reinforces with $b_1$.

iii. $(a_{1-1}\ b_{1-1}\ a_1)$, in which $a_1$ is now A's reinforcement of B's $b_{1-1}$, which was response to $a_{1-1}$.

It follows that $a_1$ may be a stimulus for B or it may be A's response to B, or it may be A's reinforcement of B.

Beyond this, however, if we consider the ambiguity of the notions "stimulus" and "response," "afferent" and "efferent"—as discussed above—we note that any $a_1$ may also be a stimulus for A; it may be A's reinforcement of self; or it may be A's response to some previous behavior of his own, as is the case in sequences of rote behavior.

This general ambiguity means in fact that the ongoing sequence of interchange between two persons is structured only by the person's own perception of the sequence as a series of contexts, each context leading into the next. The particular manner in which the sequence is structured by any particular person will be determined by that person's previous Learning II (or possibly by his genetics).

In such a system, words like "dominant" and "submissive," "succoring" and "dependent" will take on definable meaning as descriptions of segments of interchange. We shall say that "A dominates B" if A and B show by their behavior that they see their relationship as characterized by sequences of the type $a_1b_1a_2$, where $a_1$ is seen (by A and B) as a signal defining conditions of instrumental reward or punishment; $b_1$ as a signal or act obeying these conditions; and $a_2$ as a signal reinforcing $b_1$.

Similarly we shall say that "A is dependent on B" if their relationship is characterized by sequences $a_1b_1a_2$, where $a_1$ is seen as a signal of weakness; $b_1$ as a helping act; and $a_2$ as an acknowledgement of $b_1$.

But it is up to A and B to distinguish (consciously or unconsciously or not at all) between "dominance" and "dependence." A "command" can closely resemble a cry for "help."

(c) In psychotherapy, Learning II is exemplified most conspicuously by the phenomena of "transference." Orthodox Freudian theory asserts that the patient will inevitably bring to the therapy room inappropriate notions about his relationship to the therapist. These notions (conscious or unconscious) will be such that he will act and talk in a way which would press the therapist to respond in ways which would resemble the patient's picture of how some important other person (usually a parent) treated the patient in the near or distant past. In the language of the present paper, the patient will try to shape his interchange with the therapist according to the premises of his (the patient's) former Learning II.

It is commonly observed that much of the Learning II which determines a patient's transference patterns and, indeed, determines much of the relational life of all human beings, (a) *dates from early infancy*, and (b) *is unconscious*. Both of these generalizations seem to be correct and both need some explanation.

It seems probable that these two generalizations are true because of the very nature of the phenomena which we are discussing. We suggest that *what* is learned in Learning II is a way of *punctuating events*. But a *way of punctuating* is not true or false. There is nothing contained in the propositions of this learning that can be tested against reality. It is like a picture seen in an inkblot; it has neither correctness nor incorrectness. It is only a *way* of seeing the inkblot.

Consider the instrumental view of life. An organism with this view of life in a new situation will engage in trial-and-error behavior in order to make the situation provide a positive reinforcement. If he fails to get this reinforcement, his purposive philosophy is not thereby negated. His trial-and-error behavior will simply continue. The premises of "purpose" are simply not of the same logical type as the material facts of life, and therefore cannot easily be contradicted by them.

The practitioner of magic does not unlearn his magical view of events when the magic does not work. In fact, the propositions which govern punctuation have the general characteristic of being self-validating.[9] What we term "context" includes the subject's behavior as well as the external events. But this behavior is controlled by former Learning II and therefore it will be of such a kind as to mold the total context to fit the expected punctuation. In sum, this self-validating characteristic of the content of Learning II has the effect that such learning is almost ineradicable. It follows that Learning II acquired in infancy is likely to persist through life. Conversely, we must expect many of the important characteristics of an adult's punctuation to have their roots in early infancy.

In regard to the unconsciousness of these habits of punctuation, we observe that the "unconscious" includes not only repressed material but also most of the processes and *habits* of gestalt perception. Subjectively we are aware of our "dependency" but unable to say clearly how this pattern was constructed nor what cues were used in our creation of it.

## Learning III

What has been said above about the self-validating character of premises acquired by Learning II indicates that Learning III is likely to be difficult and rare even in human beings. Expectably, it will also be difficult for scientists, who are only human, to imagine or describe this process. But it is claimed that something of the sort does from time to time occur in psychotherapy, religious conversion, and in other sequences in which there is profound reorganization of character.

Zen Buddhists, Occidental mystics, and some psychiatrists

[9] J. Ruesch and G. Bateson, *Communication: The Social Matrix of Psychiatry*, New York, Norton, 1951.

assert that these matters are totally beyond the reach of language. But, in spite of this warning, let me begin to speculate about what must (logically) be the case.

First a distinction must be drawn: it was noted above that the experiments in reversal learning demonstrate Learning II whenever there is measurable learning *about* the fact of reversal. It is possible to learn (Learning I) a given premise at a given time and to learn the converse premise at a later time without acquiring the knack of reversal learning. In such a case, there will be no improvement from one reversal to the next. One item of Learning I has simply replaced another item of Learning I without any achievement of Learning II. If, on the other hand, improvement occurs with successive reversals, this is evidence for Learning II.

If we apply the same sort of logic to the relation between Learning II and Learning III, we are led to expect that there might be replacement of premises at the level of Learning II *without* the achievement of any Learning III.

Preliminary to any discussion of Learning III, it is therefore necessary to discriminate between mere replacement without Learning III and that facilitation of replacement which would be truly Learning III.

That psychotherapists should be able to aid their patients even in a mere replacement of premises acquired by Learning II is already no mean feat when we consider the self-validating character of such premises and their more or less unconscious nature. But that this much can be done there is no doubt.

Within the controlled and protected setting of the therapeutic relationship, the therapist may attempt one or more of the following maneuvers:

(*a*) to achieve a confrontation between the premises of the patient and those of the therapist—who is carefully trained not to fall into the trap of validating the old premises;

(*b*) to get the patient to act, either in the therapy room or outside, in ways which will confront his own premises;

(*c*) to demonstrate contradiction among the premises which currently control the patient's behavior;

(*d*) to induce in the patient some *exaggeration or carica-ture* (*e.g.*, in dream or hypnosis) of experience based on his old premises.

As William Blake noted, long ago, "Without Contraries is no progression." (Elsewhere I have called these contradictions at level II "double binds.")

But there are always loopholes by which the impact of contradiction can be reduced. It is a commonplace of learning psychology that while the subject will learn (Learning I) more rapidly if he is reinforced every time he responds correctly, such learning will disappear rather rapidly if reinforcement ceases. If, on the other hand, reinforcement is only occasional, the subject will learn more slowly but the resulting learning will not easily be extinguished when reinforcement ceases altogether. In other words, the subject may learn (Learning II) that the context is such that absence of reinforcement does not indicate that his response was wrong or inappropriate. His view of the context was, in fact, correct until the experimenter changed his tactics.

The therapist must certainly so support or hedge the contraries by which the patient is driven that loopholes of this and other kinds are blocked. The Zen candidate who has been assigned a paradox (*koan*) must labor at his task "like a mosquito biting on an iron bar."

I have argued elsewhere ("Style, Grace, and Information in Primitive Art," see p. 128) that an essential and necessary function of all habit formation and Learning II is an *economy* of the thought processes (or neural pathways) which are used for problem-solving or Learning I. The premises of what is commonly called "character"—the definitions of the "self" —save the individual from having to examine the abstract, philosophical, aesthetic, and ethical aspects of many sequences of life. "I don't know whether it's good music; I only know whether I like it."

But Learning III will throw these unexamined premises open to question and change.

Let us, as was done above for Learning I and II, list some of the changes which we shall be willing to call Learning III.

(*a*) The individual might learn to form more readily those habits the forming of which we call Learning II.

(*b*) He might learn to close for himself the "loopholes" which would allow him to avoid Learning III.

(*c*) He might learn to change the habits acquired by Learning II.

(*d*) He might learn that he is a creature which can and does unconsciously achieve Learning II.

(*e*) He might learn to limit or direct his Learning II.

(*f*) If Learning II is a learning of the contexts of Learning I, then Learning III should be a learning of the contexts of those contexts.

But the above list proposes a paradox. Learning III (*i.e.*, learning *about* Learning II) may lead either to an increase in Learning II or to a limitation and perhaps a reduction of that phenomenon. Certainly it must lead to a greater flexibility in the premises acquired by the process of Learning II —a *freedom* from their bondage.

I once heard a Zen master state categorically: "To become accustomed to anything is a terrible thing."

But any freedom from the bondage of habit must also denote a profound redefinition of the self. If I stop at the level of Learning II, "I" am the aggregate of those characteristics which I call my "character." "I" am my habits of acting in context and shaping and perceiving the contexts in which I act. Selfhood is a product or aggregate of Learning II. To the degree that a man achieves Learning III, and learns to perceive and act in terms of the contexts of contexts, his "self" will take on a sort of irrelevance. The concept of "self" will no longer function as a nodal argument in the punctuation of experience.

This matter needs to be examined. In the discussion of Learning II, it was asserted that all words like "dependency," "pride," "fatalism," refer to characteristics of the self which are learned (Learning II) in sequences of relationship. These words are, in fact, terms for "roles" in relationships and refer to something artificially chopped out of interactive sequences. It was also suggested that the correct way to assign rigorous meaning to any such words is to spell out the formal structure of the sequence in which the named characteristic might have been learned. Thus the interactive sequence of Pavlovian learning was proposed as a paradigm for a certain sort of "fatalism," etc.

But now we are asking about the contexts of these contexts of learning, *i.e.*, about the larger sequences within which such paradigms are embedded.

Consider the small item of Learning II which was mentioned above as providing a "loophole" for escape from Learning III. A certain characteristic of the self—call it "persistence"—is generated by experience in multiple sequences among which reinforcement is sporadic. We must now ask about the larger context of such sequences. How are such sequences generated?

The question is explosive. The simple stylized experimental sequence of interaction in the laboratory is generated by and partly determines a network of contingencies which goes out in a hundred directions leading out of the laboratory into the processes by which psychological research is designed, the interactions between psychologists, the economics of research money, etc., etc.

Or consider the same formal sequence in a more "natural" setting. An organism is searching for a needed or missing object. A pig is rooting for acorns, a gambler is feeding a slot machine hoping for a jackpot, or a man must find the key to his car. There are thousands of situations where living things must persist in certain sorts of behavior precisely *because* reinforcement is sporadic or improbable. Learning II will simplify the universe by handling these instances as a single category. But if Learning III be concerned with the contexts of these instances, then the categories of Learning II will be burst open.

Or consider what the word "reinforcement" means at the various levels. A porpoise gets a fish from the trainer when he does what the trainer wants. At level I, the fact of the fish is linked with the "rightness" of the particular action. At level II, the fact of the fish confirms the porpoise's understanding of his (possibly instrumental or dependent) relationship with the trainer. And note that at this level, if the porpoise hates or fears the trainer, pain received from the latter may be a positive reinforcement confirming that hate. ("If it's not the way I want it, I'll prove it.")

But what of "reinforcement" at level III (for porpoise or for man)?

If, as I have suggested above, the creature is driven to level III by "contraries" generated at level II, then we may expect that it is the resolving of these contraries that will constitute positive reinforcement at level III. Such resolution can take many forms.

Even the attempt at level III can be dangerous, and some fall by the wayside. These are often labeled by psychiatry as psychotic, and many of them find themselves inhibited from using the first person pronoun.

For others, more successful, the resolution of the contraries may be a collapsing of much that was learned at level II, revealing a simplicity in which hunger leads directly to eating, and the identified self is no longer in charge of organizing the behavior. These are the incorruptible innocents of the world.

For others, more creative, the resolution of contraries reveals a world in which personal identity merges into all the processes of relationship in some vast ecology or aesthetics of cosmic interaction. That any of these can survive seems almost miraculous, but some are perhaps saved from being swept away on oceanic feeling by their ability to focus in on the minutiae of life. Every detail of the universe is seen as proposing a view of the whole. These are the people for whom Blake wrote the famous advice in the "Auguries of Innocence:"

> *To see the World in a Grain of Sand,*
> *And a Heaven in a Wild Flower,*
> *Hold Infinity in the palm of your hand,*
> *And Eternity in an hour.*

## The Role of Genetics in Psychology

Whatever can be said about an animal's learning or inability to learn has bearing upon the genetic make-up of the animal. And what has been said here about the levels of learning has bearing upon the whole interplay between genetic make-up and the changes which that individual can and must achieve.

For any given organism, there is an upper limit beyond which all is determined by genetics. Planarians can probably not go beyond Learning I. Mammals other than man are probably capable of Learning II but incapable of Learning III. Man may sometimes achieve Learning III.

This upper limit for any organism is (logically and presumably) set by genetic phenomena, not perhaps by individual genes or combinations of genes, but by whatever factors control the development of basic phylar characteristics.

For every change of which an organism is capable, there is the *fact* of that capability. This fact may be genetically determined; or the capability may have been learned. If the latter, then genetics may have determined the capability of learning the capability. And so on.

This is in general true of all somatic changes as well as of those behavioral changes which we call learning. A man's skin tans in the sun. But where does genetics enter this picture? Does genetics completely determine his *ability* to tan? Or can some men increase their ability to tan? In the latter case, the genetic factors evidently have effect at a higher logical level.

The problem in regard to any behavior is clearly not "Is it learned or is it innate?" but "Up to what logical level is learning effective and down to what level does genetics play a determinative or partly effective role?"

The broad history of the evolution of learning seems to have been a slow pushing back of genetic determinism to levels of higher logical type.

## A Note on Hierarchies

The model discussed in this paper assumes, tacitly, that the logical types can be ordered in the form of a simple, unbranching ladder. I believe that it was wise to deal first with the problems raised by such a simple model.

But the world of action, experience, organization, and learning cannot be completely mapped onto a model which excludes propositions about the relation *between* classes of different logical type.

If $C_1$ is a class of propositions, and $C_2$ is a class of propositions about the members of $C_1$; $C_3$ then being a class of propositions about the members of $C_2$; how then shall we classify propositions about the relation *between* these classes? For example, the proposition "As members of $C_1$ are to members of $C_2$, so members of $C_2$ are to members of $C_3$" cannot be classified within the unbranching ladder of types.

The whole of this essay is built upon the premise that the relation between $C_2$ and $C_3$ can be compared with the relation between $C_1$ and $C_2$. I have again and again taken a stance to the side of my ladder of logical types to discuss the structure of this ladder. The essay is therefore itself an example of the fact that the ladder is not unbranching.

It follows that a next task will be to look for examples of learning which cannot be classified in terms of my hierarchy of learning but which fall to the side of this hierarchy as learning about the relation between steps of the hierarchy. I have suggested elsewhere ("Style, Grace, and Information in Primitive Art") that art is commonly concerned with learning of this sort, *i.e.*, with bridging the gap between the more or less unconscious premises acquired by Learning II and the more episodic content of consciousness and immediate action.

It should also be noted that the structure of this essay is *inductive* in the sense that the hierarchy of orders of learning is presented to the reader from the bottom upward, from level zero to level III. But it is not intended that the explanations of the phenomenal world which the model affords shall be unidirectional. In explaining the model to the reader, a unidirectional approach was necessary, but within the model it is assumed that higher levels are explanatory of lower levels and vice versa. It is also assumed that a similar reflexive relation—both inductive and deductive—obtains among ideas and items of learning as these exist in the lives of the creatures which we study.

Finally, the model remains ambiguous in the sense that while it is asserted that there are explanatory or determinative relations between ideas of adjacent levels both upward and downward, it is not clear whether direct explanatory relations exist between separated levels, *e.g.*, between level III and level I or between level zero and level II.

This question and that of the status of propositions and ideas collateral to the hierarchy of types remains unexamined.

# The Cybernetics of "Self": A Theory of Alcoholism*

The "logic" of alcoholic addiction has puzzled psychiatrists no less than the "logic" of the strenuous spiritual regime whereby the organization Alcoholics Anonymous is able to counteract the addiction. In the present essay it is suggested: (1) that an entirely new epistemology must come out of cybernetics and systems theory, involving a new understanding of mind, self, human relationship, and power; (2) that the addicted alcoholic is operating, when sober, in terms of an epistemology which is conventional in Occidental culture but which is not acceptable to systems theory; (3) that surrender to alcoholic intoxication provides a partial and subjective short cut to a more correct state of mind; and (4) that the theology of Alcoholics Anonymous coincides closely with an epistemology of cybernetics.

The present essay is based upon ideas which are, perhaps all of them, familiar either to psychiatrists who have had dealings with alcoholics, or to philosophers who have thought about the implications of cybernetics and systems theory. The only novelty which can be claimed for the thesis here offered derives from treating these ideas seriously as premises of argument and from the bringing to-

*This article appeared in *Psychiatry*, Vol. 34, No. 1, pp. 1–18, 1971. Copyright © 1971 by the William Alanson White Psychiatric Foundation. Reprinted by permission of *Psychiatry*.

gether of commonplace ideas from two too separate fields of thought.

In its first conception, this essay was planned to be a systems-theoretic study of alcoholic addiction, in which I would use data from the publications of Alcoholics Anonymous, which has the only outstanding record of success in dealing with alcoholics. It soon became evident, however, that the religious views and the organizational structure of AA presented points of great interest to systems theory, and that the correct scope of my study should include not only the premises of alcoholism but also the premises of the AA system of treating it and the premises of AA organization.

My debt to AA will be evident throughout—also, I hope, my respect for that organization and especially for the extraordinary wisdom of its cofounders, Bill W. and Dr. Bob.

In addition, I have to acknowledge a debt to a small sample of alcoholic patients with whom I worked intensively for about two years in 1949–52, in the Veterans Administration Hospital, Palo Alto, California. These men, it should be mentioned, carried other diagnoses—mostly of "schizophrenia"—in addition to the pains of alcoholism. Several were members of AA. I fear that I helped them not at all.

## The Problem

It is rather generally believed that "causes" or "reasons" for alcoholism are to be looked for in the sober life of the alcoholic. Alcoholics, in their sober manifestations, are commonly dubbed "immature," "maternally fixated," "oral," "homosexual," "passive-aggressive," "fearful of success," "oversensitive," "proud," "affable," or simply "weak." But the logical implications of this belief are usually not examined:

(1) If the sober life of the alcoholic somehow drives him to drink or proposes the first step toward intoxication, it is not to be expected that any procedure which reinforces his particular style of sobriety will reduce or control his alcoholism.

(2) If his style of sobriety drives him to drink, then that style must contain error or pathology; and intoxication must provide some—at least subjective—correction of this error. In other words, compared with his sobriety, which is in

some way "wrong," his intoxication must be in some way "right." The old tag *In vino veritas* may contain a truth more profound than is usually attributed to it.

(3) An alternative hypothesis would suggest that when sober, the alcoholic is somehow more sane than the people around him, and that this situation is intolerable. I have heard alcoholics argue in favor of this possibility, but I shall ignore it in this essay. I think that Bernard Smith, the non-alcoholic legal representative of AA, came close to the mark when he said, "the [AA] member was never enslaved by alcohol. Alcohol simply served as an escape from *personal* enslavement to the false ideals of a materialistic society."[1] It is not a matter of revolt against insane ideals around him but of escaping from his own insane premises, which are continually reinforced by the surrounding society. It is possible, however, that the alcoholic is in some way more vulnerable or sensitive than the normal to the fact that his insane (but conventional) premises lead to unsatisfying results.

(4) The present theory of alcoholism, therefore, will provide a *converse matching* between the sobriety and the intoxication, such that the latter may be seen as an appropriate subjective correction for the former.

(5) There are, of course, many instances in which people resort to alcohol and even to extreme intoxication as an anesthetic giving release from ordinary grief, resentment, or physical pain. It might be argued that the anesthetic action of alcohol provides a sufficient converse matching for our theoretical purposes. I shall, however, specifically exclude these cases from consideration as being not relevant to the problem of addictive or repetitive alcoholism; and this in spite of the undoubted fact that "grief," "resentment," and "frustration" are commonly used by addicted alcoholics as *excuses* for drinking.

I shall demand, therefore, a converse matching between sobriety and intoxication more specific than that provided by mere anesthesia.

---

[1] [Alcoholics Anonymous], *Alcoholics Anonymous Comes of Age*, New York, Harper, 1957, p. 279. (Italics added.)

## Sobriety

The friends and relatives of the alcoholic commonly urge him to be "strong," and to "resist temptation." What they mean by this is not very clear, but it is significant that the alcoholic himself—while sober—commonly agrees with their view of his "problem." He believes that he could be, or, at least, ought to be "the captain of his soul."[2] But it is a cliché of alcoholism that after "that first drink," the motivation to stop drinking is zero. Typically the whole matter is phrased overtly as a battle between "self" and "John Barleycorn." Covertly the alcoholic may be planning or even secretly laying in supplies for the next binge, but it is almost impossible (in the hospital setting) to get the sober alcoholic to plan his next binge in an overt manner. He cannot, seemingly, be the "captain" of his soul and overtly will or command his own drunkenness. The "captain" can only command sobriety —and then not be obeyed.

Bill W., the cofounder of Alcoholics Anonymous, himself an alcoholic, cut through all this mythology of conflict in the very first of the famous "Twelve Steps" of AA. The first step demands that the alcoholic agree that he is powerless over alcohol. This step is usually regarded as a *"surrender"* and many alcoholics are either unable to achieve it or achieve it only briefly during the period of remorse following a binge. AA does not regard these cases as promising: they have not yet "hit bottom"; their despair is inadequate and after a more or less brief spell of sobriety they will again attempt to use "self-control" to fight the "temptation." They will not or cannot accept the premise that, drunk or sober, the total personality of an alcoholic is an alcoholic personality which cannot conceivably fight alcoholism. As an AA leaflet

---

[2] This phrase is used by AA in derision of the alcoholic who tries to use will power against the bottle. The quotation, along with the line, "My head is bloody but unbowed," comes from the poem "Invictus" by William Ernest Henley, who was a cripple but not an alcoholic. The use of the will to conquer pain and physical disability is probably not comparable to the alcoholic's use of will.

puts it, "trying to use will power is like trying to lift yourself by your bootstraps."

The first two steps of AA are as follows:

> 1. We admitted we were powerless over alcohol—that our lives had become unmanageable.
> 2. Came to believe that a Power greater than ourselves could restore us to sanity.[3]

Implicit in the combination of these two steps is an extraordinary—and I believe correct—idea: the experience of defeat not only serves to convince the alcoholic that change is necessary; it *is* the first step in that change. To be defeated by the bottle and to know it is the first "spiritual experience." The myth of self-power is thereby broken by the demonstration of a greater power.

In sum, I shall argue that the "sobriety" of the alcoholic is characterized by an unusually disastrous variant of the Cartesian dualism, the division between Mind and Matter, or, in this case, between conscious will, or "self," and the remainder of the personality. Bill W.'s stroke of genius was to break up with the first "step" the structuring of this dualism.

Philosophically viewed, this first step is *not* a surrender; it is simply a change in epistemology, a change in how to know about the personality-in-the-world. And, notably, the change is from an incorrect to a more correct epistemology.

## Epistemology and Ontology

Philosophers have recognized and separated two sorts of problem. There are first the problems of how things are, what is a person, and what sort of a world this is. These are the problems of ontology. Second, there are the problems of how we know anything, or more specifically, how we know what sort of a world it is and what sort of creatures we are that can know something (or perhaps nothing) of this matter. These are the problems of epistemology. To

[3] [Alcoholics Anonymous], *Alcoholics Anonymous*, New York, Works Publishing, 1939.

these questions, both ontological and epistemological, philosophers try to find true answers.

But the naturalist, observing human behavior, will ask rather different questions. If he be a cultural relativist, he may agree with those philosophers who hold that a "true" ontology is conceivable, but he will not ask whether the ontology of the people he observes is "true." He will expect their epistemology to be culturally determined or even idiosyncratic, and he will expect the culture as a whole to make sense in terms of their particular epistemology and ontology.

If, on the other hand, it is clear that the local epistemology is *wrong*, then the naturalist should be alert to the possibility that the culture as a whole will never really make "sense," or will make sense only under restricted circumstances, which contact with other cultures and new technologies might disrupt.

In the natural history of the living human being, ontology and epistemology cannot be separated. His (commonly unconscious) beliefs about what sort of world it is will determine how he sees it and acts within it, and his ways of perceiving and acting will determine his beliefs about its nature. The living man is thus bound within a net of epistemological and ontological premises which—regardless of ultimate truth or falsity—become partially self-validating for him.[4]

It is awkward to refer constantly to both epistemology and ontology and incorrect to suggest that they are separable in human natural history. There seems to be no convenient word to cover the combination of these two concepts. The nearest approximations are "cognitive structure" or "character structure," but these terms fail to suggest that what is important is a body of habitual assumptions or premises implicit in the relationship between man and environment, and that these premises may be true or false. I shall therefore use the single term "epistemology" in this essay to cover both aspects of the net of premises which govern adaptation (or maladaptation) to the human and physical environment. In George Kelly's vocabulary, these are the rules by which an individual "construes" his experience.

[4] J. Ruesch and G. Bateson, *Communications: The Social Matrix of Psychiatry*, New York, Norton, 1951.

I am concerned especially with that group of premises upon which Occidental concepts of the "self" are built, and conversely, with premises which are corrective to some of the more gross Occidental errors associated with that concept.

## The Epistemology of Cybernetics

What is new and surprising is that we now have partial answers to some of these questions. In the last twenty-five years extraordinary advances have been made in our knowledge of what sort of thing the environment is, what sort of thing an organism is, and, especially, what sort of thing a *mind* is. These advances have come out of cybernetics, systems theory, information theory, and related sciences.

We now know, with considerable certainty, that the ancient problem of whether the mind is immanent or transcendent can be answered in favor of immanence, and that this answer is more economical of explanatory entities than any transcendent answer: it has at least the negative support of Occam's Razor.

On the positive side, we can assert that *any* ongoing ensemble of events and objects which has the appropriate complexity of causal circuits and the appropriate energy relations will surely show mental characteristics. It will *compare*, that is, be responsive to *difference* (in addition to being affected by the ordinary physical "causes" such as impact or force). It will "process information" and will inevitably be self-corrective either toward homeostatic optima or toward the maximization of certain variables.

A "bit" of information is definable as a difference which makes a difference. Such a difference, as it travels and undergoes successive transformation in a circuit, is an elementary idea.

But, most relevant in the present context, we know that no part of such an internally interactive system can have unilateral control over the remainder or over any other part. The mental characteristics are inherent or immanent in the ensemble as a *whole*.

Even in very simple self-corrective systems, this holistic character is evident. In the steam engine with a "governor," the very word "governor" is a misnomer if it be taken to mean that this part of the system has unilateral control. The governor is, essentially, a sense organ or transducer which receives a transform of the *difference* between the actual running speed of the engine and some ideal or preferred speed. This sense organ transforms these differences into differences in some efferent message, for example, to fuel supply or to a brake. The behavior of the governor is determined, in other words, by the behavior of the other parts of the system, and indirectly by its own behavior at a previous time.

The holistic and mental character of the system is most clearly demonstrated by this last fact, that the behavior of the governor (and, indeed, of every part of the causal circuit) is partially determined by its own previous behavior. Message material (*i.e.*, successive transforms of difference) must pass around the total circuit, and the *time* required for the message material to return to the place from which it started is a basic characteristic of the total system. The behavior of the governor (or any other part of the circuit) is thus in some degree determined not only by its immediate past, but by what it did at a time which precedes the present by the interval necessary for the message to complete the circuit. There is thus a sort of determinative *memory* in even the simplest cybernetic circuit.

The stability of the system (*i.e.*, whether it will act self-correctively or oscillate or go into runaway) depends upon the relation between the operational product of all the transformations of difference around the circuit and upon this characteristic time. The "governor" has no control over these factors. Even a human governor in a social system is bound by the same limitations. He is controlled by information from the system and must adapt his own actions to its time characteristics and to the effects of his own past action.

Thus, in no system which shows mental characteristics can any part have unilateral control over the whole. In other words, *the mental characteristics of the system are immanent, not in some part, but in the system as a whole.*

The significance of this conclusion appears when we ask, "Can a computer think?" or, "Is the mind in the brain?" And the answer to both questions will be negative unless the question is focused upon one of the few mental characteristics which are contained within the computer or the brain. A computer is self-corrective in regard to some of its internal variables. It may, for example, include thermometers or other sense organs which are affected by differences in its working temperature, and the response of the sense organ to these differences may affect the action of a fan which in turn corrects the temperature. We may therefore say that the system shows mental characteristics in regard to its internal temperature. But it would be incorrect to say that the main business of the computer—the transformation of input differences into output differences—is "a mental process." The computer is only an arc of a larger circuit which always includes a man and an environment from which information is received and upon which efferent messages from the computer have effect. This total system, or ensemble, may legitimately be said to show mental characteristics. It operates by trial and error and has creative character.

Similarly, we may say that "mind" is immanent in those circuits of the brain which are complete within the brain. Or that mind is immanent in circuits which are complete within the system, brain *plus* body. Or, finally, that mind is immanent in the larger system—man *plus* environment.

In principle, if we desire to explain or understand the mental aspect of any biological event, we must take into account the system—that is, the network of *closed* circuits, within which that biological event is determined. But when we seek to explain the behavior of a man or any other organism, this "system" will usually *not* have the same limits as the "self"—as this term is commonly (and variously) understood.

Consider a man felling a tree with an axe. Each stroke of the axe is modified or corrected, according to the shape of the cut face of the tree left by the previous stroke. This self-corrective (*i.e.*, mental) process is brought about by a total system, tree-eyes-brain-muscles-axe-stroke-tree; and it is this total system that has the characteristics of immanent mind.

More correctly, we should spell the matter out as: (differences in tree)-(differences in retina)-(differences in brain)-(differences in muscles)-(differences in movement of axe)-(differences in tree), etc. What is transmitted around the circuit is transforms of differences. And, as noted above, a difference which makes a difference is an *idea* or unit of information.

But this is *not* how the average Occidental sees the event sequence of tree felling. He says, "*I* cut down the tree" and he even believes that there is a delimited agent, the "self," which performed a delimited "purposive" action upon a delimited object.

It is all very well to say that "Billiard ball A hit billiard ball B and sent it into the pocket"; and it would perhaps be all right (if we could do it) to give a complete hard-science account of the events all around the circuit containing the man and the tree. But popular parlance includes *mind* in its utterance by invoking the personal pronoun, and then achieves a mixture of mentalism and physicalism by restricting mind within the man and reifying the tree. Finally the mind itself becomes reified by the notion that, since the "self" acted upon the axe which acted upon the tree, the "self" must also be a "thing." The parallelism of syntax between "*I* hit the billiard ball" and "The ball hit another ball" is totally misleading.

If you ask anybody about the localization and boundaries of the self, these confusions are immediately displayed. Or consider a blind man with a stick. Where does the blind man's self begin? At the tip of the stick? At the handle of the stick? Or at some point halfway up the stick? These questions are nonsense, because the stick is a pathway along which differences are transmitted under transformation, so that to draw a delimiting line *across* this pathway is to cut off a part of the systemic circuit which determines the blind man's locomotion.

Similarly, his sense organs are transducers or pathways for information, as also are his axons, etc. From a systems-theoretic point of view, it is a misleading metaphor to say that what travels in an axon is an "impulse." It would be more correct to say that what travels is a difference, or a transform of a difference. The metaphor of "impulse" suggests a hard-science line of thought which will ramify only too easily into nonsense about "psychic energy," and those who talk this kind of nonsense will disregard the information content of *quiescence*. The quiescence of an axon *differs* as much from activity as its activity does from quiescence. Therefore quiescence and activity have equal informational relevance. The message of activity can only be accepted as valid if the message of quiescence can also be trusted.

It is even incorrect to speak of the "message of activity" and the "message of quiescence." Always the fact that information is a transform of difference should be remembered, and we might better call the one message "activity —not quiescence" and the other "quiescence—not activity."

Similar considerations apply to the repentant alcoholic. He cannot simply elect "sobriety." At best he could only elect "sobriety—not drunkenness," and his universe remains polarized, carrying always both alternatives.

The total self-corrective unit which processes information, or, as I say, "thinks" and "acts" and "decides," is a *system* whose boundaries do not at all coincide with the boundaries either of the body or of what is popularly called the "self" or "consciousness"; and it is important to notice that there are *multiple* differences between the thinking system and the "self" as popularly conceived:

(1) The system is not a transcendent entity as the "self" is commonly supposed to be.

(2) The ideas are immanent in a network of causal pathways along which transforms of difference are conducted. The "ideas" of the system are in all cases at least binary in structure. They are not "impulses" but "information."

(3) This network of pathways is not bounded with consciousness but extends to include the pathways of all unconscious mentation—both autonomic and repressed, neural and hormonal.

(4) The network is not bounded by the skin but includes all external pathways along which information can travel. It also includes those effective differences which are immanent in the "objects" of such information. It includes the pathways of sound and light along which travel transforms of differences originally immanent in things and other people —and especially *in our own actions*.

It is important to note that the basic—and I believe erroneous—tenets of popular epistemology are mutually reinforcing. If, for example, the popular premise of transcendence is discarded, the immediate substitute is a premise of immanence in the body. But this alternative will be unacceptable because large parts of the thinking network are located outside the body. The so-called "Body-Mind" problem is wrongly posed in terms which force the argument toward paradox: if mind be supposed immanent in the body, then it must be transcendent. If transcendent, it must be immanent. And so on.[5]

Similarly, if we exclude the unconscious processes from the "self" and call them "ego-alien," then these processes take on the subjective coloring of "urges" and "forces"; and this pseudodynamic quality is then extended to the conscious "self" which attempts to "resist" the "forces" of the unconscious. The "self" thereby becomes itself an organization of seeming "forces." The popular notion which would equate "self" with consciousness thus leads into the notion that ideas are "forces"; and this fallacy is in turn supported by saying that the axon carries "impulses." To find a way out of this mess is by no means easy.

We shall proceed by first examining the structure of the alcoholic's polarization. In the epistemologically unsound resolution, "I will fight the bottle," what is supposedly lined up against what?

## Alcoholic "Pride"

Alcoholics are philosophers in that universal sense in which all human beings (and all mammals) are guided by highly abstract principles of which they are either quite unconscious, or unaware that the principle governing their perception and action is philosophic. A common misnomer for such principles is "feelings."[6]

This misnomer arises naturally from the Anglo-Saxon epistemological tendency to reify or attribute to the body all mental phenomena which are peripheral to consciousness. And the misnomer is, no doubt, supported by the fact that the exercise and/or frustration of these principles is often accompanied by visceral and other bodily sensations. I be-

[5] R. G. Collingwood, *The Idea of Nature*, Oxford, Oxford University Press, 1945.

[6] G. Bateson, "A Social Scientist Views the Emotions," *Expression of the Emotions in Man*, P. Knapp, ed., International University Press, 1963.

lieve, however, that Pascal was correct when he said, "The heart has its *reasons* which the reason does not at all perceive."

But the reader must not expect the alcoholic to present a consistent picture. When the underlying epistemology is full of error, derivations from it are inevitably either self-contradictory or extremely restricted in scope. A consistent corpus of theorems cannot be derived from an inconsistent body of axioms. In such cases, the attempt to be consistent leads either to the great proliferation of complexity characteristic of psychoanalytic theory and Christian theology or to the extremely narrow view characteristic of contemporary behaviorism.

I shall therefore proceed to examine the "pride" which is characteristic of alcoholics to show that this principle of their behavior is derived from the strange dualistic epistemology characteristic of Occidental civilization.

A convenient way of describing such principles as "pride," "dependency," "fatalism," and so forth, is to examine the principle as if it were a result of deutero-learning[7] and to ask what contexts of learning might understandably inculcate this principle.

(1) It is clear that the principle of alcoholic life which AA calls "pride" is not contextually structured around past achievement. They do not use the word to mean pride in something accomplished. The emphasis is not upon "I succeeded," but rather upon "I can. . . ." It is an obsessive acceptance of a challenge, a repudiation of the proposition "I cannot."

[7] This use of formal contextual structure as a descriptive device does not necessarily assume that the principle discussed is wholly or in part actually *learned* in contexts having the appropriate formal structure. The principle could have been genetically determined, and it might still follow that the principle is best described by the formal delineation of the contexts in which it is exemplified. It is precisely this fitting of behavior to context that makes it difficult or impossible to determine whether a principle of behavior was genetically determined or learned in that context; see G. Bateson, "Social Planning and the Concept of Deutero-Learning," *Conference on Science, Philosophy and Religion, Second Symposium,* New York, Harper, 1942.

(2) After the alcoholic has begun to suffer from—or be blamed for—alcoholism, this principle of "pride" is mobilized behind the proposition, "I can stay sober." But, noticeably, success in this achievement destroys the "challenge." The alcoholic becomes "cocksure," as AA says. He relaxes his determination, risks a drink, and finds himself on a binge. We may say that the contextual structure of sobriety changes with its achievement. Sobriety, at this point, is no longer the appropriate contextual setting for "pride." It is the risk of the drink that now is challenging and calls out the fatal "I can. . . ."

(3) AA does its best to insist that this change in contextual structure shall never occur. They restructure the whole context by asserting over and over again that *"Once an alcoholic, always an alcoholic."* They try to have the alcoholic place alcoholism within the self, much as a Jungian analyst tries to have the patient discover his "psychological type" and to learn to live with the strengths and weaknesses of that type. In contrast, the contextual structure of alcoholic "pride" places the alcoholism *outside* the self: "*I* can resist drinking."

(4) The challenge component of alcoholic "pride" is linked with *risk-taking*. The principle might be put in words: "I can do something where success is improbable and failure would be disastrous." Clearly this principle will never serve to maintain continued sobriety. As success begins to appear probable, the alcoholic must challenge the risk of a drink. The element of "bad luck" or "probability" of failure places failure beyond the limits of the self. "If failure occurs, it is not *mine*." Alcoholic "pride" progressively narrows the concept of "self," placing what happens outside its scope.

(5) The principle of pride-in-risk is ultimately almost suicidal. It is all very well to test once whether the universe is on your side, but to do so again and again, with increasing stringency of proof, is to set out on a project which can only prove that the universe hates you. But, still and all, the AA narratives show repeatedly that, at the very bottom of despair, *pride* sometimes prevents suicide. The final quietus must not be delivered by the "self."[8]

---

[8] See Bill's Story, *Alcoholics Anonymous, op. cit.*

## Pride and Symmetry

The so-called pride of the alcoholic always presumes a real or fictitious "other," and its complete contextual definition therefore demands that we characterize the real or imagined relationship to this "other." A first step in this task is to classify the relationship as either "symmetrical" or "complementary."[9] To do this is not entirely simple when the "other" is a creation of the unconscious, but we shall see that the indications for such a classification are clear.

An explanatory digression is, however, necessary. The primary criterion is simple:

If, in a binary relationship, the behaviors of A and B are regarded (by A and B) as *similar* and are linked so that more of the given behavior by A stimulates more of it in B, and vice versa, then the relationship is "symmetrical" in regard to these behaviors.

If, conversely, the behaviors of A and B are *dissimilar* but mutually fit together (as, for example, spectatorship fits exhibitionism), and the behaviors are linked so that more of A's behavior stimulates more of B's fitting behavior, then the relationship is "complementary" in regard to these behaviors.

Common examples of simple symmetrical relationship are armaments races, keeping up with the Joneses, athletic emulation, boxing matches, and the like. Common examples of complementary relationship are dominance-submission, sadism-masochism, nurturance-dependency, spectatorship-exhibitionism, and the like.

More complex considerations arise when higher logical typing is present. For example: A and B may compete in gift-giving, thus superposing a larger symmetrical frame upon primarily complementary behaviors. Or, conversely, a therapist might engage in competition with a patient in some sort of play therapy, placing a complementary nurturant frame around the primarily symmetrical transactions of the game.

Various sorts of "double binds" are generated when A and B perceive the premises of their relationship in different

[9] G. Bateson, *Naven,* Cambridge, Cambridge University Press, 1936.

terms—A may regard B's behavior as competitive when B thought he was helping A. And so on.

With these complexities we are not here concerned, because the imaginary "other" or counterpart in the "pride" of the alcoholic does not, I believe, play the complex games which are characteristic of the "voices" of schizophrenics.

Both complementary and symmetrical relationships are liable to progressive changes of the sort which I have called "schismogenesis."[10] Symmetrical struggles and armaments races may, in the current phrase, "escalate"; and the normal pattern of succoring-dependency between parent and child may become monstrous. These potentially pathological developments are due to undamped or uncorrected positive feedback in the system, and may—as stated—occur in either complementary or symmetrical systems. However, in *mixed* systems schismogenesis is necessarily reduced. The armaments race between two nations will be slowed down by acceptance of complementary themes such as dominance, dependency, admiration, and so forth, between them. It will be speeded up by the repudiation of these themes.

This antithetical relationship between complementary and symmetrical themes is, no doubt, due to the fact that each is the logical opposite of the other. In a merely symmetrical armaments race, nation A is motivated to greater efforts by its estimate of *the greater strength* of B. When it estimates that B is weaker, nation A will relax its efforts. But the exact opposite will happen if A's structuring of the relationship is complementary. Observing that B is *weaker* than they, A will go ahead with hopes of conquest.[11]

This antithesis between complementary and symmetrical patterns may be more than simply logical. Notably, in psychoanalytic theory,[12] the patterns which are called "libidinal" and which are modalities of the erogenous zones are all *complementary*. Intrusion, inclusion, exclusion, recep-

[10] *Ibid.*

[11] G. Bateson, "The Pattern of an Armaments Race–Part I: An Anthropological Approach," *Bulletin of Atomic Scientists*, 1946, 2(5): 10–11: also L. F. Richardson, "Generalized Foreign Politics," *British Journal of Psychology*, Monograph Supplements, 1939.

[12] E. H. Erikson, "Configurations in Play—Clinical Notes," *Psychoanalytic Quarterly*, 1937, 6: 139–214.

tion, retention, and the like—all of these are classed as "libidinal." Whereas rivalry, competition, and the like fall under the rubric of "ego" and "defense."

It is also possible that the two antithetical codes—symmetrical and complementary—may be physiologically represented by contrasting states of the central nervous system. The progressive changes of schismogenesis may reach climactic discontinuities and sudden reversals. Symmetrical rage may suddenly turn to grief; the retreating animal with tail between his legs may suddenly "turn at bay" in a desperate battle of symmetry to the death. The bully may suddenly become the coward when he is challenged, and the wolf who is beaten in a symmetrical conflict may suddenly give "surrender" signals which prevent further attack.

The last example is of special interest. If the struggle between the wolves is symmetrical—that is, if wolf A is stimulated to more aggressive behavior by the aggressive behavior of B—then if B suddenly exhibits what we may call "negative aggression," A will not be able to continue to fight unless he can quickly switch over to that complementary state of mind in which B's weakness would be a stimulus for his aggression. Within the hypothesis of symmetrical and complemetary modes, it becomes unnecessary to postulate a specifically "inhibitory" effect for the surrender signal.

Human beings who possess language can apply the label "aggression" to all attempts to damage the other, regardless of whether the attempt is prompted by the other's strength or weakness; but at the prelinguistic mammalian level these two sorts of "aggression" must appear totally different. We are told that from the lion's point of view, an "attack" on a zebra is totally different from an "attack" on another lion.[13]

Enough has now been said so that the question can be posed: Is alcoholic pride contextually structured in symmetrical or complementary form?

First, there is a very strong tendency toward symmetry in the normal drinking habits of Occidental culture. Quite apart from addictive alcoholism, two men drinking together are impelled by convention to match each other, drink for drink. At this stage, the "other" is still real and the symmetry, or rivalry, between the pair is friendly.

[13] K. Z. Lorenz, *On Aggression*, New York, Harcourt, Brace & World, 1966.

As the alcoholic becomes addicted and tries to resist drinking, he begins to find it difficult to resist the social context in which he should match his friends in their drinking. The AA says, "Heaven knows, we have tried hard enough and long enough to drink like other people!"

As things get worse, the alcoholic is likely to become a solitary drinker and to exhibit the whole spectrum of response to challenge. His wife and friends begin to suggest that his drinking is a *weakness*, and he may respond, with symmetry, both by resenting them and by asserting his strength to resist the bottle. But, as is characteristic of symmetrical responses, a brief period of successful struggle weakens his motivation and he falls off the wagon. Symmetrical effort requires continual opposition from the opponent.

Gradually the focus of the battle changes, and the alcoholic finds himself committed to a new and more deadly type of symmetrical conflict. He must now prove that the bottle cannot kill him. His "head is bloody but unbowed." He is still the "captain of his soul"—for what it's worth.

Meanwhile, his relationships with wife and boss and friends have been deteriorating. He never did like the complementary status of his boss as an authority; and now as he deteriorates his wife is more and more forced to take a complementary role. She may try to exert authority, or she becomes protective, or she shows forbearance, but all those provoke either rage or shame. His symmetrical "pride" can tolerate no complementary role.

In sum, the relationship between the alcoholic and his real or fictitious "other" is clearly symmetrical and clearly schismogenic. It escalates. We shall see that the religious conversion of the alcoholic when saved by AA can be described as a dramatic shift from this symmetrical habit, or epistemology, to an almost purely complementary view of his relationship to others and to the universe or God.

## Pride or Inverted Proof?

Alcoholics may appear to be stiff-necked, but they are not stupid. The part of the mind in which their policy is decided certainly lies too deep for the word "stupidity" to be applicable. These levels of the mind are prelinguistic and the computation which goes on there is coded in *primary process*.

Both in dream and in mammalian interaction, the only way to achieve a proposition which contains its own negation ("I will not bite you," or "I am not afraid of him") is by an elaborate imagining or acting out of the proposition to be negated, leading to a *reductio ad absurdum*. "I will not bite you" is achieved between two mammals by an experimental combat which is a "not combat," sometimes called "play." It is for this reason that "agonistic" behavior commonly evolves into friendly greeting.[14]

In this sense, the so-called pride of the alcoholic is in some degree ironic. It is a determined effort to test something like "self-control" with an ulterior but unstateable purpose of proving that "self-control" is ineffectual and absurd. "It simply won't work." This ultimate proposition, since it contains a simple negation, is not to be expressed in primary process. Its final expression is in an action—the taking of a drink. The heroic battle with the bottle, that fictitious "other," ends up in a "kiss and make friends."

In favor of this hypothesis, there is the undoubted fact that the testing of self-control leads back into drinking. And, as I have argued above, the whole epistemology of self-control which his friends urge upon the alcoholic is monstrous. If this be so, then the alcoholic is right in rejecting it. He has achieved a *reductio ad absurdum* of the conventional epistemology.

But this description of achieving a *reductio ad absurdum* verges upon teleology. If the proposition "It won't work" cannot be entertained within the coding of primary process, how then can the computations of primary process direct the organism to try out those courses of action which will demonstrate that "It won't work"?

Problems of this general type are frequent in psychiatry and can perhaps only be resolved by a model in which, under certain circumstances, the organism's discomfort activates a positive feedback loop to *increase* the behavior which preceded the discomfort. Such positive feedback would

[14] G. Bateson, "Metalogue: What Is an Instinct?," *Approaches to Animal Communication*, T. Sebeok, ed., The Hague, Mouton, 1969.

provide a verification that it was really that particular behavior which brought about the discomfort, and might increase the discomfort to some threshold level at which change would become possible.

In psychotherapy such a positive feedback loop is commonly provided by the therapist who pushes the patient in the direction of his symptoms—a technique which has been called the "therapeutic double bind." An example of this technique is quoted later in this essay, where the AA member challenges the alcoholic to go and do some "controlled drinking" in order that he may discover for himself that he has no control.

It is also usual that the symptoms and hallucinations of the schizophrenic—like dreams—constitute a corrective experience, so that the whole schizophrenic episode takes on the character of a self-initiation. Barbara O'Brien's account of her own psychosis[15] is perhaps the most striking example of this phenomenon, which has been discussed elsewhere.[16]

It will be noted that the possible existence of such a positive feedback loop, which will cause a runaway in the direction of increasing discomfort up to some threshold (which might be on the other side of death), is not included in conventional theories of learning. But a tendency to verify the unpleasant by seeking repeated experience of it is a common human trait. It is perhaps what Freud called the "death instinct."

### The Drunken State

What has been said above about the treadmill of symmetrical pride is only one half of the picture. It is the picture of the state of mind of the alcoholic *battling* with the bottle. Clearly this state is very unpleasant and clearly it is also unrealistic. His "others" are either totally imaginary or are gross distortions of persons on whom he is dependent and whom he may love. He has an alternative to this uncom-

[15] B. O'Brien, *Operators and Things: The Inner Life of a Schizophrenic*, Cambridge, Mass., Arlington Books, 1958.

[16] G. Bateson, ed., *Perceval's Narrative*, Stanford, Calif., Stanford University Press, 1961, Introduction.

fortable state—he can get drunk. Or, *"at least,"* have a drink.

With this complementary surrender, which the alcoholic will often see as an act of spite—a Parthian dart in a symmetrical struggle—his entire epistemology changes. His anxieties and resentments and panic vanish as if by magic. His self-control is lessened, but his need to compare himself with others is reduced even further. He feels the physiological warmth of alcohol in his veins and, in many cases, a corresponding psychological warmth toward others. He may be either maudlin or angry, but he has at least become again a part of the human scene.

Direct data bearing upon the thesis that the step from sobriety into intoxication is also a step from symmetrical challenge into complementarity are scarce, and always confused both by the distortions of recall and by the complex toxicity of the alcohol. But there is strong evidence from song and story to indicate that the step is of this kind. In ritual, partaking of wine has always stood for the social aggregation of persons united in religious "communion" or secular *Gemütlichkeit*. In a very literal sense, alcohol supposedly makes the individual see himself as and act as *a part of* the group. That is, it enables complementarity in the relationships which surround him.

### Hitting Bottom

AA attaches great importance to this phenomenon and regards the alcoholic who has not hit bottom as a poor prospect for their help. Conversely, they are inclined to explain their failure by saying that the individual who goes back to his alcoholism has not yet "hit bottom."

Certainly many sorts of disaster may cause an alcoholic to hit bottom. Various sorts of accidents, an attack of delirium tremens, a patch of drunken time of which he has no memory, rejection by wife, loss of job, hopeless diagnosis, and so on—any of these may have the required effect. AA says that "bottom" is different for different men and some may be dead before they reach it.[17]

It is possible, however, that "bottom" is reached many

[17] Personal communication from a member.

times by any given individual; that "bottom" is a spell of panic which provides a favorable moment for change, but not a moment at which change is inevitable. Friends and relatives and even therapists may pull the alcoholic out of his panic, either with drugs or reassurance, so that he "recovers" and goes back to his "pride" and alcoholism—only to hit a more disastrous "bottom" at some later time, when he will again be ripe for a change. The attempt to change the alcoholic in a period *between* such moments of panic is unlikely to succeed.

The nature of the panic is made clear by the following description of a "test."

> We do not like to pronounce any individual as alcoholic, but you can quickly diagnose yourself. Step over to the nearest barroom and try some controlled drinking. Try to drink and stop abruptly. Try it more than once. It will not take long for you to decide, if you are honest with yourself about it. It may be worth a bad case of jitters if you get a full knowledge of your condition.[18]

We might compare the test quoted above to commanding a driver to brake suddenly when traveling on a slippery road: he will discover fast that his control is limited. (The metaphor "skid row" for the alcoholic section of town is not inappropriate.)

The panic of the alcoholic who has hit bottom is the panic of the man who thought he had control over a vehicle but suddenly finds that the vehicle can run away with him. Suddenly, pressure on what he knows is the brake seems to make the vehicle go faster. It is the panic of discovering that *it* (the system, self *plus* vehicle) is bigger than he is.

In terms of the theory here presented, we may say that hitting bottom exemplifies systems theory at three levels:

(1) The alcoholic works on the discomforts of sobriety to a threshold point at which he has bankrupted the epistemology of "self-control." He then gets drunk—because the "system" is bigger than he is—and he may as well surrender to it.

(2) He works repeatedly at getting drunk until he proves

[18] Alcoholics Anonymous, *op. cit.*, p. 43.

that there is a still larger system. He then encounters the panic of "hitting bottom."

(3) If friends and therapists reassure him, he may achieve a further unstable adjustment—becoming addicted to their help—until he demonstrates that this system won't work, and "hits bottom" again but at a lower level. In this, as in all cybernetic systems, the sign (plus or minus) of the effect of any intrusion upon the system depends upon timing.

(4) Lastly, the phenomenon of hitting bottom is complexly related to the experience of double bind.[19] Bill W. narrates that he hit bottom when diagnosed as a hopeless alcoholic by Dr. William D. Silkworth in 1939, and this event is regarded as the beginning of AA history.[20] Dr. Silkworth also "supplied us with the tools with which to puncture the toughest alcoholic ego, those shattering phrases by which he described our illness: *the obsession of the mind* that compels us to drink and *the allergy of the body* that condemns us to go mad or die."[21] This is a double bind correctly founded upon the alcoholic's dichotomous epistemology of mind versus body. He is forced by these words back and back to the point at which only an involuntary change in deep unconscious epistemology—a spiritual experience—will make the lethal description irrelevant.

### The Theology of Alcoholics Anonymous

Some outstanding points of the theology of AA are:

(1) *There is a Power greater than the self*. Cybernetics would go somewhat further and recognize that the "self" as ordinarily understood is only a small part of a much larger trial-and-error system which does the thinking, acting, and deciding. This system includes all the informational pathways which are relevant at any given moment to any given decision. The "self" is a false reification of an improperly delimited part of this much larger field of interlocking processes. Cybernetics also recognizes that two or more persons

[19] G. Bateson, *et al.*, "Toward a Theory of Schizophrenia," *Behavioral Science*, 1956, 1: 251–64.

[20] *AA Comes of Age, op. cit.*, p. vii.

[21] *Ibid.*, p. 13. (Italics in the original)

—any group of persons—may together form such a thinking-and-acting system.

(2) This Power is felt to be personal and to be intimately linked with each person. It is "God as *you* understand him to be."

Cybernetically speaking, "my" relation to any larger system around me and including other things and persons will be different from "your" relation to some similar system around you. The relation "part of" must necessarily and logically always be complementary but the meaning of the phrase "part of" will be different for every person.[22] This difference will be especially important in systems containing more than one person. The system or "power" must necessarily appear different from where each person sits. Moreover, it is expectable that such systems, when they encounter each other, will recognize each other as systems in this sense. The "beauty" of the woods through which I walk is my recognition both of the individual trees and of the total ecology of the woods as *systems*. A similar esthetic recognition is still more striking when I talk with another person.

(3) A favorable relationship with this Power is discovered through "hitting bottom" and "surrender."

(4) By resisting this Power, men and especially alcoholics bring disaster upon themselves. The materialistic philosophy which sees "man" as pitted against his environment is rapidly breaking down as technological man becomes more and more able to oppose the largest systems. Every battle that he wins brings a threat of disaster. The unit of survival—either in ethics or in evolution—is not the organism or the species but the largest system or "power" within which the creature lives. If the creature destroys its environment, it destroys itself.

(5) But—and this is important—the Power does not reward and punish. It does not have "power" in that sense. In the biblical phrase, "All things work together for good to them that love God." And, conversely, to them that do not. The idea of power in the sense of unilateral control is foreign to AA. Their organization is strictly "democratic" (their word), and even their deity is still bound by what

---

[22] This diversity in styles of integration could account for the fact that some persons become alcoholic while others do not.

we might call a systemic determinism. The same limitation applies both to the relationship between the AA sponsor and the drunk whom he hopes to help and to the relationship between AA central office and every local group.

(6) The first two "steps" of Alcoholics Anonymous taken together identify the addiction as a manifestation of this Power.

(7) The healthy relation between each person and this Power is complementary. It is in precise contrast to the "pride" of the alcoholic, which is predicated upon a symmetrical relationship to an imagined "other." The schismogenesis is always more powerful than the participants in it.

(8) The quality and content of each person's relation to the Power is indicated or reflected in the social structure of AA. The secular aspect of this system—its governance— is delineated in "Twelve Traditions"[23] which supplement the "Twelve Steps," the latter developing man's relationship to the Power. The two documents overlap in the Twelfth Step, which enjoins aid to other alcoholics as a necessary spiritual exercise without which the member is likely to relapse. The total system is a Durkheimian religion in the sense that the relationship between man and his community parallels the relationship between man and God. "AA is a power greater than any of us."[24]

In sum, the relationship of each individual to the "Power" is best defined in the words *is part of*."

(9) Anonymity. It must be understood that anonymity means much more in AA thinking and theology than the mere protection of members from exposure and shame. With increasing fame and success of the organization as a whole, it has become a temptation for members to use the fact of their membership as a positive asset in public relations, politics, education, and many other fields. Bill W., the co-founder of the organization, was himself caught by this temptation in early days and has discussed the matter in a published article.[25] He sees first that any grabbing of the spotlight must be a personal and spiritual danger to the member, who cannot affort such self-seeking; and beyond

[23] *AA Comes of Age, op. cit.*
[24] *Ibid.*, p. 288.
[25] *Ibid.*, pp. 286–94.

this that it would be fatal for the organization as a whole to become involved in politics, religious controversy, and social reform. He states clearly that the errors of the alcoholic are the same as the "forces which are today ripping the world apart at its seams," but that it is not the business of AA to save the world. Their single purpose is "to carry the AA message to the sick alcoholic who wants it."[26] He concludes that anonymity is "the greatest symbol of self-sacrifice that we know." Elsewhere the twelfth of the "Twelve Traditions" states that "anonymity is the spiritual foundation of our traditions, ever reminding us to place principles before personalities."

To this we may add that anonymity is also a profound statement of the systemic relation, part-to-whole. Some systems theorists would go even further, because a major temptation for systems theory lies in the reification of theoretical concepts. Anatol Holt says he wants a bumper sticker which would (paradoxically) say, "Stamp out nouns."[27]

(10) Prayer. The AA use of prayer similarly affirms the complementarity of part-whole relationship by the very simple technique of asking for that relationship. They ask for those personal characteristics, such as humility, which are in fact exercised in the very act of prayer. If the act of prayer be sincere (which is not so easy), God cannot but grant the request. And this is peculiarly true of "God, *as you understand him.*" This self-affirming tautology, which contains its own beauty, is precisely the balm required after the anguish of the double binds which went with hitting bottom.

Somewhat more complex is the famous "Serenity Prayer": "God grant us the serenity to accept the things we cannot change, courage to change the things we can, and wisdom to know the difference."[28]

If double binds cause anguish and despair and destroy

---

[26] *Ibid.*

[27] M. C. Bateson, ed., *Our Own Metaphor*, Wenner-Gren Foundation, Conference on the Effects of Conscious Purpose on Human Adaptation, 1968; New York, Knopf, in press.

[28] This was not originally an AA document and its authorship is unknown. Small variations in the text occur. I have quoted the form which I personally prefer from *AA Comes of Age, op. cit.*, p. 196.

personal epistemological premises at some deep level, then it follows, conversely, that for the healing of these wounds and the growth of a new epistemology, some converse of the double bind will be appropriate. The double bind leads The Serenity Prayer explicitly frees the worshipper from these maddening bonds.
to the conclusion of despair, "There are no alternatives."

In this connection it is worth mentioning that the great schizophrenic, John Perceval, observed a change in his "voices." In the beginning of his psychosis they bullied him with "contradictory commands" (or as I would say, double binds), but later he began to recover when they offered him choice of clearly defined alternatives.[29]

(11) In one characteristic, AA differs profoundly from such natural mental systems as the family or the redwood forest. It has a *single* purpose—"to carry the AA message to the sick alcoholic who wants it"—and the organization is dedicated to the maximization of that purpose. In this respect, AA is no more sophisticated than General Motors or an Occidental nation. But biological systems, other than those premised upon Occidental ideas (and especially *money*), are multipurposed. There is no single variable in the redwood forest of which we can say that the whole system is oriented to maximizing that variable and all other variables are subsidiary to it; and, indeed, the redwood forest works toward optima, not maxima. Its needs are satiable, and too much of anything is toxic.

There is, however, this: that the single purpose of AA is directed outward and is aimed at a noncompetitve relationship to the larger world. The variable to be maximized is a complementarity and is of the nature of "service" rather than dominance.

### The Epistemological Status of Complementary and Symmetrical Premises

It was noted above that in human interaction, symmetry and complementarity may be complexly combined. It is therefore reasonable to ask how it is possible to regard

[29] Bateson, *Perceval . . . , op. cit.*

these themes as so fundamental that they shall be called "epistemological," even in a natural history study of cultural and interpersonal premises.

The answer seems to hang upon what is meant by "fundamental" in such a study of man's natural history; and the word seems to carry two sorts of meaning.

First, I call *more fundamental* those premises which are the more deeply embedded in the mind, which are the more "hard programmed" and the less susceptible to change. In this sense, the symmetrical pride or hubris of the alcoholic is fundamental.

Second, I shall call more fundamental those premises of mind which refer to the larger rather than the smaller systems or gestalten of the universe. The proposition "Grass is green" is less fundamental than the proposition "Color differences make a difference."

But, if we ask about what happens when premises are changed, it becomes clear that these two definitions of the "fundamental" overlap to a very great extent. If a man achieves or suffers change in premises which are deeply embedded in his mind, he will surely find that the results of that change will ramify throughout his whole universe. Such changes we may well call "epistemological."

The question then remains regarding what is epistemologically "right" and what is epistemologically "wrong." Is the change from alcoholic symmetrical "pride" to the AA species of complementarity a correction of his epistemology? And is complementarity *always* somehow better than symmetry?

For the AA member, it may well be true that complementarity is always to be preferred to symmetry and that even the trivial rivalry of a game of tennis or chess may be dangerous. The superficial episode may touch off the deeply embedded symmetrical premise. But this does not mean that tennis and chess propose epistemological error for everybody.

The ethical and philosophic problem really concerns only the widest universe and the deepest psychological levels. If we deeply and even unconsciously believe that our relation to the largest system which concerns us—the "Power greater than self"—is symmetrical and emulative, then we are in error.

## Limitations of the Hypothesis

Finally, the above analysis is subject to the following limitations and implications:

(1) It is not asserted that all alcoholics operate according to the logic which is here outlined. It is very possible that other types of alcoholics exist and almost certain that alcoholic addiction in other cultures will follow other lines.

(2) It is not asserted that the way of Alcoholics Anonymous is the *only* way to live correctly or that their theology is the only correct derivation from the epistemology of cybernetics and systems theory.

(3) It is not asserted that all transactions between human beings ought to be complementary, though it is clear that the relation between the individual and the larger system of which he is a part must necessarily be so. Relations between persons will (I hope) always be complex.

(4) It is, however, asserted that the nonalcoholic world has many lessons which it might learn from the epistemology of systems theory and from the ways of AA. If we continue to operate in terms of a Cartesian dualism of mind versus matter, we shall probably also continue to see the world in terms of God versus man; elite versus people; chosen race versus others; nation versus nation; and man versus environment. It is doubtful whether a species having *both* an advanced technology *and* this strange way of looking at its world can endure.

# Comment on Part III

In the essays collected in Part III, I speak of an action or utterance as occurring "in" a context, and this conventional way of talking suggests that the particular action is a "dependent" variable, while the context is the "independent" or determining variable. But this view of how an action is related to its context is likely to distract the reader—as it has distracted me—from perceiving the ecology of the ideas which together constitute the small subsystem which I call "context."

This heuristic error—copied like so many others from the ways of thought of the physicist and chemist—requires correction.

It is important to see the particular utterance or action as *part* of the ecological subsystem called context and not as the product or effect of what remains of the context after the piece which we want to explain has been cut out from it.

The mistake in question is the same formal error as that mentioned in the comment on Part II where I discuss the evolution of the horse. We should not think of this process just as a set of changes in the animal's adaptation to life on the grassy plains but as a *constancy in the relationship* between animals and environment. It is the ecology which survives and slowly evolves. In this evolution, the relata—the animals and the grass—undergo changes which are indeed adaptive from moment to moment. But if the process of adaptation were the whole story, there could be no systemic pathology. Trouble arises precisely because the "logic" of adaptation is a different "logic" from that of the survival and evolution of the ecological system.

In Warren Brodey's phrase, the "time-grain" of the adaptation is different from that of the ecology.

"Survival" means that certain descriptive statements about some living system continue to be true through some period of time; and, conversely, "evolution" refers to changes in the truth of certain descriptive statements about some living system. The trick is to define which statements about which systems remain true or undergo change.

The paradoxes (and the pathologies) of systemic process arise precisely because the constancy and survival of some larger system is maintained by changes in the constituent subsystems.

The relative constancy—the survival—of the relationship between animals and grass is maintained by changes in both relata. But any adaptive change in either of the relata, if uncorrected by some change in the other, will always jeopardize the relationship between them. These arguments propose a new conceptual frame for the "double bind" hypothesis, a new conceptual frame for thinking about "schizophrenia," and a new way of looking at context and levels of learning.

In a word, schizophrenia, deutero-learning, and the double bind cease to be matters of individual psychology and become part of the ecology of ideas in systems or "minds" whose boundaries no longer coincide with the skins of the participant individuals.

# Part IV: Biology and Evolution

# On Empty-Headedness Among Biologists and
# State Boards of Education*

My father, the geneticist William Bateson, used to read us passages of the Bible at breakfast—lest we grow up to be *empty-headed* atheists; and so I find it natural to wonder what broadening of the mind may come from the strange anti-evolutionary ruling of the State Board of Education in California.[1]

Evolution has long been badly taught. In particular, students—and even professional biologists—acquire theories of evolution without any deep understanding of what problem these theories attempt to solve. They learn but little of the evolution of evolutionary theory.

The extraordinary achievement of the writers of the first chapter of Genesis was their perception of the problem: *Where does order come from?* They observed that the land and the water were, in fact, separate and that species were separate; they saw that such separation and sorting in the universe presented a fundamental problem. In modern terms, we may say that this is the problem implicit in the Second Law of Thermodynamics: If random events lead to things getting mixed up, by what nonrandom events did things come to be sorted? And what is a "random" event?

This problem has been central to biology and to many

* This item in *BioScience*, Vol. 20, 1970, is reproduced by permission from that journal.

[1] See "California's Anti-Evolution Ruling," *BioScience*, March 1, 1970.

other sciences for the last 5000 years, and the problem is not trivial.

With what Word should we designate the principle of order which seems to be immanent in the universe?

The California ruling suggests that students be told of other attempts to solve this ancient problem. I myself collected one of these among the Stone Age head-hunters of the Iatmul tribe in New Guinea. They, too, note that the land and the water are separate even in their swampy region. They say that in the beginning there was a vast crocodile, Kavwokmali, who paddled with his front legs and paddled with his back legs, and thereby kept the mud in suspension. The culture hero, Kevembuangga, speared the crocodile, who then ceased to paddle, causing the mud and the water to separate. The result was dry land upon which Kevembuangga stamped his foot in triumph. We might say he verified that "it was good."

Our students might have their minds broadened somewhat if they would look at other theories of evolution and consider how a man's spirit must take a different shape if he believes that all sorting in the universe is due to an external agent, or if, like the Iatmul and modern scientists, he sees that the potentiality for order and pattern is immanent throughout this world.

And then the student may be forced by the new system to look at the "Great Chain of Being," with Supreme Mind at the top and the protozoa at the bottom. He will see how Mind was invoked as an explanatory principle all through the Middle Ages and how Mind later became the *problem*. Mind became that which needed explanation when Lamarck showed that the Great Chain of Being should be inverted to give an evolutionary sequence from the protozoa upward. The problem then was to explain Mind in terms of what could be known of this sequence.

And when the student reaches the mid-nineteenth century, he might be given as a textbook Philip Henry Gosse's *Creation (Omphalos): An Attempt to Untie the Geological Knot*. He will learn from this extraordinary book things about the structure of animals and plants which are today scarcely mentioned in many courses of biology; notably, that all animals and plants show a time structure, of which the rings of growth in trees are an elementary example and the cycles of life history, a more complex one. Every plant and animal is constructed upon the premise of its cyclic nature.

After all, there can be no harm in Gosse, who was a devout fundamentalist—a Plymouth Brother—as well as a distinguished marine biologist. His book was published in 1857, two years before the *Origin of Species*. He wrote it to show that the facts of the fossil record as well as those of biological homology could be made to fit with the principles of fundamentalism. It was to him inconceivable that God could have created a world in which Adam had no navel; the trees in the Garden of Eden, no rings of growth; and the rocks, no strata. Therefore, God must have created the world as though it had a past.

It will do the student no harm to wrestle with the paradoxes of Gosse's "Law of Prochronism"; if he listens carefully to Gosse's groping generalizations about the biological world, he will hear an early version of the "steady state" hypothesis.

Of course, everybody knows that biological phenomena are cyclic—from egg, to hen, to egg, to hen, etc. But not all biologists have examined the implications of this cyclic characteristic for evolutionary and ecological theory. Gosse's view of the biological world might broaden their minds.

It is silly and vulgar to approach the rich spectrum of evolutionary thought with questions only about who was right and who was wrong. We might as well assert that the amphibia and reptiles were "wrong" and the mammals and birds "right" in their solutions to the problems of how to live.

By fighting the fundamentalists, we are led into an empty-headedness analogous to theirs. The truth of the matter is that "Other men have laboured and ye are entered into their labours" (John I:38), and this text is not only a reminder of the need for humility, it is also an epitome of the vast evolutionary process into which we organisms are willy-nilly entered.

# The Role of Somatic Change in Evolution*

All theories of biological evolution depend upon at least three sorts of change: (a) change of genotype, either by mutation or by redistribution of genes; (b) somatic change under pressure of environment; and (c) changes in environmental conditions. The problem for the evolutionist is to build a theory combining these types of change into an ongoing process which, under natural selection, will account for the phenomena of adaptation and phylogeny.

Certain conventional premises may be selected to govern such theory building:

(a) *The theory shall not depend upon Lamarckian inheritance.* August Weismann's argument for this premise still stands. There is no reason to believe that either somatic change or changes in environment can, in principle, call (by physiological communication) for appropriate genotypic change. Indeed, the little that we know about communication within the multicellular[1] individual indicates that such communication from soma to gene script is likely to be rare and unlikely to be adaptive in effect. However, it is appropriate to attempt to spell out in this essay what this premise implies:

Whenever some characteristic of an organism is modifiable under measurable environmental impact or under measurable

---

* This essay appeared in the journal *Evolution*, Vol 17, 1963, and is reprinted with the editor's permission.
[1] The problems of bacterial genetics are here deliberately excluded.

impact of internal physiology, it is possible to write an equation in which the value of the characteristic in question is expressed as some function of the value of the impacting circumstance. "Human skin color is some function of exposure to sunlight," "respiration rate is some function of atmospheric pressure," etc. Such equations are constructed to be true for a variety of particular observations, and necessarily contain subsidiary propositions which are stable (*i.e.*, continue to be true) over a wide range of values of impacting circumstance and somatic characteristic. These subsidiary propositions are of different logical type from the original observations in the laboratory and are, in fact, descriptive not of the data but of *our* equations. They are statements about the form of the particular equation and about the values of the parameters mentioned within it.

It would be simple, at this point, to draw the line between genotype and phenotype by saying that the *forms and parameters* of such equations are provided by genes, while the impacts of environment, etc. determine the actual event within this frame. This would amount to saying, *e.g.*, that the *ability* to tan is genotypically determined, while the amount of tanning in a particular case depends upon exposure to sunlight.

In terms of this oversimplified approach to the overlapping roles of genotype and environment, the proposition excluding Lamarckian inheritance would read somewhat as follows: In the attempt to explain evolutionary process, there shall be no assumption that the achievement of a particular value of some variable under particular circumstances will affect, in the gametes produced by that individual, the form or parameters of the functional equation governing the relationship between that variable and its environmental circumstances.

Such a view is oversimplified, and parentheses must be added to deal with more complex and extreme cases. First, it is important to recognize that the organism, considered as a communicational system, may itself operate at multiple levels of logical typing; *i.e.*, that there will be instances in which what were above called "parameters" are subject to change. The individual organism might as a result of "training" change its ability to develop a tan under sunlight. And this type of change is certainly of very great importance in the field of animal behavior, where "learning to learn" can never be ignored.

Second, the oversimplified view must be elaborated to cover *negative* effects. An environmental circumstance may have such impact upon an organism unable to adapt to it, that the individual in question will in fact produce *no* gametes.

Third, it is expectable that some of the parameters in one equation may be subject to change under impact from some environmental or physiologic circumstance other than the circumstance mentioned in that equation.

Be all that as it may, both Weismann's objection to Lamarckian theory and my own attempt to spell the matter out share a certain parsimony: an assumption that the principles which order phenomena shall not themselves be supposed changed by those phenomena which they order. William of Occam's razor might be reformulated: in any explanation, logical types shall not be multiplied beyond necessity.

(b) *Somatic change is absolutely necessary for survival.* Any change of environment which requires adaptive change in the species will be lethal unless, by somatic change, the organisms (or some of them) are able to weather out a period of unpredictable duration, until either appropriate genotypic change occurs (whether by mutation or by redistribution of genes already available in the population), or because the environment returns to the previous normal. The premise is truistical, regardless of the magnitude of the time span involved.

(c) *Somatic change is also necessary to cope with any changes of genotype which might aid the organism in its external struggle with the environment.* The individual organism is a complex organization of interdependent parts. A mutational or other genotypic change in any one of these (however externally valuable in terms of survival) is certain to require change in many others—which changes will probably not be specified or implicit in the single mutational change of the genes. A hypothetical pregiraffe, which had the luck to carry a mutant gene "long neck," would have to adjust to this change by complex modifications of the heart and circulatory system. These collateral adjustments would have to be achieved at the somatic level. Only those pregiraffes which are (genotypically) capable of these somatic modifications would survive.

(*d*) In this essay, it is assumed that *the corpus of genotypic messages is preponderantly digital* in nature. In contrast, the soma is seen as a working system in which the genotypic recipes are tried out. Should it transpire that the genotypic corpus is also in some degree analogic—a working model of the soma—premise *c* (above) would be negated to that degree. It would then be conceivable that the mutant gene "long neck" might modify the message of those genes which affect the development of the heart. It is, of course, known that genes may have pleiotropic effect, but these phenomena are relevant in the present connection only if it can be shown, *e.g.*, that the effect of gene A upon the phenotype and its effect upon the phenotypic expression of gene B are mutually appropriate in the overall integration and adaptation of the organism.

These considerations lead to a classifying of both genotypic and environmental changes in terms of the *price* which they exact of the flexibility of the somatic system. A lethal change in either environment or genotype is simply one which demands somatic modifications which the organism cannot achieve.

But the somatic price of a given change must depend, not absolutely upon the change in question, but upon the range of somatic flexibility available to the organism at the given time. This range, in turn, will depend upon how much of the organism's somatic flexibility is already being used up in adjusting to other mutations or environmental changes. We face an *economics* of flexibility which, like any other economics, will become determinative for the course of evolution if and only if the organism is operating close to the limits set by this economics.

However, this economics of somatic flexibility will differ in one important respect from the more familiar economics of money or available energy. In these latter, each new expenditure can simply be *added* to the preceding expenditures and the economics becomes coercive when the additive total approaches the limit of the budget. In contrast, the combined effect of multiple changes, each of which exacts a price in the soma, will be *multiplicative*. This point may be stated as follows: Let S be the finite set of all possible living states of the organism. Within S, let $s_1$ be the smaller set of all states compatible with a given mutation $(m_1)$, and let $s_2$ be the set of states compatible with a second mutation $(m_2)$. It follows that the two mutations in combination will limit the organism to the logical product of $s_1$ and $s_2$, *i.e.*, to that usually smaller subset of states which is composed only of members common to both $s_1$ and $s_2$. In this way each successive mutation (or other genotypic change) will fractionate the possibilities for the somatic adjustment of the organism. And, should the one mutation require some somatic change, the exact opposite of a change required by the other, the possibilities for somatic adjustment may immediately be reduced to zero.

The same argument must surely apply to multiple environmental changes which demand somatic adjustments; and this will be true even of those changes in environment which might seem to benefit the organism. An improvement in diet, for example, will exclude from the organism's range of somatic adjustments those patterns of growth which we would call "stunted" and which might be required to meet some other exigency of the environment.

From these considerations it follows that if evolution proceeded in accordance with conventional theory, its process would be blocked. The finite nature of somatic change indicates that no ongoing process of evolution can result only from successive externally adaptive genotypic changes since these must, in combination, become lethal, demanding combinations of internal somatic adjustments of which the soma is incapable.

We turn therefore to a consideration of other classes of genotypic change. What is required to give a balanced theory of evolution is the occurrence of genotypic changes which shall *increase* the available range of somatic flexibility. When the internal organization of the organisms of a species has been limited by environmental or mutational pressure to some narrow subset of the total range of living states, further evolutionary progress will require some sort of genotypic change which will compensate for this limitation.

We note first that while the results of genotypic change are irreversible within the life of the individual organism, the opposite is usually true of changes which are achieved at the somatic level. When the latter are produced in response to special environmental conditions, a return of the environment to the previous norm is usually followed by a diminution or loss of the characteristic. (We may reasonably expect that the same would be true of those somatic adjustments which must accompany an externally adaptive mutation but, of course, it is impossible in this case to remove from the individual the impact of the mutational change.)

A further point regarding these reversible somatic changes is of special interest. Among higher organisms it is not unusual to find that there is what we may call a "defense in depth" against environmental demands. If a man is moved from sea level to 10,000 feet, he may begin to pant and his heart may race. But these first changes are swiftly reversible: if he descends the same day, they will disappear immediately. If, however, he remains at the high altitude, a second line of defense appears. He will become slowly acclimated as a result of complex physiological changes. His heart will cease to race, and he will no longer pant unless he undertakes some special exertion. If now he returns to sea level, the characteristics of the second line of defense will disappear rather slowly and he may even experience some discomfort.

From the point of view of an economics of somatic flexibility, the first effect of high altitude is to reduce the organism to a limited set of states ($s_1$) characterized by the racing of the heart and the panting. The man can still survive, but only as a comparatively inflexible creature. The later acclimation has precisely this value: it corrects for the loss of flexibility. After the man is acclimated he can use his panting mechanisms to adjust to *other* emergencies which might otherwise be lethal.

A similar "defense in depth" is clearly recognizable in the field of behavior. When we encounter a new problem for the first time, we deal with it either by trial and error or possibly by insight. Later, and more or less gradually, we form the "habit" of acting in the way which earlier experience rewarded. To continue to use insight or trial and error upon this class of problem would be wasteful. These mechanisms can now be saved for *other* problems.[2]

Both in acclimation and in habit formation the economy of flexibility is achieved by substituting a deeper and more enduring change for a more superficial and more reversible one. In the terms used above in discussing the anti-Lamarckian premise, a change has occurred in the parameters of the functional equation linking rate of respiration to external atmospheric pressure. Here it seems that the organism is behaving as we may expect any ultrastable system to behave. Ashby[3] has shown that it is a general formal characteristic of such systems that those circuits controlling the more rapidly fluctuating variables act as balancing mechanisms to protect the ongoing constancy of those variables in which change is normally slow and of small amplitude; and that any interference which fixes the values of the changeful variables must have a disturbing effect upon the constancy of the normally steady components of the system. For the man who must constantly pant at high altitudes, the respiration rate can no longer be used as a changeable quantity in the maintaining of physiological balance. Conversely, if the respiration rate is to become available again as a rapidly fluctuating variable, some change must occur among the more stable components of the system. Such a change will, in the nature of the case, be achieved comparatively slowly and be comparatively irreversible.

Even acclimation and habit formation are, however, still reversible within the life of the individual, and this very reversibility indicates a lack of communicational economy in these adaptive mechanisms. Reversibility implies that the changed value of some variable is achieved by means of homeostatic, error-activated circuits. There must be a means of detecting an undesirable or threatening change in some variable, and there must be a train of cause and effect where-

[2] G. Bateson, "Minimal Requirements for a Theory of Schizophrenia," *A.M.A. Archives of General Psychiatry*, 1960, 2: 447.

[3] W. R. Ashby, "The Effect of Controls on Stability," *Nature*, 1945, 155: 242; also Ashby, *Design for a Brain*, New York, John Wiley & Co., 1952.

by corrective action is initiated. Moreover, this entire circuit must, in some degree, be available for this purpose for the entire time during which the reversible change is maintained—a considerable using up of available message pathways.

The matter of communicational economics becomes still more serious when we note that the homeostatic circuits of an organism are not separate but complexly interlocked, *e.g.*, hormonal messengers which play a part in the homeostatic control of organ A will also affect the states of organs B, C, and D. Any special ongoing loading of the circuit controlling A will therefore diminish the organism's freedom to control B, C, and D.

In contrast, the changes brought about by mutation or other genotypic change are presumably of a totally different nature. Every cell contains a copy of the new genotypic corpus and therefore will (when appropriate) behave in the changed manner, without any change in the messages which it receives from surrounding tissues or organs. If the hypothetical pregiraffes carrying the mutant gene "long neck" could also get the gene "big heart," their hearts would be enlarged without the necessity of using the homeostatic pathways of the body to achieve and maintain this enlargement. Such a mutation will have survival value not because it enables the pregiraffe to supply its elevated head with sufficient blood, since this was already achieved by somatic change—but because it increases the overall flexibility of the organism, enabling it to survive *other* demands which may be placed upon it either by environmental or genotypic change.

It appears, then, that the process of biological evolution could be continuous if there were a class of mutations or other genotypic changes which would simulate Lamarckian inheritance. The function of these changes would be to achieve by genotypic fiat those characteristics which the organism at the given time is already achieving by the uneconomical method of somatic change.

Such a hypothesis, I believe, conflicts in no way with conventional theories of genetics and natural selection. It does, however, somewhat alter the current conventional picture of evolution as a whole, though related ideas were put forward over sixty years ago. Baldwin[4] suggested that we consider not only the operation of the external environment in natural selection but also what he called "organic selection" in which the fate of a given variation would depend upon its physiologic viability. In the same article, Baldwin attributes to Lloyd Morgan the suggestion that there might exist "coincident variations" which would simulate Lamarckian inheritance (the so-called "Baldwin effect").

According to such a hypothesis, genotypic change in an organism becomes comparable to legislative change in a society. The wise legislator will only rarely initiate a new rule of behavior; more usually he will confine himself to affirming in law that which has already become the custom of the people. An innovative rule can be introduced only at the price of activating and perhaps overloading a large number of homeostatic circuits in the society.

It is interesting to ask how a hypothetical process of evolution would work *if* Lamarckian inheritance were the rule, *i.e.*, if characteristics achieved by somatic homeostasis were inherited. The answer is simple: *it would not work*, for the following reasons:

(1) The question turns upon the concept of economy in the use of homeostatic circuits, and it would be the reverse of economical to fix by genotypic change *all* the variables which accompany a given desirable and homeostatically achieved characteristic. Every such characteristic is achieved by ancillary homeostatic changes all around the circuits, and it is most undesirable that these ancillary changes should be fixed by inheritance, as would logically happen according to any theory involving an indiscriminate Lamarckian inheritance. Those who would defend a Lamarckian theory must be prepared to suggest how in the genotype an appropriate selection can be achieved. Without such a selection, the inheritance of acquired characteristics would merely increase the proportion of nonviable genotypic changes.

(2) Lamarckian inheritance would disturb the relative timing of the processes upon which evolution must—according to the present hypothesis—depend. It is essential that there be a time lag between the uneconomical but

[4] J. M. Baldwin, "Organic Selection," *Science*, 1897, 5: 634.

reversible somatic achievement of a given characteristic and the economical but more enduring alterations of the genotype. If we look upon every soma as a working model which can be modified in various ways in the workshop, it is clear that sufficient but not infinite time must be given for these workshop trials before the results of these trials are incorporated into the final blueprint for mass production. This delay is provided by the indirection of stochastic process. It would be unduly shortened by Lamarckian inheritance.

The principle involved here is general and by no means trivial. It obtains in all homeostatic systems in which a given effect can be brought about by means of a homeostatic circuit, which circuit can, in turn, be modified in its characteristics by some higher system of control. In all such systems (ranging from the house thermostat to systems of government and administration) it is important that the higher system of control *lag behind* the event sequences in the peripheral homeostatic circuit.

In evolution two control systems are present: the homeostases of the body which deal with tolerable internal stress, and the action of natural selection upon the (genetically) nonviable members of the population. From an engineering point of view, the problem is to *limit* communication from the lower, reversible somatic system to the higher irreversible genotypic system.

Another aspect of the proposed hypothesis about which we can only speculate is the probable relative frequency of the two classes of genotypic change: those which initiate something new and those which affirm some homeostatically achieved characteristic. In the Metazoa and multicellular plants, we face complex networks of multiple interlocking homeostatic circuits, and any given mutation or gene recombination which initiates change will probably require very various and multiple somatic characteristics to be achieved by homeostasis. The hypothetical pregiraffe with the mutant gene "long neck" will need to modify not only its heart and circulatory system but also perhaps its semicircular canals, its intervertebral discs, its postural reflexes, the ratio of length and thickness of many muscles, its evasive tactics vis-à-vis predators, etc. This suggests that in such complex organisms, the merely affirmative genotypic changes must far outnumber those which initiate change, if the species is to avoid that cul-de-sac in which the flexibility of the soma approaches zero.

Conversely, this picture suggests that most organisms, at any given time, are probably in such a state that there are multiple possibilities for affirmative genotypic change. If, as seems probable, both mutation and gene redistribution are in some sense random phenomena, at least the chances are considerable that one or other of these multiple possibilities will be met.

Finally, it is appropriate to discuss what evidence is available or might be sought to support or disprove such a hypothesis. It is clear at the outset that such a testing will be difficult. The affirmative mutations upon which the hypothesis depends will usually be *invisible*. From among the many members of a population which are achieving a given adjustment to environmental circumstances by somatic change, it will not be possible immediately to pick out those few in which the same adjustment is provided by the genotypic method. In such a case, the genotypically changed individuals will have to be identified by breeding and raising the offspring under more normal conditions.

A still greater difficulty arises in cases where we would investigate those homeostatically acquired characteristics which are achieved in response to some innovative genotypic change. It will often be impossible, by mere inspection of the organism, to tell which of its characteristics are the primary results of genotypic change and which are secondary somatic adjustments to these. In the imaginary case of the pregiraffe with a somewhat elongated neck and an enlarged heart, it may be easy to *guess* that the modification of the neck is genotypic while that of the heart is somatic. But all such guesses will depend upon the very imperfect present knowledge of what an organism can achieve in way of somatic adjustment.

It is a major tragedy that the Lamarckian controversy has deflected the attention of geneticists away from the phenomenon of somatic adaptability. After all, the mechanisms, thresholds, and maxima of individual phenotypic change under stress must surely be genotypically determined.

Another difficulty, of rather similar nature, arises at the population level, where we encounter another "economics" of potential change, theoretically distinguishable from that which operates within the individual. The population of a wild species is today conventionally regarded as genotypically heterogeneous in spite of the high degree of superficial resemblance between the individual phenotypes. Such a population expectably functions as a storehouse of genotypic possibilities. The economic aspect of this storehouse of possibilities has, for example, been stressed by Simmonds.[5] He points out that farmers and breeders who demand 100 per cent phenotypic uniformity in a highly select crop are in fact throwing away most of the multiple genetic possibilities accumulated through hundreds of generations in the wild population. From this Simmonds argues that there is urgent need for institutions which shall "conserve" this storehouse of variability by maintaining unselected populations.

Lerner[6] has argued that self-corrective or buffering mechanisms operate to hold constant the composition of these mixtures of wild genotypes and to resist the effects of artificial selection. There is therefore at least a presumption that this economics of variability within the population will turn out to be of the multiplicative kind.

Now, the difficulty of discriminating between a characteristic achieved by somatic homeostasis and the same characteristic achieved (more economically) by a genotypic short cut is clearly going to be compounded when we come to consider populations instead of physiologic individuals. All actual experimentation in the field will inevitably work with populations, and, in this work, it will be necessary to discriminate the effects of that economics of *flexibility* which operates inside the individuals from the effects of the economics of *variability* which operates at the population level. These two orders of economics may be easy to separate in theory, but to separate them in experimentation will surely be difficult.

Be all that as it may, let us consider what evidential support may be available for some of the propositions which are crucial to the hypothesis:

(1) *That the phenomena of somatic adjustment are appropriately described in terms of an economics of flexi-*

[5] N. W. Simmonds, "Variability in Crop Plants, Its Use and Conservation," *Biol. Review*, 1962, 37: 422–62.

[6] I. M. Lerner, *Genetic Homeostasis*, Edinburgh, Oliver and Boyd, 1954.

*bility.* In general, we believe that the presence of stress A may reduce an organism's ability to respond to stress B and, guided by this opinion, we commonly protect the sick from the weather. Those who have adjusted to the office life may have difficulty in climbing mountains, and trained mountain climbers may have difficulty when confined to offices; the stresses of retirement from business may be lethal; and so on. But scientific knowledge of these matters, in man or other organisms, is very slight.

(2) *That this economics of flexibility has the logical structure described above—each successive demand upon flexibility fractionating the set of available possibilities.* The proposition is expectable, but so far as I know there is no evidence for it. It is, however, worthwhile to examine the criteria which determine whether a given "economic" system is more appropriately described in additive or multiplicative terms. There would seem to be two such criteria:

(a) A system will be additive insofar as the units of its currency are mutually interchangeable and, therefore, cannot meaningfully be classified into sets such as were used earlier in this paper to show that the economics of flexibility must surely be multiplicative. Calories in the economics of energy are completely interchangeable and unclassifiable, as are dollars in the individual budget. Both these systems are therefore additive. The permutations and combinations of variables which define the states of an organism are classifiable and—to this extent—noninterchangeable. The system is therefore multiplicative. Its mathematics will resemble that of information theory or negative entropy rather than that of money or energy conservation.

(b) A system will be additive insofar as the units of its currency are mutually independent. Here there would seem to be a difference between the economic system of the individual, whose budgetary problems are additive (or subtractive) and those of society at large, where the overall distribution or flow of wealth is governed by complex (and perhaps imperfect) homeostatic systems. Is there, perhaps, an economics of economic flexibility (a metaeconomics) which is multiplicative and so resembles the economics of physiological flexibility discussed above? Notice, however, that the units of this wider economics will be not dollars but patterns of distribution of wealth. Similarly, Lerner's "genetic homeostasis," insofar as it is truly homeostatic, will have multiplicative character.

The matter is, however, not simple and we cannot expect that every system will be either totally multiplicative or totally additive. There will be intermediate cases which combine the two characteristics. Specifically, where several *independent* alternative homeostatic circuits control a single variable, it is clear that the system may show additive characteristics—and even that it may pay to incorporate such alternative pathways in the system provided they can be effectively insulated from each other. Such systems of multiple alternative controls may give survival advantage insofar as the mathematics of addition and subtraction will pay better than the mathematics of logical fractionation.

(3) *That innovative genotypic change commonly makes demands upon the adjustive ability of the soma.* This proposition is orthodoxly believed by biologists but cannot in the nature of the case be verified by direct evidence.

(4) *That successive genotypic innovations make multiplicative demands upon the soma.* This proposition (which involves *both* the notion of multiplicative economics of flexibility and the notion that each innovative genotypic change has its somatic price) has several interesting and perhaps verifiable implications.

(a) We may expect that organisms in which numerous recent genotypic changes have accumulated (*e.g.*, as a result of selection, or planned breeding) will be delicate, *i.e.*, will need to be protected from environmental stress. This sensitivity to stress is to be expected in new breeds of domesticated animals and plants and experimentally produced organisms carrying either several mutant genes or unusual (*i.e.*, recently achieved) genotypic combinations.

(b) We may expect that for such organisms further genotypic innovation (of any kind other than the affirmative changes discussed above) will be progressively deleterious.

(c) Such new and special breeds should become more resistant both to environmental stress and to genotypic change, as selection works upon successive generations to favor those individuals in which "genetic assimilation of acquired characteristics" is achieved (Proposition 5).

(5) *That environmentally induced acquired characteristics may, under appropriate conditions of selection, be*

*replaced by similar characteristics which are genetically determined.* This phenomenon has been demonstrated by Waddington[7] for the bithorax phenotypes of *Drosophila.* He calls it the "genetic assimilation of acquired characteristics." Similar phenomena have also probably occurred in various experiments when the experimenters set out to prove the inheritance of acquired characteristics but did not achieve this proof through failure to control the conditions of selection. We have, however, no evidence at all as to the frequency of this phenomenon of genetic assimilation. It is worth noting, however, that, according to the arguments of this essay, it may be impossible, in principle, to exclude the factor of selection from experiments which would test "the inheritance of acquired characteristics." It is precisely my thesis that the *simulation* of Lamarckian inheritance will have survival value under circumstance of *undefined* or multiple stress.

(6). *That it is, in general, more economical of flexibility to achieve a given characteristic by genotypic than by somatic change.* Here the Waddington experiments do not throw any light, because it was the experimenter who did the selecting. To test this proposition, we need experiments in which the population of organisms is placed under double stress: (*a*) that stress which will induce the characteristic in which we are interested, and (*b*) a second stress which will selectively decimate the population, favoring, we hope, the survival of those individuals whose flexibility is more able to meet this second stress after adjusting to the first. According to the hypothesis, such a system should favor those individuals which achieve their adjustment to the first stress by genotypic process.

(7) Finally, it is interesting to consider a corollary which is the converse of the thesis of this essay. It has been argued here that simulated Lamarckian inheritance will have survival value when the population must adjust to a stress which remains constant over successive generations. This case is in fact the one which has been examined by those

[7] C. H. Waddington, "Genetic Assimilation of an Acquired Character," *Evolution,* 1953, 7: 118; also Waddington, *The Strategy of Genes,* London, Allen and Unwin, 1957.

who would demonstrate an inheritance of acquired characteristics. A converse problem is presented by those cases in which a population faces a stress which changes its intensity unpredictably and rather often—perhaps every two or three generations. Such situations are perhaps very rare in nature, but could be produced in the laboratory.

Under such variable circumstances, it might pay the organisms in survival terms to achieve the *converse* of the genetic assimilation of acquired characteristics. That is, they might profitably hand over to somatic homeostatic mechanisms the control of some characteristic which had previously been more rigidly controlled by the genotype.

It is evident, however, that such experimentation would be very difficult. Merely to establish the genetic assimilation of such characteristics as bithorax requires selection on an astronomical scale, the final population in which the genetically determined bithorax individuals can be found being a selected sample from a potential population of something like $10^{50}$ or $10^{60}$ individuals. It is very doubtful whether, after this selective process, there would still exist in the sample enough genetic heterogeneity to undergo a further converse selection favoring those individuals which still achieve their bithorax phenotype by somatic means.

Nevertheless, though this converse corollary is possibly not demonstrable in the laboratory, something of the sort seems to operate in the broad picture of evolution. The matter may be presented in dramatic form by considering the dichotomy between "regulators" and "adjusters."[8] Prosser proposes that where internal physiology contains some variable of the same dimensions as some external environmental variable, it is convenient to classify organisms according to the degree to which they hold the internal variable constant in spite of changes in the external variable. Thus, the homoiothermic animals are classified as "regulators" in regard to temperature while the poikilothermic are "adjusters." The same dichotomy can be applied to aquatic animals according to how they handle internal and external osmotic pressure.

We usually think of regulators as being in some broad evolutionary sense "higher" than adjusters. Let us now con-

[8]C. L. Prosser, "Physiological Variation in Animals," *Biol. Review*, 1955, 30: 22–262.

sider what this might mean. If there is a broad evolutionary trend in favor of regulators, is this trend consistent with what has been said above about the survival benefits which accrue when control is transferred to genotypic mechanisms?

Clearly, not only the regulators but also the adjusters must rely upon homeostatic mechanisms. If life is to go on, a large number of essential physiological variables must be held within narrow limits. If the internal osmotic pressure, for example, is allowed to change, there must be mechanisms which will defend these essential variables. It follows that the difference between adjusters and regulators is a matter of *where*, in the complex network of physiologic causes and effects, homeostatic process operates.

In the regulators, the homeostatic processes operate at or close to the input and output points of that network which is the individual organism. In the adjusters, the environmental variables are permitted to enter the body and the organism must then cope with their effects, using mechanisms which will involve deeper loops of the total network.

In terms of this analysis, the polarity between adjusters and regulators can be extrapolated another step to include what we may call "extraregulators" which achieve homeostatic controls *outside* the body by changing and controlling the environment—man being the most conspicuous example of this class.

In the earlier part of this essay, it was argued that in adjusting to high altitude there is a benefit to be obtained, in terms of an economics of flexibility, by shifting from, *e.g.*, panting to the more profound and less reversible changes of acclimation; that habit is more economical than trial and error; and that genotypic control may be more economical than acclimation. These are all *centripetal* changes in the location of control.

In the broad picture of evolution, however, it seems that the trend is in the opposite direction: that natural selection, in the long run, favors regulators more than adjusters, and extraregulators more than regulators. This seems to indicate that there is a long time evolutionary advantage to be gained by *centrifugal* shifts in the locus of control.

To speculate about problems so vast is perhaps romantic, but it is worth noting that this contrast between the overall evolutionary trend and the trend in a population faced with constant stress is what we might expect from the converse corollary here being considered. If constant stress favors centripetal shift in the locus of control, and variable stress favors centrifugal shift, then it should follow that in the vast spans of time and change which determine the broad evolutionary picture, centrifugal shift of control will be favored.

## Summary

In this essay the author uses a deductive approach. Starting from premises of conventional physiology and evolutionary theory and applying to these the arguments of cybernetics, he shows that there must be an *economics of somatic flexibility* and that this economics must, in the long run, be coercive upon the evolutionary process. External adaptation by mutation or genotypic reshuffling, as ordinarily thought of, will inevitably use up the available somatic flexibility. It follows—if evolution is to be continuous—that there must also be a class of genotypic changes which will confer a bonus of somatic flexibility.

In general, the somatic achievement of change is uneconomical because the process depends upon homeostasis, *i.e.*, upon whole circuits of interdependent variables. It follows that inheritance of acquired characteristics would be lethal to the evolutionary system because it would *fix* the values of these variables all around the circuits. The organism or species would, however, benefit (in survival terms) by genotypic change which would *simulate* Lamarckian inheritance, *i.e.*, would bring about the adaptive component of somatic homeostasis without involving the whole homeostatic circuit. Such a genotypic change (erroneously called the "Baldwin effect") would confer a bonus of somatic flexibility and would therefore have marked survival value.

Finally, it is suggested that a contrary argument can be applied in those cases where a population must acclimate to *variable* stress. Here natural selection should favor an anti-Baldwin effect.

# Problems in Cetacean and Other

# Mammalian Communication*

## *The Communication of Preverbal Mammals*

Of the Cetacea I have had little experience. I once dissected in the Cambridge Zoological Laboratories a specimen of *Phocoena* bought from the local fishmonger, and did not really encounter cetaceans again until this year, when I had an opportunity to meet Dr. Lilly's dolphins. I hope that my discussion of some of the questions that are in my mind as I approach these peculiar mammals will assist you in examining either these or related questions.

My previous work in the fields of anthropology, animal ethology, and psychiatric theory provides a theoretical framework for the transactional analysis of behavior. The premises of this theoretical position may be briefly summarized: (1) that a relationship between two (or more) organisms is, in fact, a sequence of S-R sequences (*i.e.*, of contexts in which proto-learning occurs); (2) that deutero-learning (*i.e.*, learning to learn) is, in fact, the acquiring of information about the contingency patterns of the contexts in which proto-learning occurs; and (3) that the "character" of the organism is the aggregate of its deutero-learning and

* This article appeared as Chapter 25, pp. 569–799, in *Whales, Dolphins and Porpoises*, edited by Kenneth S. Norris, University of California Press, 1966. Reprinted by permission of The Regents of the University of California.

therefore reflects the contextual patterns of past proto-learning.[1]

These premises are essentially a hierarchic structuring of learning theory along lines related to Russell's Theory of Logical Types.[2] The premises, following the Theory of Types, are primarily appropriate for the analysis of *digital* communication. To what extent they may be applicable to analogic communication or to systems that combine the digital with the analogic is problematic. I hope that the study of dolphin communication will throw light on these fundamental problems. The point is not either to discover that dolphins have complex language or to teach them English, but to close gaps in our theoretical knowledge of *communication* by studying a system that, whether rudimentary or complex, is almost certainly of a totally unfamiliar kind.

Let me start from the fact that the dolphin is a mammal. This fact has, of course, all sorts of implications for anatomy and physiology, but it is not with these that I am concerned. I am interested in his communication, in what is called his "behavior," looked at as an aggregate of data perceptible and *meaningful* to other members of the same species. It is meaningful, first, in the sense that it affects a recipient animal's behavior, and, second, in the sense that perceptible failure to achieve appropriate meaning in the first sense will affect the behavior of both animals. What I say to you may be totally ineffective, but my *ineffectiveness*, if perceptible, will affect both you and me. I stress this point because it must be remembered that in all relationships between man and some other animal, especially when that animal is a dolphin, a very large proportion of the behavior of both organisms is determined by this kind of ineffectiveness.

When I view the behavior of dolphins as communication, the mammalian label implies, for me, something very definite. Let me illustrate what I have in mind by an example from Benson Ginsburg's wolf pack in the Brookfield Zoo.

Among the Canidae, weaning is performed by the mother. When the puppy asks for milk, she presses down with her

[1] J. Ruesch and G. Bateson, *Communication: The Social Matrix of Psychiatry*, New York, Norton, 1951.

[2] A. N. Whitehead and B. Russell, *Principia Mathematica*, London, Cambridge University Press, 1910.

open mouth on the back of his neck, crushing him down to the ground. She does this repeatedly until he stops asking. This method is used by coyotes, dingoes, and the domestic dog. Among wolves the system is different. The puppies graduate smoothly from the nipple to regurgitated food. The pack comes back to the den with their bellies full. All regurgitate what they have got and all eat together. At some point the adults start to wean the puppies from these meals, using the method employed by the other Canidae; the adult crushes the puppy down by pressing its open mouth on the back of the puppy's neck. In the wolf this function is not confined to the mother, but is performed by adults of both sexes.

The pack leader of the Chicago pack is a magnificent male animal who endlessly patrols the acre of land to which the pack is confined. He moves with a beautiful trot that appears tireless, while the other eight or nine members of the pack spend most of their time dozing. When the females come in heat they usually proposition the leader, bumping against him with their rear ends. Usually, however, he does not respond, though he does act to prevent other males from getting the females. Last year one of these males succeeded in establishing coitus with a female. As in the other Canidae, the male wolf is locked in the female, unable to withdraw his penis, and this animal was helpless. Up rushed the pack leader. What did he do to the helpless male who dared to infringe the leader's prerogatives? Anthropomorphism would suggest that he would tear the helpless male to pieces. But no. The film shows that he pressed down the head of the offending male four times with his open jaws and then simply walked away.

What are the implications for research from this illustration? What the pack leader does is not describable, or only insufficiently described, in S-R terms. He does not "negatively reinforce" the other male's sexual activity. He asserts or affirms the nature of the relationship between himself and the other. If we were to translate the pack leader's action into words, the words would not be "Don't do that." Rather, they would translate the metaphoric action: "I am your senior adult male, you puppy!" What I am trying to say about wolves in particular, and about preverbal mammals in general, is that their discourse is primarily about the rules and the contingencies of relationship.

Let me offer a more familiar example to help bring home to you the generality of this view, which is by no means orthodox among ethologists. When your cat is trying to tell you to give her food, how does she do it? She has no word for food or for milk. What she does is to make movements and sounds that are characteristically those that a kitten makes to a mother cat. If we were to translate the cat's message into words, it would not be correct to say that she is crying "Milk!" Rather, she is saying something like "Mama!" Or, perhaps still more correctly, we should say that she is asserting "Dependency! Dependency!" The cat talks in terms of patterns and contingencies of relationship, and from this talk it is up to you to take a *deductive* step, guessing that it is milk that the cat wants. It is the necessity for this deductive step which marks the difference between preverbal mammalian communication and *both* the communication of bees and the languages of men.

What was extraordinary—the great new thing—in the evolution of human language was not the discovery of abstraction or generalization, but the discovery of how to be specific about something other than relationship. Indeed, this discovery, though it has been achieved, has scarcely affected the behavior even of human beings. If A says to B, "The plane is scheduled to leave at 6.30," B rarely accepts this remark as simply and solely a statement of fact about the plane. More often he devotes a few neurons to the question, "What does A's telling me this indicate for my relationship to A?" Our mammalian ancestry is very near the surface, despite recently acquired linguistic tricks.

Be that as it may, my first expectation in studying dolphin communication is that it will prove to have the general mammalian characteristic of being primarily about relationship. This premise is in itself perhaps sufficient to account for the sporadic development of large brains among mammals. We need not complain that, as elephants do not talk and whales invent no mousetraps, these creatures are not overtly intelligent. All that is needed is to suppose that large-brained creatures were, at some evolutionary stage, unwise enough to get into the game of relationship and that, once the species was caught in this game of interpreting its members' behavior toward one another as relevant to this complex and vital subject, there was survival value for those individuals who could play the game with greater ingenuity or greater wisdom. We may, then, reasonably expect to find a high complexity of communication about relationship among the Cetacea. Because they are mammals, we may expect that their communication will be about, and primarily in terms of, patterns and contingencies of relationship. Because they are social and large-brained, we may expect a high degree of complexity in their communication.

## Methodological Considerations

The above hypothesis introduces very special difficulties into the problem of how to test what is called the "psychology" (*e.g.*, intelligence, ingenuity, discrimination, etc.) of individual animals. A simple discrimination experiment, such as has been run in the Lilly laboratories, and no doubt elsewhere, involves a series of steps: (1) The dolphin may or may not perceive a difference between the stimulus objects, X and Y. (2) The dolphin may or may not perceive that this difference is a cue to behavior. (3) The dolphin may or may not perceive that the behavior in question has a good or bad effect upon reinforcement, that is, that doing "right" is conditionally followed by fish. (4) The dolphin may or may not choose to do "right," even after he knows which is right. Success in the first three steps merely provides the dolphin with a further choice point. This extra degree of freedom must be the first focus of our investigations.

It must be our *first* focus for methodological reasons. Consider the arguments that are conventionally based upon experiments of this kind. We argue always from the later steps in the series to the earlier steps. We say, "If the animal was able to achieve step 2 in our experiment, then he must have been able to achieve step 1." If he could learn to behave in the way that would bring him the reward, then he must have had the necessary sensory acuity to discriminate between X and Y, and so on.

Precisely because we want to argue from observation of the animal's success in the later steps to conclusions about the more elementary steps, it becomes of prime importance to know whether the organism with which we are dealing is capable of step 4. If it is capable, then all arguments about steps 1 through 3 will be invalidated unless appropriate methods of controlling step 4 are built into the experimental design. Curiously enough, though human beings are fully capable of step 4, psychologists working with human subjects have been able to study steps 1 through 3 without taking special care to exclude the confusions introduced by this fact. If the human subject is "cooperative and sane," he usually responds to the testing situation by repressing most of his impulses to modify his behavior according to his personal view of his relationship to the experimenter. The words *cooperative* and *sane* imply a degree of consistency at the level of step 4. The psychologist operates by a sort of *petitio principii:* if the subject is cooperative and sane (*i.e.*, if the relational rules are fairly constant), the psychologist need not worry about changes in those rules.

The problem of method becomes entirely different when the subject is noncooperative, psychopathic, schizophrenic, a naughty child, or a dolphin. Perhaps the most fascinating characteristic of this animal is derived precisely from his ability to operate at this relatively high level, an ability that is still to be demonstrated.

Let me now consider for a moment the art of the animal trainer. From conversations with these highly skilled people —trainers of both dolphins and guide dogs—my impression is that the first requirement of a trainer is that he must be able to prevent the animal from exerting choice at the level of step 4. It must continually be made clear to the animal that, when he knows what is the right thing to do in a given context, that is the only thing he *can* do, and no nonsense about it. In other words, it is a primary condition of circus success that the animal shall abrogate the use of certain higher levels of his intelligence. The art of the hypnotist is similar.

There is a story told of Dr. Samuel Johnson. A silly lady made her dog perform tricks in his presence. The Doctor seemed unimpressed. The lady said, "But Dr. Johnson, you don't know how difficult it is for the dog." Dr. Johnson replied, "Difficult, madam? Would it were impossible!"

What is amazing about circus tricks is that the animal can abrogate the use of so much of his intelligence and still have enough left to perform the trick. I regard the conscious intelligence as the greatest ornament of the human mind. But many authorities, from the Zen masters to Sigmund Freud, have stressed the ingenuity of the less conscious and perhaps more archaic level.

## Communication About Relationship

As I said earlier, I expect dolphin communication to be of an almost totally unfamiliar kind. Let me expand on this point. As mammals, we are familiar with, though largely unconscious of, the habit of communicating about our relationships. Like other terrestrial mammals, we do most of our communicating on this subject by means of kinesic and paralinguistic signals, such as bodily movements, involuntary tensions of voluntary muscles, changes of facial expression, hesitations, shifts in tempo of speech or movement, overtones of the voice, and irregularities of respiration. If you want to know what the bark of a dog "means," you look at his lips, the hair on the back of his neck, his tail, and so on. These "expressive" parts of his body tell you at what object of the environment he is barking, and what patterns of relationship to that object he is likely to follow in the next few seconds. Above all, you look at his sense organs: his eyes, his ears, and his nose.

In all mammals, the organs of sense become also organs for the transmission of messages about relationship. A blind man makes us uncomfortable, not because he cannot see— that is his problem and we are only dimly aware of it—but because he does not transmit to us through the movement of his eyes the messages we expect and need so that we may know and be sure of the state of our relationship to him. We shall not know much about dolphin communication until we know what one dolphin can read in another's use, direction, volume, and pitch of echolocation.

Perhaps it is this lack in us which makes the communication of dolphins seem mysterious and opaque, but I suspect a more profound explanation. Adaptation to life in the ocean has stripped the whales of facial expression. They have no external ears to flap and few if any erectile hairs. Even the cervical vertebrae are fused into a solid block in many species, and evolution has streamlined the body, sacrificing the expressiveness of separate parts to the locomotion of the whole. Moreover, conditions of life in the sea are such that even if a dolphin had a mobile face, the details of his expression would be visible to other dolphins only at rather short range, even in the clearest waters.

It is reasonable, then, to suppose that in these animals vocalization has taken over the communicative functions that most animals perform by facial expression, wagging tails, clenched fists, supinated hands, flaring nostrils, and the like. We might say that the whale is the communicational opposite of the giraffe; it has no neck, but has a voice. This speculation alone would make the communication of dolphins a subject of great theoretical interest. It would be fascinating, for example, to know whether or not, in an evolutionary shift from kinesics to vocalization, the same general structure of categories is retained.

My own impression—and it is only an impression unsupported by testing—is that the hypothesis that dolphins have substituted paralinguistics for kinesics does not quite fit in with my experience when I listen to their sounds. We terrestrial mammals are familiar with paralinguistic communication; we use it ourselves in grunts and groans, laughter and sobbing, modulations of breath while speaking, and so on. Therefore we do not find the paralinguistic sounds of other mammals totally opaque. We learn rather easily to recognize in them certain kinds of greeting, pathos, rage, persuasion, and territoriality, though our guesses may often be wrong. But when we hear the sounds of dolphins we cannot even guess at their significance. I do not quite trust the hunch that would explain the sounds of dolphins as merely an elaboration of the paralinguistics of other mammals. (To argue thus from our inability is, however, weaker than to argue from what we can do.)

I personally do not believe that the dolphins have anything that a human linguist would call a "language." I do not think that any animal without hands would be stupid enough to arrive at so outlandish a mode of communication.

To use a syntax and category system appropriate for the discussion of things that can be handled, while really discussing the patterns and contingencies of relationship, is fantastic. But that, I submit, is what is happening in this room. I stand here and talk while you listen and watch. I try to convince you, try to get you to see things my way, try to earn your respect, try to indicate my respect for you, challenge you, and so on. What is really taking place is a discussion of the patterns of our relationship, all according to the rules of a scientific conference about whales. So it is to be human.

I simply do not believe that dolphins have language in this sense. But I do believe that, like ourselves and other mammals, they are preoccupied with the patterns of their relationships. Let us call this discussion of patterns of relationship the μ function of the message. After all, it was the cat who showed us the great importance of this function by her mewing. Preverbal mammals communicate about things, when they must, by using what are primarily μ-function signals. In contrast, human beings use language, which is primarily oriented toward things, to discuss relationships. The cat asks for milk by saying "Dependency," and I ask for your attention and perhaps respect by talking about whales. But we do not know that dolphins, in their communication, resemble either me or the cat. They may have a quite different system.

## Analogic versus Digital Communication

There is another side of the problem. How does it happen that the paralinguistics and kinesics of men from strange cultures, and even the paralinguistics of other terrestrial mammals, are at least partly intelligible to us, whereas the verbal languages of men from strange cultures seem to be totally opaque? In this respect it would seem that the vocalizations of the dolphin resemble human language rather than the kinesics or paralinguistics of terrestrial mammals.

We know, of course, why gestures and tones of voice are partly intelligible while foreign languages are unintelligible. It is because language is *digital* and kinesics and paralinguistics are *analogic*.[3] The essence of the matter is that in digital communication a number of purely conventional signs —1, 2, 3, X, Y, and so on—are pushed around according to rules called algorithms. The signs themselves have no simple connection (*e.g.*, correspondence of magnitude) with what they stand for. The numeral "5" is not bigger than the numeral "3." It is true that if we remove the crossbar from "7" we obtain the numeral "1"; but the crossbar does not, in any sense, stand for "6." A name usually has only a purely conventional or arbitrary connection with the *class* named. The numeral "5" is only the *name* of a magnitude. It is nonsense to ask if my telephone number is larger than yours, because the telephone exchange is a purely digital computer. It is not fed with magnitudes, but only with *names* of positions on a matrix.

In analogic communication, however, real magnitudes are used, and they correspond to real magnitudes in the subject of discourse. The linked range finder of a camera is a familiar example of an analogue computer. This device is fed with an angle that has real magnitude and is, in fact, the angle that the base of the range finder subtends at some point on the object to be photographed. This angle controls a cam that in turn moves the lens of the camera forward or back. The secret of the device lies in the shape of the cam, which is an analogic representation (*i.e.*, a picture, a Cartesian graph) of the functional relationship between distance of object and distance of image.

Verbal language is almost (but not quite) purely digital. The word "big" is not bigger than the word "little"; and in general there is nothing in the pattern (*i.e.*, the system of interrelated magnitudes) in the word "table" which would correspond to the system of interrelated magnitudes in the object denoted. On the other hand, in kinesic and paralin-

---

[3] The difference between digital and analogic modes of communication may perhaps be made clear by thinking of an English-speaking mathematician confronted with a paper by a Japanese colleague. He gazes uncomprehendingly at the Japanese ideographs, but he is able partly to understand the Cartesian graphs in the Japanese publication. The ideographs, though they may originally have been analogic pictures, are now purely digital; the Cartesian graphs are analogic.

guistic communication, the magnitude of the gesture, the loudness of the voice, the length of the pause, the tension of the muscle, and so forth—these magnitudes commonly correspond (directly or inversely) to magnitudes in the relationship that is the subject of discourse. The pattern of action in the communication of the wolf pack leader is immediately intelligible when we have data about the weaning practices of the animal, for the weaning practices are themselves analogic kinesic signals.

It is logical, then, to consider the hypothesis that the vocalization of dolphins may be a *digital* expression of $\mu$ functions. It is this possibility that I especially have in mind in saying that this communication may be of an almost totally unfamiliar kind. Man, it is true, has a few words for $\mu$ functions, words like "love," "respect," "dependency," and so on. But these words function poorly in the actual discussion of relationship between participants in the relationship. If you say to a girl, "I love you," she is likely to pay more attention to the accompanying kinesics and paralinguistics than to the words themselves.

We humans become very uncomfortable when somebody starts to interpret our postures and gestures by translating them into words about relationship. We much prefer that our messages on this subject remain analogic, unconscious, and involuntary. We tend to distrust the man who can simulate messages about relationship. We therefore have no idea what it is like to be a species with even a very simple and rudimentary *digital* system whose primary subject matter would be $\mu$ functions. This system is something we terrestrial mammals cannot imagine and for which we have no empathy.

## Research Plans

The most speculative part of my paper is the discussion of plans for the testing and amplification of such a body of hypotheses. I shall be guided by the following heuristic assumptions:

(1) The epistemology in whose terms the hypotheses are constructed is itself not subject to testing. Derived from

Whitehead and Russell,[4] it serves to guide our work. Should the work prove rewarding, the success will be only a weak verification of the epistemology.

(2) We do not even know what a primitive digital system for the discussion of patterns of relationship might look like, but we can guess that it would not look like a "thing" language. (It might, more probably, resemble music.) I shall therefore not expect the techniques for cracking human linguistic codes to be immediately applicable to the vocalization of dolphins.

(3) The first requirement, then, is to identify and to classify the varieties and the components of relationship existing among the animals through detailed ethological study of their actions, interactions, and social organization. The elements of which these patterns are built are doubtless still present in the kinesics and actions of the species. We therefore begin with a listing of the kinesic signals of individual dolphins, and then try to relate them to the contexts in which they are used.

(4) No doubt, just as the pack leader's behavior tells us that "dominance" among wolves is metaphorically related to weaning, so also the dolphins will tell us their kinesic metaphors for "dominance," "dependency," and other μ functions. Gradually this system of signals will fit together piece by piece to form a picture of the varieties of relationship existing even among animals arbitrarily confined together in a tank.

(5) As we begin to understand the metaphor system of the dolphin, it will become possible to recognize and classify the contexts of his vocalization. At this point the statistical techniques for cracking codes may conceivably become useful.

(6) The assumptions regarding the hierarchic structure of the learning process—upon which this whole paper is based —provide the basis for various kinds of experimentation. The contexts of proto-learning may be variously constructed with a view to observing in what types of contexts certain types of learning most readily occur. We shall pay special attention to those contexts that involve either relationships between two or more animals and one person, or relation-

---

[4] Whitehead and Russell, *op. cit.*

ships between two or more people and one animal. Such contexts are miniature models of social organization within which the animal may be expected to show characteristic behaviors and to make characteristic attempts to modify the context (*i.e.*, to manipulate the humans).

## Comments

*Mr. Wood:* In the course of twelve years in Marine Studios in Florida, I spent a great deal of time watching what was perhaps the most natural assemblage of *Tursiops* in captivity, including animals of various ages, usually two or more of them in the process of growing up, and I saw remarkably little of what you are going to look for in a much more restricted group of animals in the Virgin Islands.

One time I saw something very interesting. Early one morning about six or six-thirty, over a period of at least half an hour, the adult male assumed a position next to one of the females in the tank who was hanging motionless in the current. He would go up occasionally and move away and then come back and assume a position beside her, and he would stroke her side with his right flipper repeatedly. There was no indication that this had sexual significance. There was no erection on the part of the male, and no observable response on the part of the female. But it was as clear-cut a nonvocal signal as I ever observed in the tank.

*Mr. Bateson:* I would like to say that the amount of signaling that goes on is much greater than is evident at first sight. There are, of course, the rather specific kinds of signals which are very important. I am not denying that. I mean the touching, and so on. But the shy individual, the traumatized female, staying almost stationary three feet below the surface while two other individuals fool around, is getting a great deal of attention just by sitting there and staying. She may not be actively transmitting, but in this business of bodily communication, you don't have to be actively transmitting in order to have your signals picked up by other people. You can just *be*, and just by being she attracts an enormous amount of attention from these other two individuals who come over, pass by, pause a little as they pass, and so on. She is, we would say, "withdrawn," but she is actually about as withdrawn as a schizophrenic who by being withdrawn becomes the center of gravity of the family. All other members of the group move around the fact of her withdrawal, which she never lets them forget.

*Dr. Ray:* I tend to agree with Mr. Bateson. We are working at the New York Aquarium with the beluga whale, and I believe these animals are much more expressive than we like to suspect. I think one of the reasons they don't do very much in captivity is that they are bored to tears most of the time. There is nothing much of interest in their tank environment, and I would like to suggest that we have to manipulate their captivity much more cleverly than we do. I don't mean handling the whales. They don't like that. But the introduction of different types of animals, or clever little things that we might do would get them to respond more. Captive cetaceans are like monkeys in a cage. They are highly intelligent and highly developed, and they are bored.

Another factor is our skill in observation, and in the beluga whale, at least, we have been able to notice visually the sounds they are making by watching the change in the shape of the melon, which is extremely marked in this animal. It can swell on one side or the other, or take several different shapes correlated with sound production. So, by very careful observation and/or skilled manipulation, I think a great deal can be done with these animals rather simply.

*Mr. Bateson:* I had meant to point out that all sense organs among mammals, and even among ants, become major organs for the transmission of messages, such as, "Where are the other fellow's eyes focused?" and, "Are his pinnae focused in one direction or another?" In this way sense organs become transmitting organs for signals.

One of the things we must absolutely acquire if we are going to understand dolphins is a knowledge of what one animal knows and can read from another animals' use of sonar. I suspect the presence of all sorts of courtesy rules in this business; it probably isn't polite to sonar scan your friends too much, just as among human beings it is not polite, really, to look at another's feet in detail. We have many taboos on observing one anothers' kinesics, because too much information can be got in that way.

*Dr. Purves:*    It seems to me that the dolphin or the cetacean must suffer from an even greater disadvantage than man has in the past, because—I have forgotten the authority—it has been said that the origin of human speech is an analogue language. In other words, if you use the word "down," you lower the hand and lower the lower jaw at the same time. If you say "up," you raise the hand and raise the lower jaw. And if you use the word "table," and, better still, pronounce it in French, your mouth widens out and you make a horizontal gesture. However complicated the human language is, it has its origin in an analogue language. The poor porpoise has nothing like this to start from. So he must have been highly intelligent to have developed a communication system completely *de novo*.

*Mr. Bateson:*    What has happened to this creature is that the information we get visually and the other terrestrial animals get visually must have been pushed into voice. I still maintain that it is appropriate for us to start by investigating what is left of the visual material.

# A Re-examination of "Bateson's Rule"*

## Introduction

Nearly eighty years ago, my father, William Bateson, became fascinated by the phenomena of symmetry and metameric regularity as exhibited in the morphology of animals and plants. It is difficult today to define precisely what he was after, but, broadly, it is clear that he believed that an entirely new concept of the nature of living things would develop from the study of such phenomena. He held, no doubt correctly, that natural selection could not be the only determinant of the direction of evolutionary change and that the genesis of variation could not be a random matter. He therefore set out to demonstrate regularity and "lawfulness" among the phenomena of variability.

In his attempt to demonstrate a sort of order which the biologists of his day had largely ignored, he was guided by the notion, never clearly formulated, that the place to look for regularity in variation would be precisely where variation had its impact upon what was already regular and repetitive. The phenomena of symmetry and metamerism, themselves strikingly regular, must surely have been brought about by regularities or "laws" within the evolutionary process and,

*This essay has been accepted for publication in the *Journal of Genetics*, and is here reproduced with the permission of that journal.

therefore, the *variations* of symmetry and metamerism should precisely exemplify these laws at work.

In the language of today, we might say that he was groping for those orderly characteristics of living things which illustrate the fact that organisms evolve and develop within cybernetic, organizational, and other communicational limitations.

It was for this study that he coined the word "genetics."[1]

He set out to examine the material in the world's museums, private collections, and journals bearing upon the teratology of animal symmetry and metamerism. The details of this survey were published in a large book[2] which is still of considerable interest.

To demonstrate regularity within the field of teratological variation, he attempted a classification of the various sorts of modification that he encountered. With this classification I am not here concerned, except that in the survey he happened upon a generalization which can be called a "discovery." This discovery came to be called "Bateson's Rule" and remains one of the unexplained mysteries of biology.

The purpose of the present note is to place Bateson's Rule in a new theoretical perspective determined by cybernetics, information theory, and the like.

Briefly, Bateson's Rule asserts in its simplest form that when an asymmetrical lateral appendage (*e.g.*, a right hand) is reduplicated, the resulting reduplicated limb will be bilaterally symmetrical, consisting of two parts each a mirror image of the other and so placed that a plane of symmetry could be imagined between them.

He himself was, however, very doubtful whether such simple reduplication ever occurs. He believed and accumulated evidence to show that, in a very large proportion of such cases, one component of the reduplicated system was itself double. He asserted that in such systems the three components are normally in one plane; that the two components of the doublet are mirror images of each other; and

[1] W. Bateson, "The Progress of Genetic Research," Inaugural Address, Royal Horticultural Society Report, 1906.

[2] W. Bateson, Materials for the Study of Variation, London, Macmillan and Co., 1894.

that that component of the doublet which is the nearer to the primary appendage is a mirror image of the primary.

This generalization was shown by my father to hold for a very large number of examples of reduplication in the vertebrates and in arthropods, and for a few cases in other phyla where the museum material was, of course, more scarce.

Ross Harrison[3] believed that Bateson underestimated the importance of simple reduplication.

Whether or not simple reduplication is a real and common phenomenon, I shall begin this essay with a discussion of the logical problems which it would present.

## The Problem Redefined

In 1894, it appeared that the problem centered around the question: What causes the development of bilateral symmetry in a context where it does not belong?

But modern theory has turned all such questions upside down. Information, in the technical sense, is that which *excludes* certain alternatives. The machine with a governor does not elect the steady state; it *prevents* itself from staying in any alternative state; and in all such cybernetic systems, corrective action is brought about by *difference*. In the jargon of the engineers, the system is "error activated." The difference between some present state and some "preferred" state activates the corrective response.

The technical term "information" may be succinctly defined as *any difference which makes a difference in some later event*. This definition is fundamental for all analysis of cybernetic systems and organization. The definition links such analysis to the rest of science, where the causes of events are commonly not differences but forces, impacts, and the like. The link is classically exemplified by the heat engine, where available energy (*i.e.*, negative entropy) is a function of a *difference* between two temperatures. In this classical instance, "information" and "negative entropy" overlap.

[3] R. G. Harrison, "On Relations of Symmetry in Transplanted Limbs," *Journal of Experimental Zoology*, 1921, 32: 1–118.

Moreover, the energy relations of such cybernetic systems are commonly inverted. Because organisms are able to store energy, it is usual that the energy expenditure is, for limited periods of time, an inverse function of energy input. The amoeba is more active when it lacks food, and the stem of a green plant grows faster on that side which is turned away from the light.

Let us therefore invert the question about the symmetry of the total reduplicated appendage: Why is this double appendage not asymmetrical like the corresponding appendages of normal organisms?

To this question a formal and general (but not particular) answer can be constructed on the following lines:

(1) An unfertilized frog's egg is radially symmetrical, with animal and vegetal poles but no differentiation of its equatorial radii. Such an egg develops into a bilaterally symmetrical embryo, but how does it select one meridian to be the plane of bilateral symmetry of that embryo? The answer is known—that, in fact, the frog's egg receives information *from the outside*. The point of entry of the spermatozoon (or the prick of a fine fiber) marks one meridian as different from all others, and that meridian is the future plane of bilateral symmetry.

Converse cases can also be cited. Plants of many families bear bilaterally symmetrical flowers. Such flowers are all clearly derived from triadic radial symmetry (as in orchids) or from pentadic symmetry (as in Labiatae, Leguminosae, etc.); and the bilateral symmetry is achieved by the differentiation of one axis (*e.g.,* the "standard" of the familiar sweet pea) of this radial symmetry. We again ask how it is possible to select one of the similar three (or five) axes. And again we find that each flower receives information *from the outside*. Such bilaterally symmetrical flowers can *only* be produced on branch stems, and the differentiation of the flower is always oriented to the manner in which the flower-bearing branch stem comes off from the main stem. Very occasionally a plant which normally bears bilaterally symmetrical flowers will form a flower at the terminus of a main stem. Such a flower is necessarily only radial in its symmetry—a cup-shaped monstrosity. (The problem of bilaterally asymmetrical flowers, *e.g.,* in the *Catasetum* group of orchids, is interesting. Presumably these must be borne, like the lateral appendages of animals, upon branches from main stems which are themselves already bilaterally symmetrical, *e.g.*, dorso-ventrally flattened.)

(2) We note then that, in biological systems, the step from radial symmetry to bilateral symmetry commonly requires a piece of information from the outside. It is, however, conceivable that some divergent process might be touched off by minute and randomly distributed differences, *e.g.*, among the radii of the frog's egg. In this case, of course, the selection of a particular meridian for special development would itself be random and could not be oriented to other parts of the organism as is the plane of bilateral symmetry in sweet peas and labiate flowers.

(3) Similar considerations apply to the step from bilateral symmetry to asymmetry. Again either the asymmetry (the differentiation of one half from the other) must be achieved by a random process or it must be achieved by information received from the outside, *i.e.*, from neighboring tissues and organs. Every lateral appendage of a vertebrate or arthropod is more or less asymmetrical[4] and the asymmetry is never set randomly in relation to the rest of the animal. Right limbs are not borne upon the left side of the body, except under experimental circumstances. Therefore the asymmetry must depend upon the outside information, presumably derived from the neighboring tissues.

(4) But if the step from bilateral symmetry to asymmetry requires additional information, then it follows that in absence of this additional information, the appendage which should have been asymmetrical can only be bilaterally symmetrical.

The problem of the bilateral symmetry of reduplicated

[4] In this connection, scales and feathers and hairs are of special interest. A feather would seem to have a very clear bilateral symmetry in which the plane of symmetry is related to the antero-posterior differentiation of the bird. Superposed on this is an asymmetry like that of the individual bilateral limbs. As in the case of lateral limbs, corresponding feathers on opposite sides of the body are mirror images of each other. Every feather is, as it were, a flag whose shape and coloring denote the values of determining variables at the point and time of its growth.

limbs thus becomes simply a problem of the *loss* of a piece of information. This follows from the general logical rule that every reduction in symmetry (from radial to bilateral or from bilateral to asymmetrical) requires *additional* information.

It is not claimed that the above argument is an explanation of all the phenomena which illustrate Bateson's Rule. Indeed, the argument is offered only to show that there are simple ways of thinking about these phenomena which have scarcely been explored. What is proposed is a *family* of hypotheses rather than a single one. A critical examination of what has been said above as if it were a single hypothesis will, however, provide a further illustration of the method.

In any given case of reduplication, it will be necessary to decide what particular piece of information has been lost, and the argument so far given should make this decision easy. A natural first guess would be that the developing appendage needs three sorts of orienting information to enable it to achieve asymmetry: proximo-distal information; dorso-ventral information; and antero-posterior information. The simplest hypothesis suggests that these might be *separately* received and therefore that *one* of these sorts of information will be lost or absent in any given case of reduplication. It should then be easy to classify cases of reduplication according to which piece of orienting information is missing. There should be at most three such types of reduplication, and these should be clearly distinct.

## Supernumerary Double Legs in Coleoptera

But in the only set of cases where this deduction can be tested, facts clearly do not fit the hypothesis. The cases are those of supernumerary pairs of appendages in beetles. About a hundred such cases were known in 1894, and of these Bateson[5] describes about half and figures thirteen.

The formal relations are remarkably uniform and leave no doubt that a single type of explanation should apply to the symmetry in all cases.

[5]W. Bateson, *Materials . . . , op. cit.*, pp. 477-503.

Typically[6] one leg (rarely more than one) of a beetle is abnormal in bearing a branch at some point in its length. This branch is regularly a doublet, consisting of two parts which may be fused at the point of branching off from the primary leg but which are commonly separate at their distal ends.

Distally from the point of branching there are thus three components—a primary leg and two supernumerary legs. These three lie in one plane and have the following symmetry: the two components of the supernumerary doublet are a complementary pair—one being a left and the other a right—as Bateson's Rule would suggest. Of these two, the leg nearest to the primary leg is complementary to it.

These relations are represented in Figure 6. (See page 345.) Each component is shown in diagrammatic cross section, and their dorsal, ventral, anterior, and posterior faces are indicated by the letters $D$, $V$, $A$, and $P$, respectively.

What is surprising about these abnormalities—in that it conflicts with the hypothesis offered above—is that there is no clear discontinuity by which the cases can be classified according to which sort of orienting information has been lost. The supernumerary doublet may be borne on any part of the circumference of the primary leg.

Figure 6 illustrates the symmetry of a doublet occurring in the dorsal region. Figure 7 (page 345) illustrates the symmetry of a doublet in the dorso-anterior region.

It appears, then, that the planes of symmetry are parallel to a tangent of the circumference of the primary leg at the point of branching but, since the points of branching may be anywhere on the circumference, a *continuous* series of possible bilateral symmetries is generated.

Figure 8 (page 343) is a machine invented by W. Bateson to demonstrate this continuous series of possible bilateral symmetries.

If the bilateral symmetry of the doublet is due to a loss of orienting information, we should expect the plane of that bilateral symmetry to be at right angles to the direction of the lost information; *i.e.*, if dorso-ventral information were lost, the resulting limbs or doublet should contain a plane of symmetry which would be at right angles to the dorso-ventral line.

[6] See Figures 4 and 5, pages 344 and 343.

(The argument for this expectation may be spelled out as follows: a gradient in a lineal sequence creates a difference between the two ends of the sequence. If this gradient is not present, then the ends of the sequence will be similar, *i.e.*, the sequence will be symmetrical about a plane of symmetry transverse to itself. Or, consider the case of the frog's egg. The two poles and the point of entry of the spermatozoon determine a plane of bilateral symmetry. To achieve asymmetry, the egg requires information *at right angles to this plane, i.e.*, something which will make the right half different from the left. If this something is lost, then the egg will revert to the original bilateral symmetry, with the original plane of symmetry transverse to the direction of the lost information.)

As noted above, the supernumerary doublets may originate from *any* face of the primary leg, and therefore all intermediates occur between the expectedly discontinuous types of loss of information. It follows that if bilateral symmetry in these doublets is due to loss of information, then the information lost cannot be classified as antero-posterior, dorso-ventral, or proximo-distal.

The hypothesis must therefore be corrected.

Let us retain the general notion of lost information, and the corollary of this that the plane of bilateral symmetry must be at right angles to the direction of the information that was lost.

The next simplest hypothesis suggests that the lost information must have been centro-peripheral. (I here retain this bipolar term rather than use the simpler "radial.")

Let us imagine, then, some centro-peripheral difference —possibly a chemical or electrical gradient—within the cross section of the primary leg; and suppose that the loss or blurring of this difference at some point along the length of the primary leg determines that any branch limb produced at this point shall fail to achieve asymmetry.

It will follow, naturally, that such a branch limb (if produced) will be bilaterally symmetrical and that its plane of bilateral symmetry will be at right angles to the direction of the lost gradient or difference.

But, clearly, a centro-peripheral difference or gradient is *not* a primary component of that information system which determined the asymmetry of the primary leg. Such a gradient might, however, inhibit branching, so that its loss or blurring would result in production of a supernumerary branch at the point of loss.

The matter becomes superficially paradoxical: the loss of a gradient which might inhibit branching results in branch formation, such that the branch cannot achieve asymmetry. It appears, then, that the hypothetical centro-peripheral gradient or difference may have two sorts of command functions: (a) to inhibit branching; and (b) to determine an asymmetry in that branch which can only come into existence at all if the centro-peripheral gradient is absent. If these two sorts of message functions can be shown to overlap or be in some sense synonymous, we shall have generated an economical hypothetical description of the phenomena.

We therefore address ourselves to the question: Is there an a priori case for expecting that the *absence* of a gradient which would prohibit branching in the primary leg will permit the formation of a branch which will lack the information necessary to determine asymmetry across a plane at right angles to the missing gradient?

The question must be inverted to fit the upside-downness of all cybernetic explanation. The concept "information necessary to determine asymmetry" then becomes "information necessary to *prohibit* bilateral symmetry."

But anything which "prohibits bilateral symmetry" will also "prohibit branching," since the two components of a branching structure constitute a symmetrical pair (even though the components may be radially symmetrical).

It therefore becomes reasonable to expect that loss or blurring of a centro-peripheral gradient which prohibits branch formation will permit the formation of a branch which will, however, itself be bilaterally symmetrical about a plane parallel to the circumference of the primary limb.

Meanwhile, within the primary limb, it is possible that a centro-peripheral gradient, by preventing branch formation, could have a function in preserving a previously determined asymmetry.

The above hypotheses provide a possible framework of explanation of the formation of the supernumerary doublet and the bilateral symmetry within it. It remains to consider the orientation of the components of that doublet. According to Bateson's Rule, the component nearest to the primary leg is in bilateral symmetry with it. In other words, that face of the supernumerary which is toward the primary is the morphological counterpart of that face of the periphery of the primary from which the branch sprang.

The simplest, and perhaps obvious, explanation of this regularity is that in the process of branching there was a sharing of morphologically differentiated structures between branch and primary and that these shared structures are, in fact, the carriers of the necessary information. However, since information carried this way will clearly have properties very different from those of information carried by gradients, it is appropriate to spell the matter out in some detail.

Consider a radially symmetrical cone with circular base. Such a figure is differentiated in the axial dimension, as between apex and base. All that is necessary to make the cone fully asymmetrical is to differentiate on the circumference of the base two points which shall be different from each other and shall not be in diametrically opposite positions, *i.e.*, the base must contain such differentiation that to name its parts in clockwise order gives a result different from the result of naming the parts in anticlockwise order.

Assume now that the supernumerary branch, by its very origin as a unit growing out from a matrix, has proximodistal differentiation, and that this differentiation is analogous to the differentiation in the axial dimension of the cone. To achieve complete asymmetry, it is then only necessary that the developing limb receive directional information in some arc of its circumference. Such information is clearly immediately available from the circumstance that, at the point of branching, the secondary limb must share some circumference with the primary. But the shared points which are in clockwise order on the periphery of the primary will be in anticlockwise order on the periphery of the branch. The information from the shared arc will therefore be such as to determine both that the resulting limb will be a mirror image of the primary and that the branch will face appropriately toward the primary.

It is now possible to construct a hypothetical sequence of events for the reduplications in the legs of beetles:

(1) A primary leg develops asymmetry, deriving the necessary information from surrounding tissues.

(2) This information, after it has had its effect, continues to exist, transformed into morphological differentiation.

(3) The asymmetry of the normal primary leg is henceforth maintained by a centro-peripheral gradient which normally prevents branching.

(4) In the abnormal specimens, this centro-peripheral gradient is lost or blurred—possibly at some point of lesion or trauma.

(5) Following the loss of the centro-peripheral gradient, branching occurs.

(6) The resulting branch is a doublet; lacking the gradient information which would have determined asymmetry, it must therefore be bilaterally symmetrical.

(7) That component of the doublet which is next to the primary is oriented to be a mirror image of the primary by the sharing of differentiated peripheral structures.

(8) Similarly each component of the doublet is itself asymmetrical, deriving the necessary information from the morphology of shared peripheries in the plane of the doublet.

The above speculations are intended to illustrate how the explanatory principle of *loss* of information might be applied to some of the regularities subsumed under Bateson's Rule. But it will be noted that the data on symmetry in the legs of beetles have, in fact, been overexplained.

Two distinct—but not mutually exclusive—types of explanation have been invoked: (*a*) the loss of information which should have been derived from a centro-peripheral gradient, and (*b*) information derived from shared peripheral morphology.

Neither of these types of explanation is sufficient by itself to explain the phenomena, but when combined the two principles overlap so that some details of the total picture can be referred simultaneously to both principles.

Such redundancy is, no doubt, the rule rather than the exception in biological systems, as it is in all other systems of organization, differentiation, and communication. In all such systems, redundancy is a major and necessary source of stability, predictability, and integration.

Redundancy within the system will inevitably appear as

overlapping between our explanations of the system. Indeed, without overlapping, our explanations will commonly be insufficient, failing to explain the facts of biological integration.

We know little about how the pathways of evolutionary change are influenced by such morphogenetic and physiological redundancies. But certainly such internal redundancies must impose nonrandom characteristics upon the phenomena of variation.[7]

### Reduplicated Limbs in Amphibia

At this point it is interesting to turn from analysis of reduplication in beetles' legs to another body of data in which reduplication commonly occurs and has been referred to Bateson's Rule.[8] These are the data on reduplication in the experimentally transplanted limbs of larval newts.

(1) There are some cases, mostly of heterotopic transplants in which the grafted limb bud develops into a simple and apparently equal binary system, in which the two components are in mirror image symmetry. I was shown about three years ago a very striking preparation by Dr. Emerson Hibbard of the California Institute of Technology. In this specimen the limb bud had been rotated through 180°, so that the anterior edge of the bud faced toward the posterior end of the host, and had been implanted in a median dorsal position on the posterior region of the head of the host. This transplant had developed into two remarkably complete legs in mirror image relationship. This binary system was connected to the head of the host only by a slender bridge of tissue.

Such preparations, where the product is binary and the parts equal, certainly look like what would be expected from a simple loss of one dimension of orienting information. (It was Dr. Hibbard's specimen that suggested to me that the

[7]G. Bateson, "The Role of Somatic Change in Evolution," *Evolution*, 1962, 17: 529–39.

[8]Harrison, *op. cit.*; also F. H. Swett, "On The Production of Double Limbs in Amphibians," *Journal of Experimental Zoology*, 1926, 44: 419–72.

hypothesis of lost information might be applicable to the amphibian material.)

(2) However, apart from these instances of equal binary reduplication, the amphibian material does not at all fit with any hypothesis that would explain the reduplication as due to a simple loss of information. Indeed, if Bateson's Rule were restricted to cases where the explanation is formally analogous to that which fits the reduplication in the beetles' legs, then the amphibian cases would probably not fall under this rubric.

The limitations of a hypothesis are, however, as important as its applications, and I shall therefore summarize here the very complex data on orthotopic transplants.

One schematic paradigm will suffice: if the right anterior limb bud is excised, turned through 180° and replaced in the wound, it will grow to be a *left* limb. But this primary limb may subsequently form secondary limb buds at its base, usually either immediately anterior or posterior to the point of insertion. The secondary will be a mirror image of the primary, and may even later develop a tertiary which will typically be formed outside the secondary, *i.e.*, on that side of the secondary which is farthest from the primary.

The formation of the left primary on the right side of the body is explained[9] by assuming that antero-posterior orientation is received by the limb bud earlier than dorso-ventral information, and that, once received, this antero-posterior information is irreversible. It is supposed that the graft is already antero-posteriorly determined at the time of grafting but later receives dorso-ventral information from the tissues with which it is now in contact. The result is a limb whose dorso-ventral orientation is correct for its new setting but whose antero-posterior orientation is reversed. It is tacitly assumed that the proximo-distal orientation of the bud is undisturbed. The result is a limb which is reversed in regard to *one* of its three sorts of asymmetry. Such a limb must logically be a left.

This explanation I accept and proceed to consider the reduplications.

These differ in four important respects from the reduplications in beetles' legs discussed above:

[9] Swett, *op. cit.;* also Harrison, *op. cit.*

(*a*) In the beetles, the reduplication is usually equal. The two halves of the supernumerary doublet are equal in size, and are usually approximately equal in size to the corresponding parts of the primary leg. Such differences as do appear among the three components are such as might expectably result from trophic differences. But in the larval newts, great differences in size occur between the components of the reduplicated system, and it appears that these differences are determined by *time*. The secondaries are smaller than the primaries because they are produced later and, similarly, the rare tertiaries are later and smaller than the secondaries. This spacing of events in time indicates clearly that the primary limb received all the information necessary to determine its own asymmetry. It received, indeed, "wrong" information and grew to be a left leg on the right side of the body but it did not suffer from such a deficiency of information as would make it immediately fail to achieve asymmetry. The reduplication cannot simply be ascribed to loss of orienting information in the primary.

(*b*) The reduplications in beetles' legs may occur at any point along the length of the leg. But those of amphibian larvae usually arise from the region of attachment of the limb to the body. It is not even sure that the secondary always shares tissue with the primary.

(*c*) In the case of the beetles, the supernumerary doublets form a continuous series, being given off from any portion of the periphery of the primary. In contrast, the reduplication of limbs in amphibian larvae is localized either anterior or posterior to the primary.

(*d*) In the beetles it is clear that the two supernumerary components form together a single unit. In many cases there is actual compounding of the two components (as in Figure 1). In no case[10] is that component of the doublet which is nearer to the primary compounded with it rather than with the other supernumerary. In the amphibian preparations, on the other hand, it is not clear that secondary and tertiary form a subunit. The relation between tertiary and secondary seems no closer than between secondary and

---

[10]Bateson (*Materials* . . . , *op. cit.*, p. 507) describes and figures one doubtful exception to this statement. This is a reduplication in the left hind tarsus of *Platycerus caraboides*.

primary. Above all, the relation is asymmetric in the time dimension.

These profound formal differences between the two bodies of data indicate that the explanations for the amphibian data must be of a different order. It would seem that the processes are located not in the shaft of the limb but in its base and the tissues surrounding the base. Tentatively we may guess that the primary in some way proposes the later formation of a secondary by a reversal of gradient information, and that the secondary similarly proposes a reversed tertiary. Models for such systems are available in cybernetic theory in those circuit structures which propose Russellian paradoxes.[11] To attempt to construct any such model at the present time would be premature.

## Summary

This essay on the symmetry of reduplicated lateral appendages starts from an explanatory principle, viz., that any step of ontogenetic differentiation which reduces the symmetry of an organ (*e.g.*, from radial to bilateral symmetry, or from bilateral symmetry to asymmetry) requires additional orienting information. From this principle it is argued that a normally asymmetrical lateral appendage, *lacking* some necessary piece of orienting information, will only be able to achieve bilateral symmetry, *i.e.*, instead of a normal asymmetrical appendage, the result will be a bilaterally symmetrical doublet.

To examine this explanatory principle, the writer has attempted to construct a hypothesis to explain Bateson's Rule as this regularity is exemplified in the rare supernumerary double legs of Coleoptera. In the construction of this hypothesis, it was assumed that morphogenetic orienting information may undergo transformation from one type of coding to another, and that each transform or code is subject to characteristic limitations:

(*a*) The information may be embodied in *gradients* (perhaps biochemical). In this coding, the information can be diffused from neighboring tissues and provide the first determinants of asymmetry in the developing appendage. It is suggested that information coded in this way is only briefly available, and that once the asymmetry of the limb is established, the information continues to exist, but transformed into morphology.

(b) It is suggested that information coded as morphological difference is essentially static. It cannot be diffused to neighboring tissues and it cannot inhibit branching. It can, however, be used by a branch which at its inception shares tissue with the primary limb from which it branches off. In this case, the information passed on by the method of shared periphery will be necessarily inverted: if the primary be a right, the branch will be a left.

(c) The information in morphological form being (by hypothesis) unable to inhibit branching, the asymmetry of a growing primary must be preserved by a centro-peripheral gradient—not itself a determinant of that asymmetry.

(d) It is suggested that the *loss* of such a centro-peripheral gradient might have two effects: that of permitting branching and that of depriving the resulting branch of one dimension of necessary orienting information; so that the branch can only be a bilaterally symmetrical unit with a plane of symmetry at right angles to the lost centro-peripheral gradient.

The data on reduplication in the experimentally transplanted limb buds of amphibia are also examined. It is argued that these data are not to be explained by simple loss of orienting information. Simple loss, it is suggested, will expectably result in equal and synchronous bilateral symmetry. The amphibian reduplicates are, in general, unequal and successive. In a few cases, synchronous and equal reduplication occurs in the amphibian experiments, especially in heterotopic implants. Such cases could perhaps be regarded as due to simple loss of orienting information.

## Postscript, 1971

Compare the bilateral symmetry in the supernumerary doublet of the beetle's leg with the bilateral symmetry in the sweet pea or orchid flower. Both in the plant and in the animal, the bilaterally symmetrical unit comes off from a point of branching.

In the plant, the morphology of the fork *provides* information enabling the flower to be not radially but bilaterally symmetrical, *i.e.*, information which will differentiate the "dorsal" standard from the ventral lip of the flower.

In the doublet on the beetle's leg, the plane of bilateral symmetry is orthogonal to that in the flower.

We might say that the information which the beetle's leg has lost is precisely that information which the plant creates by the act of branching.

## COMMENT ON PART IV

The papers placed together in this part are diverse in that while each paper is a branch from the main stem of the argument of the book, these branches come off from very different locations. "The Role of Somatic Change in Evolution" is an expansion of the thought behind "Minimal Requirements for a Theory of Schizophrenia," while "Problems in Cetacean and Other Mammalian Communication" is an application of "The Logical Categories of Learning and Communication" to a particular type of animal.

"A Re-examination of Bateson's Rule" may seem to break new ground, but is related to the remainder of the book in that it extends the notion of informational control to include the field of morphogenesis and, by discussing what happens in *absence* of needed information, brings out the importance of the context *into* which information is received.

Samuel Butler, with uncanny insight, once commented upon the analogy between dreams and parthenogenesis. We may say that the monstrous double legs of the beetles share in this analogy: they are the projection of the receptive context deprived of information which should have come from an external source.

Message material, or information, comes out of a context into a context, and in other parts of the book the focus has been on the context *out* of which information came. Here the focus is rather upon the internal state of the organism as a context *into* which the information must be received.

Of course, neither focus is sufficient by itself for our understanding of either animals or men. But it is perhaps not an accident that in these papers dealing with non-human organisms the "context" which is discussed is the obverse or complement of the "context" upon which I have focussed attention in other parts of the book.

Consider the case of the unfertilized frog's egg for which the entry point of the spermatozoon defines the plane of bilateral symmetry of the future embryo.

The prick of a hair from a camel's hair brush can be substituted and still carry the same message. From this it seems that the external context out of which the message comes is relatively undefined. From the entry point alone, the egg learns but little about the external world. But the internal context into which the message comes must be exceedingly complex.

The unfertilized egg, then, embodies an *immanent question* to which the entry point of spermatozoon provides an answer; and this way of stating the matter is the contrary or obverse of the conventional view, which would see the external context of learning as a "question" to which the "right" behavior of the organism is an answer.

We can even begin to list some of the components of the immanent question. First there are the already existing poles of the egg and, necessarily, some polarization of the intervening protoplasm towards these poles. Without some such structural conditions for the receipt of the prick of the spermatozoon, this message could have no meaning. The message must come into an appropriate *structure.*

But structure alone is not enough. It seems probable that any meridian of the frog's egg can potentially become the plane of bilateral symmetry and that, in this, all meridians are alike. It follows that there is, to this extent, no structural difference between them. But every meridian must be *ready* for the activating message, its "readiness" being given direction but otherwise unrestricted by structure. Readiness, in fact, is precisely *not-structure.* If and when the spermatozoon delivers its message, new structure is generated.

In terms of the economics of flexibility, discussed in "The Role of Somatic Change in Evolution" and later in "Ecology and Flexibility in Urban Civilization" (Part VI), this "readiness" is *uncommitted potentiality for change,* and we note here that this uncommitted potentiality is not only always finite in quantity but must be appropriately located in a structural matrix, which also must be quantitatively finite at any given time.

These considerations lead naturally into Part V, which I have titled "Epistemology and Ecology." Perhaps "epistemology" is only another word for the study of the ecology of mind.

# Part V: Epistemology and Ecology

# Cybernetic Explanation*

It may be useful to describe some of the peculiarities of cybernetic explanation.

Causal explanation is usually positive. We say that billiard ball B moved in such and such a direction because billiard ball A hit it at such and such an angle. In contrast to this, cybernetic explanation is always negative. We consider what alternative possibilities could conceivably have occurred and then ask why many of the alternatives were not followed, so that the particular event was one of those few which could, in fact, occur. The classical example of this type of explanation is the theory of evolution under natural selection. According to this theory, those organisms which were not both physiologically and environmentally viable could not possibly have lived to reproduce. Therefore, evolution always followed the pathways of viability. As Lewis Carroll has pointed out, the theory explains quite satisfactorily why there are no bread-and-butter-flies today.

In cybernetic language, the course of events is said to be subject to *restraints*, and it is assumed that, apart from such restraints, the pathways of change would be governed only by equality of probability. In fact, the "restraints" upon which cybernetic explanation depends can in all cases be regarded as factors which determine inequality of prob-

*This article is reprinted from the *American Behavioral Scientist*, Vol. 10, No. 8, April 1967, pp. 29–32, by permission of the publisher, Sage Publications, Inc.

ability. If we find a monkey striking a typewriter apparently at random but in fact writing meaningful prose, we shall look for restraints, either inside the monkey or inside the typewriter. Perhaps the monkey could not strike inappropriate letters; perhaps the type bars could not move if improperly struck; perhaps incorrect letters could not survive on the paper. Somewhere there must have been a circuit which could identify error and eliminate it.

Ideally—and commonly—the actual event in any sequence or aggregate is uniquely determined within the terms of the cybernetic explanation. Restraints of many different kinds may combine to generate this unique determination. For example, the selection of a piece for a given position in a jigsaw puzzle is "restrained" by many factors. Its shape must conform to that of its several neighbors and possibly that of the boundary of the puzzle; its color must conform to the color pattern of its region; the orientation of its edges must obey the topological regularities set by the cutting machine in which the puzzle was made; and so on. From the point of view of the man who is trying to solve the puzzle, these are all clues, *i.e.*, sources of information which will guide him in his selection. From the point of view of the cybernetic observer, they are *restraints*.

Similarly, from the cybernetic point of view, a word in a sentence, or a letter within the word, or the anatomy of some part within an organism, or the role of a species in an ecosystem, or the behavior of a member within a family—these are all to be (negatively) explained by an analysis of restraints.

The negative form of these explanations is precisely comparable to the form of logical proof by *reductio ad absurdum*. In this species of proof, a sufficient set of mutually exclusive alternative propositions is enumerated, *e.g.*, "P" and "not P," and the process of proof procedes by demonstrating that all but one of this set are untenable or "absurd." It follows that the surviving member of the set must be tenable within the terms of the logical system. This is a form of proof which the nonmathematical sometimes find unconvincing and, no doubt, the theory of natural selection sometimes seems unconvincing to nonmathematical persons for similar reasons—whatever those reasons may be.

Another tactic of mathematical proof which has its counterpart in the construction of cybernetic explanations is the use of "mapping" or rigorous metaphor. An algebraic proposition may, for example, be mapped onto a system of geometric coordinates and there proven by geometric methods. In cybernetics, mapping appears as a technique of explanation whenever a conceptual "model" is invoked or, more concretely, when a computer is used to simulate a complex communicational process. But this is not the only appearance of mapping in this science. Formal processes of mapping, translation, or transformation are, in principle, imputed to *every* step of any sequence of phenomena which the cyberneticist is attempting to explain. These *mappings* or transformations may be very complex, *e.g.*, where the output of some machine is regarded as a transform of the input; or they may be very simple, *e.g.*, where the rotation of a shaft at a given point along its length is regarded as a transform (albeit identical) of its rotation at some previous point.

The relations which remain constant under such transformation may be of any conceivable kind.

This parallel, between cybernetic explanation and the tactics of logical or mathematical proof, is of more than trivial interest. Outside of cybernetics, we look for explanation, but not for anything which would simulate logical proof. This simulation of proof is something new. We can say, however, with hindsight wisdom, that explanation by simulation of logical or mathematical proof was expectable. After all, the subject matter of cybernetics is not events and objects but the *information* "carried" by events and objects. We consider the objects or events only as proposing facts, propositions, messages, percepts, and the like. The subject matter being propositional, it is expectable that explanation would simulate the logical.

Cyberneticians have specialized in those explanations which simulate *reductio ad absurdum* and "mapping." There are perhaps whole realms of explanation awaiting discovery by some mathematician who will recognize, in the informational aspects of nature, sequences which simulate other types of proof.

Because the subject matter of cybernetics is the propositional or informational aspect of the events and objects in the natural world, this science is forced to procedures rather different from those of the other sciences. The differentiation, for example, between map and territory, which the semanticists insist that scientists shall respect in their writings must, in cybernetics, be watched for in the very phenomena about which the scientist writes. Expectably, communicating organisms and badly programmed computers will mistake map for territory; and the language of the scientist must be able to cope with such anomalies. In human behavioral systems, especially in religion and ritual and wherever primary process dominates the scene, the name often *is* the thing named. The bread *is* the Body, and the wine *is* the Blood.

Similarly, the whole matter of induction and deduction —and our doctrinaire preferences for one or the other— will take on a new significance when we recognize inductive and deductive steps not only in our own argument but in the relationships among data.

Of especial interest in this connection is the relationship between *context* and its content. A phoneme exists as such only in combination with other phonemes which make up a word. The word is the *context* of the phoneme. But the word only exists as such—only has "meaning"—in the larger context of the utterance, which again has meaning only in a relationship.

This hierarchy of contexts within contexts is universal for the communicational (or "emic") aspect of phenomena and drives the scientist always to seek for explanation in the ever larger units. It may (perhaps) be true in physics that the explanation of the macroscopic is to be sought in the microscopic. The opposite is usually true in cybernetics: without context, there is no communication.

In accord with the negative character of cybernetic explanation, "information" is quantified in negative terms. An event or object such as the letter K in a given position in the text of a message *might* have been any other of the limited set of twenty-six letters in the English language. The actual letter excludes (*i.e.*, eliminates by restraint) twenty-five alternatives. In comparison with an English letter, a Chinese ideograph would have excluded several thousand alternatives. We say, therefore, that the Chinese ideograph carries more information than the letter. The quantity of information is conventionally expressed as the log to base 2 of the improbability of the actual event or object.

Probability, being a ratio between quantities which have

similar dimensions, is itself of zero dimensions. That is, the central explanatory quantity, information, is of zero dimensions. Quantities of real dimensions (mass, length, time) and their derivatives (force, energy, etc.) have no place in cybernetic explanation.

The status of energy is of special interest. In general in communicational systems, we deal with sequences which resemble stimulus-and-response rather than cause-and-effect. When one billiard ball strikes another, there is an energy transfer such that the motion of the second ball is energized by the impact of the first. In communicational systems, on the other hand, the energy of the response is usually provided by the respondent. If I kick a dog, his immediately sequential behavior is energized by his metabolism, not by my kick. Similarly, when one neuron fires another, or an impulse from a microphone activates a circuit, the sequent event has its own energy sources.

Of course, everything that happens is still within the limits defined by the law of energy conservation. The dog's metabolism might in the end limit his response, but, in general, in the systems with which we deal, the energy supplies are large compared with the demands upon them; and, long before the supplies are exhausted, "economic" limitations are imposed by the finite number of available alternatives, *i.e.*, there is an economics of probability. This economics differs from an economics of energy or money in that probability—being a ratio—is not subject to addition or subtraction but only to multiplicative processes, such as fractionation. A telephone exchange at a time of emergency may be "jammed" when a large fraction of its alternative pathways are busy. There is, then, a low probability of any given message getting through.

In addition to the restraints due to the limited economics of alternatives, two other categories of restraint must be discussed: restraints related to "feedback" and restraints related to "redundancy."

We consider first the concept of feedback:

When the phenomena of the universe are seen as linked together by cause-and-effect and energy transfer, the resulting picture is of complexly branching and interconnecting chains of causation. In certain regions of this universe (notably organisms in environments, ecosystems, thermostats, steam engines with governors, societies, computers, and the like), these chains of causation form circuits which are *closed* in the sense that causal interconnection can be traced around the circuit and back through whatever position was (arbitrarily) chosen as the starting point of the description. In such a circuit, evidently, events at any position in the circuit may be expected to have effect at *all* positions on the circuit at later times.

Such systems are, however, always *open*: (*a*) in the sense that the circuit is energized from some external source and loses energy usually in the form of heat to the outside; and (*b*) in the sense that events within the circuit may be influenced from the outside or may influence outside events.

A very large and important part of cybernetic theory is concerned with the formal characteristics of such causal circuits, and the conditions of their stability. Here I shall consider such systems only as sources of *restraint*.

Consider a variable in the circuit at any position and suppose this variable subject to random change in value (the change perhaps being imposed by impact of some event external to the circuit). We now ask how this change will affect the value of this variable at that later time when the sequence of effects has come around the circuit. Clearly the answer to this last question will depend upon the characteristics of the circuit and will, therefore, be *not random*.

In principle, then, a causal circuit will generate a nonrandom response to a random event *at that position in the circuit at which the random event occurred.*

This is the general requisite for the creation of cybernetic restraint in any variable at any given position. The particular restraint created in any given instance will, of course, depend upon the characteristics of the particular circuit—whether its overall gain be positive or negative, its time characteristics, its thresholds of activity, etc. These will together determine the restraints which it will exert at any given position.

For purposes of cybernetic explanation, when a machine is observed to be (improbably) moving at a constant rate, even under varying load, we shall look for restraints—*e.g.*, for a circuit which will be activated by changes in rate and which, when activated, will operate upon some variable (*e.g.*, the fuel supply) in such a way as to diminish the change in rate.

When the monkey is observed to be (improbably) typing prose, we shall look for some circuit which is activated whenever he makes a "mistake" and which, when activated, will delete the evidence of that mistake at the position where it occurred.

The cybernetic method of negative explanation raises the question: Is there a difference between "being right" and "not being wrong"? Should we say of the rat in a maze that he has "learned the right path" or should we say only that he has learned "to avoid the wrong paths"?

Subjectively, I feel that I know how to spell a number of English words, and I am certainly not aware of discarding as unrewarding the letter K when I have to spell the word "many." Yet, in the first level cybernetic explanation, I should be viewed as actively discarding the alternative K when I spell "many."

The question is not trivial and the answer is both subtle and fundamental: *choices are not all at the same level.* I may have to avoid error in my choice of the word "many" in a given context, discarding the alternatives, "few," "several," "frequent," etc. But if I can achieve this higher level choice on a negative base, it follows that the word "many" and its alternatives somehow must be conceivable to me—must exist as distinguishable and possibly labeled or coded patterns in my neural processes. If they do, in some sense, exist, then it follows that, after making the higher level choice of what word to use, I shall not necessarily be faced with alternatives at the lower level. It may become unnecessary for me to exclude the letter K from the word "many." It will be correct to say that I know positively how to spell "many"; not merely that I know how to avoid making mistakes in spelling that word.

It follows that Lewis Carroll's joke about the theory of natural selection is not entirely cogent. If, in the communicational and organizational processes of biological evolution, there be something like *levels*—items, patterns, and possibly patterns of patterns—then it is logically possible for the evolutionary system to make something like positive choices. Such levels and patterning might conceivably be in or among genes or elsewhere.

The circuitry of the above mentioned monkey would be required to recognize deviations from "prose," and prose is characterized by pattern or—as the engineers call it—by redundancy.

The occurrence of the letter K in a given location in an English prose message is not a purely random event in the sense that there was ever an equal probability that any other of the twenty-five letters might have occurred in that location. Some letters are more common in English than others, and certain combinations of letters are more common than others. There is, thus, a species of patterning which partly determines which letters shall occur in which slots. As a result: if the receiver of the message had received the entire rest of the message but had not received the particular letter K which we are discussing, he might have been able, with better than random success, to guess that the missing letter was, in fact, K. To the extent that this was so, the letter K did not, for that receiver, exclude the other twenty-five letters because these were already partly excluded by information which the recipient received from the rest of the message. This patterning or predictability of particular events within a larger aggregate of events is technically called "redundancy."

The concept of redundancy is usually derived, as I have derived it, by considering first the maximum of information which might be carried by the given item and then considering how this total might be reduced by knowledge of the surrounding patterns of which the given item is a component part. There is, however, a case for looking at the whole matter the other way round. We might regard patterning or predictability as the very essence and *raison d'être* of communication, and see the single letter unaccompanied by collateral clues as a peculiar and special case.

The idea that communication *is* the creation of redundancy or patterning can be applied to the simplest engineering examples. Let us consider an *observer* who is watching A send a message to B. The purpose of the transaction (from the point of view of A and B) is to create in B's message pad a sequence of letters identical with the sequence which formerly occurred in A's pad. But from the point of view of the observer this is the creation of redundancy. If he has seen what A had on his pad, he will not get any new information about the message itself from inspecting B's pad.

Evidently, the nature of "meaning," pattern, redundancy, information and the like, depends upon where we sit. In the usual engineers' discussion of a message sent from A to B, it is customary to omit the observer and to say that B received information from A which was measurable in terms of the number of letters transmitted, reduced by such redundancy in the text as might have permitted B to do some guessing. But in a wider universe, *i.e.*, that defined by the point of view of the observer, this no longer appears as a "transmission" of information but rather as a spreading of redundancy. The activities of A and B have combined to make the universe of the observer more predictable, more ordered, and more redundant. We may say that the rules of the "game" played by A and B explain (as "restraints") what would otherwise be a puzzling and improbable coincidence in the observer's universe, namely the conformity between what is written on the two message pads.

To guess, in essence, is to face a cut or slash in the sequence of items and to predict across that slash what items might be on the other side. The slash may be spatial or temporal (or both) and the guessing may be either predictive or retrospective. A pattern, in fact, is definable as an aggregate of events or objects which will permit in some degree such guesses when the entire aggregate is not available for inspection.

But this sort of patterning is also a very general phenomenon, outside the realm of communication *between* organisms. The reception of message material by *one* organism is not fundamentally different from any other case of perception. If I see the top part of a tree standing up, I can predict —with better than random success—that the tree has roots in the ground. The percept of the tree top is redundant with (*i.e.*, contains "information" about) parts of the system which I cannot perceive owing to the slash provided by the opacity of the ground.

If then we say that a message has "meaning" or is "about" some referent, what we mean is that there is a larger universe of relevance consisting of message-plus-referent, and that redundancy or pattern or predictability is introduced into this universe by the message.

If I say to you "It is raining," this message introduces re-dundancy into the universe, message-plus-raindrops, so that from the message alone you could have guessed—with better than random success—something of what you would see if you looked out of the window. The universe, message-plus-referent, is given pattern or form—in the Shakespearean sense, the universe is *informed* by the message; and the "form" of which we are speaking is not in the message nor is it in the referent. It is a correspondence between message and referent.

In loose talk, it seems simple to locate information. The letter K in a given slot proposes that the letter in that particular slot is a K. And, so long as all information is of this very direct kind, the information can be "located": the information about the letter K is seemingly in that slot.

The matter is not quite so simple if the text of the message is redundant but, if we are lucky and the redundancy is of low order, we may still be able to point to parts of the text which indicate (carry some of the information) that the letter K is expectable in that particular slot.

But if we are asked: Where are such items of information as that: (a) "This message is in English"; and (b) "In English, a letter K often follows a letter C, except when the C begins a word"; we can only say that such information is *not* localized in any part of the text but is rather a statistical induction from the text as a whole (or perhaps from an aggregate of "similar" texts). This, after all, is metainformation and is of a basically different order—of different logical type—from the information that "the letter in this slot is K."

This matter of the localization of information has bedeviled communication theory and especially neurophysiology for many years and it is, therefore, interesting to consider how the matter looks if we start from redundancy, pattern or form as the basic concept.

It is flatly obvious that no variable of zero dimensions can be truly located. "Information" and "form" resemble contrast, frequency, symmetry, correspondence, congruence, conformity, and the like in being of zero dimensions and, therefore, are not to be located. The contrast between this white paper and that black coffee is not somewhere between the paper and the coffee and, even if we bring the paper and coffee into close juxtaposition, the contrast between them is not thereby located or pinched between them. Nor is that contrast located between the two objects and my eye. It is not even in my head; or, if it be, then it must also be in your head. But you, the reader, have not seen the paper and the coffee to which I was referring. I have in my head an image or transform or name of the contrast between them; and you have in your head a transform of what I have in mine. But the conformity between us is not localizable. In fact, information and form are not items which can be localized.

It is, however, possible to begin (but perhaps not complete) a sort of mapping of formal relations within a system containing redundancy. Consider a finite aggregate of objects or events (say a sequence of letters, or a tree) and an observer who is already informed about all the redundancy rules which are recognizable (*i.e.*, which have statistical significance) within the aggregate. It is then possible to delimit regions of the aggregate within which the observer can achieve better than random guessing. A further step toward localization is accomplished by cutting across these regions with slash marks, such that it is across these that the educated observer can guess, from what is on one side of the slash, something of what is on the other side.

Such a mapping of the distribution of patterns is, however, in principle, incomplete because we have not considered the sources of the observer's prior knowledge of the redundancy rules. If, now, we consider an observer with *no* prior knowledge, it is clear that he might discover some of the relevant rules from his perception of *less* than the whole aggregate. He could then use his discovery in predicting *rules* for the remainder—rules which would be correct even though not exemplified. He might discover that "H often follows T" even though the remainder of the aggregate contained no example of this combination. For this order of phenomenon a different order of slash mark—metaslashes —will be necessary.

It is interesting to note that metaslashes which demarcate what is necessary for the naive observer to discover a rule are, in principle, displaced relative to the slashes which would have appeared on the map prepared by an observer totally informed as to the rules of redundancy for that aggregate. (This principle is of some importance in aesthetics.

To the aesthetic eye, the form of a crab with one claw bigger than the other is not simply asymmetrical. It first proposes a rule of symmetry and then subtly denies the rule by proposing a more complex combination of rules.)

When we exclude all things and all real dimensions from our explanatory system, we are left regarding each step in a communicational sequence as a *transform* of the previous step. If we consider the passage of an impulse along an axon, we shall regard the events at each point along the pathway as a transform (albeit identical or similar) of events at any previous point. Or if we consider a series of neurons, each firing the next, then the firing of each neuron is a transform of the firing of its predecessor. We deal with event sequences which do not necessarily imply a passing on of the same energy.

Similarly, we can consider any network of neurons, and arbitrarily transect the whole network at a series of different positions, then we shall regard the events at each transection as a transform of events at some previous transection.

In considering perception, we shall not say, for example, "I see a tree," because the tree is not within our explanatory system. At best, it is only possible to see an image which is a complex but systematic transform of the tree. This image, of course, is energized by my metabolism and the nature of the transform is, in part, determined by factors within my neural circuits: "I" make the image, under various restraints, some of which are imposed by my neural circuits, while others are imposed by the external tree. An hallucination or dream would be more truly "mine" insofar as it is produced without immediate external restraints.

All that is not information, not redundancy, not form and not restraints—is noise, the only possible source of *new* patterns.

# Redundancy and Coding*

Discussion of the evolutionary and other relationships between the communication systems of men and those of other animals has made it very clear that the coding devices characteristic of verbal communication differ profoundly from those of kinesics and paralanguage. But the point has been made that there is a great deal of resemblance between the codes of kinesics and paralanguage and the codes of nonhuman mammals.

We may, I think, state categorically that man's verbal system is not derived in any simple way from these preponderantly iconic codes. There is a general popular belief that in the evolution of man, language replaced the cruder systems of the other animals. I believe this to be totally wrong and would argue as follows:

In any complex functional system capable of adaptive evolutionary change, when the performance of a given function is taken over by some new and more efficient method, the old method falls into disuse and decay. The technique of making weapons by the knapping of flint deteriorated when metals came into use.

This decay of organs and skills under evolutionary replace-

*This essay appeared as Chapter 22 in *Animal Communication: Techniques of Study and Results of Research*, edited by Thomas A. Sebeok. Copyright 1968 by Indiana University Press. Reprinted by permission of the publisher.

ment is a necessary and inevitable systemic phenomenon. If, therefore, verbal language were in any sense an evolutionary replacement of communication by means of kinesics and paralanguage, we would expect the old, preponderantly iconic systems to have undergone conspicuous decay. Clearly they have not. Rather, the kinesics of men have become richer and more complex, and paralanguage has blossomed side by side with the evolution of verbal language. Both kinesics and paralanguage have been elaborated into complex forms of art, music, ballet, poetry, and the like, and, even in everyday life, the intricacies of human kinesic communication, facial expression, and vocal intonation far exceed anything that any other animal is known to produce. The logician's dream that men should communicate only by unambiguous digital signals has not come true and is not likely to.

I suggest that this separate burgeoning evolution of kinesics and paralanguage alongside the evolution of verbal language indicates that our iconic communication serves functions totally different from those of language and, indeed, performs functions which verbal language is unsuited to perform.

When boy says to girl, "I love you," he is using words to convey that which is more convincingly conveyed by his tone of voice and his movements; and the girl, if she has any sense, will pay more attention to those accompanying signs than to the words. There are people—professional actors, confidence tricksters, and others—who are able to use kinesics and paralinguistic communication with a degree of voluntary control comparable to that voluntary control which we all think we have over the use of words. For these people who can lie with kinesics, the special usefulness of nonverbal communication is reduced. It is a little more difficult for them to be sincere and still more difficult for them to be believed to be sincere. They are caught in a process of diminishing returns such that, when distrusted, they try to improve their skill in simulating paralinguistic and kinesic sincerity. But this is the very skill which led others to distrust them.

It seems that the discourse of nonverbal communication is precisely concerned with matters of relationship—love, hate, respect, fear, dependency, etc.—between self and vis-à-vis or between self and environment and that the nature of human society is such that falsification of this discourse rapidly becomes pathogenic. From an adaptive point of view, it is therefore important that this discourse be carried on by techniques which are relatively unconscious and only imperfectly subject to voluntary control. In the language of neurophysiology, the controls of this discourse must be placed in the brain caudad of the controls of true language.

If this general view of the matter be correct, it must follow that to translate kinesics or paralinguistic messages into words is likely to introduce gross falsification due not merely to the human propensity for trying to falsify statements about "feelings" and relationship and to the distortions which arise whenever the products of one system of coding are dissected onto the premises of another, but especially to the fact that all such translation must give to the more or less unconscious and involuntary iconic message the appearance of conscious intent.

As scientists, we are concerned to build a simulacrum of the phenomenal universe in words. That is, our product is to be a verbal transform of the phenomena. It is necessary, therefore, to examine rather carefully the rules of this transformation and the differences in coding between natural phenomena, message phenomena, and words. I know that it is unusual to presume a "coding" of nonliving phenomena and, to justify this phrase, I must expand somewhat on the concept of "redundancy" as this word is used by the communications engineers.

The engineers and mathematicians have concentrated their attention rigorously upon the internal structure of message material. Typically, this material consists of a sequence or collection of events or objects (commonly members of finite sets—phonemes and the like). This sequence is differentiated from irrelevant events or objects occurring in the same region of time-space by the signal/noise ratio and by other characteristics. The message material is said to contain "redundancy" if, when the sequence is received with some items missing, the receiver is able to guess at the missing items with better than random success. It has been pointed out that, in fact, the term "redundancy" so used becomes a synonym for "patterning."[1] It is important to note that this patterning of message material always helps the receiver to differentiate between signal and noise. In fact, the regularity called signal/noise ratio is really only a special case of redundancy. Camouflage (the opposite of communication) is achieved (1) by reducing the signal/noise ratio, (2) by breaking up the patterns and regularities in the signal, or (3) by introducing similar patterns into the noise.

By confining their attention to the internal structure of the message material, the engineers believe that they can avoid the complexities and difficulties introduced into communication theory by the concept of "meaning." I would argue, however, that the concept "redundancy" is at least a partial synonym of "meaning." As I see it, if the receiver can guess at missing parts of the message, then those parts which are received must, in fact, carry a *meaning* which refers to the missing parts and is information about those parts.

If now we turn away from the narrow universe of message structure and consider the outer world of natural phenomena, we observe at once that this outer world is similarly characterized by redundancy, *i.e.*, that when an observer perceives only certain parts of a sequence or configuration of phenomena, he is in many cases able to guess, with better than random success, at the parts which he cannot immediately perceive. It is, indeed, a principal goal of the scientist to elucidate these redundancies or patternings of the phenomenal world.

If we now consider that larger universe of which these two subuniverses are parts, *i.e.*, the system: message *plus* external phenomena, we find that this larger system contains redundancy of a very special sort. The observer's ability to predict external phenomena is very much increased by his receipt of message material. If I tell you that "it is raining" and you look out the window, you will get less information from the perception of raindrops than you would have got had you never received my message. From my message you could have guessed that you would see rain.

In sum, "redundancy" and "meaning" become synonymous whenever both words are applied to the same universe of

[1] F. Attneave, *Applications of Information Theory to Psychology*, New York, Henry Holt and Co., 1959.

discourse. "Redundancy" within the restricted universe of the message sequence is not, of course, synonymous with "meaning" in the wider universe that includes both message and external referent.

It will be noted that this way of thinking about communication groups all methods of coding under the single rubric of part-for-whole. The verbal message "It is raining" is to be seen as a *part* of a larger universe within which that message creates redundancy or predictability. The "digital," the "analogic," the "iconic," the "metaphoric," and all other methods of coding are subsumed under this single heading. (What the grammarians call "synecdoche" is the metaphoric use of the name of a part in place of the name of the whole, as in the phrase "five *head* of cattle.")

This approach to the matter has certain advantages: the analyst is forced at all times to define the universe of discourse within which "redundancy" or "meaning" is supposed to occur. He is forced to examine the "logical typing" of all message material. We shall see that this broad view of the matter makes it easy to identify major steps in the evolution of communication. Let us consider the scientist who is observing two animals in a physical environment. The following components then must be considered:

(1) The physical environment contains internal patterning or redundancy, *i.e.*, the perception of certain events or objects makes other events or objects predictable for the animals and/or for the observer.

(2) Sounds or other signals from one animal may contribute redundancy to the system, *environment plus signal; i.e.*, the signals may be "about" the environment.

(3) The sequence of signals will certainly contain redundancy—one signal from an animal making another signal from the same animal more predictable.

(4) The signals may contribute redundancy to the universe; *A's signals plus B's signals, i.e.*, the signals may be *about* the interaction of which they are component parts.

(5) If all rules or codes of animal communication and understanding were genotypically fixed, the list would end at this point. But some animals are capable of *learning*, *e.g.*, the repetition of sequences may lead to their becoming effective as patterns. In logic, "every proposition proposes its own truth," but in natural history we deal always with a

converse of this generalization. The perceivable events which accompany a given percept propose that that percept shall "mean" these events. By some such steps an organism may learn to use the information contained in patterned sequences of external events. I can therefore predict with better than random success that in the universe, organism *plus* environment, events will occur to complete patterns or configurations of learned adaptation between organism and environment.

(6) The behavioral "learning" which is usually studied in psychological laboratories is of a different order. The redundancy of that universe, which consists of the animal's actions *plus* external events, is increased, from the animal's point of view, when the animal regularly responds to certain events with certain actions. Similarly, this universe gains redundancy when the animal succeeds in producing those actions which function as regular *precursors* (or causes) of specific external events.

(7) For every organism there are limitations and regularities which define what will be learned and under what circumstances this learning will occur. These regularities and patterns become basic premises for the individual adaptation and social organization of any species.

(8) Last but not least, there is the matter of phylogenetic learning and phylogeny in general. There is redundancy in the system, organism-*plus*-environment, such that from the morphology and behavior of the organism a human observer can guess with better than random success at the nature of the environment. This "information" about the environment has become lodged in the organism through a long phylogenetic process, and its coding is of a very special kind. The observer who would learn about the aquatic environment from the shape of a shark must deduce the hydrodynamics from the adaptation which copes with the water. The information contained in the phenotypic shark is implicit in forms which are complementary to characteristics of other parts of the universe, *phenotype plus environment* whose redundancy is increased by the phenotype.

This very brief and incomplete survey of some of the sorts of redundancy in biological systems and the universes of their relevance indicates that under the general rubric "part-for-whole" a number of different sorts of relationship between

part and whole are included. A listing of some of the characteristics of these formal relations is in order. We consider
some of the iconic cases:

(1) The events or objects which we here call the "part"
or "signal" may be real components of an existing sequence
or whole. A standing trunk of a tree indicates the probable
presence of invisible roots. A cloud may indicate the coming
storm of which it is a part. The bared fang of a dog may be
part of a real attack.

(2) The "part" may have only a conditional relationship
to its whole: the cloud may indicate that we shall get wet
if we don't go indoors; the bared fang may be the beginning of an attack which will be completed unless certain
conditions are met.

(3) The "part" may be completely split from the whole
which is its referent. The bared fang at the given instant
may *mention* an attack which, if and when it occurs, will
include a *new* baring of the fangs. The "part" has now
became a true iconic signal.

(4) Once a true iconic signal has evolved—not necessarily through steps 1, 2, or 3, above—a variety of other
pathways of evolution become possible:

(*a*) The "part" may become more or less digitalized, so
that magnitudes within it no longer refer to magnitudes
within the whole which is its referent but, for example,
contribute to an improvement of the signal/noise ratio.

(*b*) The "part" may take on special ritual or metaphoric
meanings in contexts where the original whole to which it
once referred is no longer relevant. The game of mutual
mouthing between mother dog and puppy which once followed her weaning of the pup may become a ritual aggregation. The actions of feeding a baby bird may become a
ritual of courtship, etc.

Throughout this series, whose branches and varieties are
here only briefly indicated, it is notable that animal communication is confined to signals which are derived from actions
of the animals themselves, *i.e.*, those which are parts of such
actions. The external universe is, as already noted, redundant in the sense that it is replete with part-for-whole
messages, and—perhaps for that reason—this basic style
of coding is characteristic of primitive animal communication. But in so far as animals can signal at all about the

external universe, they do so by means of actions which are parts of their response to that universe. The jackdaws indicate to each other that Lorenz is a "jackdaw-eater" not by simulating some part of the act of eating jackdaws but by simulating part of their aggression vis-à-vis such a creature. Occasionally actual pieces of the external environment—scraps of potential nest-building material, "trophies," and the like—are used for communication, and in these cases again the messages usually contribute redundancy to the universe *message plus the relationship between the organisms* rather than to the universe *message plus external environment*.

In terms of evolutionary theory, it is not simple to explain why over and over again genotypic controls have been evolved to determine such iconic signaling. From the point of view of the human observer such iconic signals are rather easy to interpret, and we might expect iconic coding to be comparatively easy for animals to decode—in so far as the animals must *learn* to do so. But the genome is presumed not capable of learning in this sense, and we might therefore expect genotypically determined signals to be aniconic or arbitrary rather than iconic.

Three possible explanations of the iconic nature of genotypic signals can be offered:

(1) Even genotypically determined signals do not occur as separate and isolated elements in the life of the phenotype but are necessarily components in a complex matrix of behavior some, at least, of which is learned. It is possible that the iconic coding of genotypically determined signals renders these easy to assimilate into this matrix. There may be an experiential "schoolmarm" which acts selectively to favor those genotypic changes which will give rise to iconic rather than arbitrary signaling.

(2) A signal of aggression which places the signaler in a position of readiness to attack probably has more survival value than would a more arbitrary signal.

(3) When the genotypically determined signal affects the behavior of another species—*e.g.*, eye marks or postures which have a warning effect, movements which facilitate camouflage or aposematic mimicry—clearly the signal must be iconic to the perceptive system of that other species. However, an interesting phenomenon arises in many instances where what is achieved is a secondary statistical iconicism.

*Labroides dimidiatus,* a small Indo-Pacific wrasse, which lives on the ectoparasites of other fishes, is strikingly colored and moves or "dances" in a way which is easily recognized. No doubt these characteristics attract other fish and are part of a signaling system which leads the other fish to permit the approaches of the cleaner. But there is a mimic of this species of *Labroides,* a saber-toothed blenny (*Aspidontus taeniatus*), whose similar coloring and movement permit the mimic to approach—and bite off pieces of the fins of other fishes.[2]

Clearly the coloring and movements of the mimic are iconic and "represent" the cleaner. But what of the coloring and movements of the latter? All that is primarily required is that the cleaner be conspicuous or distinctive. It is not required that it represent something else. But when we consider the statistical aspects of the system, it becomes clear that if the blennies become too numerous, the distinctive features of the wrasses will become iconic warnings and their hosts will avoid them. What is necessary is that the signals of the wrasse shall clearly and indubitably represent wrasse, *i.e.,* the signals, though perhaps aniconic in the first instance, must achieve and maintain by multiple impact a sort of autoiconicism. "When I say it three times, it is true." But this necessity for autoiconicism may also arise within the species. Genotypic control of signaling ensures the necessary repetitiveness (which might be only fortuitous if the signals had to be learned).

(4) There is a case for asserting that the genotypic determination of adaptive characteristics is, in a special sense, more economical than the achievement of similar characteristic by somatic change or phenotypic learning. This matter has been argued elsewhere.[3] Briefly it is asserted that the somatic adaptive flexibility and/or learning capacity of any organism is limited and that the demands placed upon these capacities will be reduced by genotypic change in any appropriate direction. Such changes would therefore have

[2] J. E. Randall and H. S. Randall, "Examples of Mimicry and Protective Resemblance in Tropical Marine Fishes," *Bulletin of Marine Science of the Gulf and Caribbean,* 1960, 10: 444–80.

[3] G. Bateson, "The Role of Somatic Change in Evolution," *Evolution,* 1963, 17: 529–39.

survival value because they set free precious adaptive or learning capacity for other uses. This amounts to an argument for *Baldwin* effects. An extention of this argument would suggest that the iconic character of genotypically controlled signaling characteristics may, in some cases, be explained by supposing that these characteristics were once learned. (This hypothesis does not, of course, imply any sort of Lamarckian inheritance. It is obvious (1) that to fix the value of any variable in a homeostatic circuit by such inheritance would soon gum up the homeostatic system of the body, and (2) that no amount of modification of the dependent variables in a homeostatic circuit will change the bias of the circuit.)

(5) Last, it is unclear at what level genotypic determination of behavior might act. It was suggested above that iconic codes are easier for an organism to learn than more arbitrary codes. It is possible that the genotypic contribution to such an organism might take the form, not of fixing the given behavior, but rather of making this behavior easier to learn—a change in specific learning capacity rather than a change in genotypically determined behavior. Such a contribution from the genotype would have obvious advantages in that it would work along with ontogenetic change instead of working possibly at cross-purposes with it.

To sum up the argument so far:

(1) It is understandable that an early (in an evolutionary sense) method of creating redundancy would be the use of iconic part-for-whole coding. The external nonbiological universe contains redundancy of this kind, and in evolving a code of communication it is expectable that organisms would fall into the same trick. We have noted that the "part" can be split from the whole, so that a showing of the fangs can denote a possible but as yet nonexistent fight. All this provides an explanatory background for communication by means of "intention movements" and the like.

(2) It it partly understandable that such tricks of coding by iconic parts might become genotypically fixed.

(3) It has been suggested that the survival of such primitive (and therefore involuntary) signalling in human communication about personal relationship is explained by a need for honesty in such matters.

But the evolution of aniconic verbal coding remains unexplained.

We know from studies of aphasia, from Hockett's enumeration at this meeting of the characteristics of language and from elementary common sense that the component processes of creating and understanding verbal communication are many and that language fails when any one of those component processes is interrupted. It is possible that each of these processes should be the focus of a separate study. Here, however, I shall consider only one aspect of the matter: the evolution of simple indicative assertion.

An interesting intermediate between the iconic coding of animals and the verbal coding of human speech can be recognized in human dreaming and human myth. In psychoanalytic theory, the productions of dream process are said to be characterized by "primary-process" thinking.[4] Dreams, whether verbal or not, are to be considered as metaphoric statements, *i.e.*, the referents of dream are *relationships* which the dreamer, consciously or unconsciously, perceives in his waking world. As in all metaphor, the relata remain unmentioned and in their places appear other items such that the relationships between these substitute items shall be the same as those between the relata in the waking world.

To identify the relata in the waking world to which the dream refers would convert the metaphor into a simile, and, in general, dreams contain no message material which overtly performs this function. There is no signal in the dream which tells the dreamer that this is metaphor or what the referent of the metaphor may be. Similarly, dream contains no tenses. Time is telescoped, and representations of past events in real or distorted forms may have the present as their referent—or vice versa. The patterns of dream are timeless.

In a theater, the audience is informed by the curtain and the framing of the stage that the action on the stage is "only" a play. From within that frame the producers and actors may attempt to involve the audience in an illusion of reality as seemingly direct as the experience of dream. And,

[4] O. Fenichel, *Psychoanalytic Theory of Neurosis*, New York, Norton, 1945.

as in dream, the play has metaphoric reference to the outside world. But in dream, unless the sleeper be partly conscious of the fact of sleep, there is no curtain and no framing of the action. The partial negative—"This is *only* metaphor"—is absent.

I suggest that this absence of metacommunicative frames and the persistence in dream of pattern recognition are archaic characteristics in an evolutionary sense. If this be correct, then an understanding of dream should throw light both on how iconic communication operates among animals and on the mysterious evolutionary step from the iconic to the verbal.

Under the limitation imposed by the lack of a metacommunicative frame, it is clearly impossible for dream to make an indicative statement, either positive or negative. As there can be no frame which labels the content as "metaphoric," so there can be no frame to label the content as "literal." Dream can imagine rain or drought, but it can never assert "It is raining" or "It is not raining." Therefore, as we have seen, the usefulness in imagining "rain" or "drought" is limited to their metaphoric aspects.

Dream can *propose* the applicability of pattern. It can never assert or deny this applicability. Still less can it make an indicative statement about any identified referent, since no referent is identified.

The pattern is the thing.

These characteristics of dream may be archaic, but it is important to remember that they are not obsolete: that, as kinesic and paralinguistic communication has been elaborated into dance, music, and poetry, so also the logic of dream has been elaborated into theater and art. Still more astonishing is that world of rigorous fantasy which we call mathematics, a world forever isolated by its axioms and definitions from the possibility of making an indicative statement about the "real" world. Only *if* a straight line is the shortest distance between two points is the theorem of Pythagoras asserted.

The banker manipulates numerals according to rules supplied by the mathematician. These numerals are the names of numbers, and the numbers are somehow embodied in (real or fictitious) dollars. To remember what he is doing, the banker marks his numerals with labels, such as the dollar sign, but these are nonmathematical and no computer needs them. In the strictly mathematical procedure, as in the process of dream, the pattern of relationships controls all operations, but the relata are unidentified.

We return now to the contrast between the iconic method of creating redundancy in the universe, organism *plus* other organism, by the emission of parts of interactive patterns and the linguistic device of naming the relata. We noted above that the human communication which creates redundancy in the relationships between persons is still preponderantly iconic and is achieved by means of kinesics, paralinguistics, intention movements, actions, and the like. It is in dealing with the universe, message *plus* environment, that the evolution of verbal language has made the greatest strides.

In animal discourse, redundancy is introduced into this universe by signals which are iconic parts of the signaler's probable response. The environmental items may serve an ostensive function but cannot, in general, be mentioned. Similarly, in iconic communication about relationship, the relata—the organisms themselves—do not have to be identified because the subject of any predicate in this iconic discourse is the emitter of the signal, who is always ostensively present.

It appears then that at least two steps were necessary to get from the iconic use of parts of patterns of own behavior to the naming of entities in the external environment: there was both a change in coding and a change in the centering of the subject-predicate frame.

To attempt to reconstruct these steps can only be speculative, but some remarks may be offered:

(1) Imitation of environmental phenomena makes it possible to shift the subject-predicate frame from the self to some environmental entity while still retaining the iconic code.

(2) A similar shifting of the subject-predicate frame from self to other is latent in those interactions between animals in which A proposes a pattern of interaction and B negates this with an iconic or ostensive "don't." The subject of B's message here verbalized as "don't" is A.

(3) It is possible that the paradigms of interaction which are basic to iconic signaling about relationship could serve

as evolutionary models for the paradigms of verbal grammar. We should not, I suggest, think of the earliest rudiments of verbal communication as resembling what a man does with only a few words of a foreign language and no knowledge of its grammar and syntax. Surely, at all stages of the evolution of language, the communication of our ancestors was structured and formed—complete in itself, not made of broken pieces. The antecedents of grammar must surely be as old or older than the antecedents of words.

(4) For actions of the self, iconic abbreviations are readily available, and these control the vis-à-vis by implicit reference to interactional paradigms. But all such communication is necessarily positive. To show the fangs is to mention combat, and to mention combat is to propose it. There can be no simple iconic representation of a negative: no simple way for an animal to say "I will not bite you." It is easy, however, to imagine ways of communicating negative commands if (and *only* if) the other organism will first propose the pattern of action which is to be forbidden. By threat, by inappropriate response and so on, "don't" can be communicated. A pattern of interaction, offered by one organism, is negated by the other, who disrupts the proposed paradigm.

But "don't" is very different from "not." Commonly, the important message "I will not bite you" is generated as an *agreement* between two organisms following real or ritual combat. That is, the opposite of the final message is worked through to reach a *reductio ad absurdum* which can then be the basis of mutual peace, hierarchic precedence, or sexual relations. Many of the curious interactions of animals, called "play," which resemble (but are not) combat are probably the testing and reaffirmation of such negative agreement.

But these are cumbersome and awkward methods of achieving the negative.

(5) It was suggested above that the paradigms of verbal grammar might somehow be derived from the paradigms of interaction. We, therefore, look for the evolutionary roots of the simple negative among the paradigms of interaction. The matter, however, is not simple. What is known to occur at the animal level is the simultaneous presentation of contradictory signals—postures which mention both aggression and flight, and the like. These ambiguities are, however, quite different from the phenomenon familiar among humans

where the friendliness of a man's words may be contradicted by the tension or aggressiveness of his voice or posture. The man is engaging in a sort of deceit, an altogether more complex achievement, while the ambivalent animal is offering positive alternatives. From neither of these patterns is it easy to derive a simple "not."

(6) From these considerations it appears likely that the evolution of the simple negative arose by introjection or imitation of the vis-à-vis, so that "not" was somehow derived from "don't."

(7) This still leaves unexplained the shift from communication about interaction patterns to communication about things and other components of the external world. This is the shift which determines that language would never make obsolete the iconic communication about the contingency patterns of personal relationship.

Further than that we cannot at present go. It is even possible that the evolution of verbal naming preceded the evolution of the simple negative. It is, however, important to note that evolution of a simple negative would be a decisive step toward language as we know it. This step would immediately endow the signals—be they verbal or iconic—with a degree of separateness from their referents, which would justify us in referring to the signals as "names." The same step would make possible the use of negative aspects of classification: those items which are not members of an identified class would become identifiable as nonmembers. And, lastly, simple affirmative indicative statements would become possible.

# Conscious Purpose Versus Nature*

Our civilization, which is on the block here for investigation and evaluation, has its roots in three main ancient civilizations: the Roman, the Hebrew and the Greek; and it would seem that many of our problems are related to the fact that we have an imperialist civilization leavened or yeasted by a downtrodden, exploited colony in Palestine. In this conference, we are again going to be fighting out the conflict between the Romans and the Palestinians.

You will remember that St. Paul boasted, "I was born free." What he meant was that he was born Roman, and that this had certain legal advantages.

We can engage in that old battle either by backing the downtrodden or by backing the imperialists. If you are going to fight that battle, you have to take sides in it. It's that simple.

On the other hand, of course, St. Paul's ambition, and the ambition of the downtrodden, is always to get on the side of the imperialists—to become middle-class imperialists themselves—and it is doubtful whether creating more members of the civilization which we are here criticizing is a solution to the problem.

There is, therefore, another more abstract problem. We

*This lecture was given in August, 1968, to the London Conference on the Dialectics of Liberation, and is here reprinted from *Dialectics of Liberation* by permission of the publisher, Penguin Books Inc.

426

need to understand the pathologies and peculiarities of the whole Romano-Palestinian system. It is this that I am interested in talking about. I do not care, here, about defending the Romans or defending the Palestinians—the upper dogs or the underdogs. I want to consider the dynamics of the whole traditional pathology in which we are caught, and in which we shall remain as long as we continue to struggle within that old conflict. We just go round and round in terms of the old premises.

Fortunately our civilization has a third root—in Greece. Of course Greece got caught up in a rather similar mess, but still there was a lot of clean, cool thinking of a quite surprising kind which was different.

Let me approach the bigger problem historically. From St. Thomas Aquinas to the eighteenth century in Catholic countries, and to the Reformation among Protestants (because we threw out a lot of Greek sophistication with the Reformation), the structure of our religion was Greek. In mid-eighteenth century the biological world looked like this: there was a supreme mind at the top of the ladder, which was the basic explanation of everything downwards from that—the supreme mind being, in Christianity, God; and having various attributes at various philosophic stages. The ladder of explanation went downwards deductively from the Supreme to man to the apes, and so on, down to the infusoria.

This hierarchy was a set of deductive steps from the most perfect to the most crude or simple. And it was rigid. It was assumed that every species was unchanging.

Lamarck, probably the greatest biologist in history, turned that ladder of explanation upside down. He was the man who said it starts with the infusoria and that there were changes leading up to man. His turning the taxonomy upside down is one of the most astonishing feats that has ever occurred. It was the equivalent in biology of the Copernican revolution in astronomy.

The logical outcome of turning the taxonomy upside down was that the study of evolution might provide an explanation of *mind*.

Up to Lamarck, mind was the explanation of the biological world. But, hey presto, the question now arose: Is the biological world the explanation of mind? That which was the explanation now became that which was to be explained. About three quarters of Lamarck's *Philosophie Zoologique* (1809) is an attempt, very crude, to build a comparative psychology. He achieved and formulated a number of very modern ideas: that you cannot attribute to any creature psychological capacities for which it has no organs; that mental process must always have physical representation; and that the complexity of the nervous system is related to the complexity of mind.

There the matter rested for 150 years, mainly because evolutionary theory was taken over, not by a Catholic heresy but by a Protestant heresy, in the mid-nineteenth century. Darwin's opponents, you may remember, were not Aristotle and Aquinas, who had some sophistication, but fundamentalist Christians whose sophistication stopped with the first chapter of Genesis. The question of the nature of mind was something which the nineteenth-century evolutionists tried to exclude from their theories, and the matter did not come up again for serious consideration until after World War II. (I am doing some injustice to some heretics along the road, notably to Samuel Butler—and others.)

In World War II it was discovered what sort of complexity entails mind. And, since that discovery, we know that: wherever in the Universe we encounter that sort of complexity, we are dealing with mental phenomena. It's as materialistic as that.

Let me try to describe for you that order of complexity, which is in some degree a technical matter. Russel Wallace sent a famous essay to Darwin from Indonesia. In it he announced his discovery of natural selection, which coincided with Darwin's. Part of his description of the struggle for existence is interesting:

> The action of this principle [the struggle for existence] is exactly like that of the steam engine, which checks and corrects any irregularities almost before they become evident; and in like manner no unbalanced deficiency in the animal kingdom can ever reach any conspicuous magnitude, because it would make itself felt at the very first step, by rendering existence difficult and extinction almost sure to follow.

The steam engine with a governor is simply a circular train of causal events, with somewhere a link in that chain such that the more of something, the less of the next thing in the circuit. The *wider* the balls of the governor diverge, the *less* the fuel supply. If causal chains with that general characteristic are provided with energy, the result will be (if you are lucky and things balance out) a self-corrective system.

Wallace, in fact, proposed the first cybernetic model.

Nowadays cybernetics deals with much more complex systems of this general kind; and we know that when we talk about the processes of civilization, or evaluate human behavior, human organization, or any biological system, we are concerned with self-corrective systems. Basically these systems are always *conservative* of something. As in the engine with a governor, the fuel supply is changed to conserve—to keep constant—the speed of the flywheel, so always in such systems changes occur to conserve the truth of some descriptive statement, some component of the *status quo*. Wallace saw the matter correctly, and natural selection acts primarily to keep the species unvarying; but it may act at higher levels to keep constant that complex variable which we call "survival."

Dr. Laing noted that the obvious can be very difficult for people to see. That is because people are self-corrective systems. They are self-corrective against disturbance, and if the obvious is not of a kind that they can easily assimilate without internal disturbance, their self-corrective mechanisms work to sidetrack it, to hide it, even to the extent of shutting the eyes if necessary, or shutting off various parts of the process of perception. Disturbing information can be framed like a pearl so that it doesn't make a nuisance of itself; and this will be done, according to the understanding of the system itself of what would be a nuisance. This too—the premise regarding what would cause disturbance—is something which is learned and then becomes perpetuated or conserved.

At this conference, fundamentally, we deal with three of these enormously complex systems or arrangements of conservative loops. One is the human individual. Its physiology and neurology conserve body temperature, blood chemistry, the length and size and shape of organs during growth and embryology, and all the rest of the body's characteristics. This is a system which conserves descriptive statements about the human being, body or soul. For the same is true of the psychology of the individual, where learning occurs to conserve the opinions and components of the *status quo*.

Second, we deal with the society in which that individual lives—and that society is again a system of the same general kind.

And third, we deal with the ecosystem, the natural biological surroundings of these human animals.

Let me start from the natural ecosystems around man. An English oak wood, or a tropical forest, or a piece of desert, is a community of creatures. In the oak wood perhaps 1000 species, perhaps more; in the tropical forest perhaps ten times that number of species live together.

I may say that very few of you here have ever seen such an undisturbed system; there are not many of them left; they've mostly been messed up by *Homo sapiens* who either exterminated some species or introduced others which became weeds and pests, or altered the water supply, etc., etc. We are rapidly, of course, destroying all the natural systems in the world, the balanced natural systems. We simply make them unbalanced—but still natural.

Be that as it may, those creatures and plants live together in a combination of competition and mutual dependency, and it is that combination that is the important thing to consider. Every species has a primary Malthusian capacity. Any species that does not, potentially, produce more young than the number of the population of the parental generation is out. They're doomed. It is absolutely necessary for every species and for every such system that its components have a potential positive gain in the population curve. But, if every species has potential gain, it is then quite a trick to achieve equilibrium. All sorts of interactive balances and dependencies come into play, and it is these processes that have the sort of circuit structure that I have mentioned.

The Malthusian curve is exponential. It is the curve of population growth and it is not inappropriate to call this the population *explosion*.

You may regret that organisms have this explosive characteristic, but you may as well settle for it. The creatures that don't are out.

On the other hand, in a balanced ecological system whose underpinnings are of this nature, it is very clear that any monkeying with the system is likely to disrupt the equilibrium. Then the exponential curves will start to appear. Some plant will become a weed, some creatures will be exterminated, and the system as a *balanced* system is likely to fall to pieces.

What is true of the species that live together in a wood is also true of the groupings and sorts of people in a society, who are similarly in an uneasy balance of dependency and competition. And the same truth holds right inside you, where there is an uneasy physiological competition and mutual dependency among the organs, tissues, cells, and so on. Without this competition and dependency you would not be, because you cannot do without any of the competing organs and parts. If any of the parts did not have the expansive characteristics they would go out, and you would go out, too. So that even in the body you have a liability. With improper disturbance of the system, the exponential curves appear.

In a society, the same is true.

I think you have to assume that all important physiological or social change is in some degree a slipping of the system at some point along an exponential curve. The slippage may not go far, or it may go to disaster. But in principle if, say, you kill off the thrushes in a wood, certain components of the balance will run along exponential curves to a new stopping place.

In such slippage there is always danger—the possibility that some variable, *e.g.*, population density, may reach such a value that further slippage is controlled by factors which are inherently harmful. If, for example, population is finally controlled by available food supply, the surviving individuals will be half starved and the food supply overgrazed, usually to a point of no return.

Now let me begin to talk about the individual organism. This entity is similar to the oak wood and its controls are represented in the *total* mind, which is perhaps only a reflection of the total body. But the system is segmented in various ways, so that the effects of something in your food life, shall we say, do not totally alter your sex life, and things in your sex life do not totally change your kinesic life, and so on. There is a certain amount of compartmentalization, which is no doubt a necessary economy. There is one compartmentalization which is in many ways mysterious but certainly of crucial importance in man's life. I refer to the "semipermeable" linkage between consciousness and the remainder of the total mind. A certain limited amount of information about what's happening in this larger part of the mind seems to be relayed to what we may call the screen of consciousness. But what gets to consciousness is selected; it is a systematic (not random) sampling of the rest.

Of course, the *whole* of the mind could not be reported in a *part* of the mind. This follows logically from the relationship between part and whole. The television screen does not give you total coverage or report of the events which occur in the whole television process; and this not merely because the viewers would not be interested in such a report, but because to report on any extra part of the total process would require extra circuitry. But to report on the events in this extra circuitry would require a still further addition of more circuitry, and so on. Each additional step toward increased consciousness will take the system farther from total consciousness. To add a report on events in a given part of the machine will actually *decrease* the percentage of total events reported.

We therefore have to settle for very limited consciousness, and the question arises: How is the selecting done? On what principles does your mind select that which "you" will be aware of? And, while not much is known of these principles, something is known, though the principles at work are often not themselves accessible to consciousness. First of all, much of the input is consciously scanned, but only *after* it has been processed by the totally unconscious process of perception. The sensory events are packaged into images and these images are then "conscious."

I, the conscious I, see an unconsciously edited version of a small percentage of what affects my retina. I am guided in my perception by *purposes*. I see who is attending, who is not, who is understanding, who is not, or at least I get a myth about this subject, which may be quite correct. I am interested in getting that myth as I talk. It is relevant to my purposes that you hear me.

What happens to the picture of a cybernetic system—an

oak wood or an organism—when that picture is selectively drawn to answer only questions of purpose?

Consider the state of medicine today. It's called medical science. What happens is that doctors think it would be nice to get rid of polio, or typhoid, or cancer. So they devote research money and effort to focusing on these "problems," or purposes. At a certain point Dr. Salk and others "solve" the problem of polio. They discover a solution of bugs which you can give to children so that they don't get polio. This is the solution to the problem of polio. At this point, they stop putting large quantities of effort and money into the problem of polio and go on to the problem of cancer, or whatever it may be.

Medicine ends up, therefore, as a total science, whose structure is essentially that of a bag of tricks. Within this science there is extraordinarily little knowledge of the sort of things I'm talking about; that is, of the body as a systemically cybernetically organized self-corrective system. Its internal interdependencies are minimally understood. What has happened is that *purpose* has determined what will come under the inspection or consciousness of medical science.

If you allow purpose to organize that which comes under your conscious inspection, what you will get is a bag of tricks—some of them very valuable tricks. It is an extraordinary achievement that these tricks have been discovered; all that I don't argue. But still we do not know two-penn'orth, really, about the total network system. Cannon wrote a book on *The Wisdom of the Body*, but nobody has written a book on the wisdom of medical science, because wisdom is precisely the thing which it lacks. Wisdom I take to be the knowledge of the larger interactive system—that system which, if disturbed, is likely to generate exponential curves of change.

Consciousness operates in the same way as medicine in its sampling of the events and processes of the body and of what goes on in the total mind. It is organized in terms of purpose. It is a short-cut device to enable you to get quickly at what you want; not to act with maximum wisdom in order to live, but to follow the shortest logical or causal path to get what you next want, which may be dinner; it may be a Beethoven sonata; it may be sex. Above all, it may be money or power.

But you may say: "Yes, but we have lived that way for a million years." Consciousness and purpose have been characteristic of man for at least a million years, and may have been with us a great deal longer than that. I am not prepared to say that dogs and cats are not conscious, still less that porpoises are not conscious.

So you may say: "Why worry about that?"

But what worries me is the addition of modern technology to the old system. Today the purposes of consciousness are implemented by more and more effective machinery, transportation systems, airplanes, weaponry, medicine, pesticides, and so forth. Conscious purpose is now empowered to upset the balances of the body, of society, and of the biological world around us. A pathology—a loss of balance—is threatened.

I think that much of what brings us here today is basically related to the thoughts that I have been putting before you. On the one hand, we have the systemic nature of the individual human being, the systemic nature of the culture in which he lives, and the systemic nature of the biological, ecological system around him; and, on the other hand, the curious twist in the systemic nature of the individual man whereby consciousness is, almost of necessity, blinded to the systemic nature of the man himself. Purposive consciousness pulls out, from the total mind, sequences which do not have the loop structure which is characteristic of the whole systemic structure. If you follow the "common-sense" dictates of consciousness you become, effectively, greedy and unwise—again I use "wisdom" as a word for recognition of and guidance by a knowledge of the total systemic creature.

Lack of systemic wisdom is always punished. We may say that the biological systems—the individual, the culture, and the ecology—are partly living sustainers of their component cells or organisms. But the systems are nonetheless punishing of any species unwise enough to quarrel with its ecology. Call the systemic forces "God" if you will.

Let me offer you a myth.

There was once a Garden. It contained many hundreds of species—probably in the subtropics—living in great fertility and balance, with plenty of humus, and so on. In that garden, there were two anthropoids who were more intelligent than the other animals.

On one of the trees there was a fruit, very high up, which the two apes were unable to reach. So they began to *think*. That was the mistake. They began to think purposively.

By and by, the he ape, whose name was Adam, went and got an empty box and put it under the tree and stepped on it, but he found he still couldn't reach the fruit. So he got another box and put it on top of the first. Then he climbed up on the two boxes and finally he got that apple.

Adam and Eve then became almost drunk with excitement. *This* was the way to do things. Make a plan, ABC and you get D.

They then began to specialize in doing things the planned way. In effect, they cast out from the Garden the concept of their own total systemic nature and of its total systemic nature.

After they had cast God out of the Garden, they really went to work on this purposive business, and pretty soon the topsoil disappeared. After that, several species of plants became "weeds" and some of the animals became "pests"; and Adam found that gardening was much harder work. He had to get his bread by the sweat of his brow and he said, "It's a vengeful God. I should never have eaten that apple."

Moreover, there occurred a qualitative change in the relationship between Adam and Eve, after they had discarded God from the Garden. Eve began to resent the business of sex and reproduction. Whenever these rather basic phenomena intruded upon her now purposive way of living, she was reminded of the larger life which had been kicked out of the Garden. So Eve began to resent sex and reproduction, and when it came to parturition she found this process very painful. She said this, too, was due to the vengeful nature of God. She even heard a Voice say "In pain shalt thou bring forth" and "Thy desire shall be unto thy husband, and he shall rule over thee."

The biblical version of this story, from which I have borrowed extensively, does not explain the extraordinary perversion of values, whereby the woman's capacity for love comes to seem a curse inflicted by the deity.

Be that as it may. Adam went on pursuing his purposes and finally invented the free-enterprise system. Eve was not, for a long time, allowed to participate in this because she was a woman. But she joined a bridge club and there found an outlet for her hate.

In the next generation, they again had trouble with love. Cain, the inventor and innovator, was told by God that "His [Abel's] desire shall be unto thee and thou shalt rule over him." So he killed Abel.

A parable, of course, is not data about human behavior. It is only an explanatory device. But I have built into it a phenomenon which seems to be almost universal when man commits the error of purposive thinking and disregards the systemic nature of the world with which he must deal. This phenomenon is called by the psychologists "projection." The man, after all, has acted according to what he thought was common sense and now he finds himself in a mess. He does not quite know what caused the mess and he feels that what has happened is somehow unfair. He still does not see himself as part of the system in which the mess exists, and he either blames the rest of the system or he blames himself. In my parable Adam combines two sorts of nonsense: the notion "I have sinned" and the notion "God is vengeful."

If you look at the real situations in our world where the systemic nature of the world has been ignored in favor of purpose or common sense, you will find a rather similar reaction. President Johnson is, no doubt, fully aware that he has a mess on his hands, not only in Vietnam but in other parts of the national and international ecosystems; and I am sure that from where he sits it appears that he followed his purposes with common sense and that the mess must be due either to the wickedness of others or to his own sin or to some combination of these, according to his temperament.

And the terrible thing about such situations is that inevitably they shorten the time span of all planning. Emergency is present or only just around the corner; and long-term wisdom must therefore be sacrificed to expediency, even though there is a dim awareness that expediency will never give a long-term solution.

Morever, since we are engaged in diagnosing the machinery of our own society, let me add one point: our politicians—both those in a state of power and those in a state of protest or hunger for power—are alike utterly ignorant of the matters which I have been discussing. You can search the Congressional Record for speeches which show awareness that the problems of government are biological problems, and you will find very, very few that apply biological insight. Extraordinary!

In general, governmental decisions are made by persons who are as ignorant of these matters as pigeons. Like the famous Dr. Skinner, in *The Way of All Flesh*, they "combine the wisdom of the dove with the harmlessness of the serpent."

But we are met here not only for diagnosis of some of the world's ills but also to think about remedies. I have already suggested that no simple remedy to what I called the Romano-Palestinian problem can be achieved by backing the Romans against the Palestinians or vice versa. The problem is systemic and the solution must surely depend upon realizing this fact.

First, there is humility, and I propose this not as a moral principle, distasteful to a large number of people, but simply as an item of a scientific philosophy. In the period of the Industrial Revolution, perhaps the most important disaster was the enormous increase of scientific arrogance. We had discovered how to make trains and other machines. We knew how to put one box on top of the other to get that apple, and Occidental man saw himself as an autocrat with complete power over a universe which was made of physics and chemistry. And the biological phenomena were in the end to be controlled like processes in a test tube. Evolution was the history of how organisms learned more tricks for controlling the environment; and man had better tricks than any other creature.

But that arrogant scientific philosophy is now obsolete, and in its place there is the discovery that man is only a part of larger systems and that the part can never control the whole.

Goebbels thought that he could control public opinion in Germany with a vast communication system, and our own public relations men are perhaps liable to similar delusions. But in fact the would-be controller must always have his spies out to tell him what the people are saying about his propaganda. He is therefore in the position of being *responsive* to what they are saying. Therefore he cannot have a simple lineal control. We do not live in the sort of universe in which simple lineal control is possible. Life is not like that.

Similarly, in the field of psychiatry, the family is a cybernetic system of the sort which I am discussing and usually when systemic pathology occurs, the members blame each other, or sometimes themselves. But the truth of the matter is that both these alternatives are fundamentally arrogant. Either alternative assumes that the individual human being has total power over the system of which he or she is a part.

Even within the individual human being, control is limited. We can in some degree set ourselves to learn even such abstract characteristics as arrogance or humility, but we are not by any means the captains of our souls.

It is, however, possible that the remedy for ills of conscious purpose lies with the individual. There is what Freud called the royal road to the unconscious. He was referring to dreams, but I think we should lump together dreams and the creativity of art, or the perception of art, and poetry and such things. And I would include with these the best of religion. These are all activities in which the whole individual is involved. The artist may have a conscious purpose to sell his picture, even perhaps a conscious purpose to make it. But in the making he must necessarily relax that arrogance in favor of a creative experience in which his conscious mind plays only a small part.

We might say that in creative art man must experience himself—his total self—as a cybernetic model.

It is characteristic of the 1960s that a large number of people are looking to the psychedelic drugs for some sort of wisdom or some sort of enlargement of consciousness, and I think this symptom of our epoch probably arises as an attempt to compensate for our excessive purposiveness. But I am not sure that wisdom can be got that way. What is required is not simply a relaxation of consciousness to let the unconscious material gush out. To do this is merely to exchange one partial view of the self for the other partial view. I suspect that what is needed is the synthesis of the two views and this is more difficult.

My own slight experience of LSD led me to believe that Prospero was wrong when he said, "We are such stuff as dreams are made on." It seemed to me that pure dream was, like pure purpose, rather trivial. It was not the stuff of which we are made, but only bits and pieces of that stuff. Our conscious purposes, similarly, are only bits and pieces.

The systemic view is something else again.

# Effects of Conscious Purpose on Human Adaptation*

"Progress," "learning," "evolution," the similarities and differences between phylogenetic and cultural evolution, and so on, have been subjects for discussion for many years. These matters become newly investigable in the light of cybernetics and systems theory.

In this Wenner-Gren conference, a particular aspect of this wide subject matter will be examined, namely the role of *consciousness* in the ongoing process of human adaptation.

Three cybernetic or homeostatic systems will be considered: the individual human organism, the human society, and the larger ecosystem. Consciousness will be considered as an important component in the *coupling* of these systems.

A question of great scientific interest and perhaps grave importance is whether the information processed through consciousness is adequate and appropriate for the task of human adaptation. It may well be that consciousness contains systematic distortions of view which, when implemented by modern technology, become destructive of the balances between man, his society and his ecosystem.

*This essay was prepared as the author's position paper for Wenner-Gren Foundation Conference on "Effects of Conscious Purpose on Human Adaptation." The author was chairman of this conference, which was held in Burg Wartenstein, Austria, July 17–24, 1968. The proceedings of the conference as a whole are to be published by Knopf & Co. under the title *Our Own Metaphor*, edited by Mary Catherine Bateson.

To introduce this question the following considerations are offered:

(1) All biological and evolving systems (*i.e.*, individual organisms, animal and human societies, ecosystems, and the like) consist of complex cybernetic networks, and all such systems share certain formal characteristics. Each system contains subsystems which are potentially regenerative, *i.e.*, which would go into exponential "runaway" if uncorrected. (Examples of such regenerative components are Malthusian characteristics of population, schismogenic changes of personal interaction, armaments races, etc.) The regenerative potentialities of such subsystems are typically kept in check by various sorts of governing loops to achieve "steady state." Such systems are "conservative" in the sense that they tend to conserve the truth of propositions about the values of their component variables—especially they conserve the values of those variables which otherwise would show exponential change. Such systems are homeostatic, *i.e.*, the effects of small changes of input will be negated and the steady state maintained by *reversible* adjustment.

(2) But *"plus c'est la même chose, plus ça change."* This converse of the French aphorism seems to be the more exact description of biological and ecological systems. A constancy of some variable is maintained by changing other variables. This is characteristic of the engine with a governor: the constancy of rate of rotation is maintained by altering the fuel supply. *Mutatis mutandis,* the same logic underlies evolutionary progress: those mutational changes will be perpetuated which contribute to the constancy of that complex variable which we call "survival." The same logic also applies to learning, social change, etc. The ongoing truth of certain descriptive propositions is maintained by altering other propositions.

(3) In systems containing many interconnected homeostatic loops, the changes brought about by an external impact may slowly spread through the system. To maintain a given variable ($V_1$) at a given value, the values of $V_2$, $V_3$, etc., undergo change. But $V_2$ and $V_3$ may themselves be subject to homeostatic control or may be linked to variables ($V_4$, $V_5$, etc.) which are subject to control. This second-order homeostasis may lead to change in $V_6$, $V_7$, etc. And so on.

(4) This phenomenon of spreading change is in the widest

sense a sort of *learning*. Acclimation and addiction are special cases of this process. Over time, the system becomes dependent upon the continued presence of that original external impact whose immediate effects were neutralized by the first order homeostasis.

Example: under the impact of Prohibition, the American social system reacted homeostatically to maintain the constancy of the supply of alcohol. A new profession, the bootlegger, was generated. To control this profession, changes occurred in the police system. When the question of repeal was raised, it was expectable that certainly the bootleggers and possibly the police would be in favor of maintaining Prohibition.

(5) In this ultimate sense, all biological change is conservative and all learning is aversive. The rat, who is "rewarded" with food, accepts that reward to neutralize the changes which hunger is beginning to induce; and the conventionally drawn distinction between "reward" and "punishment" depends upon a more or less arbitrary line which we draw to delimit that subsystem which we call the "individual." We call an external event "reward" if its occurrence corrects an "internal" change which would be punishing. And so on.

(6) Consciousness and the "self" are closely related ideas, but the ideas (possibly related to genotypically determined premises of territory) are crystallized by that more or less arbitrary line which delimits the individual and defines a logical difference between "reward" and "punishment." When we view the individual as a servosystem coupled with its environment, or as a part of the larger system which is individual + environment, the whole appearance of adaptation and purpose changes.

(7) In extreme cases, change will precipitate or permit some runaway or slippage along the potentially exponential curves of the underlying regenerative circuits. This may occur without total destruction of the system. The slippage along exponential curves will, of course, always be limited, in extreme cases, by breakdown of the system. Short of this disaster, other factors may limit the slippage. It is important, however, to note that there is a danger of reaching levels at which the limit is imposed by factors which are in themselves deleterious. Wynne-Edwards has pointed out—what

every farmer knows—that a population of healthy individuals cannot be directly limited by the available food supply. If starvation is the method of getting rid of the excess population, then the survivors will suffer if not death at least severe dietary deficiency, while the food supply itself will be reduced, perhaps irreversibly, by overgrazing. In principle, the homeostatic controls of biological systems must be activated by variables which are not in themselves harmful. The reflexes of respiration are activated not by oxygen deficiency but by relatively harmless $CO_2$ excess. The diver who learns to ignore the signals of $CO_2$ excess and continues his dive to approach oxygen deficiency runs serious risks.

(8) The problem of coupling self-corrective systems together is central in the adaptation of man to the societies and ecosystems in which he lives. Lewis Carroll long ago joked about the nature and order of *randomness* created by the inappropriate coupling of biological systems. The problem, we may say, was to create a "game" which should be random, not only in the restricted sense in which "matching pennies" is random, but meta-random. The randomness of the moves of the two players of "matching pennies" is restricted to a finite set of known alternatives, namely "heads" or "tails" in any given play of the game. There is no possibility of going outside this set, no meta-random choice among a finite or infinite set of sets.

By imperfect coupling of biological systems in the famous game of croquet, however, Carroll creates a meta-random game. Alice is coupled with a flamingo, and the "ball" is a hedgehog.

The "purposes" (if we may use the term) of these contrasting biological systems are so discrepant that the randomness of play can no longer be delimited with finite sets of alternatives, known to the players.

Alice's difficulty arises from the fact that she does not "understand" the flamingo, *i.e.*, she does not have systemic information about the "system" which confronts her. Similarly, the flamingo does not understand Alice. They are at "cross-purposes." The problem of coupling man through consciousness with his biological environment is comparable. If consciousness lacks information about the nature of man and the environment, or if the information is distorted and inappropriately selected, then the coupling is likely to generate meta-random sequence of events.

(9) We presume that consciousness is not entirely without effect—that it is not a mere collateral resonance without feedback into the system, an observer behind a one-way mirror, a TV monitor which does not itself affect the program. We believe that consciousness has feedback into the remainder of mind and so an effect upon action. But the effects of this feedback are almost unknown and urgently need investigation and validation.

(10) It is surely true that the content of consciousness is no random sample of reports on events occurring in the remainder of mind. Rather, the content of the screen of consciousness is systematically selected from the enormously great plethora of mental events. But of the rules and preferences of this selection, very little is known. The matter requires investigation. Similarly the limitations of verbal language require consideration.

(11) It appears, however, that the system of selection of information for the screen of consciousness is importantly related to "purpose," "attention," and similar phenomena which are also in need of definition, elucidation, etc.

(12) If consciousness has feedback upon the remainder of mind (9, above), and if consciousness deals only with a skewed sample of the events of the total mind, then there must exist a *systematic* (*i.e.*, nonrandom) difference between the conscious views of self and the world, and the true nature of self and the world. Such a difference must distort the processes of adaptation.

(13) In this connection, there is a profound difference between the processes of cultural change and those of phylogenetic evolution. In the latter, the Weismannian barrier between soma and germ plasm is presumed to be totally opaque. There is no coupling from environment to genome. In cultural evolution and individual learning, the coupling through consciousness is present, incomplete and probably distortive.

(14) It is suggested that the specific nature of this distortion is such that *the cybernetic nature of self and the world tends to be imperceptible to consciousness*, insofar as the contents of the "screen" of consciousness are determined by considerations of purpose. The argument of purpose tends

to take the form "*D* is desirable; *B* leads to *C*; *C* leads to *D*; so *D* can be achieved by way of *B* and *C*." But, if the total mind and the outer world do not, in general, have this lineal structure, then by forcing this structure upon them, we become blind to the cybernetic circularities of the self and the external world. Our conscious sampling of data will not disclose whole circuits but only arcs of circuits, cut off from their matrix by our selective attention. Specifically, the attempt to achieve a change in a given variable, located either in self or environment, is likely to be undertaken without comprehension of the homeostatic network surrounding that variable. The considerations outlined in paragraphs 1 to 7 of this essay will then be ignored. It may be essential for *wisdom* that the narrow purposive view be somehow corrected.

(15) The function of consciousness in the coupling between man and the homeostatic systems around him is, of course, no new phenomenon. Three circumstances, however, make the investigation of this phenomenon an urgent matter.

(16) First, there is man's habit of changing his environment rather than changing himself. Faced with a changing variable (*e.g.*, temperature) within itself which it should control, the organism may make changes *either* within itself *or* in the external environment. It may adapt to the environment or adapt the environment to itself. In evolutionary history, the great majority of steps have been changes within the organism itself; some steps have been of an intermediate kind in which the organisms achieved change of environment by change of locale. In a few cases organisms other than man have achieved the creation of modified microenvironments around themselves, *e.g.*, the nests of hymenoptera and birds, concentrated forests of conifers, fungal colonies, etc.

In all such cases, the logic of evolutionary progress is toward ecosystems which sustain *only* the dominant, environment-controlling species, and its symbionts and parasites.

Man, the outstanding modifier of environment, similarly achieves single-species ecosystems in his cities, but he goes one step further, establishing special environments for his symbionts. These, likewise, become single-species ecosystems: fields of corn, cultures of bacteria, batteries of fowls, colonies of laboratory rats, and the like.

(17) Secondly, the power ratio between purposive con-

sciousness and the environment has changed rapidly in the last one hundred years, and the *rate* of change in this ratio is certainly rapidly increasing with technological advance. Conscious man, as a changer of his environment, is now fully able to wreck himself and that environment—with the very best of conscious intentions.

(18) Third, a peculiar sociological phenomenon has arisen in the last one hundred years which perhaps threatens to isolate conscious purpose from many corrective processes which might come out of less conscious parts of the mind. The social scene is nowadays characterized by the existence of a large number of self-maximizing entities which, in law, have something like the status of "persons"—trusts, companies, political parties, unions, commercial and financial agencies, nations, and the like. In biological fact, these entities are precisely *not* persons and are not even aggregates of whole persons. They are aggregates of *parts* of persons. When Mr. Smith enters the board room of his company, he is expected to limit his thinking narrowly to the specific purposes of the company or to those of that part of the company which he "represents." Mercifully it is not entirely possible for him to do this and some company decisions are influenced by considerations which spring from wider and wiser parts of the mind. But ideally, Mr. Smith is expected to act as a pure, uncorrected consciousness—a dehumanized creature.

(19) Finally, it is appropriate to mention some of the factors which may act as correctives—areas of human action which are not limited by the narrow distortions of coupling through conscious purpose and where wisdom can obtain.

(*a*) Of these, undoubtedly the most important is love. Martin Buber has classified interpersonal relationships in a relevant manner. He differentiates "I-Thou" relations from "I-It" relations, defining the latter as the normal pattern of interaction between man and inanimate objects. The "I-It" relationship he also regards as characteristic of human relations wherever purpose is more important than love. But if the complex cybernetic structure of societies and ecosystems is in some degree analogous to animation, then it would follow that an "I-Thou" relationship is conceivable between man and his society or ecosystem. In this connection, the formation of "sensitivity groups" in many depersonalized organizations is of special interest.

(b) The arts, poetry, music, and the humanities similarly are areas in which more of the mind is active than mere consciousness would admit. *"Le coeur a ses raisons que la raison ne connaît point."*

(c) Contact between man and animals and between man and the natural world breeds, perhaps—sometimes—wisdom.

(d) There is religion.

(20) To conclude, let us remember that Job's narrow piety, his purposiveness, his common sense, and his worldly success are finally stigmatized, in a marvelous totemic poem, by the Voice out of the Whirlwind:

> *Who is this that darkeneth counsel by words*
> *without understanding . . .*
> *Dost thou know when the wild goats of the*
> *rock bring forth?*
> *Or canst thou tell when the hinds do calve?*

# Form, Substance, and Difference*

Let me say that it is an extraordinary honor to be here tonight, and a pleasure. I am a little frightened of you all, because I am sure there are people here who know every field of knowledge that I have touched much better than I know it. It is true that I have touched a number of fields, and I probably can face any one of you and say I have touched a field that you have not touched. But I am sure that for every field I have touched, there are people here who are much more expert than I. I am not a well-read philosopher, and philosophy is not my business. I am not a very well-read anthropologist, and anthropology is not exactly my business.

But I have tried to do something which Korzybski was very much concerned with doing, and with which the whole semantic movement has been concerned, namely, I have studied the area of impact between very abstract and formal philosophic thought on the one hand and the natural history of man and other creatures on the other. This overlap between formal premises and actual behavior is, I assert, of quite dreadful importance today. We face a world which is threatened not only with disorganization of many kinds, but also with the destruction of its environment, and we, today,

*This was the Nineteenth Annual Korzybski Memorial Lecture, delivered January 9, 1970, under the auspices of the Institute of General Semantics. It is here reprinted from the *General Semantics* Bulletin, No. 37, 1970, by permission of the Institute of General Semantics.

are still unable to think clearly about the relations between an organism and its environment. What sort of a thing is this, which we call "organism plus environment"?

Let us go back to the original statement for which Korzybski is most famous—the statement that *the map is not the territory*. This statement came out of a very wide range of philosophic thinking, going back to Greece, and wriggling through the history of European thought over the last 2000 years. In this history, there has been a sort of rough dichotomy and often deep controversy. There has been a violent enmity and bloodshed. It all starts, I suppose, with the Pythagoreans versus their predecessors, and the argument took the shape of "Do you ask what it's made of—earth, fire, water, etc?" Or do you ask, "What is its *pattern?*" Pythagoras stood for inquiry into pattern rather than inquiry into *substance*.[1] That controversy has gone through the ages, and the Pythagorean half of it has, until recently, been on the whole the submerged half. The Gnostics follow the Pythagoreans, and the alchemists follow the Gnostics, and so on. The argument reached a sort of climax at the end of the eighteenth century when a Pythagorean evolutionary theory was built and then discarded—a theory which involved Mind.

The evolutionary theory of the late eighteenth century, the Lamarckian theory, which was the first organized transformist theory of evolution, was built out of a curious historical background which has been described by Lovejoy in *The Great Chain of Being*. Before Lamarck, the organic world, the living world, was believed to be hierarchic in structure, with Mind at the top. The chain, or ladder, went down through the angels, through men, through the apes, down to the infusoria or protozoa, and below that to the plants and stones.

What Lamarck did was to turn that chain upside down. He observed that animals changed under environmental pressure. He was incorrect, of course, in believing that those changes were inherited, but in any case, these changes were for him the evidence of evolution. When he turned the lad-

[1] R. G. Collingwood has given a clear account of the Pythagorean position in *The Idea of Nature*, Oxford, 1945.

der upside down, what had been the explanation, namely, the Mind at the top, now became that which had to be explained. His problem was to explain Mind. He was convinced about evolution, and there his interest in it stopped. So that if you read the *Philosophie Zoologique* (1809), you will find that the first third of it is devoted to solving the problem of evolution and the turning upside down of the taxonomy, and the rest of the book is really devoted to comparative psychology, a science which he founded. *Mind* was what he was really interested in. He had used habit as one of the axiomatic phenomena in his theory of evolution, and this of course also took him into the problem of comparative psychology.

Now mind and pattern as the explanatory principles which, above all, required investigation were pushed out of biological thinking in the later evolutionary theories which were developed in the mid-nineteenth century by Darwin, Huxley, etc. There were still some naughty boys, like Samuel Butler, who said that mind could not be ignored in this way—but they were weak voices, and incidentally, they never looked at organisms. I don't think Butler ever looked at anything except his own cat, but he still knew more about evolution than some of the more conventional thinkers.

Now, at last, with the discovery of cybernetics, systems theory, information theory, and so on, we begin to have a formal base enabling us to think about mind and enabling us to think about all these problems in a way which was totally heterodox from about 1850 through to World War II. What I have to talk about is how the great dichotomy of epistemology has shifted under the impact of cybernetics and information theory.

We can now say—or at any rate, can begin to say—what we think a mind is. In the next twenty years there will be other ways of saying it and, because the discoveries are new, I can only give you my personal version. The old versions are surely wrong, but which of the revised pictures will survive, we do not know.

Let us start from the evolutionary side. It is now empirically clear that Darwinian evolutionary theory contained a very great error in its identification of the unit of survival under natural selection. The unit which was believed to be crucial and around which the theory was set up was either the breeding individual or the family line or the sub-species or some similar homogeneous set of conspecifics. Now I suggest that the last hundred years have demonstrated empirically that if an organism or aggregate of organisms sets to work with a focus on its own survival and thinks that that is the way to select its adaptive moves, its "progress" ends up with a destroyed environment. If the organism ends up destroying its environment, it has in fact destroyed itself. And we may very easily see this process carried to its ultimate *reductio ad absurdum* in the next twenty years. The unit of survival is not the breeding organism, or the family line, or the society.

The old unit has already been partly corrected by the population geneticists. They have insisted that the evolution-ary unit is, in fact, not homogeneous. A wild population of any species consists always of individuals whose genetic constitution varies widely. In other words, potentiality and readiness for change is already built into the survival unit. The heterogeneity of the wild population is already one-half of that trial-and-error system which is necessary for dealing with environment.

The artificially homogenized populations of man's domestic animals and plants are scarcely fit for survival.

And today a further correction of the unit is necessary. The flexible environment must also be included along with the flexible organism because, as I have already said, the organism which destroys its environment destroys itself. The unit of survival is a flexible organism-in-its-environment.

Now, let me leave evolution for a moment to consider what is the unit of mind. Let us go back to the map and the territory and ask: "What is it in the territory that gets onto the map?" We know the territory does not get onto the map. That is the central point about which we here are all agreed. Now, if the territory were uniform, nothing would get onto the map except its boundaries, which are the points at which it ceases to be uniform against some larger matrix. What gets onto the map, in fact, is *difference*, be it a difference in altitude, a difference in vegetation, a dif-ference in population structure, difference in surface, or what-ever. Differences are the things that get onto a map.

But what is a difference? A difference is a very peculiar

and obscure concept. It is certainly not a thing or an event. This piece of paper is different from the wood of this lectern. There are many differences between them—of color, texture, shape, etc. But if we start to ask about the localization of those differences, we get into trouble. Obviously the difference between the paper and the wood is not in the paper; it is obviously not in the wood; it is obviously not in the space between them, and it is obviously not in the time between them. (Difference which occurs across time is what we call "change.")

A difference, then, is an abstract matter.

In the hard sciences, effects are, in general, caused by rather concrete conditions or events—impacts, forces, and so forth. But when you enter the world of communication, organization, etc., you leave behind that whole world in which effects are brought about by forces and impacts and energy exchange. You enter a world in which "effects"—and I am not sure one should still use the same word—are brought about by *differences*. That is, they are brought about by the sort of "thing" that gets onto the map from the territory. This is difference.

Difference travels from the wood and paper into my retina. It then gets picked up and worked on by this fancy piece of computing machinery in my head.

The whole energy relation is different. In the world of mind, nothing—that which is *not*—can be a cause. In the hard sciences, we ask for causes and we expect them to exist and be "real." But remember that zero is different from one, and because zero is different from one, zero can be a cause in the psychological world, the world of communication. The letter which you do not write can get an angry reply; and the income tax form which you do not fill in can trigger the Internal Revenue boys into energetic action, because they, too, have their breakfast, lunch, tea, and dinner and can react with energy which they derive from their metabolism. The letter which never existed is no source of energy.

It follows, of course, that we must change our whole way of thinking about mental and communicational process. The ordinary analogies of energy theory which people borrow from the hard sciences to provide a conceptual frame upon which they try to build theories about psychology and behavior—that entire Procrustean structure—is non-sense. It is in error.

I suggest to you, now, that the word "idea," in its most elementary sense, is synonymous with "difference." Kant, in the *Critique of Judgment*—if I understand him correctly—asserts that the most elementary aesthetic act is the selection of a fact. He argues that in a piece of chalk there are an infinite number of potential facts. The *Ding an sich*, the piece of chalk, can never enter into communication or mental process because of this infinitude. The sensory receptors cannot accept it; they filter it out. What they do is to select certain *facts* out of the piece of chalk, which then become, in modern terminology, information.

I suggest that Kant's statement can be modified to say that there is an infinite number of *differences* around and within the piece of chalk. There are differences between the chalk and the rest of the universe, between the chalk and the sun or the moon. And within the piece of chalk, there is for every molecule an infinite number of differences between its location and the locations in which it *might* have been. Of this infinitude, we select a very limited number, which become information. In fact, what we mean by information—the elementary unit of information—is a *difference which makes a difference*, and it is able to make a difference because the neural pathways along which it travels and is continually transformed are themselves provided with energy. The pathways are ready to be triggered. We may even say that the question is already implicit in them.

There is, however, an important contrast between most of the pathways of information inside the body and most of the pathways outside it. The differences between the paper and the wood are first transformed into differences in the propagation of light or sound, and travel in this form to my sensory end organs. The first part of their journey is energized in the ordinary hard-science way, from "behind." But when the differences enter my body by triggering an end organ, this type of travel is replaced by travel which is energized at every step by the metabolic energy latent in the protoplasm which *receives* the difference, recreates or transforms it, and passes it on.

When I strike the head of a nail with a hammer, an impulse is transmitted to its point. But it is a semantic error, a misleading metaphor, to say that what travels in an axon is an "impulse." It could correctly be called "news of a difference."

Be that as it may, this contrast between internal and external pathways is not absolute. Exceptions occur on both sides of the line. Some external chains of events are energized by relays, and some chains of events internal to the body are energized from "behind." Notably, the mechanical interaction of muscles can be used as a computational model.[2]

In spite of these exceptions, it is still broadly true that the coding and transmission of differences outside the body is very different from the coding and transmission inside, and this difference must be mentioned because it can lead us into error. We commonly think of the external "physical world" as somehow separate from an internal "mental world." I believe that this division is based on the contrast in coding and transmission inside and outside the body.

The mental world—the mind—the world of information processing—is not limited by the skin.

Let us now go back to the notion that the transform of a difference traveling in a circuit is an elementary idea. If this be correct, let us ask what a mind is. We say the map is different from the territory. But what is the territory? Operationally, somebody went out with a retina or a measuring stick and made representations which were then put upon paper. What is on the paper map is a representation of what was in the retinal representation of the man who made the map; and as you push the question back, what you find is an infinite regress, an infinite series of maps. The territory never gets in at all. The territory is *Ding an sich* and you can't do anything with it. Always the process of representation will filter it out so that the mental world is only maps of

---

[2] It is interesting to note that digital computers depend upon transmission of energy "from behind" to send "news" along wire from one relay to the next. But each relay has its own energy source. Analogic computers, *e.g.*, tide machines and the like, are commonly entirely driven by energy "from behind." Either type of energization can be used for computational purposes.

maps of maps, ad infinitum.[3] All "phenomena" are literally "appearances."

Or we can follow the chain forward. I receive various sorts of mappings which I call data or information. Upon receipt of these I act. But my actions, my muscular contractions, are transforms of differences in the input material. And I receive again data which are transforms of my actions. We get thus a picture of the mental world which has somehow jumped loose from our conventional picture of the physical world.

This is not new, and for historic background we go again to the alchemists and Gnostics. Carl Jung once wrote a very curious little book, which I recommend to all of you. It is called *Septem Sermones ad Mortuos*, Seven Sermons to the Dead.[4] In his *Memoirs, Dreams and Reflections*, Jung tells us that his house was full of ghosts, and they were noisy. They bothered him, they bothered his wife, and they bothered the children. In the vulgar jargon of psychiatry, we might say that everybody in the house was as psychotic as hooty owls, and for quite good reason. If you get your epistemology confused, you go psychotic, and Jung was going through an epistemological crisis. So he sat down at his desk and picked up a pen and started to write. When he started to write the ghosts all disappeared, and he wrote this little book. From this he dates all his later insight. He signed it "Basilides," who was a famous Gnostic in Alexandria in the second century.

He points out that there are two worlds. We might call

[3] Or we may spell the matter out and say that at every step, as a difference is transformed and propagated along its pathway, the embodiment of the difference before the step is a "territory" of which the embodiment after the step is a "map." The map-territory relation obtains at every step.

[4] Written in 1916, translated by H. G. Baynes and privately circulated in 1925. Republished by Stuart & Watkins, London, and by Random House, 1961. In later work, Jung seems to have lost the clarity of the Seven Sermons. In his "Answer to Job," the archetypes are said to be "pleromatic." It is surely true, however, that constellations of ideas may seem subjectively to resemble "forces" when their ideational character is unrecognized.

them two worlds of explanation. He names them the *pleroma* and the *creatura*, these being Gnostic terms. The pleroma is the world in which events are caused by forces and impacts and in which there are no "distinctions." Or, as I would say, no "differences." In the creatura, effects are brought about precisely by difference. In fact, this is the same old dichotomy between mind and substance.

We can study and describe the pleroma, but always the distinctions which we draw are attributed *by us* to the pleroma. The pleroma knows nothing of difference and distinction; it contains no "ideas" in the sense in which I am using the word. When we study and describe the creatura, we must correctly identify those differences which are effective within it.

I suggest that "pleroma" and "creatura" are words which we could usefully adopt, and it is therefore worthwhile to look at the bridges which exist between these two "worlds." It is an oversimplification to say that the "hard sciences" deal only with the pleroma and that the sciences of the mind deal only with the creatura. There is more to it than that.

First, consider the relation between energy and negative entropy. The classical Carnot heat engine consists of a cylinder of gas with a piston. This cylinder is alternately placed in contact with a container of hot gas and with a container of cold gas. The gas in the cylinder alternately expands and contracts as it is heated or cooled by the hot and cold sources. The piston is thus driven up and down.

But with each cycle of the engine, the *difference* between the temperature of the hot source and that of the cold source is reduced. When this difference becomes zero, the engine will stop.

The physicist, describing the pleroma, will write equations to translate the temperature difference into "available energy," which he will call "negative entropy," and will go on from there.

The analyst of the creatura will note that the whole system is a sense organ which is triggered by temperature difference. He will call this difference which makes a difference "information" or "negative entropy." For him, this is only a special case in which the effective difference happens to be a matter of energetics. He is equally interested in all differences which can activate some sense organ. For him, any such difference is "negative entropy."

Or consider the phenomenon which the neurophysiologists call "synaptic summation." What is observed is that in certain cases, when two neurons, A and B, have synaptic connection to a third neuron, C, the firing of neither neuron by itself is sufficient to fire C; but that when both A and B fire simultaneously (or nearly so), their combined "impulses" will cause C to fire.

In pleromatic language, this combining of events to surmount a threshold is called "summation."

But from the point of view of the student of creatura (and the neurophysiologist must surely have one foot in the pleroma and the other in creatura), this is not summation at all. What happens is that the system operates to create differences. There are two differentiated *classes* of firings by A: those firings which are accompanied by B and those which are unaccompanied. Similarly there are two classes of firings by B.

The so-called "summation," when both fire, is not an additive process from this point of view. It is the formation of a logical product—a process of fractionation rather than summation.

The creatura is thus the world seen as mind, wherever such a view is appropriate. And wherever this view is appropriate, there arises a species of complexity which is absent from pleromatic description: creatural description is always hierarchic.

I have said that what gets from territory to map is transforms of difference and that these (somehow selected) differences are elementary ideas.

But there are differences between differences. Every effective difference denotes a demarcation, a line of classification, and all classification is hierarchic. In other words, differences are themselves to be differentiated and classified. In this context I will only touch lightly on the matter of classes of difference, because to carry the matter further would land us in problems of *Principia Mathematica*.

Let me invite you to a psychological experience, if only to demonstrate the frailty of the human computer. First note that differences in texture are *different* (*a*) from differences in color. Now note that differences in size are *different*

(b) from differences in shape. Similarly ratios are different (c) from subtractive differences.

Now let me invite you, as disciples of Korzybski, to define the differences between "different (a)," "different (b)," and "different (c)" in the above paragraph.

The computer in the human head boggles at the task.

But not all classes of difference are as awkward to handle.

One such class you are all familiar with. Namely, the class of differences which are created by the process of transformation whereby the differences immanent in the territory become differences immanent in the map. In the corner of every serious map you will find these rules of transformation spelled out—usually in words. Within the human mind, it is absolutely essential to recognize the differences of this class, and, indeed, it is these that form the central subject matter of "Science and Sanity."

An hallucination or a dream image is surely a transformation of something. But of what? And by what rules of transformation?

Lastly there is that hierarchy of differences which biologists call "levels." I mean such differences as that between a cell and a tissue, between tissue and organ, organ and organism, and organism and society.

These are the hierarchies of units or *Gestalten*, in which each subunit is a part of the unit of next larger scope. And, always in biology, this difference or relationship which I call "part of" is such that certain differences in the part have informational effect upon the larger unit, and vice versa.

Having stated this relationship between biological part and whole, I can now go on from the notion of creatura as Mind in general to the question of what is *a* mind.

What do I mean by "my" mind?

I suggest that the delimitation of an individual mind must always depend upon what phenomena we wish to understand or explain. Obviously there are lots of message pathways outside the skin, and these and the messages which they carry must be included as part of the mental system whenever they are relevant.

Consider a tree and a man and an axe. We observe that the axe flies through the air and makes certain sorts of gashes in a pre-existing cut in the side of the tree. If now we want to explain this set of phenomena, we shall be concerned with differences in the cut face of the tree, differences in the retina of the man, differences in his central nervous system, differences in his efferent neural messages, differences in the behavior of his muscles, differences in how the axe flies, to the differences which the axe then makes on the face of the tree. Our explanation (for certain purposes) will go round and round that circuit. In principle, if you want to explain or understand anything in human behavior, you are always dealing with total circuits, completed circuits. This is the elementary cybernetic thought.

The elementary cybernetic system with its messages in circuit is, in fact, the simplest unit of mind; and the transform of a difference traveling in a circuit is the elementary idea. More complicated systems are perhaps more worthy to be called mental systems, but essentially this is what we are talking about. The unit which shows the characteristic of trial and error will be legitimately called a mental system.

But what about "me"? Suppose I am a blind man, and I use a stick. I go tap, tap, tap. Where do *I* start? Is my mental system bounded at the handle of the stick? Is it bounded by my skin? Does it start halfway up the stick? Does it start at the tip of the stick? But these are nonsense questions. The stick is a pathway along which transforms of difference are being transmitted. The way to delineate the system is to draw the limiting line in such a way that you do not cut any of these pathways in ways which leave things inexplicable. If what you are trying to explain is a given piece of behavior, such as the locomotion of the blind man, then, for this purpose, you will need the street, the stick, the man; the street, the stick, and so on, round and round.

But when the blind man sits down to eat his lunch, his stick and its messages will no longer be relevant—if it is his eating that you want to understand.

And in addition to what I have said to define the individual mind, I think it necessary to include the relevant parts of memory and data "banks." After all, the simplest cybernetic circuit can be said to have memory of a dynamic kind—not based upon static storage but upon the travel of information around the circuit. The behavior of the governor of a steam engine at Time 2 is partly determined by what it did at Time 1—where the interval between Time 1 and

Time 2 is that time necessary for the information to complete the circuit.

We get a picture, then, of mind as synonymous with cybernetic system—the relevant total information-processing, trial-and-error completing unit. And we know that within Mind in the widest sense there will be a hierarchy of sub-systems, any one of which we can call an individual mind.

But this picture is precisely the same as the picture which I arrived at in discussing *the unit of evolution*. I believe that this identity is the most important generalization which I have to offer you tonight.

In considering units of evolution, I argued that you have at each step to include the completed pathways outside the protoplasmic aggregate, be it DNA-in-the-cell, or cell-in-the-body, or body-in-the-environment. The hierarchic structure is not new. Formerly we talked about the breeding individual or the family line or the taxon, and so on. Now each step of the hierarchy is to be thought of as a *system*, instead of a chunk cut off and visualized as *against* the surrounding matrix.

This identity between the unit of mind and the unit of evolutionary survival is of very great importance, not only theoretical, but also ethical.

It means, you see, that I now localize something which I am calling "Mind" immanent in the large biological system—the ecosystem. Or, if I draw the system boundaries at a different level, then mind is immanent in the total evolutionary structure. If this identity between mental and evolutionary units is broadly right, then we face a number of shifts in our thinking.

First, let us consider ecology. Ecology has currently two faces to it: the face which is called bioenergetics—the economics of energy and materials within a coral reef, a redwood forest, or a city—and, second, an economics of information, of entropy, negentropy, etc. These two do not fit together very well precisely because the units are differently bounded in the two sorts of ecology. In bioenergetics it is natural and appropriate to think of units bounded at the cell membrane, or at the skin; or of units composed of sets of conspecific individuals. These boundaries are then the frontiers at which measurements can be made to determine the additive-subtractive budget of energy for the given unit. In contrast, informational or entropic ecology deals with the budgeting of pathways and of probability. The resulting budgets are fractionating (not subtractive). The boundaries must enclose, not cut, the relevant pathways.

Moreover, the very meaning of "survival" becomes different when we stop talking about the survival of something bounded by the skin and start to think of the survival of the system of ideas in circuit. The contents of the skin are randomized at death and the pathways within the skin are randomized. But the ideas, under further transformation, may go on out in the world in books or works of art. Socrates as a bioenergetic individual is dead. But much of him still lives as a component in the contemporary ecology of ideas.[5]

It is also clear that theology becomes changed and perhaps renewed. The Mediterranean religions for 5000 years have swung to and fro between immanence and transcendence. In Babylon the gods were transcendent on the tops of hills; in Egypt, there was god immanent in Pharoah; and Christianity is a complex combination of these two beliefs.

The cybernetic epistemology which I have offered you would suggest a new approach. The individual mind is immanent but not only in the body. It is immanent also in pathways and messages outside the body; and there is a larger Mind of which the individual mind is only a subsystem. This larger Mind is comparable to God and is perhaps what some people mean by "God," but it is still immanent in the total interconnected social system and planetary ecology.

Freudian psychology expanded the concept of mind inwards to include the whole communication system within the body—the autonomic, the habitual, and the vast range of unconscious process. What I am saying expands mind outwards. And both of these changes reduce the scope of the conscious self. A certain humility becomes appropriate, tem-

---

[5] For the phrase "ecology of ideas," I am indebted to Sir Geoffrey Vickers' essay "The Ecology of Ideas" in *Value Systems and Social Process,* Basic Books, 1968. For a more formal discussion of the survival of ideas, see Gordon Pasks' remarks in Wenner-Gren Conference on "Effects of Conscious Purpose on Human Adaptation," 1968.

pered by the dignity or joy of being part of something much bigger. A part—if you will—of God.

If you put God outside and set him vis-à-vis his creation and if you have the idea that you are created in his image, you will logically and naturally see yourself as outside and against the things around you. And as you arrogate all mind to yourself, you will see the world around you as mindless and therefore not entitled to moral or ethical consideration. The environment will seem to be yours to exploit. Your survival unit will be you and your folks or conspecifics against the environment of other social units, other races and the brutes and vegetables.

If this is your estimate of your relation to nature *and you have an advanced technology*, your likelihood of survival will be that of a snowball in hell. You will die either of the toxic by-products of your own hate, or, simply, of over-population and overgrazing. The raw materials of the world are finite.

If I am right, the whole of our thinking about what we are and what other people are has got to be restructured. This is not funny, and I do not know how long we have to do it in. If we continue to operate on the premises that were fashionable in the precybernetic era, and which were especially underlined and strengthened during the Industrial Revolution, which seemed to validate the Darwinian unit of survival, we may have twenty or thirty years before the logical *reductio ad absurdum* of our old positions destroys us. Nobody knows how long we have, under the present system, before some disaster strikes us, more serious than the destruction of any group of nations. The most important task today is, perhaps, to learn to think in the new way. Let me say that I don't know how to think that way. Intellectually, I can stand here and I can give you a reasoned exposition of this matter; but if I am cutting down a tree, I still think "Gregory Bateson" is cutting down the tree. *I* am cutting down the tree. "Myself" is to me still an excessively concrete object, different from the rest of what I have been calling "mind."

The step to realizing—to making habitual—the other way of thinking—so that one naturally thinks that way when one reaches out for a glass of water or cuts down a tree—that step is not an easy one.

And, quite seriously, I suggest to you that we should trust no policy decisions which emanate from persons who do not yet have that habit.

There are experiences and disciplines which may help me to imagine what it would be like to have this habit of correct thought. Under LSD, I have experienced, as have many others, the disappearance of the division between self and the music to which I was listening. The perceiver and the thing perceived become strangely united into a single entity. This state is surely more correct than the state in which it seems that "I hear the music." The sound, after all, is *Ding an sich*, but my perception of it is a part of mind.

It is told of Johann Sebastian Bach that when somebody asked him how he played so divinely, he answered, "I play the notes, in order, as they are written. It is God who makes the music." But not many of us can claim Bach's correctness of epistemology—or that of William Blake, who knew that the Poetic Imagination was the only reality. The poets have known these things all through the ages, but the rest of us have gone astray into all sorts of false reifications of the "self" and separations between the "self" and "experience."

For me another clue—another moment when the nature of mind was for a moment clear—was provided by the famous experiments of Adelbert Ames, Jr. These are optical illusions in depth perception. As Ames' guinea pig, you discover that those mental processes by which you create the world in three-dimensional perspective are within your mind but totally unconscious and utterly beyond voluntary control. Of course, we all know that this is so—that mind creates the images which "we" then see. But still it is a profound epistemological shock to have direct experience of this which we always knew.

Please do not misunderstand me. When I say that the poets have always known these things or that most of mental process is unconscious, I am not advocating a greater use of emotion or a lesser use of intellect. Of course, if what I am saying tonight is approximately true, then our ideas about the relation between thought and emotion need to be revised. If the boundaries of the "ego" are wrongly drawn or even totally fictitious, then it may be nonsense to regard emotions or dreams or our unconscious computations of perspective as "ego-alien."

We live in a strange epoch when many psychologists try to "humanize" their science by preaching an anti-intellectual gospel. They might, as sensibly, try to physicalize physics by discarding the tools of mathematics.

It is the attempt to *separate* intellect from emotion that is monstrous, and I suggest that it is equally monstrous—and dangerous—to attempt to separate the external mind from the internal. Or to separate mind from body.

Blake noted that "A tear is an intellectual thing," and Pascal asserted that "The heart has its *reasons* of which the reason knows nothing." We need not be put off by the fact that the reasonings of the heart (or of the hypothalamus) are accompanied by sensations of joy or grief. These computations are concerned with matters which are vital to mammals, namely, matters of *relationship*, by which I mean love, hate, respect, dependency, spectatorship, performance, dominance, and so on. These are central to the life of any mammal and I see no objection to calling these computations "thought," though certainly the units of relational computation are different from the units which we use to compute about isolable things.

But there are bridges between the one sort of thought and the other, and it seems to me that the artists and poets are specifically concerned with these bridges. It is not that art is the expression of the unconscious, but rather that it is concerned with the relation *between* the levels of mental process. From a work of art it may be possible to analyze out some unconscious thoughts of the artist, but I believe that, for example, Freud's analysis of Leonardo's *Virgin on the Knees of St. Anne* precisely misses the point of the whole exercise. Artistic skill is the combining of many levels of mind —unconscious, conscious, and external—to make a statement of their combination. It is not a matter of expressing a single level.

Similarly, Isadora Duncan, when she said, "If I could say it, I would not have to dance it," was talking nonsense, because her dance was about combinations of saying and moving.

Indeed, if what I have been saying is at all correct, the whole base of aesthetics will need to be re-examined. It seems that we link feelings not only to the computations of the heart but also to computations in the external pathways of the mind. It is when we recognize the operations of creatura in the external world that we are aware of "beauty" or "ugliness." The "primrose by the river's brim" is beautiful because we are aware that the combination of differences which constitutes its appearance could only be achieved by information processing, *i.e.*, by *thought*. We recognize another mind within our own external mind.

And last, there is death. It is understandable that, in a civilization which separates mind from body, we should either try to forget death or to make mythologies about the survival of transcendent mind. But if mind is immanent not only in those pathways of information which are located inside the body but also in external pathways, then death takes on a different aspect. The individual nexus of pathways which I call "me" is no longer so precious because that nexus is only part of a larger mind.

The ideas which seemed to be me can also become immanent in you. May they survive—if true.

## COMMENT ON PART V

In the final essay of this part, "Form, Substance and Difference," much of what has been said in earlier parts of the book falls into place. In sum, what has been said amounts to this: that in addition to (and always in conformity with) the familiar physical determinism which characterises our universe, there is a mental determinism. This mental determinism is in no sense supernatural. Rather it is of the very nature of the macroscopic° world that it exhibit mental characteristics. The mental determinism is not transcendent but immanent and is especially complex and evident in those sections of the universe which are alive or which include living things.

But so much of occidental thinking is shaped on the premise of transcendent deity that it is difficult for many people to rethink their theories in terms of immanence. Even Darwin from time to time wrote about Natural Selection in phrases which almost ascribed to this process the characteristics of transcendence and purpose.

---

° I do not agree with Samuel Butler, Whitehead, or Teilhard de Chardin that it follows from this mental character of the macroscopic world that the single atomies must have mental character or potentiality. I see the mental as a function only of complex *relationship*.

It may be worthwhile, therefore, to give an extreme sketch of the difference between the belief in transcendence and that in immanence.

Transcendent mind or deity is imagined to be personal and omniscient, and as receiving information by channels separate from the earthly. He sees a species acting in ways which must disrupt its ecology and, either in sorrow or in anger, He sends the wars, the plagues, the pollution, and the fallout.

Immanent mind would achieve the same final result but without either sorrow or anger. Immanent mind has no separate and unearthly channels by which to know or act and, therefore, can have no separate emotion or evaluative comment. The immanent will differ from the transcendent in greater determinism.

St. Paul (Galatians VI) said that "God is not mocked," and immanent mind similarly is neither vengeful nor forgiving. It is of no use to make excuses; the immanent mind is not "mocked."

But since our minds—and this includes our tools and actions—are only parts of the larger mind, its computations can be confused by our contradictions and confusions. Since it contains our insanity, the immanent mind is inevitably subject to possible insanity. It is in our power, with our technology, to create insanity in the larger system of which we are parts.

In the final section of the book, I shall consider some of these mentally pathogenic processes.

# Part VI: Crisis in the Ecology of Mind

# From Versailles to Cybernetics*

I have to talk about recent history as it appears to me in my generation and to you in yours and, as I flew in this morning, words began to echo in my mind. These were phrases more thunderous than any I might be able to compose. One of these groups of words was, "The fathers have eaten bitter fruit and the children's teeth are set on edge." Another was the statement of Joyce that "history is that nightmare from which there is no awakening." Another was, "The sins of the fathers shall be visited on the children even to the third and fourth generation of those that hate me." And lastly, not so immediately relevant, but still I think relevant to the problem of social mechanism, "He who would do good to another must do it in Minute Particulars. General Good is the plea of the scoundrel, hypocrite, and flatterer."

We are talking about serious things. I call this lecture "From Versailles to Cybernetics," naming the two historic events of the twentieth century. The word "cybernetics" is familiar, is it not? But how many of you know what happened at Versailles in 1919?

The question is, *What* is going to count as important in the history of the last sixty years? I am sixty-two, and, as I began to think about what I have seen of history in my life-

*Previously unpublished. This lecture was given April 21, 1966, to the "Two Worlds Symposium" at Sacramento State College.

time, it seemed to me that I had really only seen two moments that would rate as really important from an anthropologist's point of view. One was the events leading up to the Treaty of Versailles, and the other was the cybernetic breakthrough. You may be surprised or shocked that I have not mentioned the A-bomb, or even World War II. I have not mentioned the spread of the automobile, nor of the radio and TV, nor many other things that have occurred in the last sixty years.

Let me state my criterion of historical importance:

Mammals in general, and we among them, care extremely, not about episodes, but about the patterns of their relationships. When you open the refrigerator door and the cat comes up and makes certain sounds, she is not talking about liver or milk, though you may know very well that that is what she wants. You may be able to guess correctly and give her that—if there is any in the refrigerator. What she actually says is something about the relationship between herself and you. If you translated her message into words, it would be something like, "dependency, dependency, dependency." She is talking, in fact, about a rather abstract pattern within a relationship. From that assertion of a pattern, you are expected to go from the general to the specific—to deduce "milk" or "liver."

This is crucial. This is what mammals are about. They are concerned with patterns of relationship, with where they stand in love, hate, respect, dependency, trust, and similar abstractions, vis-à-vis somebody else. This is where it hurts us to be put in the wrong. If we trust and find that that which we have trusted was untrustworthy; or if we distrust, and find that that which we distrusted was in fact trustworthy, we feel *bad*. The pain that human beings and all other mammals can suffer from this type of error is extreme. If, therefore, we really want to know what are the significant points in history, we have to ask which are the moments in history when attitudes were changed. These are the moments when people are hurt because of their former "values."

Think of the house thermostat in your home. The weather changes outdoors, the temperature of the room falls, the thermometer switch in the living room goes through its business and switches on the furnace; and the furnace warms the room and when the room is hot, the thermometer switch turns it off again. The system is what is called a homeostatic circuit or a servocircuit. But there is also a little box in the living room on the wall by which you *set* the thermostat. If the house has been too cold for the last week, you must move it up from its present setting to make the system now oscillate around a new level. No amount of weather, heat or cold or whatever, will change that setting, which is called the "bias" of the system. The temperature of the house will oscillate, it will get hotter and cooler according to various circumstances, but the setting of the mechanism will not be changed by those changes. But when *you* go and *you* move that bias, you will change what we may call the "attitude" of the system.

Similarly, the important question about history is: Has the bias or setting been changed? The episodic working out of events under a single stationary setting is really trivial. It is with this thought in mind that I have said that the two most important historic events in my life were the Treaty of Versailles and the discovery of cybernetics.

Most of you probably hardly know how the Treaty of Versailles came into being. The story is very simple. World War I dragged on and on; the Germans were rather obviously losing. At this point, George Creel, a public relations man—and I want you not to forget that this man was a granddaddy of modern public relations—had an idea: the idea was that maybe the Germans would surrender if we offered them soft armistice terms. He therefore drew up a set of soft terms, according to which there would be no punitive measures. These terms were drawn up in fourteen points. These Fourteen Points he passed on to President Wilson. If you are going to deceive somebody, you had better get an honest man to carry the message. President Wilson was an almost pathologically honest man and a humanitarian. He elaborated the points in a number of speeches: there were to be "no annexations, no contributions, no punitive damages . . ." and so on. And the Germans surrendered.

We, British and Americans—especially the British—continued of course to blockade Germany because we didn't want them to get uppity before the Treaty was signed. So, for another year, they continued to starve.

The Peace Conference has been vividly described by

Maynard Keynes in *The Economic Consequences of the Peace* (1919).

The Treaty was finally drawn up by four men: Clemenceau, "the tiger," who wanted to crush Germany; Lloyd George, who felt it would be politically expedient to get a lot of reparations out of Germany, and some revenge; and Wilson, who had to be bamboozled along. Whenever Wilson would wonder about those Fourteen Points of his, they took him out into the war cemeteries and made him feel ashamed of not being angry with the Germans. Who was the other? Orlando was the other, an Italian.

This was one of the great sellouts in the history of our civilization. A most extraordinary event which led fairly directly and inevitably into World War II. It also led (and this is perhaps more interesting than the fact of its leading to World War II) to the total demoralization of German politics. If you promise your boy something, and renege on him, framing the whole thing on a high ethical plane, you will probably find that not only is he very angry with you, but that *his* moral attitudes deteriorate as long as he feels the unfair whiplash of what you are doing to him. It's not only that World War II was the appropriate response of a nation which had been treated in this particular way; what is more important is the fact that the demoralization of that nation was expectable from this sort of treatment. From the demoralization of Germany, we, too, became demoralized. This is why I say that the Treaty of Versailles was an attitudinal turning point.

I imagine that we have another couple of generations of aftereffects from that particular sellout to work through. We are, in fact, like members of the house of Atreus in Greek tragedy. First there was Thyestes' adultery, then Atreus' killing of Thyestes' three children, whom he served to Thyestes at a peace-making feast. Then the murder of Atreus' son, Agamemnon, by Thyestes' son, Aegistheus; and finally the murder of Aegistheus and Clytemnestra by Orestes.

It goes on and on. The tragedy of oscillating and self-propagating distrust, hate, and destruction down the generations.

I want you to imagine that you come into the middle of one of these sequences of tragedy. How is it for the middle generation of the house of Atreus? They are living in a crazy universe. From the point of view of the people who started the mess, it's not so crazy; they know what happened and how they got there. But the people down the line, who were not there at the beginning, find themselves living in a crazy universe, and find themselves crazy, precisely because they do not know how they got that way.

To take a dose of LSD is all right, and you will have the experience of being more or less crazy, but this will make quite good sense because you *know* you took the dose of LSD. If, on the other hand, you took the LSD by accident, and then find yourself going crazy, not knowing how you got there, this is a terrifying and horrible experience. This is a much more serious and terrible experience, very different from the trip which you can enjoy if you know you took the LSD.

Now consider the difference between my generation and you who are under twenty-five. We all live in the same crazy universe whose hate, distrust, and hypocrisy relates back (especially at the international level) to the Fourteen Points and the Treaty of Versailles.

We older ones know how we got here. I can remember my father reading the Fourteen Points at the breakfast table and saying, "By golly, they're going to give them a decent armistice, a decent peace," or something of the kind. And I can remember, but I will not attempt to verbalize, the sort of thing he said when the Treaty of Versailles came out. It wasn't printable. So I know more or less how we got here.

But from your point of view, we are absolutely crazy, and you don't know what sort of historic event led to this craziness. "The fathers have eaten bitter fruit and the children's teeth are set on edge." It's all very well for the fathers, they know what they ate. The children don't know what was eaten.

Let us consider what is to be expected of people in the aftermath of a major deception. Previous to World War I, it was generally assumed that compromise and a little hypocrisy are a very important ingredient in the ordinary comfortableness of life. If you read Samuel Butler's *Erewhon Revisited*, for example, you will see what I mean. All the principal characters in the novel have got themselves into an awful mess: some are due to be executed, and others are due for public scandal, and the religious system of the nation is threatened with collapse. These disasters and tangles are smoothed out by Mrs. Ydgrun (or, as we would say, "Mrs. Grundy"), the guardian of Erewhonian morals. She carefully reconstructs history, like a jigsaw puzzle, so that nobody is really hurt and nobody is disgraced—still less is anybody executed. This was a very comfortable philosophy. A little hypocrisy and a little compromise oil the wheels of social life.

But after the great deception, this philosophy is untenable. You are perfectly correct that something is wrong; and that the something wrong is of the nature of a deceit and a hypocrisy. You live in the midst of corruption.

Of course, your natural responses are puritanical. Not sexual puritanism, because it is not a sexual deceit that lies in the background. But an extreme puritanism against compromise, a puritanism against hypocrisy, and this ends up as a reduction of life to little pieces. It is the big integrated structures of life that seem to have carried the lunacy, and so you try to focus down on the smallest things. "He who would do good to another must do it in Minute Particulars. General Good is the plea of the scoundrel, hypocrite, and flatterer." The general good smells of hypocrisy to the rising generation.

I don't doubt that if you asked George Creel to justify the Fourteen Points, he would urge the general good. It is possible that that little operation of his saved a few thousand American lives in 1918. I don't know how many it cost in World War II, and since in Korea and Vietnam. I recall that Hiroshima and Nagasaki were justified by the general good and saving American lives. There was a lot of talk about "unconditional surrender," perhaps because we could not trust ourselves to honor a conditional armistice. Was the fate of Hiroshima determined at Versailles?

Now I want to talk about the other significant historical event which has happened in my lifetime, approximately in 1946–47. This was the growing together of a number of ideas which had developed in different places during World War II. We may call the aggregate of these ideas cybernetics, or communication theory, or information theory, or systems theory. The ideas were generated in many places: in Vienna by Bertalanffy, in Harvard by Wiener, in Princeton by von Neumann, in Bell Telephone labs by Shannon, in Cambridge by

Craik, and so on. All these separate developments in different intellectual centers dealt with communicational problems, especially with the problem of what sort of a thing is an organized system.

You will notice that everything I said about history and about Versailles is a discussion of organized systems and their properties. Now I want to say that we are developing a certain amount of rigorous scientific understanding of these very mysterious organized systems. Our knowledge today is way ahead of anything that George Creel could have said. He was an applied scientist before the science was ripe to be applied.

One of the roots of cybernetics goes back to Whitehead and Russell and what is called the Theory of Logical Types. In principle, the name is not the thing named, and the name of the name is not the name, and so on. In terms of this powerful theory, a message *about* war is not part *of* the war.

Let me put it this way: the message "Let's play chess" is not a move in the game of chess. It is a message in a more abstract language than the language of the game on the board. The message "Let's make peace on such and such terms" is not within the same ethical system as the deceits and tricks of battle. They say that all is fair in love and war, and that may be true *within* love and war, but outside and about love and war, the ethics are a little different. Men have felt for centuries that treachery in a truce or peace-making is worse than trickery in battle. Today this ethical principle receives rigorous theoretical and scientific support. The ethics can now be looked at with formality, rigor, logic, mathematics, and all that, and stands on a different sort of basis from mere invocational preachments. We do not have to feel our way; we can sometimes *know* right from wrong.

I included cybernetics as the second historic event of importance in my lifetime because I have at least a dim hope that we can bring ourselves to use this new understanding with some honesty. If we understand a little bit of what we're doing, maybe it will help us to find our way out of the maze of hallucinations that we have created around ourselves.

Cybernetics is, at any rate, a contribution to change—not simply a change in attitude, but even a change in the understanding of what an attitude is.

The stance that I have taken in choosing what is important in history—saying that the important things are the moments at which attitude is determined, the moments at which the bias of the thermostat is changed—this stance is derived directly from cybernetics. These are thoughts shaped by events from 1946 and after.

But pigs do not go around ready-roasted. We now have a lot of cybernetics, a lot of games theory, and the beginnings of understanding of complex systems. But any understanding can be used in destructive ways.

I think that cybernetics is the biggest bite out of the fruit of the Tree of Knowledge that mankind has taken in the last 2000 years. But most of such bites out of the apple have proved to be rather indigestible—usually for cybernetic reasons.

Cybernetics has integrity within itself, to help us to not be seduced by it into more lunacy, but we cannot trust *it* to keep us from sin.

For example, the state departments of several nations are today using games theory, backed up by computers, as a way of deciding international policy. They identify first what seem to be the rules of the game of international interaction; they then consider the distribution of strength, weapons, strategic points, grievances, etc., over the geography and the identified nations. They then ask the computers to compute what should be our next move to minimize the chances of our losing the game. The computer then cranks and heaves and gives an answer, and there is some temptation to obey the computer. After all, if you follow the computer you are a little *less responsible* than if you made up your own mind.

But if you do what the computer advises, you assert by that move that you support the *rules of the game* which you fed into the computer. You have affirmed the rules of that game.

No doubt nations of the other side also have computers and are playing similar games, and are affirming the rules of the game that they are feeding to their computers. The result is a system in which the rules of international interaction become more and more rigid.

I submit to you that what is wrong with the international field is that the *rules* need changing. The question is not what is the best thing to do within the rules as they are at the moment. The question is how can we get away from the rules within which we have been operating for the last ten or twenty years, or since the Treaty of Versailles. The problem is to *change* the rules, and insofar as we let our cybernetic inventions—the computers—lead us into more and more rigid situations, we shall in fact be maltreating and abusing the first hopeful advance since 1918.

And, of course, there are other dangers latent in cybernetics and many of these are still unidentified. We do not know, for example, what effects may follow from the computerization of all government dossiers.

But this much is sure, that there is also latent in cybernetics the means of achieving a new and perhaps more human outlook, a means of changing our philosophy of control and a means of seeing our own follies in wider perspective.

# Pathologies of Epistemology*

First, I would like you to join me in a little experiment. Let me ask you for a show of hands. How many of you will agree that *you see me*? I see a number of hands—so I guess insanity loves company. Of course, *you* don't "really" see *me*. What you "see" is a bunch of pieces of information about me, which you synthesize into a picture image of me. You make that image. It's that simple.

The proposition "I see you" or "You see me" is a proposition which contains within it what I am calling "epistemology." It contains within it assumptions about how we get information, what sort of stuff information is, and so forth. When you say you "see" me and put up your hand in an innocent way, you are, in fact, agreeing to certain propositions about the nature of knowing and the nature of the universe in which we live and how we know about it.

I shall argue that many of these propositions happen to be false, even though we all share them. In the case of such epistemological propositions, error is not easily detected and is not very quickly punished. You and I are able to get along in the world and fly to Hawaii and read papers on psychiatry and find our places around these tables and in general

*This paper was given at the Second Conference on Mental Health in Asia and the Pacific, 1969, at the East-West Center, Hawaii. Copyright © 1972 by the East-West Center Press. It will also appear in the report of that conference and is here reprinted by permission of the East-West Center Press, Hawaii.

function reasonably like human beings in spite of very deep error. The erroneous premises, in fact, *work*.

On the other hand, the premises work only up to a certain limit, and, at some stage or under certain circumstances, if you are carrying serious epistemological errors, you will find that they do not work any more. At this point you discover to your horror that it is exceedingly difficult to get rid of the error, that it's sticky. It is as if you had touched honey. As with honey, the falsification gets around; and each thing you try to wipe it off on gets sticky, and your hands still remain sticky.

Long ago I knew intellectually, and you, no doubt, all know intellectually, that you do not see me; but I did not really encounter this truth until I went through the Adelbert Ames experiments and encountered circumstances under which my epistemological error led to errors of action.

Let me describe a typical Ames experiment with a pack of Lucky Strike cigarettes and a book of matches. The Lucky Strikes are placed about three feet from the subject of experiment supported on a spike above the table and the matches are on a similar spike six feet from the subject. Ames had the subject look at the table and say how big the objects are and where they are. The subject will agree that they are where they are, and that they are as big as they are, and there is no apparent epistemological error. Ames then says, "I want you to lean down and look through this plank here." The plank stands vertically at the end of the table. It is just a piece of wood with a round hole in it, and you look through the hole. Now, of course, you have lost use of one eye, and you have been brought down so that you no longer have a crow's-eye view. But you still see the Lucky Strikes where they are and of the size which they are. Ames then said, "Why don't you get a parallax effect by sliding the plank?" You slide the plank sideways and suddenly your image changes. You see a little tiny book of matches about half the size of the original and placed three feet from you; while the pack of Lucky Strikes appears to be twice its original size, and is now six feet away.

This effect is accomplished very simply. When you slid the plank, you in fact operated a lever under the table which you had not seen. The lever reversed the parallax effect; that is, the lever caused the thing which was closer to you to travel with you, and that which was far from you to get left behind.

Your mind has been trained or genotypically determined —and there is much evidence in favor of training—to do the mathematics necessary to use parallax to create an image in depth. It performs this feat without volition and without your consciousness. You cannot control it.

I want to use this example as a paradigm of the sort of error that I intend to talk about. The case is simple; it has experimental backing; it illustrates the intangible nature of epistemological error and the difficulty of changing epistemological habit.

In my everyday thinking, *I see you*, even though I know intellectually that I don't. Since about 1943 when I saw the experiment, I have worked to practice living in the world of truth instead of the world of epistemological fantasy; but I don't think I've succeeded. Insanity, after all, takes psychotherapy to change it, or some very great new experience. Just one experience which ends in the laboratory is insufficient.

This morning, when we were discussing Dr. Jung's paper, I raised the question which nobody was willing to treat seriously, perhaps because my tone of voice encouraged them to smile. The question was whether there are *true* ideologies. We find that different peoples of the world have different ideologies, different epistemologies, different ideas of the relationship between man and nature, different ideas about the nature of man himself, the nature of his knowledge, his feelings, and his will. But if there were a truth about these matters, then only those social groups which thought according to that truth could reasonably be stable. And if no culture in the world thinks according to that truth, then there would be no stable culture.

Notice again that we face the question of how long it takes to come up against trouble. Epistemological error is often reinforced and therefore self-validating. You can get along all right in spite of the fact that you entertain at rather deep levels of the mind premises which are simply false.

I think perhaps the most interesting—though still incomplete—scientific discovery of the twentieth century is the discovery of the nature of *mind*. Let me outline some of the ideas which have contributed to this discovery. Immanuel

Kant, in the *Critique of Judgment,* states that the primary act of aesthetic judgment is selection of a fact. There are, in a sense, no facts in nature; or if you like, there are an infinite number of potential facts in nature, out of which the judgment selects a few which become truly facts by that act of selection. Now, put beside that idea of Kant Jung's insight in *Seven Sermons to the Dead,* a strange document in which he points out that there are two worlds of explanation or worlds of understanding, the *pleroma* and the *creatura.* In the pleroma there are only forces and impacts. In the creatura, there is difference. In other words, the pleroma is the world of the hard sciences, while the creatura is the world of communication and organization. A difference cannot be localized. There is a difference between the color of this desk and the color of this pad. But that difference is not in the pad, it is not in the desk, and I cannot pinch it between them. The difference is not in the space between them. In a word, *a difference is an idea.*

The world of creatura is that world of explanation in which effects are brought about by ideas, essentially by differences.

If now we put Kant's insight together with that of Jung, we create a philosophy which asserts that there is an infinite number of *differences* in this piece of chalk but that only a few of these differences make a difference. This is the epistemological base for information theory. The unit of information is difference. In fact, the unit of psychological input is difference.

The whole energy structure of the pleroma—the forces and impacts of the hard sciences—have flown out the window, so far as explanation within creatura is concerned. After all, zero differs from one, and zero therefore can be a cause, which is not admissible in hard science. The letter which you did not write can precipitate an angry reply, because zero can be one-half of the necessary bit of information. Even sameness can be a cause, because sameness differs from difference.

These strange relations obtain because we organisms (and many of the machines that we make) happen to be able to store energy. We happen to have the necessary circuit structure so that our energy expenditure can be an inverse function of energy input. If you kick a stone, it moves with energy which it got from your kick. If you kick a dog, it moves with the energy which it got from its metabolism. An amoeba will, for a considerable period of time, move *more* when it is hungry. Its energy expenditure is an inverse function of energy input.

These strange creatural effects (which do not occur in the pleroma) depend also upon *circuit structure,* and a circuit is a closed pathway (or network of pathways) along which *differences* (or transforms of differences) are transmitted.

Suddenly, in the last twenty years, these notions have come together to give us a broad conception of the world in which we live—a new way of thinking about what a *mind* is. Let me list what seem to me to be those essential minimal characteristics of a system, which I will accept as characteristics of mind:

(1) The system shall operate with and upon *differences.*

(2) The system shall consist of closed loops or networks of pathways along which differences and transforms of differences shall be transmitted. (What is transmitted on a neuron is not an impulse, it is news of a difference.)

(3) Many events within the system shall be energized by the respondent part rather than by impact from the triggering part.

(4) The system shall show self-correctiveness in the direction of homeostasis and/or in the direction of runaway. Self-correctiveness implies trial and error.

Now, these minimal characteristics of mind are generated whenever and wherever the appropriate circuit structure of causal loops exists. Mind is a necessary, an inevitable function of the appropriate complexity, wherever that complexity occurs.

But that complexity occurs in a great many other places besides the inside of my head and yours. We'll come later to the question of whether a man or a computer has a mind. For the moment, let me say that a redwood forest or a coral reef with its aggregate of organisms interlocking in their relationships has the necessary general structure. The energy for the responses of every organism is supplied from its metabolism, and the total system acts self-correctively in various ways. A human society is like this with closed loops of causation. Every human organization shows both the self-corrective characteristic and has the potentiality for runaway.

Now, let us consider for a moment the question of whether a computer thinks. I would state that it does not. What "thinks" and engages in "trial and error" is the man *plus* the computer *plus* the environment. And the lines between man, computer, and environment are purely artificial, fictitious lines. They are lines *across* the pathways along which information or difference is transmitted. They are not boundaries of the thinking system. What thinks is the total system which engages in trial and error, which is man plus environment.

But if you accept self-correctiveness as the criterion of thought or mental process, then obviously there is "thought" going on inside the man at the autonomic level to maintain various internal variables. And similarly, the computer, if it controls its internal temperature, is doing some simple thinking within itself.

Now we begin to see some of the epistemological fallacies of Occidental civilization. In accordance with the general climate of thinking in mid-nineteenth-century England, Darwin proposed a theory of natural selection and evolution in which the unit of survival was either the family line or the species or subspecies or something of the sort. But today it is quite obvious that this is not the unit of survival in the real biological world. The unit of survival is *organism* plus *environment*. We are learning by bitter experience that the organism which destroys its environment destroys itself.

If, now, we correct the Darwinian unit of survival to include the environment and the interaction between organism and environment, a very strange and surprising identity emerges: *the unit of evolutionary survival turns out to be identical with the unit of mind.*

Formerly we thought of a hierarchy of taxa—individual, family line, subspecies, species, etc.—as units of survival. We now see a different hierarchy of units—gene-in-organism, organism-in-environment, ecosystem, etc. Ecology, in the widest sense, turns out to be the study of the interaction and survival of ideas and programs (*i.e.*, differences, complexes of differences, etc.) in circuits.

Let us now consider what happens when you make the epistemological error of choosing the wrong unit: you end up with the species versus the other species around it or versus the environment in which it operates. Man against nature. You end up, in fact, with Kaneohe Bay polluted, Lake Erie a slimy green mess, and "Let's build bigger atom bombs to kill off the next-door neighbors." There is an ecology of bad ideas, just as there is an ecology of weeds, and it is characteristic of the system that basic error propagates itself. It branches out like a rooted parasite through the tissues of life, and everything gets into a rather peculiar mess. When you narrow down your epistemology and act on the premise "What interests me is me, or my organization, or my species," you chop off consideration of other loops of the loop structure. You decide that you want to get rid of the by-products of human life and that Lake Erie will be a good place to put them. You forget that the eco-mental system called Lake Erie is a part of *your* wider eco-mental system—and that if Lake Erie is driven insane, its insanity is incorporated in the larger system of *your* thought and experience.

You and I are so deeply acculturated to the idea of "self" and organization and species that it is hard to believe that man might view his relations with the environment in any other way than the way which I have rather unfairly blamed upon the nineteenth-century evolutionists. So I must say a few words about the history of all this.

Anthropologically, it would seem from what we know of the early material, that man in society took clues from the natural world around him and applied those clues in a sort of metaphoric way to the society in which he lived. That is, he identified with or empathized with the natural world around him and took that empathy as a guide for his own social organization and his own theories of his own psychology. This was what is called "totemism."

In a way, it was all nonsense, but it made more sense than most of what we do today, because the natural world around us really has this general systemic structure and therefore is an appropriate source of metaphor to enable man to understand himself in his social organization.

The next step, seemingly, was to reverse the process and to take clues from himself and apply these to the natural world around him. This was "animism," extending the notion of personality or mind to mountains, rivers, forests, and such things. This was still not a bad idea in many ways. But the next step was to separate the notion of mind from the natural world, and then you get the notion of gods.

But when you separate mind from the structure in which it is immanent, such as human relationship, the human society, or the ecosystem, you thereby embark, I believe, on fundamental error, which in the end will surely hurt you.

Struggle may be good for your soul up to the moment when to win the battle is easy. When you have an effective enough technology so that you can really act upon your epistemological errors and can create havoc in the world in which you live, then the error is lethal. Epistemological error is all right, it's fine, up to the point at which you create around yourself a universe in which that error becomes immanent in monstrous changes of the universe that you have created and now try to live in.

You see, we're not talking about the dear old Supreme Mind of Aristotle, St. Thomas Aquinas, and so on down through ages—the Supreme Mind which was incapable of error and incapable of insanity. We're talking about immanent mind, which is only too capable of insanity, as you all professionally know. This is precisely why you're here. These circuits and balances of nature can only too easily get out of kilter, and they inevitably get out of kilter when certain basic errors of our thought become reinforced by thousands of cultural details.

I don't know how many people today really believe that there is an overall mind separate from the body, separate from the society, and separate from nature. But for those of you who would say that that is all "superstition," I am prepared to wager that I can demonstrate with them in a few minutes that the habits and ways of thinking that went with those supersitions are still in their heads and still determine a large part of their thoughts. The idea that *you can see me* still governs your thought and action in spite of the fact that you may know intellectually that it is not so. In the same way we are most of us governed by epistemologies that we know to be wrong. Let us consider some of the implications of what I have been saying.

Let us look at how the basic notions are reinforced and expressed in all sorts of detail of how we behave. The very fact that I am monologuing to you—this is a norm of our academic subculture, but the idea that I can teach you, *unilaterally*, is derivative from the premise that the mind controls the body. And whenever a psychotherapist lapses into unilateral therapy, he is obeying the same premise. I, in fact, standing up in front of you, am performing a subversive act by reinforcing in your minds a piece of thinking which is really nonsense. We all do it all the time because it's built into the detail of our behavior. Notice how I stand while you sit.

The same thinking leads, of course, to theories of control and to theories of power. In that universe, if you do not get what you want, you will blame somebody and establish either a jail or a mental hospital, according to taste, and you will pop them in it if you can identify them. If you cannot identify them, you will say, "It's the system." This is roughly where our kids are nowadays, blaming the establishment, but you know the establishments aren't to blame. They are part of the same error, too.

Then, of course, there is the question of weapons. If you believe in that unilateral world and you think that the other people believe in that world (and you're probably right; they do), then, of course, the thing is to get weapons, hit them hard, and "control" them.

They say that power corrupts; but this, I suspect, is nonsense. What is true is that the *idea of power* corrupts. Power corrupts most rapidly those who believe in it, and it is they who will want it most. Obviously our democratic system tends to give power to those who hunger for it and gives every opportunity to those who don't want power to avoid getting it. Not a very satisfactory arrangement if power corrupts those who believe in it and want it.

Perhaps there is no such thing as unilateral power. After all, the man "in power" depends on receiving information all the time from outside. He responds to that information just as much as he "causes" things to happen. It is not possible for Goebbels to control the public opinion of Germany because in order to do so he must have spies or legmen or public opinion polls to tell him what the Germans are thinking. He must then trim what he says to this information; and then again find out how they are responding. It is an interaction, and not a lineal situation.

But the *myth* of power is, of course, a very powerful myth and probably most people in this world more or less believe in it. It is a myth which, if everybody believes in it, becomes to that extent self-validating. But it is still epistemological lunacy and leads inevitably to various sorts of disaster.

Last, there is the question of urgency. It is clear now to many people that there are many catastrophic dangers which have grown out of the Occidental errors of epistemology. These range from insecticides to pollution, to atomic fallout, to the possibility of melting the Antarctic ice cap. Above all, our fantastic compulsion to save individual lives has created the possibility of world famine in the immediate future.

*Perhaps* we have an even chance of getting through the next twenty years with no disaster more serious than the mere destruction of a nation or group of nations.

I believe that this massive aggregation of threats to man and his ecological systems arises out of errors in our habits of thought at deep and partly unconscious levels.

As therapists, clearly we have a duty.

First, to achieve clarity in ourselves; and then to look for every sign of clarity in others and to implement them and reinforce them in whatever is sane in them.

And there are patches of sanity still surviving in the world. Much of Oriental philsophy is more sane than anything the West has produced, and some of the inarticulate efforts of our own young people are more sane than the conventions of the establishment.

# The Roots of Ecological Crisis*

*Summary:* Other testimony has been presented regarding bills to deal with particular problems of pollution and environmental degradation in Hawaii. It is hoped that the proposed Office of Environmental Quality Control and the Environmental Center at the University of Hawaii will go beyond this *ad hoc* approach and will study the more basic causes of the current rash of environmental troubles.

The present testimony argues that these basic causes lie in the *combined* action of (*a*) technological advance; (*b*) population increase; and (*c*) conventional (but wrong) ideas about the nature of man and his relation to the environment.

It is concluded that the next five to ten years will be a period like the Federalist period in United States history in which the whole philosophy of government, education, and technology must be debated.

*We submit:*

(1) That all *ad hoc* measures leave uncorrected the deeper causes of the trouble and, worse, usually permit those

*This document was testimony on behalf of the University of Hawaii Committee on Ecology and Man, presented in March, 1970, before a Committee of the State Senate of Hawaii, in favor of a bill (S.B. 1132). This bill proposed the setting up of an Office of Environmental Quality Control in Government and an Environmental Center in the University of Hawaii. The bill was passed.

causes to grow stronger and become compounded. In medicine, to relieve the symptoms without curing the disease is wise and sufficient *if and only if* either the disease is surely terminal *or* will cure itself.

The history of DDT illustrates the fundamental fallacy of *ad hoc* measures. When it was invented and first put to use, it was itself an *ad hoc* measure. It was discovered in 1939 that the stuff was an insecticide (and the discoverer got a Nobel Prize). Insecticides were "needed" (*a*) to increase agricultural products; and (*b*) to save people, especially troops overseas, from malaria. In other words, DDT was a symptomatic cure for troubles connected with the increase of population.

By 1950, it was known to scientists that DDT was seriously toxic to many other animals (Rachel Carson's popular book *Silent Spring* was published in 1962).

But in the meanwhile, (*a*) there was a vast industrial commitment to DDT manufacture; (*b*) the insects at which DDT was directed were becoming immune; (*c*) the animals which normally ate those insects were being exterminated; (*d*) the population of the world was permitted by DDT to increase.

In other words, the world became *addicted* to what was once an *ad hoc* measure and is now known to be a major danger. Finally in 1970, we begin to prohibit or control this danger. And we still do not know, for example, whether the human species on its present diet can surely survive the DDT which is already circulating in the world and will be there for the next twenty years even if its use is immediately and totally discontinued.

It is now reasonably certain (since the discovery of significant amounts of DDT in the penguins of Antarctica) that *all* the fish-eating birds as well as the land-going carnivorous birds and those which formerly ate insect pests are doomed. It is probable that all the carnivorous fish[1] will soon contain too much DDT for human consumption and may themselves become extinct. It is possible that the earthworms, at least in forests and other sprayed areas, will vanish—with what ef-

---

[1] Ironically, it turns out that fish will probably become poisonous as carriers of mercury rather than DDT. [G.B. 1971]

fect upon the forests is anybody's guess. The plankton of the high seas (upon which the entire planetary ecology depends) is believed to be still unaffected.

That is the story of one blind application of an *ad hoc* measure; and the story can be repeated for a dozen other inventions.

(2) That the proposed combination of agencies in State Government and in the University should address itself to diagnosing, understanding and, if possible, suggesting remedies for the wider processes of social and environmental degradation in the world and should attempt to define Hawaii's policy in view of these processes.

(3) That *all* of the many current threats to man's survival are traceable to three root causes:

    (*a*) technological progress

    (*b*) population increase

    (*c*) certain errors in the thinking and attitudes of Occidental culture. Our "values" are wrong.

We believe that all three of these fundamental factors are necessary conditions for the destruction of our world. In other words, we *optimistically* believe that the correction of any *one* of them would save us.

(4) That these fundamental factors certainly interact. The increase of population spurs technological progress and creates that anxiety which sets us against our environment as an enemy; while technology both facilitates increase of population and reinforces our arrogance, or "hubris," vis-à-vis the natural environment.

The attached diagram illustrates the interconnections. It will be noted that in this diagram each corner is clockwise, denoting that each is by itself a self-promoting (or, as the scientists say, "autocatalytic") phenomenon: the bigger the population, the faster it grows; the more technology we have, the faster the rate of new invention; and the more we believe in our "power" over an enemy environment, the more "power" we seem to have and the more spiteful the environment seems to be.

Similarly the pairs of corners are clockwise connected to make three self-promoting subsystems.

The problem facing the world and Hawaii is simply how to introduce some anticlockwise processes into this system.

How to do this should be a major problem for the pro-

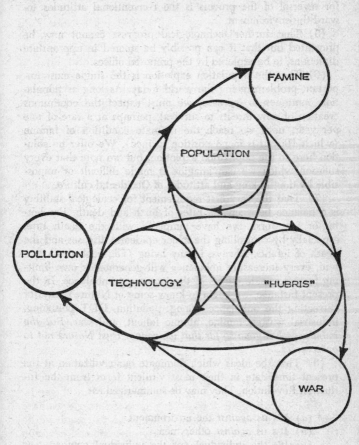

Figure 3. The Dynamics of Ecological Crisis

posed State Office of Environmental Quality Control and the University Environmental Center.

It appears, at present, that the only possible entry point for reversal of the process is the conventional attitudes toward the environment.

(5) That further technological progress cannot now be prevented but that it can possibly be steered in appropriate directions, to be explored by the proposed offices.

(6) That the population explosion is the single most important problem facing the world today. As long as population continues to increase, we must expect the continuous creation of new threats to survival, perhaps at a rate of one per year, until we reach the ultimate condition of famine (which Hawaii is in no position to face). We offer no solution here to the population explosion, but we note that every solution which we can imagine is made difficult or impossible by the thinking and attitudes of Occidental culture.

(7) That the very first requirement for ecological stability is a balance between the rates of birth and death. For better or for worse, we have tampered with the death rate, especially by controlling the major epidemic diseases and the death of infants. Always, in any living (*i.e.*, ecological) system, every increasing imbalance will generate its own limiting factors as side effects of the increasing imbalance. In the present instance, we begin to know some of Nature's ways of correcting the imbalance—smog, pollution, DDT poisoning, industrial wastes, famine, atomic fallout, and war. *But the imbalance has gone so far that we cannot trust Nature not to overcorrect.*

(8) That the ideas which dominate our civilization at the present time date in their most virulent form from the Industrial Revolution. They may be summarized as:

(a) It's us *against* the environment.

(b) It's us *against* other men.

(c) It's the individual (or the individual company, or the individual nation) that matters.

(d) We *can* have unilateral control over the environment and must strive for that control.

(e) We live within an infinitely expanding "frontier."

(f) Economic determinism is common sense.

(g) Technology will do it for us.

We submit that these ideas are simply proved *false* by the great but ultimately destructive achievements of our technology in the last 150 years. Likewise they appear to be false under modern ecological theory. *The creature that wins against its environment destroys itself.*

(9) That other attitudes and premises—other systems of human "values"—have governed man's relation to his environment and his fellow man in other civilizations and at other times. Notably, the ancient Hawaiian civilization and the Hawaiians of today are unconcerned about Occidental "hubris." In other words, our way is not the only possible human way. *It is conceivably changeable.*

(10) That change in our thinking has already begun—among scientists and philosophers, and among young people. But it is not only long-haired professors and long-haired youth who are changing their ways of thought. There are also many thousands of businessmen and even legislators who *wish* they could change but feel that it would be unsafe or not "common sense" to do so. The changes will continue as inevitably as technological progress.

(11) That these changes in thought will impact upon our government, economic structure, educational philosophy, and military stance because the old premises are deeply built into all these sides of our society.

(12) That nobody can predict what new patterns will emerge from these drastic changes. We hope that the period of change may be characterized by wisdom, rather than by either violence or the fear of violence. Indeed, the ultimate goal of this bill is to make such a transition possible.

(13) We conclude that the next five to ten years will be a period comparable to the Federalist period in United States history. New philosophies of government, education, and technology must be debated both inside the government and in the public press, and especially among leading citizens. The University of Hawaii and the State Government could take a lead in these debates.

# Ecology and Flexibility in Urban Civilization*

First, it will be convenient to have, not a specific or ultimate goal, but an abstract idea of what we might mean by ecological health. Such a general notion will both guide the collection of data and guide the evaluation of observed trends.

I suggest then that a healthy ecology of human civilization would be defined somewhat as follows:

A single system of *environment combined with high human civilization* in which the flexibility of the civilization shall match that of the environment to create an ongoing complex system, open-ended for slow change of even basic (hard-programmed) characteristics.

We now proceed to consider some of the terms in this definition of systemic health and to relate them to conditions in the existing world.

*In October, 1970, the author convened and chaired a small five-day conference on "Restructuring the Ecology of a Great City," sponsored by the Wenner-Gren Foundation. A purpose of the conference was to join with planners in the office of John Lindsay, mayor of New York City, in examining relevant components of ecological theory. This essay was written for this conference and subsequently edited. Section VI on the Transmission of Theory has been added and represents afterthoughts following the conference.

## *"A High Civilization"*

It appears that the man-environment system has certainly been progressively unstable since the introduction of metals, the wheel, and script. The deforestation of Europe and the man-made deserts of the Middle East and North Africa are evidence for this statement.

Civilizations have risen and fallen. A new technology for the exploitation of nature or a new technique for the exploitation of other men permits the rise of a civilization. But each civilization, as it reaches the limits of what can be exploited in that particular way, must eventually fall. The new invention gives elbow room or flexibility, but the using up of that flexibility is death.

Either man is too clever, in which case we are doomed, or he was not clever enough to limit his greed to courses which would not destroy the ongoing total system. I prefer the second hypothesis.

It becomes then necessary to work toward a definition of "high."

(*a*) It would not be wise (even if possible) to return to the innocence of the Australian aborigines, the Eskimo, and the Bushmen. Such a return would involve loss of the wisdom which prompted the return and would only start the whole process over.

(*b*) A "high" civilization should therefore be presumed to have, on the technological side, whatever gadgets are necessary to promote, maintain (and even increase) wisdom of this general sort. This may well include computers and complex communication devices.

(*c*) A "high" civilization shall contain whatever is necessary (in educational and religious institutions) to maintain the necessary wisdom in the human population and to give physical, aesthetic, and creative satisfaction to people. There shall be a matching between the flexibility of people and that of the civilization. There shall be diversity in the civilization, not only to accommodate the genetic and experiential diversity of persons, but also to provide the flexibility and "preadaptation" necessary for unpredictable change.

(*d*) A "high" civilization shall be limited in its transactions

with environment. It shall consume unreplaceable natural resources *only* as a means to facilitate necessary change (as a
chrysalis in metamorphosis must live on its fat). For the rest,
the metabolism of the civilization must depend upon the
energy income which Spaceship Earth derives from the sun.
In this connection, great technical advance is necessary. With
present technology, it is probable that the world could only
maintain a small fraction of its present human population,
using as energy sources only photosynthesis, wind, tide, and
water power.

## Flexibility

To achieve, in a few generations, anything like the healthy
system dreamed of above or even to get out of the grooves
of fatal destiny in which our civilization is now caught, very
great *flexibility* will be needed. It is right, therefore, to examine this concept with some care. Indeed, this is a crucial
concept. We should evaluate not so much the values and
trends of relevant variables as the relation between these
trends and ecological flexibility.

Following Ross Ashby, I assume that any biological system (*e.g.*, the ecological environment, the human civilization, and the system which is to be the combination of these
two) is describable in terms of interlinked variables such
that for any given variable there is an upper and a lower
threshold of tolerance beyond which discomfort, pathology,
and ultimately death must occur. Within these limits, the
variable can move (and is moved) in order to achieve
*adaptation*. When, under stress, a variable must take a value
close to its upper or lower limit of tolerance, we shall say,
borrowing a phrase from the youth culture, that the system
is "up tight" in respect to this variable, or lacks "flexibility"
in this respect.

But, because the variables are interlinked, to be up tight
in respect to one variable commonly means that other variables cannot be changed without pushing the up-tight variable. The loss of flexibility thus spreads through the system.
In extreme cases, the system will only accept those changes
which *change the tolerance limits* for the up-tight variable.
For example, an overpopulated society looks for those

changes (increased food, new roads, more houses, etc.) which will make the pathological and pathogenic conditions of overpopulation more comfortable. But these *ad hoc* changes are precisely those which in longer time can lead to more fundamental ecological pathology.

The pathologies of our time may broadly be said to be the accumulated results of this process—the eating up of flexibility in response to stresses of one sort or another (especially the stress of population pressure) and the refusal to bear with those by-products of stress (*e.g.*, epidemics and famine) which are the age-old correctives for population excess.

The ecological analyst faces a dilemma: on the one hand, if any of his recommendations are to be followed, he must first recommend whatever will give the system a positive budget of flexibility; and on the other hand, the people and institutions with which he must deal have a natural propensity to eat up all available flexibility. He must create flexibility and prevent the civilization from immediately expanding into it.

It follows that while the ecologist's goal is to increase flexibility, and to this extent he is less tyrannical than most welfare planners (who tend to increase legislative control), he must also exert authority to preserve such flexibility as exists or can be created. At this point (as in the matter of unreplaceable natural resources), his recommendations must be tyrannical.

Social flexibility is a resource as precious as oil or titanium and must be budgeted in appropriate ways, to be spent (like fat) upon needed change. Broadly, since the "eating up" of flexibility is due to regenerative (*i.e.*, escalating) subsystems within the civilization, it is, in the end, these that must be controlled.

It is worth noting here that flexibility is to specialization as entropy is to negentropy. Flexibility may be defined as *uncommitted potentiality for change*.

A telephone exchange exhibits maximum negentropy, maximum specialization, maximum information load, and maximum rigidity when so many of its circuits are in use that one more call would probably jam the system. It exhibits maximum entropy and maximum flexibility when none of its pathways are committed. (In this particular example, the state of nonuse is not a committed state.)

It will be noted that the budget of flexibility is fractionating (not subtractive, as is a budget of money or energy).

## The Distribution of Flexibility

Again following Ashby, the *distribution* of flexibility among the many variables of a system is a matter of very great importance.

The healthy system, dreamed of above, may be compared to an acrobat on a high wire. To maintain the ongoing truth of his basic premise ("I am on the wire"), he must be free to move from one position of instability to another, *i.e.*, certain variables such as the position of his arms and the rate of movement of his arms must have great flexibility, which he uses to maintain the stability of other more fundamental and general characteristics. If his arms are fixed or paralyzed (isolated from communication), he must fall.

In this connection, it is interesting to consider the ecology of our legal system. For obvious reasons, it is difficult to control by law those basic ethical and abstract principles upon which the social system depends. Indeed, historically, the United States was founded upon the premise of freedom of religion and freedom of thought—the separation of Church and State being the classic example.

On the other hand, it is rather easy to write laws which shall fix the more episodic and superficial details of human b avior. In other words, as laws proliferate, our acrobat is progressively limited in his arm movement but is given free permission to fall off the wire.

Note, in passing, that the analogy of the acrobat can be applied at a higher level. During the period when the acrobat is *learning* to move his arms in an appropriate way, it is necessary to have a safety net under him, *i.e.*, precisely to give him the freedom to fall off the wire. Freedom and flexibility in regard to the most basic variables may be necessary during the process of learning and creating a new system by social change.

These are paradoxes of order and disorder which the ecological analyst and planner must weigh.

Be all that as it may, it is at least arguable that the trend of social change in the last one hundred years, especially in the USA, has been towards an inappropriate distribution of flexibility among the variables of the civilization. Those variables which should be flexible have been pegged, while those which should be comparatively steady, changing only slowly, have been cast loose.

But, even so, the law is surely not the appropriate method for stabilizing the fundamental variables. This should be done by the processes of education and character formation —those parts of our social system which are currently *and expectably* undergoing maximum perturbation.

## The Flexibility of Ideas

A civilization runs on ideas of all degrees of generality. These ideas are present (some explicit, some implicit) in the actions and interactions of persons—some conscious and clearly defined, others vague, and many unconscious. Some of these ideas are widely shared, others differentiated in various subsystems of the society.

If a budget of flexibility is to be a central component of our understanding of how the environment-civilization works, and if a category of pathology is related to unwise spending of this budget, then surely the flexibility of ideas will play an important role in our theory and practice.

A few examples of basic cultural ideas will make the matter clear:

"The Golden Rule," "An eye for an eye," and "Justice."

"The common sense of scarcity economics" versus "The common sense of affluence."

"The name of that thing is 'chair'" and many of the reifying premises of language.

"The survival of the fittest" versus "The survival of organism-*plus*-environment."

Premises of mass production, challenge, pride, etc.

The premises of transference, ideas about how character is determined, theories of education, etc.

Patterns of personal relatedness, dominance, love, etc.

The ideas in a civilization are (like all other variables) interlinked, partly by some sort of psycho-logic and partly by consensus about the quasi-concrete effects of action.

It is characteristic of this complex network of determination of ideas (and actions) that particular links in the net are often weak but that any given idea or action is subject to multiple determination by many interwoven strands. We turn off the light when we go to bed, influenced partly by the economics of scarcity, partly by premises of transference, partly by ideas of privacy, partly to reduce sensory input, etc.

This multiple determination is characteristic of all biological fields. Characteristically, every feature of the anatomy of an animal or plant and every detail of behavior is determined by a multitude of interacting factors at both the genetic and physiological levels; and, correspondingly, the processes of any ongoing ecosystem are the outcome of multiple determination.

Moreover, it is rather unusual to find that any feature of a biological system is at all directly determined by the need which it fulfills. Eating is governed by appetite, habit, and social convention rather than by hunger, and respiration is governed by $CO_2$ excess rather than by oxygen lack. And so on.

In contrast, the products of human planners and engineers are constructed to meet specified needs in a much more direct manner, and are correspondingly less viable. The multiple causes of eating are likely to ensure the performance of this necessary act under a large variety of circumstances and stresses whereas, if eating were controlled only by hypoglycaemia, any disturbance of the single pathway of control would result in death. Essential biological functions are not controlled by lethal variables, and planners will do well to note this fact.

Against this complex background, it is not easy to construct a theory of flexibility of ideas and to conceive of a *budget* of flexibility. There are, however, two clues to the major theoretical problem. Both of these are derived from the stochastic process of evolution or learning whereby such interlocked systems of ideas come into being. First we consider the "natural selection" which governs which ideas shall survive longest; and second we shall consider how this process sometimes works to create evolutionary culs-de-sac.

(More broadly, I regard the grooves of destiny into which our civilization has entered as a special case of evolutionary cul-de-sac. Courses which offered short-term advantage have been adopted, have become rigidly programmed, and have begun to prove disastrous over longer time. This is the paradigm for extinction by way of loss of flexibility. And this paradigm is more surely lethal when the courses of action are chosen in order to maximize single variables.)

In a simple learning experiment (or any other experience), an organism, especially a human being, acquires a vast variety of information. He learns something about the smell of the lab; he learns something about the patterns of the experimenter's behavior; he learns something about his own capacity to learn and how it feels to be "right" or "wrong"; he learns that there is "right" and "wrong" in the world. And so on.

If he now is subjected to another learning experiment (or experience), he will acquire some new items of information: some of the items of the first experiment will be repeated or affirmed; some will be contradicted.

In a word, some of the ideas acquired in the first experience will *survive* the second experience, and natural selection will tautologically insist that those ideas which survive will survive longer than those which do not survive.

But in mental evolution, there is also an economy of flexibility. Ideas which survive repeated use are actually handled in a special way which is different from the way in which the mind handles new ideas. The phenomenon of *habit formation* sorts out the ideas which survive repeated use and puts them in a more or less separate category. These trusted ideas then become available for immediate use without thoughtful inspection, while the more flexible parts of the mind can be saved for use on newer matters.

In other words, the *frequency* of use of a given idea becomes a determinant of its survival in that ecology of ideas which we call Mind; and beyond that the survival of a frequently used idea is further promoted by the fact that habit formation tends to remove the idea from the field of critical inspection.

But the survival of an idea is also certainly determined by

its relations with other ideas. Ideas may support or contradict each other; they may combine more or less readily. They may influence each other in complex unknown ways in polarized systems.

It is commonly the more generalized and abstract ideas that survive repeated use. The more generalized ideas thus tend to become *premises* upon which other ideas depend. These premises become relatively inflexible.

In other words, in the ecology of ideas there is an evolutionary process, related to the economics of flexibility, and this process determines which ideas shall become hard programmed.

The same process determines that these hard-programmed ideas become nuclear or nodal within constellations of other ideas, because the survival of these other ideas depends on how they fit with the hard-programmed ideas.[1] It follows that any change in the hard-programmed ideas may involve change in the whole related constellation.

But frequency of validation of an idea within a given segment of time is not the same as *proof* that the idea is either true or pragmatically useful over long time. We are discovering today that several of the premises which are deeply ingrained in our way of life are simply untrue and become pathogenic when implemented with modern technology.

## Exercise of Flexibility

It is asserted above that the overall flexibility of a system depends upon keeping many of its variables in the middle of their tolerable limits. But there is a partial converse of this generalization:

> [1] Analogous relations certainly obtain in the ecology of a redwood forest or a coral reef. The most frequent or "dominant" species are likely to be nodal to constellations of other species, because the survival of a newcomer to the system will commonly be determined by how its way of life fits with that of one or more dominant species.
>
> In these contexts—both ecological and mental—the word "fit" is a low-level analogue of "matching flexibility."

Owing to the fact that inevitably many of the subsystems of the society are regenerative, the system as a whole tends to "expand" into any area of unused freedom.

It used to be said that "Nature abhors a vacuum," and indeed something of the sort seems to be true of unused potentiality for change in any biological system.

In other words, if a given variable remains too long at some middle value, other variables will encroach upon its freedom, narrowing the tolerance limits until its freedom to move is zero or, more precisely, until any future movement can only be achieved at the price of disturbing the encroaching variables.

In other words, the variable which does not change its value becomes *ipso facto* hard programmed. Indeed, this way of stating the genesis of hard-programmed variables is only another way of describing *habit formation*.

As a Japanese Zen master once told me, *"To become accustomed to anything is a terrible thing."*

From all of this it follows that to maintain the flexibility of a given variable, either that flexibility must be *exercised,* or the encroaching variables must be directly controlled.

We live in a civilization which seems to prefer prohibition to positive requirement, and therefore we try to legislate (*e.g.,* with antitrust laws) against the encroaching variables; and we try to defend "civil liberties" by legally slapping the wrists of encroaching authority.

We try to prohibit certain encroachments, but it might be more effective to encourage people to know their freedoms and flexibilities and to use them more often.

In our civilization, the exercise of even the physiological body, whose proper function is to maintain the flexibility of many of its variables by pushing them to extreme values, becomes a "spectator sport," and the same is true of the flexibility of social norms. We go to the movies or the courts —or read newspapers—for vicarious experience of exceptional behavior.

## The Transmission of Theory

A first question in all application of theory to human problems concerns the education of those who are to carry out the plans. This paper is primarily a presentation of theory to planners; it is an attempt at least to make some theoretical ideas available to them. But in the restructuring of a great city over a period of ten to thirty years, the plans and their execution must pass through the heads and hands of hundreds of persons and dozens of committees.

Is it important that the right things be done for the right reasons? Is it necessary that those who revise and carry out plans should understand the ecological insights which guided the planners? Or should the original planners put into the very fabric of their plan collateral incentives which will seduce those who come later into carrying out the plan for reasons quite different from those which inspired the plan?

This is an ancient problem in ethics and one which (for example) besets every psychiatrist. Should he be satisfied if his patient makes a readjustment to conventional life for neurotic or inappropriate reasons?

The question is not only ethical in the conventional sense, it is also an ecological question. The means by which one man influences another are a part of the ecology of ideas in their relationship, and part of the larger ecological system within which that relationship exists.

The hardest saying in the Bible is that of St. Paul, addressing the Galatians: *"God is not mocked,"* and this saying applies to the relationship between man and his ecology. It is of no use to plead that a particular sin of pollution or exploitation was only a little one or that it was unintentional or that it was committed with the best intentions. Or that "If I didn't, somebody else would have." The processes of ecology are not mocked.

On the other hand, surely the mountain lion when he kills the deer is not acting to protect the grass from overgrazing.

In fact, the problem of how to transmit our ecological reasoning to those whom we wish to influence in what seems to us to be an ecologically "good" direction is itself an ecological problem. We are not outside the ecology for which we plan—we are always and inevitably a part of it.

Herein lies the charm and the terror of ecology—that the ideas of this science are irreversibly becoming a part of our own ecosocial system.

We live then in a world different from that of the mountain lion—he is neither bothered nor blessed by having ideas about ecology. We are.

I believe that these ideas are not evil and that our greatest (ecological) need is the propagation of these ideas as they develop—and as they are developed by the (ecological) process of their propagation.

If this estimate is correct, then the ecological ideas implicit in our plans are more important than the plans themselves, and it would be foolish to sacrifice these ideas on the altar of pragmatism. It will not in the long run pay to "sell" the plans by superficial *ad hominem* arguments which will conceal or contradict the deeper insight.

# The Published Work of Gregory Bateson

Prepared by Vern Carroll

## I. Books, Reviews and Articles

1926      "On certain aberrations of the red-legged partridges *Alectoris rufa* and *saxatilis.*" *Journal of Genetics* 16: 101–23. (with W. Bateson).

1932a      "Further notes on a snake dance of the Baining." *Oceania* 2: 334–41.

1932b      "Social structure of the Iatmul people of the Sepik River (Parts I and II)." *Oceania* 2: 245–91.

1932c      "Social structure of the Iatmul people of the Sepik River (Part III)." *Oceania* 2: 401–53.

1935a      "Music in New Guinea." *Eagle* 47, no. 214: 158–70. ["The Eagle . . . a magazine supported by members of St. John's College, Cambridge, England. Printed at the University Press for subscribers only."]

*1935b      "Culture contact and schismogenesis." *Man* 35: 178–83 (art. 199).

1936      *Naven: A Survey of the Problems Suggested by a Composite Picture of the Culture of a New Guinea Tribe Drawn from Three Points of View.* Cambridge: Cambridge University Press. Reprint. New York: Macmillan Co., 1937.

1937      "An old temple and a new myth." *Djawa* 17: 291–307. Text reprinted in *Traditional Balinese Culture*, edited by Jane Belo, pp. 111–36. New York and London: Columbia University Press, 1970. [Note: the reprint excludes five of the eight original photographs and adds two photographs which do not appear in the original, but which pertain to two of the same subjects appearing in the original.]

---

° Articles marked with an asterisk have been included in this volume. As a matter of historical interest, the occasion for which each paper was prepared has been noted. Reprintings of articles have generally been excluded. Readers failing to find a book in this bibliography listed in a library catalog under either the volume editor's name or the volume title should try looking under the title of the conference or symposium, which is listed immediately preceeding the editor's name.

*1941a    "Experiments in thinking about observed ethnological material." *Philosophy of Science* 8: 53–68. Paper read at the Seventh Conference on Methods in Philosophy and the Sciences, 28 April 1940, at the New School for Social Research, New York, New York.

1941b    "Age conflicts and radical youth." Mimeographed. New York: Institute for Intercultural Studies. Prepared for the Committee for National Morale.

1941c    "The frustration-aggression hypothesis and culture." *Psychological Review* 48: 350–55. Paper read at the 1940 meeting of the Eastern Psychological Association in the Symposium on the Effects of Frustration.

1941d    "Principles of morale building." *Journal of Educational Sociology* 15: 206–20. (with Margaret Mead).

1941e    Review of *Conditioning and Learning*, by Ernest R. Hilgard and Donald G. Marquis. *American Anthropologist* 43: 115–16.

1941f    Review of *Mathematico-Deductive Theory of Rote Learning*, by Clark L. Hull et al. *American Anthropologist* 43: 116–18.

1942a    *Balinese Character: A Photographic Analysis*. Special Publications of the New York Academy of Sciences, vol. 2. New York: New York Academy of Sciences. (with Margaret Mead).

1942b    "Some systematic approaches to the study of culture and personality." *Character and Personality* 11: 76–82. Reprinted in *Personal Character and Cultural Milieu*, edited by Douglas G. Haring, pp. 71–77. Syracuse, New York, 1948. Rev. ed. Syracuse Univ. Press, 1949.

*1942c    Comment on "The comparative study of culture and the purposive cultivation of democratic values," by Margaret Mead. In *Science, Philosophy and Religion; Second Symposium* (held 8-11 September 1941, at New York, New York). Conference on Science, Philosophy and Religion. Edited by Lyman Bryson and Louis Finkelstein, pp. 81–97. New York: Conference on Science, Philosophy and Religion in Their Relation to the Democratic Way of Life, Inc. Reprinted widely under the title "Social planning and the concept of deutero-learning.

*1942d    "Morale and national character." In *Civilian Morale*. Society for the Psychological Study of Social Issues, Second Yearbook. Edited by Goodwin Watson, pp. 71–91. Boston: Houghton Mifflin Co. (for Reynal & Hitchcock, New York).

1943a    "Cultural and thematic analysis of fictional films."

*Transactions of the New York Academy of Sciences,* series 2, vol. 5, no. 4: 72–78. An address to the New York Academy of Sciences, 18 January 1943. Reprinted in *Personal Character and Cultural Milieu,* edited by Douglas G. Haring, pp. 117–23. Syracuse, New York, 1948.

1943b "An analysis of the film *Hitlerjunge Quex* (1933)." Mimeographed. New York: Museum of Modern Art Film Library. Microfilm copy made in 1965 by Graphic Microfilm Co. Abstracted in *The Study of Culture at a Distance,* edited by Margaret Mead and Rhoda Métraux, pp. 302–14. Chicago: University of Chicago Press, 1953. A copy of the first three reels of this film, with analytic titles by Gregory Bateson, is in the Museum of Modern Art Film Library.

1943c "Human dignity and the varieties of civilization." In *Science, Philosophy and Religion; Third Symposium,* (held 27-31 August 1942, at New York, New York). Conference on Science, Philosophy and Religion. Edited by Lyman Bryson and Louis Finkelstein, pp. 245–55. New York: Conference on Science, Philosophy and Religion in Their Relation to the Democratic Way of Life, Inc.

1943d Discussion concerning "The science of decency." *Philosophy of Science* 10: 140–42.

1944a "Psychology—in the War and after (Part VII): Material on contemporary peoples." *Junior College Journal* 14: 308–11.

1944b "Pidgin English and cross-cultural communication." *Transactions of the New York Academy of Sciences,* series 2, vol. 6, no. 4: 137–41. Paper read to the New York Academy of Sciences, Section of Anthropology, 24 January 1944.

1944c "Cultural determinants of personality." In *Personality and the Behavior Disorders,* vol. 2, edited by Joseph McV. Hunt, pp. 714–35. New York: Ronald Press Co.

1944d "Form and function of the dance in Bali." In *The Function of Dance in Human Society: A Seminar Directed by Franziska Boas,* pp. 46–52. Boas School. New York: The Boas School. (with Clair Holt). Reprinted in *Traditional Balinese Culture,* edited by Jane Belo, pp. 322–30. New York and London: Columbia University Press, 1970.

1944e "A Melanesian culture-contact myth in pidgin English." *Journal of American Folklore* 57, no. 226: 255–62. (with Robert Hall, Jr.).

1946a "Physical thinking and social problems." *Science* 103, no. 2686 (21 June 1946): 717–18.

1946b "Arts of the South Seas." *Art Bulletin* 28: 119–23. Review of an exhibit held 29 January 1946—19 May 1946, at the Museum of Modern Art, New York, New York.

1946c "The pattern of an armaments race, Part I: An anthropological approach." *Bulletin of the Atomic Scientists* 2, nos. 5 & 6: 10–11. Reprinted in *Personal Character and Cultural Milieu*, edited by Douglas G. Haring, pp. 85–88. Syracuse, New York, 1948.

1946d "The pattern of an armaments race, Part II: An analysis of nationalism." *Bulletin of the Atomic Scientists* 2, nos. 7 & 8: 26–28. Reprinted in *Personal Character and Cultural Milieu*, edited by Douglas G. Haring, pp. 89–93. Syracuse, New York, 1948.

1946e "From one social scientist to another." *American Scientist* 34 (October 1946): 648 ff.

1946f "Protecting the future." Letter to the *New York Times*, 8 December 1946, section 4, p. 10.

1947a "Sex and culture." *Annals of the New York Academy of Sciences* 47: 647–60. Paper read to the Conference on Physiological and Psychological Factors in Sex Behavior, New York Academy of Sciences, Sections of Biology and Psychology, 1 March 1946. Reprinted in *Personal Character and Cultural Milieu*, edited by Douglas G. Haring, pp. 94–107. Syracuse, New York, 1948.

1947b "Atoms, nations, and cultures." *International House Quarterly* 11, no. 2: 47–50. Lecture delivered 23 March 1947, at International House, Columbia University.

1947c Review of *The Theory of Human Culture*, by James Fiebleman. *Political Science Quarterly* 62: 428–30.

•1949a "Bali: The value system of a steady state." In *Social Structure: Studies Presented to A. R. Radcliffe-Brown*, edited by Meyer Fortes, pp. 35–53. Oxford: Clarendon Press. Reprint. New York: Russell & Russell, 1963.

1949b "Structure and process in social relations." *Psychiatry* 12: 105–24. (with Jurgen Ruesch).

1951a *Communication: The Social Matrix of Psychiatry.* New York: W. W. Norton & Co.; Toronto: George McLeod. (with Jurgen Ruesch). Reprint. New York: Norton, 1968.

°1951b "Metalogue: Why do Frenchmen?" In *Impulse, Annual of Contemporary Dance, 1951*, edited by Marian Van Tuyl. San Francisco: Impulse Publications, 1951. Reprinted in *ETC.: A Review of General Semantics* 10 (1953): 127–30. Reprinted also in *Anthology of Impulse, Annual of Contemporary Dance, 1951–1966*, edited by Marian Van Tuyl. Brooklyn: Dance Horizons, 1969.

1952 "Applied metalinguistics and international relations." *ETC.: A Review of General Semantics* 10: 71–73.

1953a "An analysis of the Nazi film *Hitlerjunge Quex*." In *The Study of Culture at a Distance*, edited by Margaret Mead and Rhoda Métraux, pp. 302–14. Chicago: University of Chicago Press. Abstract by Margaret Mead of "An Analysis of The Film *Hitlerjunge Quex* (1933)," by Gregory Bateson. (cf. Bateson 1943b).

1953b "The position of humor in human communication." In *Cybernetics: Circular Causal and Feedback Mechanisms in Biological and Social Sciences; Transactions of the Ninth Conference* (held 20–21 March 1952, at New York, New York). Conference on Cybernetics. Edited by Heinz Von Foerster, pp. 1–47. New York: Josiah Macy, Jr. Foundation.

°1953c "Metalogue: About games and being serious." *ETC.: A Review of General Semantics* 10: 213–17.

°1953d "Metalogue: Daddy, how much do you know?" *ETC.: A Review of General Semantics* 10: 311–15. Reprinted herein as "Metalogue: How much do you know?"

°1953e "Metalogue: Why do things have outlines?" *ETC.: A Review of General Semantics* 11: 59–63.

°1954 "Metalogue: Why a swan?" In *Impulse, Annual of Contemporary Dance, 1954*, edited by Marian Van Tuyl, pp. 23–26. San Francisco: Impulse Publications. Reprinted in *Anthology of Impulse, Annual of Contemporary Dance, 1951–1966*, edited by Marian Van Tuyl, pp. 95–99. Brooklyn: Dance Horizons, 1969.

°1955a "A theory of play and fantasy; a report on theoretical aspects of the project for study of the role of paradoxes of abstraction in communication." *Approaches to the Study of Human Personality*, pp. 39–51. American Psychiatric Association. Psychiatric Research Reports, no. 2. Paper delivered to a symposium of the American Psychiatric Association on Cultural, Anthropological, and Communications Approaches, 11 March 1954, at Mexico City.

°1955b      "How the deviant sees his society." In *The Epidemiology of Mental Health*, pp. 25–31. Mimeographed. An Institute Sponsored by the Departments of Psychiatry and Psychology of the University of Utah, and by the Veterans Administration Hospital, Fort Douglas Division, Salt Lake City, Utah, May 1955, at Brighton, Utah. Reprinted herein, edited, as "The epidemiology of a schizophrenia."

1956a      "The message 'This is play'." In *Group Processes: Transactions of the Second Conference* (held 9-12 October 1955, at Princeton, New Jersey). Conference on Group Processes. Edited by Bertram Schaffner, pp. 145–242. New York: Josiah Macy, Jr. Foundation.

1956b      "Communication in occupational therapy." *American Journal of Occupational Therapy* 10: 188.

°1956c      "Toward a theory of schizophrenia." *Behavioral Science* 1: 251–64. (with Don D. Jackson, Jay Haley, and John Weakland).

1958a      *Naven: A Survey of the Problems Suggested by a Composite Picture of the Culture of a New Guinea Tribe Drawn from Three Points of View.* 2nd ed., with added "Epilogue 1958." Stanford: Stanford University Press; London: Oxford University Press. Reprint. Stanford: Stanford University Press, 1965; London: Oxford University Press, 1965. (cf. Bateson 1936).

1958b      "Language and psychotherapy—Frieda Fromm-Reichmann's last project." *Psychiatry* 21: 96–100. The Frieda Fromm-Reichmann Memorial Lecture, delivered 3 June 1957, at the Veterans Administration Hospital, Palo Alto, Cailfornia.

1958c      "Schizophrenic distortions of communication." In *Psychotherapy of Chronic Schizophrenic Patients.* Sea Island Conference on Psychotherapy of Chronic Schizophrenic Patients, sponsored by Little, Brown & Co., 15–17 October 1955, at Sea Island, Georgia. Edited by Carl A. Whitaker, pp. 31–56. Boston and Toronto: Little, Brown & Co.; London: J. & A. Churchill.

1958d      "Analysis of group therapy in an admission ward, United States Naval Hospital, Oakland, California." In *Social Psychiatry in Action: A Therapeutic Community,* by Harry A. Wilmer, pp. 334–49. Springfield, Illinois: Charles C. Thomas.

1958e      "The new conceptual frames for behavioral research." In *Proceedings of the Sixth Annual Psychiatric Institute* (held 17 September 1958, at the New Jersey

Neuro-Psychiatric Institute, Princeton, New Jersey), pp. 54–71. n.p.

1959a    Letter in response to "Role and status of anthropological theories," by Sidney Morganbesser. *Science* 129 (6 February 1959): 294–98.

1959b    Panel Review. In *Individual and Familial Dynamics.* Vol. 2, *Science and Psychoanalysis.* [Report of a conference held in May 1958, at the Academy of Psychoanalysis, Chicago.] Academy of Psychoanalysis, Chicago. Edited by Jules H. Masserman, pp. 207–11. New York: Grune & Stratton.

1959c    "Cultural problems posed by a study of schizophrenic process." In *Schizophrenia; an Integrated Approach.* [American Psychiatric Association symposium of the Hawaiian Divisional Meeting, 1958, San Francisco.] Symposium on Schizophrenia. Edited by Alfred Auerback, pp. 125–48. New York: Ronald Press Co.

°1960a    "The group dynamics of schizophrenia." In *Chronic Schizophrenia; Explorations in Theory and Treatment.* Institute on Chronic Schizophrenia and Hospital Treatment Programs, State Hospital, Osawatomie, Kansas, 1–3 October 1958. Edited by Lawrence Appleby, Jordan M. Scher, and John Cumming, pp. 90–105. Glencoe, Illinois: Free Press; London: Collier-Macmillan.

°1960b    "Minimal requirements for a theory of schizophrenia." *Archives of General Psychiatry* 2: 477–91. Second annual Albert D. Lasker Memorial Lecture, delivered 7 April 1959, at the Institute for Psychosomatic and Psychiatric Research and Training of the Michael Reese Hospital, Chicago.

1960c    Discussion of "Families of schizophrenic and of well children," by Samuel J. Beck. *American Journal of Orthopsychiatry* 30: 263–66. 36th Annual Meeting of the American Orthopsychiatric Association, 30 March–1 April 1959, San Francisco.

1961a    *Perceval's Narrative: A Patient's Account of His Psychosis, 1830–1832,* by John Perceval. Edited and with an Introduction by Gregory Bateson. Stanford: Stanford University Press; London: Hogarth Press, 1962.

1961b    "The biosocial integration of behavior in the schizophrenic family." In *Exploring the Base for Family Therapy.* M. Robert Gomberg Memorial Conference (held 2-3 June 1960, at the New York Academy of Medicine). Edited by Nathan W. Ackerman, Frances

L. Beatman, and Sanford N. Sherman, pp. 116–22. New York: Family Service Association of America.

1961c "Formal research in family structure." In *Exploring the Base for Family Therapy*. M. Robert Gomberg Memorial Conference (held 2-3 June 1960, at the New York Academy of Medicine). Edited by Nathan W. Ackerman, Frances L. Beatman, and Sanford N. Sherman, pp. 136–40. New York: Family Service Association of America.

1963a "A social scientist views the emotions." In *Expression of the Emotions in Man*. Symposium on Expression of the Emotions in Man (held at the meeting of the American Association for the Advancement of Science, 29-30 December, at New York, New York). Edited by Peter H. Knapp, pp. 230–36. New York: International Universities Press.

1963b "Exchange of information about patterns of human behavior." In *Information Storage and Neural Control*. Houston Neurological Society Tenth Annual Scientific Meeting, 1962, jointly sponsored by the Department of Neurology, Baylor University College of Medicine, Texas University Medical Center. Edited by William S. Fields and Walter Abbott, pp. 173–86, Springfield, Illinois; Charles C. Thomas.

1963c "A note on the double bind." In *Family Process* 2: 154–61. (with Don D. Jackson, Jay Haley, and John H. Weakland).

•1963d "The role of somatic change in evolution." *Evolution* 17: 529–39.

1964 "Some varieties of pathogenic organization." In *Disorders of Communication*. Proceedings of the Association, 7 & 8 December 1962, at New York, New York. Association for Research in Nervous and Mental Disease, Research Publications, vol. 42. Edited by David McK. Rioch and Edwin A. Weinstein, pp. 270–90. Baltimore: Williams & Wilkins Co.; Edinburgh: E. & S. Livingstone. (with Don D. Jackson).

1966a "Communication theories in relation to the etiology of the neuroses." In *The Etiology of the Neuroses*. [Report of a symposium sponsored by the Society of Medical Psychoanalysts, 17–18 March 1962, at New York, New York.] Edited by Joseph H. Merin, pp. 28–35, Palo Alto, California: Science & Behavior Books.

1966b "Slippery theories." Comment on "Family interaction and schizophrenia: A review of current theories," by Elliot G. Mishler and Nancy E. Waxler. *International Journal of Psychiatry* 2: 415–17. Reprinted in *Family*

*Processes and Schizophrenia*, edited by Elliot G. Mishler and Nancy E. Waxler. New York: Science House, 1969.

°1966c    "Problems in cetacean and other mammalian communication." In *Whales, Dolphins, and Porpoises*. International Symposium on Cetacean Research (sponsored by the American Institute of Biological Sciences, August 1963, Washington, D.C.). Edited by Kenneth S. Norris, pp. 569–79. Berkeley and Los Angeles: University of California Press.

°1967a    "Cybernetic explanation." *American Behavioral Scientist* 10, no. 6 (April 1967): 29–32.

1967b    Review of *Person, Time, and Conduct in Bali*, by Clifford Geertz. *American Anthropologist* 69: 765–66.

°1968a    "Redundancy and coding." In *Animal Communication; Techniques of Study and Results of Research*. [Report of the Wenner-Gren Conference on Animal Communication, held 13–22 June 1965, at Burg Wartenstein, Austria.] Edited by Thomas A. Sebeok, pp. 614–26. Bloomington, Indiana and London: Indiana University Press.

1968b    Review of *Primate Ethology*, edited by Desmond Morris. *American Anthropologist* 70: 1035.

°1968c    "Conscious purpose *versus* nature." In *The Dialectics of Liberation*, edited by David Cooper, pp. 34–49. Congress on the Dialectics of Liberation, held 15–30 July 1967, at London. Harmondsworth, England; Baltimore, Maryland; Victoria, Australia: Penguin Books, Pelican Books. Reprinted under title: *To Free a Generation; the Dialectics of Liberation*. New York: Macmillan Co., Collier Books, 1969.

°1969a    "Metalogue: What is an instinct?" In *Approaches to Animal Communication*, edited by Thomas A. Sebeok and Alexandra Ramsay, pp. 11–30. The Hague and Paris: Mouton & Co.

1969b    Comment on "The study of language and communication across species," by Harvey B. Sarles. *Current Anthropology* 10: 215.

1970a    "An open letter to Anatol Rapoport." *ETC.: A Review of General Semantics* 27: 359–63.

°1970b    "On empty-headedness among biologists and state boards of education." *BioScience* 20: 819.

°1970c    "Form, substance and difference." *General Semantics Bulletin* vol. 37. 19th Annual Alfred Korzybski Memorial Lecture, delivered 9 January 1970, at New York, New York.

1970d     "The message of reinforcement." In *Language Behavior: A Book of Readings in Communication*, edited by Johnnye Akin et al., pp. 62–72 Janua Linguarum, series maior, 41. The Hague: Mouton & Co.

\*1971a     "The cybernetics of 'self': A theory of alcoholism." *Psychiatry* 34: 1–18.

\*1971b     "A re-examination of 'Bateson's Rule'." *Journal of Genetics*, in press.

1971c     "A systems approach." Evaluation of "Family therapy," by Jay Haley. *International Journal of Psychiatry* 9: 242–44.

1971d     "Introduction" to *The Natural History of an Interview*. University of Chicago Library Microfilm Collection of Manuscripts in Cultural Anthropology, series 15, nos. 95–98.

\*1971e     "Metalogue: Why do things get in a muddle?" Previously unpublished. (written 1948).

\*1971f     "From Versailles to cybernetics." Lecture given to the Two Worlds Symposium, 21 April 1966, at Sacramento State College, California. Previously unpublished.

\*1971g     "Style, grace and information in primitive art." In *The Study of Primitive Art*. [Report of the Wenner-Gren Symposium on Primitive Art and Society, held 27 June–5 July 1967, at Burg Wartenstein, Austria.] Edited by Anthony Forge. New York: Oxford University Press, forthcoming.

\*1971h     "The logical categories of learning and communication, and the acquisition of world views." Paper given at the Wenner-Gren Symposium on World Views: Their Nature and Their Role in Culture, 2–11 August 1968, at Burg Wartenstein, Austria. Previously unpublished. Published herein as "The logical categories of learning and communication."

\*1971i     "Pathologies of epistemology." In *Mental Health Research in Asia and the Pacific*, vol. 2. [Report of the Second Conference on Culture and Mental Health in Asia and the Pacific, held 17–21 March 1969, at Honolulu, Hawaii.] Edited by William P. Lebra. Honolulu: East-West Center Press, forthcoming.

\*1971j     "Double bind, 1969." Paper given at the Annual Meeting of the American Psychological Association, 2 September 1969, at Washington, D.C. Previously unpublished.

\*1971k     "Statement on problems which will confront the proposed Office of Environmental Quality Control in government and an Environmental Center at the University of Hawaii." Prepared for the University of Hawaii Committee on Ecology and Man, as testimony before a committee of the Hawaii State Senate, 1970. Previously unpublished. Published herein as "The roots of ecological crisis."

°1971l    "Restructuring the ecology of a great city." Paper prepared for the Wenner-Gren Symposium on Restructuring the Ecology of a Great City, held 26–31 October 1970, in New York City. Previously unpublished. Published herein as "Ecology and flexibility in urban civilization."

°1971m    "The science of mind and order." In *Steps to an Ecology of Mind*, by Gregory Bateson. San Francisco: Chandler. New York: Ballantine Books.

1971n    *La cérémonie du naven: les problèmes posés par la description sous trois rapports d'une tribu de nouvelle-guinée.* Translated by Jean-Paul Latouche and Nimet Safouan; translation edited by Jean-Claude Chamboredon and Pascale Maididier. Paris: Les Editions de Minuit.

forthcoming

Our Own Metaphor, edited by M.C. Bateson. [Report of the Wenner-Gren Conference on the Effects of Conscious Purpose on Human Adaptation, held 17–24 July 1968, at Burg Wartenstein, Austria; Gregory Bateson, Chairman.] New York: Alfred A. Knopf, forthcoming.

"Effects of conscious purpose on human adaptation." In *Our Own Metaphor*, edited by M. C. Bateson. New York: Alfred A. Knopf, forthcoming. Paper given at the Wenner-Gren Symposium on Effects of Conscious Purpose on Human Adaptation, 17–24 July 1968, at Burg Wartenstein, Austria.

## II. Films

The following films in the series Character Formation in Different Cultures, produced in collaboration with Margaret Mead for the Institute for Intercultural Studies, were released in 1951 by the New York University Film Library, New York, New York 10003. All are 16 mm, black and white, sound:

*A Balinese Family*, 2 reels.
*Bathing Babies in Three Cultures*, 1 reel.

*Childhood Rivalry in Bali and New Guinea,* 2 reels.
*First Days in the Life of a New Guinea Baby,* 2 reels.
*Karba's First Years,* 2 reels.
*Trance and Dance in Bali,* 2 reels.

The following films, produced by Gregory Bateson, are as yet not commercially available. Both are 16mm, black and white, sound:

*Communication in Three Families,* 2 reels.
*The Nature of Play—Part I: River Otters,* 1 reel.

# INDEX

Abel, 442

Acclimation, 351-352, 442
reversibility of, 351f.

Acculturation, 62-72

Adam, 345
and Eve, 435-436

Adaptation, 253f., 273f., 314, 338-339, 346-363, 440f., 495f.
and consciousness, 440-447
hierarchic characteristics of, 274-276
*See also* Biological evolution

Addiction, 309-337, 442, 489

Aegistheus, 472

Aesthetics, 148, 265-267, 306, 332, 409-410, 453, 464, 495
as modulation of communication, 231-232
and morality, 265f.
and non-verbal communication, 232
and scientific truth, 265f.
*See also* Art

Agamemnon, 472

Aggression, 325, 424
"negative" aggression, 325
and surrender, 53, 325

Alcoholic pride, 320f.

Alcoholics Anonymous, 309-313, 321, 322, 325, 328-337

Alcoholism, 309-337

and anesthesia, 311
and challenge, 321f.
and complementary relationship, 325f.
epistemology of, 310f.
and hitting bottom, 312, 329-332
intoxication in, 310-312
pride in, 321f.
and religious conversion, 326, 331f.
schismogenesis in, 322f.
and sobriety, 310f.
and symmetrical relationship, 322f.

Alexander, Franz, 93

*Alice in Wonderland*, 30
Alice and the flamingo, 30, 443

Allegory, 136

Altamira cave paintings, 130, 144

Ames, Adalbert, Jr., 135, 463, 479f.

Analogic coding, *see* Coding

Analogy, 153-155

Andaman Islands, 141, 182

Animism, 484

Anonymity, 333-334

Anthropology, xviii, xxi, 61f., 146-147, 160-161, 170, 202, 253

Appleby, Lawrence, 231

Aquinas, St. Thomas, 427, 428, 485

# Psychology Bestsellers from BALLANTINE

Before there was est, before there was assertiveness training, before anyone thought about whether or not they were OK, there was Dr. Eric Berne and the *Games People Play*.

16                                                                    G-11

# Learn to live with somebody... yourself.